THE ULTIMATE
BEATLES
QUIZ BOOK II

ALSO BY

MICHAEL J. HOCKINSON

The Ultimate Beatles Quiz Book

THE ULTIMATE BEATLES QUIZ BOOK II

MICHAEL J. HOCKINSON

ST. MARTIN'S GRIFFIN ❧ NEW YORK

www.stmartins.com

Design by Heidi T. Eriksen

Library of Congress Cataloging-in-Publication Data

Hockinson, Michael J.
    The ultimate Beatles quiz book II / Michael J. Hockinson.
      p. cm.
    ISBN 0-312-26406-2
    1. Beatles—Miscellanea. 2. Rock musicians—England—
Biography. I. Title.

ML421.B4 H62 2000
782.42166'092'2—dc21
[B]

00-031815

First Edition: November 2000

10 9 8 7 6 5 4 3 2 1

This one is for Jeanna Borisch, without whose great love, humor, and support this book never could have been written.

Many of the illustrations featured in this book come from the collection of Patti Mecham, a first-generation Beatles/McCartney fan of the highest order. On 19 August 1999, Patti passed away while I was still in the process of editing this manuscript. It is to her memory that I also dedicate *The Ultimate Beatles Quiz Book II*.

LOVERS & FRIENDS I STILL CAN RECALL . . .

Paul "Hippie" Addis, Josh Bass, Doug "Sir Douglas" Brown, Keith Brown, Mark "Equinox" Brown, Mike Downey, Margy Dunn, Margo Graham, Peggie Guzman, Mike Hawkinson, Lynn Hoskins, Russ Hunt, Donna "Candy" Kane, Curtis Malasky, Karen Pederson, Tom Moran, Kevin Nettleingham, Beverly Palmer, Suzan Parker, Wayne Pernu, Lori E. Pollock, Tanaz Polson, Joe Ramsey, Lori St. James, Mary Jo Schimelpfenig, Dan Swan, Leslie Verduin, and Robert Wolk.

My sincerest thanks to the following writers, without whose diligent efforts in Beatles research my own book would not have been possible: Mark Lewisohn, Bill King, Keith Badman, Scott Belmer, Jim Berkenstadt, Harry Castleman, Ray Coleman, Hunter Davies, Kristopfer K. Engelhardt, Tony Fletcher, Hans Olof Gottfridsson, Bill Harry, Allan Kozinn, Dan Matovina, Barry Miles, Philip Norman, Walter J. Podrazik, John Robertson, Tom Schultheiss, Ray Schweighardt, Bruce Spizer, Doug Sulpy, Steve Turner, and Allen J. Wiener.

Special thanks to my parents, Donald and Mary, and my brother, Patrick. To my three editors at St. Martin's: Calvert D. Morgan, Jr. (who just *asked me* one day if I was interested in writing another quiz book), Dana Albarella (who actually did the editing), and Bryan Cholfin (who saw it to fruition). Last, but not least, to Tom Chartrand, who photographed all the memorabilia.

"My songs are not there to be digested and pulled apart like the Mona Lisa."
—John Lennon, 1972

"Funniest thing is that we don't always agree on the memories, because it was thirty years ago. You've just got to laugh. It's fucking human, so real. We forget—who cares? We did some great stuff. But exact analysis was never our bag."
—Paul McCartney, 1995

"Unlike the experts who wallow in Beatle trivia, I spend a lot of time getting the junk out of my mind through meditation, so I don't know or remember—I don't want to know or remember—every last detail because it was trivial pursuit."
—George Harrison, 1998

THE ULTIMATE
BEATLES
QUIZ BOOK II

1100–1956

1. Dating back to at least the 12th century, it began as a footpath leading from Lisson Green to Kilburn Priory, but Beatle fans know this North London lane today by what name?

2. When Ringo's great-grandmother remarried, she changed her surname to Starkey. Had Starr's grandfather, John, not followed his mother's lead, what would have been the last name on Ringo's birth certificate?

3. Jack Lennon, John's grandfather, made his living for a time as a professional entertainer. Singing, dancing, and playing banjo, Jack made a name for himself working in America on the vaudeville circuit. What group was he a founding member of?

4. What were the maiden names of the Beatles' mothers (John, Paul, George, Ringo, and Stuart)?

5. Who were the Masked Melody Makers?

6. Abbey Road studios was officially opened 12 November 1931—what was the first piece of music recorded there?

7. Who are the Four Tune Tellers?

8. Randolph Peter Best was born in Madras, India, 24 November 1941, to John and Mona Best. What was Mona's first name?

9. Which Beatle nicknamed his brother "Sea-legs"?

10. Who is Ingrid Pedersen?

11. In March 1946, John was sent to live with his Aunt Mimi and Uncle George at "Mendips" (named after the Welsh hills), 251 Menlove Avenue. Who lived just off Menlove Avenue in a semidetached home called "Vega"?

12. Among John's aunts, what was his nickname until around the age of twelve?

13. In 1946, in a boardinghouse in Blackpool, five-year-old John was forced to decide between staying with his mother, Julia, or going with his father, Freddie. Initially he chose his father, but his mother's departure in tears quickly changed his mind. Freddie had planned to emigrate with his son. Had John stayed with his father, where might he have ended up?

14. Who is Marie Maguire?

15. Who are Sally and Prince?

16. While attending Joseph Williams Primary School in Naylorsfield Road, Belle Vale, eleven-year-old Paul McCartney received his very first one from classmate Grace Pendleton. What did Grace give him?

17. Students of Quarry Bank High School were divided into one of five "houses." When John enrolled there in September 1952, which house did he belong to?

18. In September 1952, Ringo was attending Dingle Vale Secondary Modern School. Which house did he belong to?

19. After passing the eleven-plus examination at Blackmoor Park Primary School, Pete Best won a scholarship to Liverpool Collegiate grammar school in Shaw Street where he achieved five "O" (Ordinary) levels. Had Mona Best not thought of turning the cellar of the family residence at 8 Hayman's Green into the Casbah Coffee Club, Pete might have gone with his original career choice—what was that?

20. In 1953, eleven-year-old Paul auditioned for Ronald Woan, resident choirmaster of the Choristers of Liverpool Cathedral. Why didn't McCartney pass the audition?

21. "Four thousand Hindu carrots have been found, eaten by the dreaded IRA. Does this mean that dad will have to work again? It could only be the work of the Phantom!" Where does this early example of Lennon reportage appear?

22. One of John's most treasured possessions as a boy was his bicycle. What make and model did Lennon own?

23. Who bought George his first guitar? What kind was it?

24. In 1956, Paul went to Rushworth and Draper's and traded in his first instrument, a trumpet, to get his first guitar, a Zenith acoustic. He found the instrument difficult to play at first. "Nobody talked about being left-handed," he recalled to journalist Tony Bacon. "So I tried it right-handed, and I couldn't get any rhythm because it was the wrong hand doing it. Then I saw a picture of (*) in one of the music papers. I found out he was left-handed so I thought that's good, you can have it the other way 'round." Which singer/guitarist had McCartney seen a picture of?

25. In September 1956, William Edward Pobjoy (or "Popeye," as he was known to the students) took over as headmaster at Quarry Bank High School. What comment did Mr. Pobjoy write at the bottom of John's last report card?

ANSWERS

1. The lane which led from Lisson Green to Kilburn Priory (also known as Kilburn Abbey), eventually came to be known as Abbey Road.

2. Had his grandfather, John Alfred, not changed his last name to Starkey, Ringo would have been born as Richard Parkin.

(When Ringo's daughter Lee was born at Queen Charlotte's Hospital in London, 11 November 1970, she was given the middle name Parkin.)

3. Jack Lennon was a founding member of the Kentucky Minstrels.

4. Julia Stanley (John); Mary Patricia Mohin (Paul); Louise French (George); Elsie Gleave (Ringo); Martha "Millie" Cronin (Stuart).

5. The Masked Melody Makers was the first name given to the band formed in 1919 by Paul's father, Jim McCartney.

(The MMMs wore highwayman masks until the masks melted on their faces one night, during a particularly strenuous performance. McCartney then changed their name to Jim Mac's Band.)

6. The first piece of music recorded at Abbey Road studios was "Pomp and Circumstance March No. 2."

(Sir Edward Elgar, the composer of the work, conducted the London Symphony Orchestra in Studio One. An excerpt of Elgar and the LSO's recording was used to open *The Beatles at Abbey Road*, a ninety-minute film, video and slide documentary presentation, shown in Studio Two, from 18 July to 11 September 1983.)

7. The Four Tune Tellers was the name of the first group formed by fifteen-year-old George Martin in 1941, initially to play dances put on by The Quavers, the amateur dramatic society he belonged to.

(When the four-piece became a quintet, the name was changed to George Martin and the Four Tune Tellers.)

8. Mona Best's first name was Alice.

9. When Pete Best's brother Rory was born in 1944, he spent so much time hanging onto his older brother as he learned to walk that Pete called him "Sea-legs."

10. Ingrid Pedersen is the adopted name given to John Lennon's half-sister, Victoria Elizabeth Lennon, whom Julia gave birth to in a Salvation Army hostel in Liverpool, 19 June 1945.

(Victoria's name was changed to Ingrid when she was adopted by Peder Pedersen, a Norwegian sailor and his Liverpool wife, Margaret. The father is believed to have been a Welsh soldier known as Taffy Williams. Despite efforts to locate her, John never met Victoria, whose existence he had been aware of since 1964.)

11. Quarry Men tea chest bassist Ivan Vaughan lived at "Vega" in Vale Road, just off Menlove Avenue.

12. Among his aunts (which, along with Julia, comprised his immediate family), John's nickname until around the age of twelve was Stinker.

13. Freddie Lennon had planned to emigrate to New Zealand.

14. In 1947, eleven-year-old Marie Maguire, with the aid of Chambers Primary Readers, taught Ringo to read and write.

(At seven, Ritchie had been unable to do either, having fallen behind after spending over a year at Myrtle Street Children's Hospital recovering from a burst appendix and the resulting peritonitis.)

15. Sally (a mutt) and Prince (a half-breed sheepdog) are the respective names of dogs John and Paul owned as boys.

16. Grace gave Paul his first kiss.

17. Named for the part of Liverpool you lived in, John was in Woolton house at Quarry Bank.

(The other four houses at Quarry Bank were Childwall, Allerton, Wavertree and Aigburth.)

18. Ringo's house at Dingle Vale was Gibraltar.

19. Pete Best had considered becoming a teacher.

20. Paul's father, Jim, who had encouraged his oldest son to join, believed he didn't win a spot in the Liverpool Cathedral Choir because he purposely cracked his voice so that he would fail the audition.

(Another reason given was that Paul couldn't sight-read music.)

21. Under the headline, "Could This be the Work of the Phantom?" this early example of Lennon wit is an entry from *The Daily Howl*, John's Quarry Bank High School notebook.

22. John rode a Raleigh Lenton.

(At the time of their first meeting, 6 July 1957, Paul owned a Raleigh three-speed racing bike.)

23. Louise Harrison gave George the £3 necessary to buy his first six-string guitar from a schoolmate, an Egmond steel-strung Spanish-style.

(On 28 August 1986, Harrison's Egmond, sporting a broken neck and no tuning knobs, sold for $5,755 at Sotheby's in London.)

24. McCartney had seen a picture of Slim Whitman playing guitar left-handed.

25. "The boy is bound to fail."

1957–1959

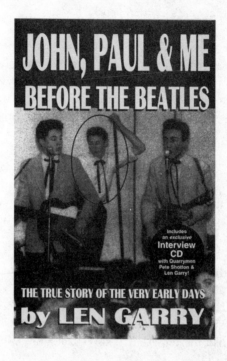

JOHN, PAUL & ME

BEFORE THE BEATLES

Includes an *exclusive* Interview CD with Quarrymen Pete Shotton & Len Garry!

THE TRUE STORY OF THE VERY EARLY DAYS

by LEN GARRY

1. On 9 June 1957, the Quarry Men auditioned for Carroll Levis at Liverpool's Empire Theatre, hoping for a spot on his *TV Star Search* show. What song did the group perform?

2. What make of banjo did Rod Davis play in the Quarry Men?

3. In 1957, Ringo joined the Eddie Clayton Skiffle Group, playing the new drum kit his Grandfather Starkey had lent him the £50 deposit to buy the previous year. Where was their first gig?

4. Who are Arthur and Martha?

5. Thirteen-year-old Sally Wright was among those on the field behind St. Peter's Church when the Quarry Men played from a makeshift stage as part of the afternoon's entertainment at the annual Garden Fête, 6 July 1957. Why was Sally there?

6. Who was also on the bill with the Quarry Men at the Grand Dance the evening of 6 July 1957 at the church hall of St. Peter's Church, the closing event of that year's Garden Fête?

7. A member of St. Peter's youth club, Bob Molyneaux was sixteen years old in 1957 when he recorded the Quarry Men at the Grand Dance on his portable Grundig TK8 3-inch reel tape recorder. A surviving reel from that historic evening (along with the recorder) was auctioned by Sotheby's in London, 15 September 1994. What two songs by the Quarry Men did Molyneaux preserve on this reel?

8. The group consisted of George Harrison, his older brother Peter, and noted British actor Arthur Kelly on guitars, along with Alan Williams (not the Beatles' first agent) and a fifth member (whose name is lost in the mists of time) playing tea-chest bass and washboard. What was the name of this skiffle outfit, George's first band?

9. Which of the future Beatles was the first to play the Cavern Club?

10. During McCartney's enrollment at the Liverpool Institute, the school play one year was George Bernard Shaw's *Saint Joan*, directed by the school's English master, Alan "Dusty" Durband. What role did Paul keenly audition for?

11. "The very first thing John and I tried to write was a play," Paul once told journalist Mat Snow. Written on the lined paper of a school exercise book, Lennon and McCartney's play revolved around a character (never seen) who believes he's the born-again son of God. What was his name?

12. What dubious honor does the instrumental "Guitar Boogie" hold for Paul McCartney?

13. In early 1958, during morning break from classes at the Liverpool Institute, Paul asked his mate John "Duff" Lowe if he wanted to play piano in the Quarry Men. Lowe could join, but only if he could play the opening of what Jerry Lee Lewis song?

14. What was Percy Phillips's connection to the Quarry Men?

15. Who was last the person to see John's mother Julia alive, 15 July 1958?

16. Why did tea-chest bassist Len Garry drop out of the Quarry Men?

17. While attending Liverpool College of Art, John's girlfriend for six months following summer holidays in 1958 was sixteen-year-old Thelma Pickles. Whom did she eventually marry?

18. What might Paul have been if he hadn't become a musician? Upon entering his sixth form at the Liverpool Institute in 1958, McCartney was handed a multiple-page form to complete where he listed his interests (swimming, church youth club, modern and ancient architecture), the number and subjects of his GCE (General Certificate of Education) O-level passes (which would come to include Spanish, French, and German) and career choices. What two vocations did the sixteen-year-old Quarry Man list?

19. A forerunner of his *Mersey Beat* newspaper, Liverpool Art College student Bill Harry edited and contributed local gig and concert reviews for a publication funded by Frank Hessy's Music Store, where many a Beatle guitar was purchased, including Stuart Sutcliffe's Hofner President bass. What was the name of this publication?

20. What group was George playing guitar in prior to rejoining the Quarry Men on the opening night of Mona Best's Casbah Coffee Club, 29 August 1959? At which club did this group have a residency?

21. Several weeks after its opening, a write-up on the Casbah Coffee Club appeared in the *West Derby Reporter*, "Kasbah (sic) Has A New Meaning For Local Teenagers." In describing the Casbah's "Eastern atmosphere," the uncredited writer notes "a large dragon painted along the length of one wall." Who painted this dragon?

22. Before joining the Beatles, Pete Best had been playing drums in the Blackjacks, a group he'd formed in October 1959. Who was in the original lineup?

23. In the fall of 1959, John Lennon had three people in mind for the job of bassist in the Quarry Men—Stuart Sutcliffe and two other art school mates—asking each if they could join (which meant securing a bass guitar) without telling the others. Dave May, who played with Ken Dallas & the Silhouettes was tempted, but couldn't afford the instrument's cost. Had Sutcliffe not sold his canvas at the John Moores Exhibition, who might have become a Beatle?

24. What is the title of the Stuart Sutcliffe canvas, selected for display at the John Moores Exhibition at Liverpool's Walker Gallery, which Moores himself would buy for £65? (Sutcliffe would subsequently use a portion of this money to make a deposit at Frank Hessy's on a Hofner President 500/5 bass guitar and become a "Beatal.")

25. What song did Johnny and the Moondogs sing during the final round of Carroll Levis's northwest *TV Star Search*, held Sunday evening, 15 November 1959, at the Hippodrome Theatre, Manchester?

ANSWERS

1. Quarry Man banjoist Rod Davis remembers the group performing "Worried Man Blues" at their Carroll Levis audition, a song the group had learned from a Burl Ives 78 record belonging to Davis.

2. Rod played a Windsor World banjo, which he purchased for £6 from a family in Denbigh, Wales.

(John's guitar at this time was a Gallotone Champion six-string acoustic.)

3. The Eddie Clayton Skiffle Group's first gig was at the Labour Club, Peel Street, Liverpool.

4. Iris Caldwell was twelve years old in 1957 when George (then fourteen) became her first boyfriend. George was often accompanied on his visits to the Caldwell residence by his former Rebels bandmate Arthur Kelly, who was seeing Iris's best friend. Iris's mother Vi dubbed the pair Arthur and Martha.

5. Sally Wright was crowned 1957 Rose Queen at the Garden Fete by Mrs. Thelwall Jones.

6. The Quarry Men shared the bill that evening with the George Edwards Band.

(It was while the Quarry Men were setting up in the hall for their evening performance that tea-chest bassist Ivan Vaughan introduced John Lennon to Paul McCartney.)

7. Standing by the side of the stage with his Grundig plugged into the mains, Molyneaux's hand mike recorded John singing the first two songs from the Quarry Men's second set that evening, Arthur Gunter's "Baby, Let's Play House" (an Elvis Presley B-side) and Lonnie Donegan's "Puttin' on the Style."

(Tea-chest bassist Len Garry remembers the second set continued with "Jailhouse Rock," "Worried Man Blues," "Cumberland Gap," "Midnight Special," and "Come Go With Me." Molyneaux's tape also includes two numbers by the George Edwards Band. The recording was bought for EMI by David Hughes, a Thorn EMI vice president in London for $122,770.)

8. George's first group was the Rebels.

(The Rebels' sole gig was in the summer of 1957 at the British Legion Club in Speke.)

9. Ringo Starr was the first of the Beatles to play the Cavern.

(Ringo's debut is believed to have been with the Eddie Clayton Skiffle Group at an evening session [which included a Miss Cavern Bathing Beauty Contest], 31 July 1957. Starr was known to have sat in during this period with the Darktown Skiffle Group, so it is also possible his debut at the venue may have been earlier that summer. John Lennon would not make his Cavern debut with the Quarrymen until 7 August 1957. McCartney, while a member of the group, was away at scout camp on this date and would not play the club until 24 January 1958. The Beatles as a group made their unadvertised debut at the Cavern [along with George] at a lunchtime session, 9 February 1961.)

10. Paul auditioned for the role of Richard De Beauchamp, Earl of Warwick.

(Paul was quite upset when he lost the role to Peter Sissons, future anchorman and interviewer for ITN. Durband ended up giving McCartney a nonspeaking role as a monk in scene vi.)

11. Pilchard.

(Discouraged by their lack of knowledge in the mechanics of playwriting, John and Paul's first collaboration expired after only two pages were written.)

12. Debuting with the Quarry Men at the Conservative Club's rock and skiffle night at the New Clubmoor Hall, Norris Green, 18 October 1957, Paul got "sticky fingers" during his solo on "Guitar Boogie," a hit in 1946 for Arthur Smith.

13. "Duff's" ability to play the rolling arpeggio up the keyboard that opens "Mean Woman Blues" was enough to get him into the Quarry Men.

14. Percy Phillips ran Phillips Sound Recording Service out of his living room at 38, Kensington, Liverpool. In late spring or early summer 1958, the Quarry Men made their first studio recording there.

(For his fee of 17s/6d, Phillips recorded the group onto a 78 rpm shellac disk as they performed Buddy Holly's "That'll Be The Day" and the McCartney/Harrison composition "In Spite Of All The Danger." Both songs were included on disc one of *Anthology 1*, released by EMI/Capitol in November 1995.)

15. Former Quarry Men manager Nigel Whalley was the last person to see Julia alive, having walked with her the last two hundred yards from her sister Mimi's house to her bus stop. Crossing Menlove Avenue, Julia, 44, was struck and killed by a car driven by an off-duty policeman.

(Julia's last words to her sister that evening were "Don't worry.")

16. In August 1958, Len fell unconscious at his family's Liverpool home. As the Quarry Men carried on, Garry spent the next seven months recovering in Fazakerly Hospital from tubercular meningitis.

(Ironically, during this same period, former Quarry Man Nigel Whalley was recovering from pleurisy in a different section of the hospital.)

17. Thelma Pickles married poet Roger McGough.

(From 1963 to 1974, McGough was part of the musical/comedy trio The Scaffold, which included John Gorman and Paul's brother, Mike.)

18. McCartney's listed career choices were "teaching" (university or training college) and "architect."

(Paul would list his father Jim's occupation as "lead guitarist with Rory Shakin' Blackwell," before crossing it out to list his correct occupation of cotton salesman.)

19. Frank Hessy's music magazine was called *Frank Comments*.

20. The Les Stewart Quartet, featuring guitarist George Harrison, had a residency at the Lowlands Club, just fifty yards up from the Casbah on the opposite side of Hayman's Green.

(When Les Stewart refused a residency at the Casbah, following an argument with bassist Ken Brown, George approached John and Paul, reforming the Quarry Men, who had been mostly idle since late January.

On opening night, Brown remembers John singing "Three Cool Cats" and Paul singing "Long Tall Sally."

21. The dragon at the Casbah was painted by Mona Best.

(The spiderwebs painted on the club's walls were created by John's future wife, Cynthia Powell.)

22. The Blackjacks featured Pete Best on drums, Ken Brown (recently sacked by the Quarry Men) on guitar and vocals, Bill Barlow on lead guitar and Charlie "Chas" Newby on bass guitar.

23. Rod Murray, who shared Flat 3 with John and Stu at Hillary Mansions in Gambier Terrace, was in the process of making a bass guitar to join the Quarry Men when Stuart got the nod.

(George had tried to recruit his schoolmate, noted British actor Arthur Kelly, to be the Quarry Men's bassist but, like Dave May, he found the purchase price prohibitive.)

24. Sutcliffe's canvas was titled "Summer Painting."

(Only half of "Summer Painting" was actually displayed at the Walker Gallery when the Moores exhibition ran from 17 November 1959 to 17 January 1960. The second half—which would have measured out the work to 8' × 8'—was left exposed to the elements in the backyard at Hillary Mansions until Stuart's mother and sisters finally retrieved it.)

25. Graham Nash (who was also performing for Carroll Levis that night with future Hollies bandmate Allan Clarke), remembers Johnny and the Moondogs singing Buddy Holly's "Think It Over."

(Also performing that night were Billy Fury and Freddie Garritty—later of Freddie & the Dreamers.)

1960

LIVERPOOL MAY 1960

JOHN
PAUL
GEORGE
AND STU

2-RECORD SET! OVER 80 MINUTES OF VINTAGE HOME RECORDINGS
including I'll Follow the Sun, Hallelujah, I Love Her So and The One After 909

1. If one of the other Beatles wanted to get Paul's attention, he might've called him by his nickname, "Macca." Though neither ever enjoyed the widespread use the variation on Paul's surname has, John and George both had similar nicknames—what are they?

2. "Well don't leave me alone, my dear/Have courage and follow me, my dear." These lyrics were long gone by the time the Beatles recorded this song in 1964, but not so in April 1960, when Paul was captured on tape rehearsing it with the Beatals/Silver Beetles in the front parlor of the McCartney's home on Forthlin Road. What is the song?

3. "My darlin', when you burnt that toast the other mornin', I looked into your eyes and I could see your National Health eyeball. And I loved you, like I've never done, like I've never done before." These heartfelt sentiments, captured on an early recording, were spoken by John during the middle eight break of what McCartney/Lennon composition?

4. Organized by Allan Williams, flyers for this event at Liverpool Stadium, 3 May, billed it as "The Greatest Show Ever to Be Staged." Ringo Starr even took part in the evening—who was the headliner?

5. Around 5 May, Allan Williams, acting on a suggestion from Brian Cassar, secured Tommy Moore as the Beatals' new drummer. At his Gambier Terrace audition, the thirty-six-year-old forklift driver at Garston Bottle Works remembers that it was his ability to reproduce the slow, skipping beat of this Everly Brothers song that got him the nod. What was the song?

6. Five groups auditioned for Larry Parnes at the Wyvern Social Club, 10 May, for the opportunity to back Billy Fury—Cass and the Cassanovas, Derry and the Seniors, Gerry and the Pacemakers, Cliff Roberts and the Rockers, and the Silver Beetles. Which group did Parnes select?

7. Who is Ricky Damone and what was his connection to Larry Parnes' Wyvern auditions?

8. When the Silver Beetles backed Johnny Gentle on a tour of Scotland, 20–28 May, nearly every member of the group adopted a new stage name. Paul became Paul Ramon, George became Carl Harrison (in honor of Carl Perkins), and Stu Sutcliffe became Stuart de Stael, after the Russian-born French painter Nicholas de Stael. While John has vehemently denied it, Paul now maintains that Lennon also adopted a stage name—what was it?

9. While the engagement never materialized, Larry Parnes considered sending the Silver Beetles back to Scotland in mid-July to back another singer from his "stable"—which one?

10. Who is Big Ronnie?

11. Promoters wishing to book "Rock and Rhythm" group Gerry and the Peacemakers in 1960 contacted Flag Productions at 8 Menzies Street in Liverpool. If you wanted to engage Rory Storm and the Hurricanes, Ringo's group at the time, who would you call?

12. A "startling investigation" in the Sunday 24 July edition of *The People* reported on the "unsavoury cult" of "beatniks of Britain." Peter Forbes's expose included a spotlight on "a group that inhabits a three-room flat in decaying Gambier Terrace, in the heart of Liverpool"—Rod Murray, Rod

Jones, and John Lennon. A staged photo taken in Murray's room shows John lying on the floor amid the carefully staged squalor listening to the "magnificent home-built hi-fi record player, blaring the cool jazz." What was the title of the article?

13. Who contacted Pete Best to ask him if he'd like to audition for the Beatles on 12 August?

14. What was the name of the first Liverpool group Allan Williams contracted to Bruno Koschmider, thus paving the way for the Beatles' first Hamburg stint, forty-eight nights at the Indra Club, beginning 17 August?

15. Conversely, when Bruno Koschmider requested a second Liverpool group to play the Indra, the Beatles' story might have gone quite differently if the first band Allan Williams asked had said yes. Who were they?

16. When Paul McCartney first accompanied the Beatles to Hamburg, he played guitar. What kind was it?

17. Stuart often sang one of two Elvis Presley songs during his vocal spotlight in the Silver Beetles/Silver Beatles/Beatles—what were their titles?

18. During their first trip to Hamburg, George accompanied John to the Musikhaus Rotthoff where Lennon sold his Hofner Club 40 electric hollow body guitar to buy his first model of what guitar?

19. The Beatles excelled at three-part harmonies, as songs like "That Boy," "Here There and Everywhere," and "Because" well attest. "We learned three-part harmony from singing (this song)," remembers Paul. What song was it?

20. When Klaus Voormann wandered onto the cobbled Grosse Freiheit (Great Freedom) in Hamburg's St. Pauli district one night in October, he was drawn to the Kaiserkeller by the sounds of rock and roll emanating from within. What group was playing onstage when he entered that first time?

21. Accompanied by his girlfriend, Astrid Kirchherr, Klaus first introduced himself to John during a break in the Beatles' set a few nights later. Voormann recalls "connecting" with Lennon when he showed him the first sleeve he ever produced. What West German release had Voorman designed it for?

22. Following their introduction to the group, Jurgen Vollmer remembers that from then on, whenever the Beatles spotted their Exi (existentialist) friends in the Kaiserkeller, they would finish the song they were playing and break immediately into what?

23. Who, in the Beatles' circle of friends, lived at 42A Eimsbutteler Strasse, Altona in Hamburg?

24. Following his return from Hamburg, 1 December, Paul secured gainful employment through the Labour Exchange—what did he do?

25. "For only me to see/Your lips, your lovely eyes/Are the key to paradise/A guiding star that's what you are." These lyrics were written by Stuart Sutcliffe in 1960 while a member of the Silver Beetles/Silver Beatles/Beatles—what did he title them?

ANSWERS

1. John and George's nicknames are "Lennie" and "Hazza," respectively.

2. "I'll Follow The Sun."

3. Loving gazes into National Health eyeballs feature in "You'll Be Mine."

(Included on disc one of *Anthology 1*, a practice session during an Easter holiday in April 1960 provided the occasion for this recording by the Beatals/Silver Beetles (with Stuart Sutcliffe on bass) on a borrowed Grundig TK12 tape recorder at the McCartney home at 20 Forthlin Road.)

4. Gene Vincent was the headliner at Allan Williams' rock show at Liverpool Stadium, 3 May.

(Ringo Starr numbered among the many support acts on the bill, drumming for Rory Storm and the Hurricanes. Eddie Cochran had also been scheduled to headline the show, when a car accident near Chippenham, 17 April, claimed his life. Vincent, who had also been riding in the car, still honored the Liverpool engagement, despite a broken collarbone and ribs.)

5. It was Moore's drumming on Phil and Don Everly's song "Cathy's Clown" that convinced the Beatals he should join the group.

6. None of the groups who auditioned at the Wyvern that day were selected to back Fury.

7. Ricky Damone was the first stage name adopted by John Askew. When Askew joined Larry Parnes's stable of pop singers, Parnes changed his name to Johnny Gentle. A result of the Wyvern audition was the booking Parnes subsequently offered the Silver Beetles, backing Gentle on a seven-show tour of Scotland, 20–28 May.

(Askew had taken the name Ricky from Ricky Nelson, whom he cites as an early influence. Parnes had initially wanted to rename him Tim McGee, on the assumption that everyone who came from Liverpool sounded Irish, but Askew refused.)

8. In volume one of the *Anthology* video set, McCartney maintains that John took the stage name "Long John" on the Scottish tour.

(It was Brian Cassar [Cass, of Cass and the Casanovas] who suggested the group change their name from Beatles to Long John and the Silver Beetles, having first suggested Long John and his Pieces of Eight. In a 1996 phone interview with the BBC, McCartney said that for a short time during this year he considered taking the stage name Paul James.)

9. Parnes considered sending the Silver Beetles on a tour backing Dickie Pride.

(Parnes died in London, 30 July 1989, at the age of 59.)

10. Tommy Moore having essentially left the group, the Silver Beetles were drummerless before an engagement at the Grosvenor Ballroom in Wallasey, 11 June. Not expecting any takers, John Lennon petitioned the audience for a replacement. Seventeen-year-old Big Ronnie was an exceptionally large, red-headed Teddy Boy who took up Lennon's invitation to "play" the empty kit set up on stage. The results were reported to be less than musical.

11. Downbeat Promotions handled bookings for Rory Storm and the Hurricanes at Stoneycroft-3324.

12. Originally presented to the Gambier Terrace residents as a feature on the difficulties of making ends meet on student grants, *The People* ran their article on pages 2 and 3 under the headline "This Is the Beatnik Horror!"

13. Paul McCartney phoned 8 Haymans Green to ask Pete if he would like to audition for the Beatles.

(Best auditioned for the group on 12 August at the Wyvern Social Club.)

14. The Beatles owned their Hamburg apprenticeship to the favorable impression made at the Kaiserkeller by Derry (Wilkie) and the Seniors.

15. The first group Williams asked to play the Indra was Gerry and the Peacemakers.

(The group would decline, which in the end only delayed their Hamburg apprenticeship by a few months. Williams's first choice for the job had been Rory Storm and the Hurricanes, but they were already up in Pwllheli in North Wales, playing the summer season at a Butlin's holiday camp.)

16. McCartney's guitar on the Beatles' first trip to Hamburg was a Dutch-made Rosetti Lucky Seven.

("It was like one of the worst ever made," Paul told Vic Garbarini. "It was just a hunk of plywood with a pick (guard) on it. Worst action going. But it looked good.")

17. Stuart's Elvis Presley vocal spotlights were Lieber-Stoller's "Loving You" and the Presley/Matson-credited "Love Me Tender" (though actually written by Ken Darby.)

18. Lennon purchased his first Rickenbacker 325 guitar at the Musikhaus Rotthoff, a 1958 or 1959 Capri model in a natural maple finish.

19. John, Paul and George perfected their three-part harmonies singing the Phil Spector composition "To Know Him Is to Love Him," a hit for the Teddy Bears in 1958.

(The Beatles would sing the song as "To Know Her Is to Love Her." "That was the first three-part we ever did," remembers Paul. "[We] learned that in my dad's house in Liverpool.")

20. Rory Storm and the Hurricanes were finishing up their set when Voormann first entered the Kaiserkeller that fateful night in October.

(Erwin Ross's handpainted posters for the engagement at the club touted the "Festival Der Rock 'n Roll Fans," with "Rory Storm and his Hurrican und the Beatles.")

21.   Voorman showed Lennon his artwork for the sleeve of a cover version of the Ventures' "Walk Don't Run" by the Typhoons.

(That was my first cover," Voorman would tell *Beatlefan* contributing editor Rip Rense in 1996. "Just a black-and-white cover of a man walking in the street. And John said, 'Go to Stuart; he's the arty one.' ")

22.   When the Beatles spotted Astrid, Jurgen and Klaus in the Kaiserkeller, they would break into "Stay," Maurice Williams's 1960 U.S. hit with the Zodiacs.)

23.   Astrid Kirchherr was living at this address (her family home) when she first saw the Beatles playing at the Kaiserkeller, in October 1960. Klaus Voormann, her boyfriend at the time, was also a lodger in the attic there.

24.   Paul earned £7 a week during the Christmas rush as a truck driver's mate, delivering packages for the Speedy Prompt Delivery Company.

25.   Sutcliffe's lyrics were titled "Heavenly."

1961

SOTHEBY'S

ROCK & ROLL MEMORABILIA
1956~1983

Thursday, 1st September, 1983

1. Had relations between Bruno Koschmider and the Beatles gone better, the group might well have followed up the completion of their residency at the Kaiserkeller, 31 December 1960, with a four-week engagement at a club in what city, starting 7 January?

2. The evening of 17 February, Casbah Promotions held "a rock 'n' roll dance" at St. John's Hall in Liverpool featuring the Beatles and Gene Day and the Jango Beats. Who ran Casbah Promotions?

3. Who were the Bulldog Gang?

4. In March, Paul was supplementing his Beatles gigs at the Cavern and the Casbah with a job at what firm?

5. During their thirteen-week stay at Hamburg's Top Ten Club (starting 1 April), Paul went to the second floor of Steinway's music shop to purchase his first one of these for 350 German Marks (about £30)—what was it?

6. Following a visit to the Top Ten Club in April 1961, this German rocker's recommendation to Bert Kaempfert eventually led to Tony Sheridan and the Beatles recording for the famous bandleader and composer. Who is he?

7. What was GAR-6922?

8. What is the name of the song Tony Sheridan has said he composed with Paul McCartney in Hamburg in June 1961?

9. Who is Dan Sherry and what did he do in June 1961 to secure himself a prominent place in the Beatles' history?

10. Stuart Sutcliffe started a novel whose central character was a young artist "living with a friend in a seedy flat in 'Puke Street,'" based after John and himself, which he first named "John" and later changed to "Nhoke." What was to have been the book's title?

11. What is "STOP THE WORLD—and listen to everything in it"?

12. The Beatles' appearance at the Aintree Institute, 19 August, was supplemented by Joan Pratt, Maureen O'Donnell and Marie Williams. By what name were they better known?

13. Sponsored by Cavern Club owner Ray McFall, the Beatles played four "Riverboat Shuffles" on the River Mersey, the first, 25 August, in support of Acker Bilk's Paramount Jazz Band. These performances "over the water" were held on what boat?

14. "I stay home on Friday night/Go to bed at eight/On Saturday night I'm all alone/I don't have a date." What is the title of this Sutcliffe composition, one of several songs written by Stuart during this period?

15. Liverpool promoter Brian Kelly regularly booked the Beatles at such venues as the Aintree Institute and Litherland Town Hall. Compering these appearances was Cavern DJ Bob Wooler, who often introduced the group while spinning a record of what piece of music as the curtains parted?

16. In Bob Wooler's *Mersey Beat* column for 31 August, he describes the Beatles as "the stuff screams are made of," singling out Pete Best for his "mean, moody magnificence." While Pete was neither mean nor moody, the tag stuck. Wooler has said this phrase originated from a movie-poster description of actress Jane Russell—what was the film?

17. On 30 September, funded by £100 Lennon had received from an aunt in Scotland for his twenty-first birthday, John and Paul began a fourteen day hitchhiking holiday to Paris. It was while passing through London that the two first acquired what noted item of Beatles apparel?

18. Who were the Beatmakers?

19. Brian Epstein's autobiography, A *Cellarful of Noise*, opens with eighteen-year-old Raymond Jones walking into his Whitechapel record store at about three o'clock on Saturday, 28 October. "There's a record I want. It's 'My Bonnie' and it was made in Germany. Have you got it?" This would certainly appear to be an historic date in Beatles history—the request that would lead Epstein to the group he would eventually manage. But NEMS record store regularly stocked *Mersey Beat* newspaper (beginning with the first issue, published 6 July). Brain was aware of the local groups reported in its pages (including the Beatles) through regular discussions with its publisher, Bill Harry. Who is Raymond Jones—why has he never come forward?

20. Brain Epstein visited the Cavern for the first time on Thursday, 9 November, taking in part of a lunchtime session with his personal assistant at NEMS, Alistair Taylor. The Beatles were already onstage when the pair arrived; the first song Brian heard them play was a Lennon/McCartney composition—which one?

21. While it might seem obvious, who was the first member of the Quarry Men to perform on a commercially issued recording in Britain?

22. Cavern Club compere Bob Wooler was affectionately known for his "Woolerisms," the phrases he would confer on Liverpool music personalities. Brian Epstein was known as "The Nemperor," Derry Wilke (of Derry and the Seniors) was "Big Daddy," and Faron Young (of Faron and the Flamingos), the "Panda-footed Prince of Prance." Who did Bob "Big Beat" Wooler dub "Mr. Showmanship" and "Mr. Personality"?

23. On 10 December, the Beatles met with Brian Epstein at the Casbah Coffee Club and agreed in principle to sign a management contract with him. The news came as a disappointment to this Liverpool promoter, who had hoped to release the Beatles' first single on his own "Troubadour Records" label. Who is he?

24. Whom did John refer to as "Curly"?

25. As the year came to a close, to whom did Stuart sell his Hofner President 500/5 bass?

ANSWERS

1. On 16 October, Koschmider extended the Beatles' engagement at the Kaiserkeller through 31 December. Had the Beatles not fallen out with Bruno (who had received reports of the group playing at rival Peter Eckhorn's Top Ten Club), it appeared the group's next stop would have been West Berlin, starting 7 January 1961.

(In a letter written over September and October 1960 to his friend and former Rebels bandmate Arthur Kelly, Harrison mentions, "I can speak gut German now and we are staying here until Christ[mas] and then we are going with a man to Berlin. We are earning £18 a week now and after Crimble when we go to Berlin we will earn 60 marks a night [£30 a week]." Another letter written by Stuart Sutcliffe that November also mentioned a Berlin destination after Christmas.)

2. Casbah Promotions was run by Pete Best's mother, Mona.

(Mona ran dances from St. John's Hall on several occasions, as it was not far from her West Derby home.)

3. The Bulldog Gang were one of several cliques formed by the girls who frequented the Cavern Club to see the Beatles.

(Other groups included the Cement Mixers, the Woodentops and one group of eight girls John nicknamed the "Beatletts.")

4. Paul worked briefly for Massey & Coggins Ltd.

(McCartney first swept the yard at the Edge Hill Works site on Bridge Road; a short time later he was promoted to winding cogs.)

5. Paul's purchase at Steinway's was his first left-handed Hofner Violin bass guitar.

(The Hofner Company was founded by Karl Hofner in 1887; it was Karl's son, Walter, who had the idea for a short-scale electric bass guitar made in the "viol family" shape. McCartney's bass, a 1961 model 500/1, with separate machine head gears, "rugby-ball"-shaped tuning knobs, and close pickups, was manufactured at the Hofner plant at Schonbacher Strasse 56, Beubenreuth. In February 1998, he had it insured for £2,000,000.)

6. Tommy Kent.

(Kent's recommendation along with that of producer Alfred Schacht would convince Kaempfert to hear Sheridan and the Beatles at the Top Ten Club. By 1 July, both had signed recording contracts with "Der Bert Kaempfert Producktion.")

7. In the Liverpool telephone directory for 1961, GARston-6922 was Paul McCartney's telephone number at 20 Forthlin Road, 18, listed under J(ames) McCartney, his father.

(George [formerly at GAR-4596] can be heard reciting this number ["GARston six nine double two"] at the end of "Miss O'Dell," the B-side of his May 1973 Apple single "Give Me Love [Give Me Peace On Earth].")

8. Tony's Sheridan/McCartney composition is titled "Tell Me If You Can."

9. When Philips in Germany issued the LP *Twist Im Star-Club Hamburg* in March 1963, among its various artists recorded live at the venue were two cuts featuring Tony Sheridan. As Sheridan was under contract to Polydor at the time, the vocals were credited under the pseudonym Dan Sherry.

(From 22–23 June 1961, the Beatles backed "Sherry Dan" on sessions at the Friedrich Ebert Halle in Hamburg, including "My Bonnie" and "The Saints.")

10. Sutcliffe's unfinished novel was titled *Spotlight on Johnny*.

(This manuscript was sold at Sotheby's in London, 1 September 1983, for £1045. Stuart had also expressed plans to write a play centering around a bus conductor and his "subconscious inspector" which he intended to title *Mister Man and Queen Elsie*.)

11. "STOP THE WORLD—and listen to everything in it" was the title of Brian Epstein's record review column for *Mersey Beat* music paper.

(Brian's column appeared in issue number three, dated August 3–17, 1961. Among the new releases he reviewed were "show albums" for *Beyond the Fringe* [on Parlophone, produced by George Martin], *The Music*

Man [available from NEMS as both a Capitol import and HMV domestic], as well as the latest singles from Elvis Presley, Bobby Rydell, and Chubby Checker.)

12. Joan, Maureen and Marie were dancers better known as the Shimmy-Shimmy Girls, a name coined by Bob Wooler.

13. Ray McFall's Riverboat Shuffles were held aboard the MV *Royal Iris*.

14. "Everybody's Ever Got Somebody Caring."
(Other songs written by Sutcliffe during this time include "Ooh Ooh Ooh," "Peace of Mind," and "Yeah 'Cos You're a Sure a Bet to Win My Lips.")

15. Wooler would often bring on the Beatles to the opening bars of Gioacchino Rossini's "William Tell Overture."

16. Bob Wooler remembered a movie poster description of Jane Russell as "mean, moody and magnificent" in her role as Rio in the 1943 Howard Hughes Western, *The Outlaw*.

17. Wandering along Charing Cross Road in London, Lennon and McCartney acquired their first pairs of what would one day be known as Beatle boots, the flamenco-style, calf-length black boots with Cuban heels and a tag at the back, which they'd seen in the windows of specialist shoe retailers Annello and Davide.

18. The Beatles and Gerry and the Pacemakers performed onstage together as the Beatmakers at Litherland Town Hall, 19 October, the only occasion both groups performed together.
(Lead vocals were handled by Gerry Marsden and Karl Terry, the latter on the bill that evening as leader of his group, Karl Terry and the Cruisers.)

19. Raymond Jones never existed; he was created by Alistair Taylor, Epstein's personal assistant at the time.
(In a fax to the author dated 6 June 1997, George Gunby, Taylor's personal manager, related how fans at NEMS were asking for "My Bonnie" by the Beatles, but no one would place a specific order for it. "Alistair felt that the shop was missing sales. Brian would not order the record without a specific customer order. So Alistair used a little initiative and wrote an order out for a customer, using the name Raymond Jones. When the Beat-

les broke, Alistair had joined PYE Records in London. Brian noted the Raymond Jones name and used it in his press releases and interviews. Alistair never bothered to correct the impression, as it was a useful tale to include in the Beatles myth."

"It gave us a hook to hang a story on when interest grew and the press began asking questions," wrote Taylor in a letter printed in the July 1997 issue of *Mojo* magazine.)

20. Alistair Taylor remembers the first Beatles song he and Brian heard at the Cavern was "Hello Little Girl," sung by Paul.

21. As a member of the Trad Grads, Rod Davis played on Decca single 45-F 11403, "Runnin' Shoes"/"Rag-Day Jazz-Band Ball," issued in Britain in November 1961.

(The Beatles would wait until January 1962 for their first English release, when Polydor issued Tony Sheridan's "My Bonnie" [with English introduction] backed with "The Saints" [When The Saints Go Marching In]. The single is also of note as the first commercial recording to be issued in Britain to bear the name "Beatles.")

22. "Mr. Showmanship" and "Mr. Personality" were Woolerisms for Rory Storm and Gerry Marsden, respectively.

(During this period Wooler often copromoted shows at Hambleton Hall with Vic Anton. A classified ad in the *Liverpool Echo* announcing an appearance by the Beatles at the venue 26 November supplied Woolerisms for each Beatle: "The Singing Rage" [John], "The Rockin' Riot" [Paul], "Sheik of Araby" [George], and "The Bashful Beat" [Pete Best].)

23. Sam Leach.

(Leach, who had staged three Operation Big Beat shows at New Brighton's Tower Ballroom in 1961 featuring the group, had wanted the Beatles to record "Twist and Shout" and "Stand By Me.")

24. As he was balding at the forehead, John nicknamed Liverpool wedding photographer Albert Marrion "Curly."

(At Brian Epstein's request, Marrion took the first official photographs of the Beatles, dressed in their leathers, at his studio at 268 Wallasey Village, Wallasey, 17 December.)

25. Stuart sold his Hofner to Klaus Voormann to buy paints.

1962

1962 THE AUDITION TAPES

1.   What was the name of the first U.S. publication to mention the Beatles by name?

2.   What did the Beatles do over individual six-pence postage revenue stamps of Great Britain in the offices of NEMS, 24 January?

3.   During January and February, Stuart played a few times with this German group, who had recently lost their bass player to Tony Sheridan. Though Stuart was offered the vacancy, he declined. What was the name of the group?

4.   The Beatles' appearance at the Aintree Institute, 27 January, was the last time Brian Kelly promoted a Beatles engagement—why was that?

5.   "An unusual group, not as 'Rocky' as most, more C&W with a tendency to play music." Who wrote this assessment of the group on their audition application, 12 February?

6. Stuart Sutcliffe made his last visit to Liverpool in February, visiting the Cavern with sister Pauline to see the Beatles and having dinner with Brian Epstein. On his return to Hamburg, Sutcliffe received a letter from Brian with an interesting offer—what was it?

7. In March, Polydor had planned to release a followup single to "My Bonnie"/"The Saints" (Polydor NH 24757), which was later cancelled. What songs would have comprised the single?

8. Stuart Sutcliffe died in Hamburg of a brain hemorrhage, 10 April. His body was laid to rest in Parish Church Cemetary in the Liverpool suburb of Huyton. Who does Stu share his gravestone with?

9. When Manfred Weissleder opened his new Star-Club at 2 P.M., 13 April, the Beatles were there to begin a seven-week stint. What business had previously occupied the site at Grosse Freiheit 39, before Weissleder gutted it (beginning in 1961), to create Hamburg's most famous rock club?

10. What does Pete Best remember as the working title of "Love Me Do"?

11. "Created" during the Beatles' seven-week residency at the Star-Club, what was nicknamed "The Thing"?

12. Before he would release the Beatles from their contract with him, Bert Kaempfert required the group to back Tony Sheridan one last time, 24 May. The session, at the Studio Rahlstedt, Hamburg, was intended to produce a single release for Polydor, with "Sweet Georgia Brown" on the A-side. According to the "Aufnahmeprotokoll" (release protocol) document in Polydor's archive, who was the arranger for this song?

13. Brian Epstein's second signing after the Beatles were Gerry and the Pacemakers in June. What was Gerry's nickname for the Beatles?

14. Not surprisingly, George was the first among the Beatles to acquire a car—what kind was it?

15. A strong contender for the drum stool Pete Best was to lose 16 August was suggested by Bob Wooler. "I wouldn't join the Beatles for a gold clock," was his response. Who is he?

16. Ringo's departure from the Hurricanes left Rory Storm without a drummer and another eleven days left on their engagement at Butlin's in Skegness. Who was deputized as a Hurricane for those dates?

17. Ringo had been planning to leave Rory Storm and the Hurricanes at the conclusion of their season at Butlin's at the end of August and had already accepted an offer from another group (then playing in Hamburg) when Brian Epstein's phone call changed everything. Had things gone differently, who might Starr have been drumming for?

18. Following Best's sacking, Brian Epstein was dining at the Cabaret Club with Ted Knibbs, manager of Billy J. Kramer, and Bob Wooler when Wooler announced that he was "going to tell the *true* Pete Best story," the article likely to have appeared in *Mersey Beat*. Wooler regrets never having written the piece, which Knibbs convinced him to drop—what was he going to title it?

19. What two groups did Pete Best decline offers to join before settling with Lee Curtis and the All Stars?

20. The Beatles were filmed for television for the first time 22 August, when Granada Television captured performances of "Some Other Guy" and "Kansas City"/"Hey-Hey-Hey-Hey!" at a Cavern lunchtime session. The footage had been intended for a program called *Know the North* and would also have spotlighted what other group?

21. Adam Faith, Johnny Angel, and the Beatles all passed on this song by Lionel Michael Stitcher, but not Gerry and the Pacemakers—what is it?

22. John and George both special ordered Gibson J-160E acoustic guitars from Rushworth's Music in Liverpool during the summer of 1962. The guitars were flown in from the U.S. by jet, the two Beatles taking delivery from John Rushworth, 10 September. What was the first Beatles song Lennon recorded with his Gibson?

23. It's unlikely John ever knew Elizabeth Ann Barton, but he sure knew how to cover the song she inspired; after its composer released it as a single on the Dot label, 17 September 1962, the Beatles added it to their live shows. The following year, they performed it twice on BBC radio and included it on their debut LP. What is this song's title?

24. In 1962, Parlophone's release schedule included 45-R 4919, "My Tears Will Turn to Laughter"/"I've Just Fallen for Someone," by Darren Young. Besides sporting the same red label Parlophone would use on the Beatles' first single, "Love Me Do"/"P.S. Love You" (45-R 4949), what is the Beatles connection to Young's single?

25. When EMI purchased a ninety-five percent interest in Capitol Records for $8.5 million in January 1955, the deal gave Capitol first right of refusal on recordings issued by EMI artists. When George Martin submitted the Beatles' Parlophone single "Love Me Do"/"P.S. I Love You" for consideration, he had to contend with the judgment of this producer, whom Capitol Records president Alan Livingston had given the assignment of listening to all EMI submissions to determine their suitability for the American market. Who was this man, responsible for Capitol passing not only on "Love Me Do," but on the group's two subsequent UK chart toppers?

ANSWERS

1. Music trade paper *Cash Box* was the first publication in the U.S. to mention the Beatles by name.

(Noted in the International Section of the issue dated 13 January was the release of "My Bonnie" on the Polydor label by the "new rock and roll team, Tony Sheridan and the Beatles.")

2. As witnessed by Brian's personal assistant, Alistair Taylor, the Beatles affixed their signatures to their first management contract with Epstein over individual six-pence postage revenue stamps displaying a Dorothy Wilding portrait of Queen Elizabeth II in reddish purple.

(Though Taylor's signature attests to having "witnessed" it, Epstein did not sign over his stamp on the contract until October.)

3. Stuart was dissuaded by Astrid and her mother from considering the bass vacancy recently opened in the Bats.

4. Kelly offended Brian Epstein by paying the Beatles' £15 fee in loose change.

("[S]ixpences and florins and even halfpennies," Epstein recalled in *A Cellarful of Noise*, "and I kicked up an awful fuss not because £15 isn't £15 in any currency, but because I thought it was disrespectful to the Beatles.")

5. This assessment of the Beatles was written by BBC teen radio program producer Peter Pilbeam on the group's "Application for an Audition by Variety Department."

(Having passed their audition that day at Broadcasting House in Manchester, the group were subsequently booked for their first BBC appearance, *Teenager's Turn—Here We Go*, recorded at the Playhouse Theatre, Manchester, 7 March, and broadcast the following afternoon.)

6. Epstein's letter inquired if Stuart would be interested in working for NEMS Enterprises helping to manage the Beatles.

7. Information discovered on the original master tape cover indicates that Polydor had planned a followup single featuring "Why" backed with the Harrison/Lennon instrumental "Cry for a Shadow."

8. Stu's gravestone also marks the final resting place of his father, Charles, who died 18 March 1966 at the age of sixty.

9. Before the Star-Club, Grosse Freiheit 39 was the address of the Stern Kino, an adult cinema where many Weissleder-financed films were shown.

10. Best recalls the working title of "Love Me Do" as "Love, Love Me Do."

(Pete remembers John and Paul working on the song in the Beatles' flat on the Gross Freiheit one afternoon in April prior to beginning their residency at the Star-Club. "The title started out as *Love, Love Me Do*, but was quickly abbreviated by popular agreement.")

11. During their residency at the Star-Club, the Beatles had their own flat on the Grosse Freiheit, across the street from the venue. Following a night of heavy drinking, George vomited onto the floor at the side of his bed. Festooned with cigarette butts and bits of food, the mess, which Harrison and the cleaning lady both refused to clean, soon grew until, as Pete Best recounted in *Beatle!* ". . . it assumed the look of a hedgehog; we christened it The Thing."

12. The arranger of "Sweet Georgia Brown" at the Beatles' last session with Tony Sheridan was Paul McCartney.

(Polydor never issued this single, which was to include a cover of "Swanee River," also recorded at this session, as its B-side. According to Kaempfert's widow, this version [as opposed to the released version recorded by the non-Beatles Beat Brothers in December 1961] is said to no longer exist, having been destroyed—along with all his other recordings—in a fire.)

13.   Gerry Marsden referred to the Beatles as "The Beats."

14.   George's first car (license plate 935 MPF) was a Ford Anglia. (Paul's first car was a Ford Classic.)

15.   Big Three drummer Johnny Hutchinson was considered as Pete Best's replacement in the Beatles.

(When Pete Best was sacked by Brian Epstein, 16 August, the Beatles still had three bookings to honor before Ringo could join them on the 18th. It was Hutchinson who drummed on these interim engagements, at the Riverpark Ballroom, Chester on the 16th, and the Majestic Ballroom, Birkenhead, and New Brighton's Tower Ballroom on the 17th.)

16.   Rory Storm and the Hurricanes recruited Anthony Ashdown, an actor who could play drums, to finish their third summer season at Butlin's.

17.   Starr had already accepted an offer from Ted "Kingsize" Taylor to drum in his Dominoes when Epstein called.

18.   Wooler's article on Pete Best's sacking was to have been titled "Odd Man—Out."

19.   According to guitarist Johnny Byrne, Pete was offered the drum seat vacated by Ringo in Rory Storm and the Hurricanes. Shortly after the sacking, Brian Epstein had another meeting with Best where he offered him the opportunity to drum for the Merseybeats, whom he was considering for management.

20.   *Know the North* would also have focused on the Brighouse and Rastrick Brass Band.

(The program was shelved when the Beatles footage was judged unsuitable for broadcast. Granada also realized that were they to air the film, they would have to pay the B&R Brass Band the prevailing Musicans Union rates.)

21.   Stitcher's song (composed under the name Mitch Murray) was "How Do You Do It."

(Johnny Angel passed on the song in favor of another Murray composition, "Better Luck Next Time." While the Beatles got as far as recording the song [Studio Two, 4 September], their version would not be officially released until *Anthology 1* in 1995, merely serving at the time as the demo Gerry and the Pacemakers would follow, taking the song to number one in March 1963.)

22. The next morning, 11 September, Lennon took his J-160E to Abbey Road, playing it on the Beatles' remake of "Love Me Do" in Studio Two.

(Lennon's first J-160E was stolen in December 1963. In *A Hard Day's Night*, John is seen using George's Gibson for "If I Fell" and "And I Love Her.")

23. Elizabeth Ann Barton inspired the song "Anna (Go To Him)."

("Damn, the Beatles playing me," composer Arthur Alexander exclaimed when he first heard their version of "Anna" while playing pool. "That line, 'All of my life I've searching for a girl' is true. I was real young and naive, and when I got to that part, that thrilled me so much." "Anna" relates the end of his marriage to Elizabeth Ann Barton, whom Alexander had met in 1960. "She never said to me she wanted to go with another guy, but I could tell. You can tell from the way the relationship was going, because in my mind she wanted to be free. I had given her rings and stuff. She never gave 'em back, even though we separated." Alexander died of heart failure, 9 June 1993, age fifty-three.)

24. In 1962, Darren Young was the stage name of singer Johnny Gentle. Gentle has maintained that during his tour of Scotland backed by the Silver Beetles in May 1960, Lennon had an uncredited hand in helping him write the middle eight of "I've Just Fallen for Someone" in a hotel room in Inverness.

25. Acting on behalf of Capitol, Dave Dexter passed on the Beatles' first three Parlophone singles: "Love Me Do," "Please Please Me," and "She Loves You."

(In late October/early November of 1963, Dexter had in fact recommended passing on "I Want To Hold Your Hand," as well. Following a London phone call from Brian Epstein to Alan Livingston urging him to give the group a listen, the Capitol president agreed to release the song.)

1963

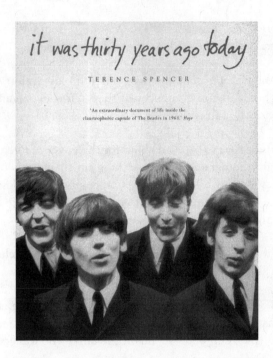

it was thirty years ago today

TERENCE SPENCER

'An extraordinary document of life inside the
claustrophobic capsule of The Beatles in 1963.' *Mojo*

1. What journalist did John Lennon once refer to as "the Just William woman"?

2. Unimpressed with EMI publisher Ardmore & Beechwood's lack of promotion on "Love Me Do"/"P.S. I Love You," Brian Epstein ended up giving Dick James the publishing rights to the Beatles' next single, "Please Please Me"/"Ask Me Why" (issued on Parlophone, 11 January). James established Northern Songs with the Beatles and Brian to administer their compositions. Epstein's original plan however, had been to go with an American publisher—who?

3. When Neil Aspinall came down with the flu during the third week of January, who was deputized as the Beatles' road manager for shows on the 18th (at the Floral Ballroom, Morecambe) and the 19th (at the Town Hall Ballroom, Shropshire)?

4. When Capitol turned down the Beatles' second Parlophone single, "Please Please Me"/"Ask Me Why," New York attorney Paul Marshall acting on behalf of EMI, next offered the record to this label, who also rejected it as being "derivative and not pure," according the label head's secretary. What label was it?

5. The lyrics were inspired by "I'm Wishing," from Disney's 1937 film *Snow White and the Seven Dwarfs*. Can you name the song?

6. What brand of throat lozenges did John use before attempting "Twist and Shout," the final number of their ten-song marathon session for *Please Please Me*, 11 February?

7. Several ideas were bandied about for the cover of *Please Please Me*. Dezo Hoffman photographed them kicking up their heels on the front steps of Abbey Road, while EMI staff photographer John Dove had them posing on the outside spiral stairwell of EMI House. Where had George Martin suggested they pose for the cover shot?

8. What was the working title for "Thank You Girl," released in the UK 11 April as the B-side of "From Me to You"?

9. On 18 April, the Beatles appeared for the first time at the Royal Albert Hall as part of the live BBC radio concert, *Swinging Sound '63*. On this occasion, the group were second on the bill—who was first?

10. What song did the Beatles record with Angus Mackenzie?

11. What song did John compose during his twelve-day holiday in Spain with Brian Epstein, beginning 28 April?

12. What label released the first Lennon/McCartney composition to hit the charts in the U.S.?

13. Actress Catherine (Katie) Boyle was the only person to do this with both John and Ringo—what did she do?

14. George Martin has described this Lennon/McCartney composition as ". . . a brilliant song, one of the most vital songs they had." Yet when he produced it, he initially thought the song's ending, on a major sixth, "banal" and "corny," telling them it was almost like a Glenn Miller arrangement. "Do you have to do that?" he asked them, "I've heard it so many times in my life." What song was Martin referring to?

15. What Beatles song had the working title of "Get You in the End"?

16.   Whom did the Beatles refer to as "Uncle Walter"?

17.   It's midday in the dining room of the Palace Court hotel, where the Beatles are staying during their six-day residency at the Gaumont Cinema, 19 to 24 August. The boys are seated against a deep maroon curtain save Ringo, who is kneeling on a stool. What is the occasion?

18.   In order to avoid the appearance of cashing in on his brother's rapidly rising star and "to retain a little dignity," Mike McCartney decided change his last name as he pursued his own show business career as a member of the Scaffold. Before deciding on Mike McGear ("gear" being Liverpool slang for "great"), two other surnames were "close contenders." What were they?

19.   George became the first Beatle to visit the United States 16 September, when he and his brother, Peter, flew out of London to visit their sister, Louise, in Benton, Illinois. Before their return, 2 October, George performed with what local band?

20.   Recorded in Studio Two, 17 October, the Beatles' first fan club flexidisk, *The Beatles' Christmas Record*, was sent out to 31,000 paid members beginning 6 December. Who came up with the idea of the group issuing a Christmas message?

21.   Whom did Paul often refer to as "the Man with the Shiny Shoes"?

22.   In November, John, Cynthia and Julian moved into flat #3 at 13 Emperor's Gate, their first address on their own in London (the Lennons would move to Weybridge the following July). What name was listed on their doorbell in an (unsuccessful) attempt to elude their fans? Who were the Lennons' neighbors on the floor below in flat #2?

23.   While it may appear obvious, what was the title of the first Beatles LP issued by Capitol in North America?

24.   As of this writing, what is the title of the only song on *With the Beatles* to which Paul McCartney owns the publishing rights?

25.   Ringo called it "Good, but not as good as the original by Chan Romero." Paul disagreed: "Doesn't matter about Chan Romero's disk. Nobody remembers. It's as good as a new song." "It's a popular song around Liverpool," noted George. "We used to do it. Could be hit." The Beatles' comments, taken from their appearance as the entire panel on BBC-TV's *Juke Box Jury*, 7 December, are in reference to what song?

ANSWERS

1. John Lennon called *London Evening Standard* journalist Maureen Cleave "the Just William woman."

(Cleave first wrote about the Beatles in January 1963, after traveling to Liverpool to interview them before a concert at the Grafton Rooms, 10 January. Maureen discovered then that she shared a love of Richmal Crompton's *Just William* books with Lennon. After the article appeared, John would tell her, "You write like that woman who did the William books.")

2. Epstein was planning to go with Hill and Range, telling George Martin it was "because they're jolly good publishers, and besides, they do all the Elvis Presley stuff."

(Martin discouraged the idea, suggesting Dick James as the kind of "hungry" publisher Epstein needed to give the Beatles' records that extra push in promotion. In 1952, James had been one of the first artists George had recorded of his own initiative, producing several hits for the band singer, including "Robin Hood" and "Tenderly.")

3. Les Hurst, road manager for Gerry and the Pacemakers, stepped in for the ailing Neil Aspinall at Beatles shows on 18 and 19 January.

(When Les was unavailable 20 January to drive the Beatles to London to record appearances for Radio Luxembourg and the BBC [on the 21st and 22nd, respectively], twenty-six-year-old Cavern bouncer and GPO telephone technician Mal Evans was first deputized to work for the group. Evans officially joined the Beatles as their road manager on 11 August.)

4. Saying they were only interested in "authentic American music," Jerry Wexler's Atlantic Records passed on the chance to release "Please Please Me" in the U.S.

(Following Atlantic's rejection, Paul Marshall would offer the recordings to Vee-Jay, who were also a client of the attorney. [The label's previous acquisition from Marshall, Frank Ifield's "I Remember You" had gone top 5, after MGM had passed on the disk.] Issued 20 February 1963, VJ 498 became the first record released in the U.S. to bear the name Beatles, albeit misspelled "Beattles.")

5. "Do You Want to Know a Secret?"

(John remembers his mother Julia singing "I'm Wishing" to him when he was a boy one or two years old.)

6. Suffering from the effects of a heavy cold, Lennon prepared his voice for "Twist and Shout" by gargling with milk and sucking on a couple of *Zubes* throat lozenges.

7. As a fellow at the London Zoo, George Martin tried to get permission to have the Beatles pose outside the zoo's insect house. The Zoological Society of London refused, deeming the activity to be in poor taste.

(Martin eventually brought in theatrical photographer Angus McBean, who would photograph them at EMI House looking down over the first floor railing to the building's entrance.)

8. "Thank You Little Girl."

(McCartney now sees it as "a bit of a hack song really, but all good practice.")

9. First billed on *Swinging Sound '63* was Del Shannon.

(Paul first met his future fiancee Jane Asher at this broadcast.)

10. The Beatles recorded "Side by Side" with Scottish musician Angus Mackenzie, who recorded professionally under the name Karl Denver.

(Denver's Karl Denver Trio was the resident group on the BBC radio series *Side by Side*, presented by John Dunn. On three occasions in 1963, the Beatles were guests on the show [22 April, 13 May, and 24 June]. The opening and closing theme, a version of the 1927 composition by Harry Wood, was performed together by both groups.)

11. Lennon composed "Bad To Me" (given to Billy J. Kramer) during his Spanish holiday with Brian Epstein.

12. On 3 June, Big Top issued Del Shannon's version of "From Me to You" (backed with "Two Silhouettes"), which became the first Lennon/McCartney song to chart in the U.S., entering the *Billboard* Hot 100 at 96 on 29 June, peaking 20 July at 77.

(On its original release, the Beatles' version didn't fare as well. Issued 6 May as Vee-Jay single 522, "From Me to You"/"Thank You Girl" debuted on *Billboard* at 125, 3 August, peaking 10 August at 116.)

13. Boyle appeared on the four-person panel on the two respective occasions Lennon and Starr appeared on BBC-TV's *Juke Box Jury*.

(Katie appeared on the panel with John in the edition taped 22 June 1963 and with Ringo on 25 July 1964.)

14. Despite George Martin's constructive criticism, John, Paul and George were quite enamoured with the major sixth chord with which they ended "She Loves You", and kept it the way they recorded it, 1 July in Studio Two.

15. "I'll Get You."

(According to Paul, the chord progression to the lyric, "It's not like me to pretend" [from D flat to A flat minor], was "nicked" from the song "All My Trials," which McCartney owned a version of on record by Joan Baez.)

16. When Brian Epstein moved his NEMS organization to London in the summer of 1963, he appointed the accounting firm Bryce, Hanmer and Isherwood to handle the Beatles' finances. "Uncle Walter" was the Beatles' name for Dr. Walter Strach, a senior member of the firm who was put in charge of the Beatles' account.

17. Dressed in their black polo-neck sweaters, the Beatles are posing for Robert Freeman's famous "half shadow" group portrait, used for the cover of *With the Beatles* in the UK and *Meet the Beatles* in the U.S.

(The original proposal for *With the Beatles* had been to reproduce Freeman's photo across the entire front of the album without any logos or lettering.)

18. Mike Dangerfield (a character in J. P. Donleavey's *The Ginger Man*) and Mike McFab were close contenders for Mike McCartney's new Scaffold surname.

19. Harrison performed with a group billed as the Four Vests.

(Playing mostly Hank Williams and Chuck Berry tunes, Harrison joined the group on two occasions, at the VFW Hall in El Dorado, IL and later at the Boneyard Boccie Ball Club in Benton, Illinois.)

20. Tony Barrow, PR and publicity chief at NEMS Enterprises, came up with the idea of a fan club Christmas disk.

21. Paul called Alistair Taylor "The Man With The Shiny Shoes."

(Brian hired Taylor as general manager of NEMS Enterprises in October 1963. He would remain in the service of the Beatles [earning the nickname "Mr. Fixit"] until 1969, when he became a victim of Allen Klein's mass firings at Apple.)

22. The Lennons' family pseudonym at Emperor's Gate was Hadley. Their neighbors in flat #2 were photographer Robert Freeman and his wife.

23. The first Beatles album issued on Capitol in North America was *Beatlemania with the Beatles*, issued by Capitol of Canada, 25 November.

(Capitol of Canada was also the first label to release a Beatles single in North America, "Love Me Do"/"P.S. I Love You," on 4 February. The first U.S. single, "Please Please Me"/"Ask Me Why," wasn't released on Vee-Jay until 20 February.)

24. The only song on *With the Beatles* that Paul owns the publishing rights to is Meredith Willson's "Till There Was You," written for *The Music Man*.)

(MPL Communications acquired the rights to the song when they purchased Meredith Willson Music.)

25. The Beatles were critiquing the Swinging Blue Jeans' version of "The Hippy Hippy Shake," which they declared a hit (which it was) peaking at number two in January 1964.

(A staple of the group's repertoire from 1961–63, the Beatles performed the song five times for BBC radio shows, their rendition from *Pop Goes the Beatles*, transmitted 30 July, is included on disc two of *The Beatles Live at the BBC*, released by EMI/Capitol in December 1994.)

1964

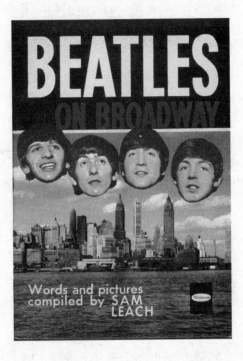

1. What is the significance of the phrase "Get Off You Nit!"?

2. "What's Happening in Beatleland," is the title of a Capitol Records press release issued 29 January. The release stated that Voyle Gilmore, artists and repertoire vice president for the label, "would fly to New York and personally record the Carnegie Hall concerts. The resulting album . . . will probably be issued in April." What was that album to be titled?

3. Quoted in George Harrison's column for London's *Daily Express*, which popular performer said of the Beatles' first visit to America, "I thought the Beatles would die in New York. I was surprised by the reception they got. I was wrong."

4. The Beatles' instant popularity in the U.S. meant that designer Jim Houlihan and his staff at Milton Bradley had only three weeks before the annual Toy Fair convention to invent a game based on the group. What is the name of this classic piece of Beatles memorabilia?

5. Who was director Richard Lester's first choice for writing the screenplay for *A Hard Day's Night*?

6. Who was Richard Lester's first choice for the role of Paul's grandfather, John McCartney?

7. According to Richard Lester, Victor Spinetti's paranoid TV director was actually "based on a real television director that both Alun (Owen) and I have worked with." Who is he?

8. Before the Beatles could act in *A Hard Day's Night*, they had to become members of Equity, the actor's union. Who proposed their membership? Who seconded it?

9. Bumped in favor of "Can't Buy Me Love," what song was originally planned to accompany the Beatles' romp through a field in *A Hard Day's Night*?

10. It could have been called *Stop One and Buy Me* or *The Transistor Negro*. What was it?

11. Pairing each of the Beatles with a chorus girl (from the Lionel Blair Dancers), Richard Lester attempted to film a stop-frame animation sequence for *A Hard Day's Night*. With film frames hand-cranked two at a time, the Beatles and their partners would move their bodies (but not their feet) in a series of Busby Berkeley patterns. What Beatles song was to have accompanied this sequence?

12. While Ringo is credited with coming up with the title "A Hard Day's Night," who thought up the line "What would you call that hairstyle you're wearing?—'Arthur'?"

13. Legend has it that many titles were suggested for the Beatles' first film before Ringo came up with "A Hard Day's Night"—can you name three?

14. First aired on ATV 18 April (but recorded back on 2 December 1963), what song did the Beatles, decked out in boaters and striped jackets, sing with Eric Morecambe and Ernie Wise at the close of that edition of *The Morecambe and Wise Show*?

15. Who is Isla Blair?

16. Derek Taylor (then writing for the *Daily Express*) had not been Brian Epstein's first choice to ghost his autobiography, *A Cellarful of Noise*—who had been?

17. Paul played the weaver, Nick Bottom, and John became Francis Flute, a bellows mender. The tailor, Robin Starveling, was played by George, while Ringo was a joiner (carpenter) named Snug. Rounding out the cast was Tom Snout the tinker, played by Trevor Peacock. What was the occasion?

18. "I'll be waiting here all alone/Just like I've always done/Hoping you will need me somehow./'Til that day I'll keep loving you/Just like I love you now./Don't forget me when you need someone." John wrote this unused verse for which Beatles song?

19. "Good George Martin is our friend/Buddy Pal and Mate./Buy this record and he'll send/A dog for your front gate." Sung to the tune of "Old Macdonald Had An Arm," for which album did John include this verse as part of his accompanying sleeve notes?

20. Kansas City A's (Athletics) owner Charles O. Finley paid the Beatles a then-record $150,000 for an unscheduled appearance at the city's Municipal Stadium, 17 September. On this one occasion, the group departed from their standard opener, "Twist and Shout." What did they play instead?

21. Which Beatles song did John describe as "sort of my version of 'Silhouettes'"?

22. To parody Breck shampoo's portrait ads, *Mad* associate editor Nick Meglin selected Ringo to become "the non-Breck boy . . . the ugliest of the Beatles, with a big nose, and the long hair." The result was the "Blecch" portrait ad, featured in the October 1964 issue of *Mad* magazine. Whom did Meglin commission to paint the ad?

23. What two albums did Vee-Jay Records reissue when they created their "International Battle of the Century," *The Beatles vs. the Four Seasons*?

24. While Harold Wilson's Labour Party ended up winning the General Election, 16 October, one interesting candidate standing against him in the Liverpool constituency of Huyton was quoted in the *Daily Mirror* supporting a platform of "votes at eighteen, no victimization of long hair, a knighthood for the Beatles and legalizing (pirate) radio stations." Who was this candidate?

25.   After knocking on a brass doorknocker in the shape of a nude woman, visitors to "Kenwood," John's home in Weybridge on the St. George's Hill Estate, would encounter Sydney in the entrance hall. Who was he?

ANSWERS

1.   These were the words on the placards held by Paul, George, Ringo, and John, respectively, in a skit they performed with compere Bruce Forsyth during their second appearance on *Val Parnell's Sunday Night at the London Palladium*, broadcast live, 12 January.

2.   *The Beatles at Carnegie Hall.*

(It is believed that the American Federation of Musicians union blocked the recording of the two shows, which took place 12 February. Carnegie's archive contains a copy of the contract between Capitol and the venue, giving the label permission to record the group for a fee of

$300. The contract was unsigned. The main page of the program booklet from the evening's shows has Paul's name listed as "John McCartney.")

3. Frank Sinatra "thought the Beatles would die in New York," in a quote from George Harrison's column for the *Daily Express*.

(Harrison's column, which was usually ghosted by Derek Taylor, was likely written on this occasion by the Express' U.S. correspondent, David English.)

4. Jim Houlihan and his staff had created the rules for *The Beatles Flip Your Wig Game* so quickly that when the artwork was returned to them, they discovered they had forgotten how to play the game!

5. Richard Lester's first choice for screenwriter on *A Hard Day's Night* was Johnny Speight, who had written for Lester's TV series *Idiot's Weekly, Price 2d*.

(Speight had previously authored *French Dressing*, released in 1963 by director Ken Russell. Notable among the cast was Roy Kinnear as Henry, who would later play Algernon in Lester's *Help!* Prior commitments prevented Speight from accepting. Richard's second choice, Liverpudlian playwright Alun Owen, first worked with Lester as an actor on *The Dick Lester Show* [1955]. Owen died 6 December 1994 at the age of sixty-nine.)

6. Lester first considered Irish actor Dermot Kelly for the role of Paul's grandfather.

(Kelly played a con man in the Herman's Hermits film *Mrs. Brown, You've Got a Lovely Daughter*, released in 1968. The film is notable for two additional Beatles people in supporting roles—Lance Percival, the voice of Paul and Ringo in *The Beatles* cartoon series and Old Fred in *Yellow Submarine*, and Nat Jackley, who played Happy Nat the Rubber Man in *Magical Mystery Tour*, as a pub singer.)

7. Victor Spinetti's character in *A Hard Day's Night* was based on television/film director Philip Saville.

(In the fifties, Saville and Lester had worked together for Associated Rediffusion [ARTV], notably on the latter's television special, *The Dick Lester Show*. Saville, who also directed several of Alun Owen's television plays, went on to direct such feature films as *Secrets* [1971]; *Fellow Traveler* [1989]; *Family Pictures* [1993] and *The Buccaneers* [1995].)

8. The Beatles' membership to Equity (made 2 March on the platform of London's Paddington Station just minutes before boarding their train for the first day of shooting), was proposed by Norman Rossington (Norm) and seconded by John Junkin (Shake).

(Rossington died of cancer at age seventy, 21 May 1999.)

9. "I'll Cry Instead" was originally set to accompany the Beatles' field antics, filmed at a helicopter launch pad at Gatwick Airport, South Surrey, 13 March, and at Thornburry Playing Fields, Isleworth, on 23 April.

10. These were two of John's suggested titles for his first book, *In His Own Write*, first published by Jonathan Cape, 23 March. The title, by the way, was thought up by Paul.

(Tom Maschler, the editor at Jonathan Cape responsible for publishing Lennon's two books, was first exposed to John's poems and drawings by New York journalist Michael Braun, the author of *Love Me Do: The Beatles' Progress*.)

11. Lester wanted to film "You Can't Do That" as a stop-frame animation sequence.

(Lacking the particular claw-foot camera needed in 1964 to film stop-motion properly, Lester attempted to fake it with the equipment on hand, the results proving unsatisfactory. Lester returned to "You Can't Do That," filming the Beatles miming to the song during the TV performance sequence filmed at the Scala Theatre, 31 March. While this sequence was cut from the final film, it was shown on *The Ed Sullivan Show*, 24 May.)

12. Used in the press party sequence filmed 2 April at the Scala Theatre, London, "What would you call that hairstyle you're wearing?" was thought up by George.

13. Among the many suggestions for the title of the Beatles' first film: *Beatlemania; The Beatles Film; Beatles No. 1; It's A Daft, Daft, Daft, Daft, Daft World; Let's Go; Moving On; Oh, What a Lovely Wart; Travelling On*, and *What Little Old Man?*

14. The Beatles and Morecambe and Wise sang the Edward Madden/Percy Wenrich composition "Moonlight Bay."

(Their performance can be heard on disc two of *Anthology 1*.)

15. Isla Blair played the actress dressed in eighteenth-century period costume in Paul McCartney's solo scene in *A Hard Day's Night*.

(Filmed 20–21 April at the Jack Billings TV School of Dancing, located on the second floor of the Bush public house, the scene was cut when Lester felt that it slowed the pace of the film. "I think the scene was a bit suspect, a little po-faced, with the camera swirling round and round," wrote McCartney in his introduction to Andrew Yule's book on Richard Lester. In 1970, Blair starred in the film *Taste the Blood of Dracula*. Starring Christopher Lee in the title role, it also featured Roy Kinnear, who played Algernon in *Help!* and Musketeer Clapper in *How I Won the War*.)

16. Epstein had originally wanted another former *Daily Express* staff writer Tony Stratton Smith to ghost his autobiography.

(At their meeting at the Amsterdam Hilton, Smith, who was writing *The Rebel Nun* at the time, told Epstein he wouldn't be able to start on his book for at least three to six months. Anxious to undertake the book immediately, Epstein eventually contracted Derek Taylor.)

17. Opening Jack Good's *Around the Beatles* TV special (first aired in the UK by Rediffusion, 6 May) was a spoof of the Interlude from Shakespeare's *A Midsummer Night's Dream* (Act V, Scene I) in which the Beatles portray this group of Athenian workmen, the "mechanicals," as they stage their play, *Pyramus and Thisbe*, assuming the roles of Pyramus (Paul), Thisbe (John), Moonshine (George), Lion (Ringo) and the Wall (Trevor Peacock).

18. "Anytime At All."

19. Lennon's new version of "Old Macdonald Had a Farm" ("With an arf, arf, here, and an arf, arf there, etc.") were part of the liner notes he penned for George Martin's instrumental album of Beatles songs, *Off the Beatle Track*, first issued by Parlophone in the U.K., 10 July.

(*Off the Beatle Track* had been Martin's suggestion for the title of the Beatles' first album, *Please Please Me*.)

20. The Beatles opened their Kansas City show with Little Richard's medley arrangement of "Kansas City"/"Hey, Hey, Hey, Hey."

21. John's version of the Rays' 1957 hit "Silhouettes" is "No Reply."

("I had that image of walking down the street and seeing her silhouetted in the window and not answering the phone . . .")

22. The "Blecch" portrait of Ringo in *Mad #90* was painted by Frank Frazetta.

23. Released 1 October, *The Beatles vs. the Four Seasons* reissued *Introducing the Beatles* and *The Golden Hits of the Four Seasons*.

(The Beatles nearly did share the bill with the Four Seasons on their third UK package tour, 18 May–9 June 1963. When original headliner Duane Eddy ran into problems, promoter Kennedy Street Enterprises had planned at one point to book Ben E. King and the Four Seasons as his replacements [the engagement eventually went to Roy Orbison]. On the fade of "Genuine Imitation Life," from the Four Seasons' January 1969 concept album, *Genuine Imitation Life Gazette*, you can hear the group quoting from the fade of "Hey Jude.")

24. Knighthood for the Beatles was part of the platform of National Teenage Party candidate and rock 'n' roll artistocrat David Edward "Screaming Lord" Sutch.

(Sutch hanged himself in his Harrow, Middlesex, home, 16 June 1999.)

25. Sydney was the name John gave the suit of armor which visitors encountered in Kenwood's entrance hall.

(A Robert Freeman photo of John posing behind Sydney is perched atop John's ear in Klaus Voormann's *Revolver* cover collage, and in Richard Hamilton's poster collage for the *White Album*. In the latter, Sydney is in Kenwood's entrance hall, in front of a mural based on a drawing Lennon originally included in *In His Own Write* to illustrate "Neville Club.")

1965

HELP!
THE BEATLES

Released by United Artists
A Random House Book

1. Where did Ringo propose marriage to Maureen Cox?

2. Marc Behm first submitted his original screenplay for *Help!* to which actor?

3. What were the working titles of *Help!*?

4. During the filming of *Help!* Paul was constantly at work on this song, "...slowly driving everyone mad as it came together piece by piece," writes Andrew Yule in his biography of director Richard Lester. "If I hear that once more," he told Paul only half jokingly, "I'll have that bloody piano taken away. What's it called anyway?" What was McCartney's response?

5. What was the name of the Indian restaurant in *Help!* the Beatles approach on London's Blandford Street "seeking enlightenment as to rings"?

6. In the *Doctor Who* episode titled "The Executioners" (first aired in the U.K. on 22 May), the Beatles are seen for approximately twenty-five seconds through a "space-time visualizer" in the Doctor's Tardis. What song are they performing?

7. On 3 June, John and Cynthia and George and Pattie attended this noted poet's thirty-ninth birthday party at the Chester Square basement flat of Barry Miles. Arriving to the party late, they found the birthday boy drunk and . . . naked! After paying their respects, Beatles and wives quickly departed. Whose party was it?

8. "Can't explain or name I think it's pain, but again/I'm ashamed the flame of love is maimed, now and then/I'll complain in vain, and I'll still love you." These unused lyrics were penned by John during the composition of which Beatles song?

9. The Beatles only played in Italy during their 1965 European tour, performing a total of eight shows, from 24 to 28 June, in Milan, Genoa, and Rome. Owing to his size and strength, what nickname did Mal Evans earn among the other touring acts on this leg of the tour?

10. *Help!* had its royal premiere 29 July at the London Pavilion, with Princess Margaret and Lord Snowdon in attendance. Which film preceeded the premiere?

11. What does *Help!* have in common with the popular English television series *The Prisoner?*

12. The Beatles spent most of 14 August at CBS Studio 50, rehearsing their appearance on *The Ed Sullivan Show* before taping their six songs before a live audience at 8:30 that evening. What noted musician attended the dress rehearsal at 2:30 that afternoon?

13. What a celluloid coup this might have been—an attempt was made to get the Beatles to appear in Elvis's latest film, the group to sing a song with Presley at the picture's conclusion. What movie was this proposed for?

14. On 13 September, Ringo and Maureen's first child, Zak, was born at Queen Charlotte's Hospital in London. Zak had not been Ringo's first choice for his son's name—what was?

At 10:30 A.M. Eastern Standard Time on the morning of 25 September, *The Beatles* cartoon series debuted in the U.S. on ABC-TV. Produced by King Features, seventy-eight five-and one-half minute episodes were made, each titled after a song written or covered by the group, along with thirty-three sing-along segments. In the next four questions, can you recall each story's title from the plot synopsis?

15. He can sing soprano, compute in algebra, and write in Swahili—he's Mr. Marvelous, a Hollywood studio's star ape. John questions why he should be kept in a cage and sets Mr. Marvelous free to roam the town. Now it's up to the Beatles to find him.

16. Rehearsal space being at a premium during a visit to Rome, the group set up in the Coliseum, but the ancient columns and statuary don't stand a chance against the vibrations caused by their performance of this song.

17. While in Japan, police caution the boys to be on the lookout for Anyface, a jewel-thief master of disguise. When John, George, and Ringo discover there are now two Pauls, they look into the cave of truth to determine which is the real Macca.

18. The boys visit an orphanage to try and cheer up its young residents.

19. What was the working title of "Norwegian Wood (This Bird Has Flown)"?

20. After hearing this parody/homage to "Norwegian Wood," John reportedly felt a little paranoid that Bob Dylan was making fun of his attempts to diversify his songwriting. What is the song?

21. What song has John said inspired the distinctive opening guitar riff on "Day Tripper"?

22. In his book *I Me Mine*, George describes the guitar line on "If I Needed Someone" as "like a million other songs written around the D chord." Harrison actually based it on the twelve-string figure from what song?

23. It was Quarry Man Ivan Vaughan who first introduced John to Paul, 6 July 1957. His wife, Jan, made a significant contribution to *Rubber Soul*—what was the contribution?

24. What Beatles song was recorded under the working title "Won't Be There With You"?

25. *Paul's Christmas Album* had a limited pressing of three acetates (made by Dick James) which McCartney gave to John, George, and Ringo. Featuring his experimental music and tape loops (which he prepared on a pair of Brenell tape recorders), what song introduces the album?

ANSWERS

1. Ringo proposed on bended knee to Maureen at the Ad Lib, the night club on the fourth floor of the Prince Charles Theatre, 7 Leicester Place, at 3 A.M. one morning in January.

2. Behm first submitted his original screenplay for *Help!* (then titled *Eight Arms to Hold You*) to Peter Sellers.

3. Before acquiring its title, *Help!* was known to the cast and crew as *Beatles 2*. Call sheets (detailing the actors to be present and requirements of a day's shooting) also refer to the movie as *Eight Arms to Hold You*.

(Another presumably facetious suggestion from the group for the movie's title was *High-Heeled Knickers*.)

4. McCartney told Richard Lester he was working on "Scrambled Eggs," the working title of "Yesterday."

5. The restaurant the Beatles visit in *Help!* is the Rajahama.

(The Beatles were actually filmed in front of the Dolphin Restaurant, 9 May, sporting the spuriously created Rajahama sign.)

6. During a demonstration of the "space-time visualizer," Vicki, the Doctor's assistant (Maureen O'Brien), selects to view the Beatles miming to "Ticket to Ride" from their final appearance on *Top of the Pops*, first aired 15 April.

(Remarking upon the group's performance, Vicki is surprised that "they play classical music.")

7. Allen Ginsberg.

8. These lyrics were from an early draft of "It's Only Love."

9. On the Beatles' 1965 Italian dates, Mal was referred to as "Il Elefante" (the Elephant).

10. A travelog on Venice by Harold Baim preceded the royal premiere of *Help!*

11. Patrick Cargill (who played Superintendant Gluck in *Help!*) appeared in several episodes of *The Prisoner* as Number Two. Leo McKern (who played Clang), also played Number Two in the seventeenth and final episode, "Fall Out."

(In the final episode, Number Six [Patrick McGoohan] is led through various underground corridors toward his meeting with Number One. Passing through one room, McGoohan is serenaded by a line of jukeboxes all playing the Beatles' "All You Need Is Love." McGoohan's original script for this scene described the music issuing from these jukeboxes as a "wailing cacophony" of sound. Songs he indicated for possible use in this sound collage included "Yellow Submarine," "Little Boxes," "Toot-Toot-Tootsie Goodbye," "Hello Dolly," as well as "All You Need Is Love.")

12. Composer/conductor Leonard Bernstein attended the Beatles' *Ed Sullivan Show* dress rehearsal.

(The Beatles' appearance was first aired 12 September.)

13. There was a proposal made to try to get the Beatles to appear with Elvis in *Paradise, Hawaiian Style*.

(The Beatles' contract with United Artists prevented them from appearing with Elvis.)

14. Believing names "were boring for people," Ringo told Beatles biographer Hunter Davies that when Zak was born, "I really wanted to call him 'XL.' " Needless to say, Maureen refused.

(Had their first child been a girl, her name would have been Lee, which they remembered when Maureen gave birth to a daughter, 11 November 1970, naming her Lee Parkin.)

15. "There's A Place."

16. "I Should Have Known Better."

17. "No Reply."

("No Reply" was animated by Chris Cuddington and Kevin Degue at the Graphik Animation studio in Paddington Sydney, Australia. Chris and Kevin also animated the cartoons for "If I Fell," and "I'll Be Back.")

18. "Strawberry Fields Forever."

(A nice example of tying the story to the song—Strawberry Field being the name of the Salvation Army orphanage at Beaconsfield Road, Woolton, Liverpool, on whose grounds John attended summer fêtes as a child. "Strawberry Fields Forever" and "Penny Lane" were the last new episodes created for the series, aired on 4 November 1967.)

19. "This Bird Has Flown" was the working title for "Norwegian Wood."

(McCartney remembers the title as a reference to the decor of Peter Asher's bedroom, which was done in pine. "Norwegian wood. It was pine really, cheap pine. But it's not as good a title, 'Cheap Pine,' baby.")

20. John viewed "Fourth Time Around" as a parody of "Norwegian Wood," a dig by Dylan at the expense of his efforts on *Rubber Soul* to diversify his songwriting with lyrics that were more autobiographical.

(Calling on Bob with a copy of *Revolver* at London's Mayfair Hotel, 4 May 1966, McCartney was the first Beatle to hear "Fourth Time Around" when Dylan played him the acetate of his forthcoming *Blonde On Blonde* LP. Al Kooper, the musical director on the album, remarked to Dylan how much "Fourth" sounded like "Norwegian Wood." Replied Dylan, "Well actually, 'Norwegian Wood' sounds a lot like this! I'm afraid they took it from me, and I feel that I have to, y'know, record it.")

21. Playing some of his favorite platters on New York's WNEW-FM, 28 September 1974, Lennon spun "Watch Your Step" by Bobby Parker, telling DJ Dennis Elsas that it had been the inspiration for the riff on "Day Tripper."

22. According to George, the guitar line for "If I Needed Someone" is "based on the twelve-string figure from 'The Bells of Rhymney' from the Byrds."

23. Paul queried Jan Vaughan, who made her living teaching French, for suitable French phrases to compliment the lyrics he was writing for "Michelle."

24. "Won't Be There With You" was the working title for "Think For Yourself."

25. "I did one once called 'Unforgettable,'" Paul told Barry Miles, "and used the 'Unforgettable'—Nat King Cole—'Is what you are . . .' as the intro. Then did a sort of 'Hello, hello . . .' like a radio show."

(In the Winter 94/95 issue of *Club Sandwich*, McCartney specifically titled his 1965 Christmas album *Unforgettable*.)

1966

1. When Paul wrote "Woman" for Peter and Gordon, he used the pseudonym Bernard Webb ". . . just to see if it was the Lennon-McCartney bit that sold our songs." According to the story invented for the press, where was Mr. Webb living at the time and what was his occupation?

2. "While listening to (this album) I got the feeling that these songs had been written specifically with Chet in mind. The fact that they were not proves his eminence as an artist—the perfect example being *Yesterday*." This quote by George Harrison was drawn from the liner notes he penned for which album by Chet Atkins, released by RCA in March?

3. On 25 March, Bob Whitaker shot his famous "Butcher" photographs of the group, featured on first run copies of "*Yesterday*" . . . *and Today* (issued by Capitol in the U.S. on 20 June and quickly withdrawn). Whitaker had originally envisioned the photos as part of a triptych for a "double-fold album" of the group, presented like a Russian religious icon commenting on "the mass adulation of the group and the illusory nature of stardom." What was Whitaker's name for this triptych?

4. If you were a friend of Paul's during this period, you would have been encouraged to use his secret name when sending him a letter to distinguish your missive from the stacks of fan mail he regularly waded through. What was his secret name?

5. Which song on *Revolver* has Paul said ". . . is actually an ode to pot"?

6. Before the green Granny Smith apple became the logo of Apple Records in 1968, George was using the name "Granny Smith" in 1966 to designate something else—what?

7. What song did John call "son of Day Tripper"?

8. Before Paul came up with *Revolver*, several names were suggested as the title of their seventh studio album, including "Abracadabra," "Beatles on Safari," "Bobby," "Fat Man," "Four Sides to the Circle," "Magic Circle," and "Pendulums." What was Ringo's suggestion?

9. What song included on *Revolver* was this unused lyric couplet written for: "Now what I let you keep for free/Won't take long to get back to me?"

10. For this track's guitar solo, he played an Epiphone Casino '64 with a Bigsby tailpiece. Which Beatle? Which song from *Revolver*?

11. Whose score, featured in a film playing in London cinemas at the time, inspired George Martin's double-string quartet arrangement for "Eleanor Rigby"?

12. Where were the Beatles when Bob Whitaker took the photograph used for the back cover of *Revolver*?

13. Returning to EMI studios from a lunch break at the Genevieve restaurant on Thayer Street, 19 May, the Beatles met with the owner from what boutique to select fabrics for their new stage outfits?

14. "(This album) was probably the big influence that set me thinking when we recorded *Pepper*; it set me off on a period I had then for a couple of years of nearly always writing quite melodic bass lines." What album is McCartney referring to?

15. What song on *Revolver* had originally been recorded with a spoken introduction by Ringo to the sound of marching feet, alluding to the walk for charity by Dr. Barbara Moore, from Land's End (the southernmost tip of England) to John O'Groats (the northernmost tip of Scotland)?

16. When Bert Kaempfert and his wife paid a call on the Beatles backstage at the Merck Halle in Hamburg, 26 June, what song did John sing the opening line from?

17. During their concert stop in Tokyo (30 June–2 July), the Beatles created a four-man painting in the Presidential Suite (Room 1005) of the Tokyo Hilton. Executed on a large piece of hand-made Japanese paper, what music did the group listen to as they painted?

18. A restricted memo sent by the ambassador at the British Embassy in Tokyo, 15 July, reported that Nationalists were upset that the Beatles' appearance at the Nippon Budokan would desecrate the hall, which they considered sacred. "The main financial backers of the Beatles' visit," noted the ambassador, "were the *Yomiuri* newspaper, whose proprietor, Mr. Matsutaro Shoriki, is a leading Buddhist." Pressure from some members of the government nearly resulted in Mr. Shoriki cancelling the "Biitoruzu" concerts. How was the situation resolved?

19. Why would it be an understatement to say that Birmingham, Alabama disk jockey Tommy James was not very popular with the Beatles in 1966?

20. Bobby Hart got the idea for The Monkees' first hit single, "Last Train To Clarkville," after hearing just the fade-out of which Beatles song for the first time?

21. "Here Come the Beatles" declared Wes Wilson's poster for the Beatles' last concert at Candlestick Park, 29 August 1966. Support acts listed included the Cyrkle, the Ronettes, the Remains, "plus two other acts to be determined." Who were they?

22. In September, Kenneth Tynan, artistic director of the National Theatre, asked Paul if he would write some music for an upcoming production. What play was it?

23. What does the 1966 film *Tobruk* (starring Rock Hudson and George Peppard) have in common with *A Hard Day's Night*?

24. Paul and Jane attended the premiere of *The Family Way*, 18 December, at London's Warner Theatre. McCartney received his first screen credit as a solo composer for the twenty-eight minutes of music featured in the film. What was the film's working title?

25. Who is Hiram J. Pipesucker Jr. and what is his connection to John Lennon?

ANSWERS

1. According to Paul, Bernard Webb ". . . was a student in Paris and very unavailable for interviews."

("Woman" was first issued as a single by Capitol in the U.S., 10 January. On some U.S. pressings, the songwriting credit was assigned to "A. Smith.")

2. George's liner notes were for *Chet Atkins Picks on the Beatles*.

3. Whitaker called his Beatles triptych "A Somnambulant Adventure."

(Citing the surrealistic influence of Salvador Dali, the photographer had envisioned a photo of the group holding a string of sausages [symbolizing the birth of the Beatles and its attendant umbilical cord] as the album's front cover.)

4. McCartney's secret name was Ian Iachimoe.

(Paul came by his alias when he played his name backwards on one of the two Brenell tape recorders he owned. Ian Iachimoe's name appeared during this period in the pages of the *International Times* [IT] in its staff box as a way of thanking McCartney for his frequent financial support.)

5. "Got To Get You Into My Life" is a song about marijuana.

("It's really a song about that," Paul told Barry Miles, "it's not to a person, it's actually about pot.")

6. Recording sheets from *Abbey Road* note the working title of George's "Love You To" as "Granny Smith."

7. "Son of Day Tripper" was how John described Paul's song "Paperback Writer."

8. Ringo's suggested album title was *After Geography*, a pun on the Rolling Stones' latest album *Aftermath*, which Decca released 15 April.

9. "Taxman."

10. Paul played his Epiphone Casino for the solo on "Taxman," recorded during a lengthy session in Abbey Road's Studio Two, 21 April.

11. Of his score for "Eleanor Rigby," George Martin has said, "I was very much inspired by Bernard Herrmann, in particular a score he did for the (Francois) Truffaut film *Fahrenheit 451*."

12. On 19 May, the Beatles were in Studio One at Abbey Road, shooting promotional clips for "Paperback Writer" and "Rain."

13. The Beatles' stage outfits (featured on their final American tour beginning 12 August), were made by the *Hung on You* boutique.

14. Paul was talking about the Beach Boys' *Pet Sounds* album, first released by Capitol in the U.S., 16 May 1966.

(Paul first heard *Pet Sounds*, along with John and Keith Moon, in May 1966, when Bruce Johnston, on a solo visit to London, played his assembled guests an advance pressing in his suite at the Waldorf in Aldwych. "I've often played [it] and cried. It's that kind of an album for me," said Paul in a 1990 interview with David Leaf. "[I] . . . bought my kids each a copy of it for their education in life—I figure no one is educated musically 'til they've heard that album.")

15. A spoken introduction was recorded for "Yellow Submarine," 1 June, in Studio Two.

(A unique mix of the song, which includes the spoken introduction, was released as a bonus track on the "Real Love" single, issued by Capitol, 6 March 1996.)

16. John greeted the group's first producer with the opening line of the Kaempfert composition "Strangers in the Night."

17. As witnessed by photographer Bob Whitaker, the Beatles continuously played an acetate of *Revolver* as they painted, deciding as they did on the album's final track order in the U.K.

18. A letter from the chairman of the executive board of the Budokan, a leading member of the government party, promoting the Beatles' respectability, was published in *Yomiuri* prior to the concerts.

(According to the ambassador's memo, the chairman "argued that the respectability of the Beatles was beyond any doubt, the proof being that they had all received decorations from Her Majesty the Queen. This well-aimed salvo silenced all but the hardcore of extremists.")

19. Following the publication (out of context) of Lennon's remarks on the Beatles "being more popular than Jesus" on the cover of the teen magazine *Datebook*, 29 July, WAQY disk jockey James drew national attention by reading Lennon's remarks over the air. This had the effect of outraging Christian fundamentalists and prompting Beatle record boycotts and bonfires around the country just as the group was preparing to embark upon their final U.S. tour, beginning 12 August in Chicago.

20. "Paperback Writer."

("I only heard the fade out," remembers Hart, "and although they were singing 'Paperback Writer,' I heard it as, 'Take the last train . . .' something. Because their song had nothing to do with trains, as I discovered when I heard it again, I thought we [he and songwriting partner, Tommy Boyce] should consider writing a train song." "Last Train" was issued as a single 16 August [Colgems 1001] and topped the *Billboard* singles chart on 5 November.)

21. Had Wes Wilson's poster of the Beatles' final live concert been accurate, there would only have been *one* other act to be determined— Bobby Hebb, who sang four songs, including "Sunny," his big hit at the time.

(Hebb went on second that evening, preceded by the Remains [who also backed him during his slot], and followed by the Cyrkle and the Ronettes, sans Ronnie Spector. Tempo Productions, who promoted the show, were forced by the American Federation of Musicians Local 6 to hire Del Courtney and twenty-five musicians to sit in the stands of Candlestick [as standby musicians] and play "The Star Spangled Banner" at a cost of $1072.)

22. Tynan asked McCartney if he would compose some music for the National Theatre's production of Shakespeare's *As You Like It*, starring Sir Laurence Olivier.

(McCartney would decline the offer. Responding to a letter Tynan had written 28 September, asking him to reconsider, Paul replied that he could not write the music because, "I don't really like words by Shake-speare." Alluding to Olivier's role in the production, he closed his letter, "Maybe I could write the National Theatre Stomp sometime, or the Bal-lad of Larry O.")

23. Liverpudlian actor Norman Rossington worked in both films, play-ing Norm in A *Hard Day's Night* and Alfie in *Tobruk* (1966), a role he secured on the strength of his performance in *AHDN*, which the produc-ers screened prior to hiring him.

(While Rossington was in Hollywood filming *Tobruk*, he was able to land the role of Arthur Babcock in the Elvis Presley film *Double Trouble* [1967], making him the only actor to have worked with both the Beatles and the King.)

24. When it was announced 14 October that Paul had been working on the score for the new Hayley Mills film, its working title was *Wedlocked or All in Good Time*.

(*The Family Way* was based on Bill Naughton's play *All in Good Time*.)

25. Hiram J. Pipesucker Jr. is the name of the character played by Peter Cook in a men's night-club sketch from *Not Only . . . But Also*, first aired Boxing Day (26 December) on BBC2.

(Mr. Pipesucker, an American TV presenter, gains entrance to the "Ad Lav" by slipping a fiver to Dan, the club's uniformed doorman, played by John Lennon.)

1967

1.   When the Beatles began recording "A Day in the Life" in Studio Two, 19 January, what was the song's working title?

2.   "He blew his mind out in a car./He didn't notice that the lights had changed." Drawing on an actual event, who was John referring to in this lyric couplet from "A Day in the Life"?

3.   What is "One Down, Six to Go"?

4.   What event at London's Roundhouse touted "music composed by Paul McCartney and Delta Music Plus"?

5.   Who is William Darby and what was his connection to *Sgt. Pepper*?

6.   In McCartney's initial draft for this song, he ". . . showed them how to please a crowd. The man's a leader and he's made them proud." Who?

7.   In "Penny Lane" there is "a barber showing photographs of every head he's had the pleasure to know," while "on the corner there's a banker with a motor car." Written by Paul based on real places in Liverpool, what was the name of the bank and barber shop in Penny Lane at the time of the song's release in the U.K. (as a double A-sided single with "Strawberry Fields Forever"), 17 February?

8. In one of Paul's early drafts of this song, she was "writing all the numbers in her little black book"—who is she?

9. Who is Melanie Coe and what is her connection to *Sgt. Pepper*?

10. While the title and initial impetus for John and Paul to write "Lucy in the Sky With Diamonds" originated from a drawing made by four-year-old Julian Lennon of his Heath House nursery school classmate, Lucy O'Donnell, what other work did John cite as his inspiration for the psychedelic imagery of the song's lyrics?

11. How does a 1961 recording of the *Beyond the Fringe* comedy revue (starring Peter Cook, Dudley Moore, Jonathan Miller, and Alan Bennett) figure into the making of *Sgt. Pepper*?

12. Which song on *Sgt. Pepper* was composed on a pedal harmonium at Klaus Voormann's house in Hampstead, London?

13. Who was George Martin producing a session for that led an impatient Paul McCartney in early March to invite freelance producer/arranger Mike Leander over to his Cavendish home to arrange an orchestral score for "She's Leaving Home"?

14. Where did Peter Blake and Jann Haworth find the picture of Dion Di Mucci they used for the cover of *Sgt. Pepper*?

15. While the Beatles' *Sgt. Pepper* suits were made to order by Berman's Theatrical Outfitters, who made the shoes worn with them?

16. Against a yellow background, freelance designer Stephen Weaver, sixty-two, painted images of fall dahlias, chrysanthemums, and delphiniums on the doors of John's Rolls-Royce Phantom V. Weaver's work was part of a six-week £1,000 respray commissioned by John in April to J. P. Fallon Ltd. bodyworks company in Chertsey, Surrey. The theme of the paint job was October, the month of his birth. What image adorns the roof?

17. "There's several days' work on that tape. For perhaps the hundredth time, the engineer runs it back to the start for yet another stage in the making of an almost certain hit record. The supervisor is George Martin, the musical brain behind all the Beatles records. There's the orchestra coming into the studio now, and you'll notice that the musicians are not rock-and-roll youngsters. The Beatles get on best with symphony men."

Do they now? This was the live commentary of BBC reporter Steve Race from Studio One at Abbey Road. What was the occasion?

18. Who did the Beatles nickname "Miss Freak-out" during the filming of *Magical Mystery Tour*?

19. What vehicle of Beatles-note had the license plate URO 913E?

20. Who recommended to Paul that he should use the (then unknown) Bonzo Dog Doo-Dah Band in *Magical Mystery Tour*?

21. Okay, once and for all, who was the Walrus: John or Paul?

22. For the Beatles' appearance on the cover of this magazine, Paul is wearing a jacket "made of pure-gold-threaded fabric originally woven for the ceremonial robes of the Dalai Lama." Their hair was "styled" by Gerald, courtesy of London's *Daily Mail*. What is the magazine?

23. What is the title of the song by the Monkees that references the Beatles?

24. It was to have been made for the Beatles by Peacock Productions Limited, directed by Keith Green from a screenplay by Ian Dallas. What was it?

25. Where did Apple Films production chief, Denis O'Dell, get the cloud footage the Beatles subsequently color-filtered for the "Flying" sequence in *Magical Mystery Tour*?

ANSWERS

1. The working title for "A Day in the Life" was "In the Life of . . ."

2. The man who "blew his mind out in a car" was Terry Doran, the Liverpool car dealer who would go on to become the managing director of Apple Music when Apple Corp. was launched in 1968.

(Once while visiting Lennon at Kenwood, Doran remembers John announcing that they were going to a "love-in at Ally Pally" [London's Alexander Palace]. Before departing Weybridge, both took acid. Passing through Hammersmith with Doran driving, they came to the junction at the bottom by what was then Moscow Mansions:

"We were stopped at the lights and I said, 'I can't move,' and John was saying 'Come on, come on.' All these people were coming across the road and looking at us and at the car. Everyone behind was honking at us because I'd blown my mind and didn't notice that the lights had changed. That's where the line from 'A Day in the Life' came from—John and I did it together. Everybody thinks it's about Tara Browne, but it's nothing to do with him.")

3. According to Tony Bramwell, "One Down, Six To Go," was the working title for *Sgt. Pepper*, a facetious reference to the new contract they had signed with EMI, 27 January.

4. On consecutive Saturdays, 28 January and 4 February, the design team of Binder, Edwards and Vaughan presented their *Carnival of Light Rave* at the Roundhouse. At David Vaughan's request, Paul contributed "Carnival of Light," which the Beatles recorded in Studio Two, 5 January.

5. Born in Norwich in 1796, William Darby became the first black circus proprietor in Britain. Beginning in the 1830s, he went by the name Pablo Fanque. On 31 January 1967, John obtained a circus poster from an antique shop in Sevenoaks, Kent (following completion of filming for the "Strawberry Fields Forever" promotional film in nearby Knole Park), advertising and appearance by Pablo Fanque's Circus Royal in Town-Meadows, Rochdale, 14 February 1843. Lennon based the lyrics for "Being For The Benefit of Mr. Kite!" on this poster.

(Mr. Kite's first name, by the way, was also William.)

6. Sgt. Pepper.
(From a early draft of "Sgt. Pepper's Lonely Hearts Club Band.")

7. In the Penny Lane roundabout, the bank on the corner was Martin's Bank. The barber shop was called Bioletti's.

8. "Lovely Rita."

(Paul wrote the words to "Rita" during an evening walk near brother Michael's home in Gayton, in the Wirral, near Liverpool. This same early draft also offers Rita "filling in a ticket with her little blue pen.")

9. On 27 February, McCartney read an article in the *Daily Mail* about the disappearance of seventeen-year-old Melanie Coe from her parents' home in Amhurst Park, Stamford Hill, North, London. "I cannot imagine why she should run away," said Melanie's father, John Coe, "She has everything here." Paul used this article as the basis for the song "She's Leaving Home."

(In real life, Melanie didn't meet "a man from the motor trade," but a croupier from a gambling club named David. Terry Doran, who was personal assistant to John and George at the time, claims he was the man from the motor trade referred to in the song. "I was hanging around with Paul while he was doing this song and he sang 'meeting a man from . . .' and then he just looked up at me and laughed and sang ' . . . from the motor trade.' McCartney has since stated that ". . . it was just fiction, like the sea captain in 'Yellow Submarine,' they weren't real people.")

10. Lennon's psychedelic imagery in "Lucy" can be traced to Lewis Carroll's *Through the Looking Glass (And What Alice Found There)*, specifically Chapter 5, "Wool and Water."

("It was Alice in the boat," Lennon told David Sheff. "She is buying an egg and it turns into Humpty Dumpty [Chapter 6]. The woman serving in the shop turns into a sheep and the next minute they are rowing in a rowing boat somewhere and I was visualizing that.")

11. In Abbey Road's sound effects archive, "Volume 6: Applause and Laughter" was compiled from a recording of the *Beyond the Fringe* comedy revue at the Fortune Theatre, London in 1961. When stereo and mono mixes of "Sgt. Pepper's Lonely Hearts Club Band" were made 6 March 1967, this tape was utilized to good effect (along with "Volume 28: Audience Applause and Atmosphere, Royal Albert Hall and Queen Elizabeth Hall") to give the album's opening cut the appropriate live ambience.

12. George composed "Within You Without You" on Klaus Voormann's pedal harmonium following a dinner party Voormann gave, attended by George and wife Pattie.

13.   Martin was producing a session for Cilla Black.

(Leander would work with the Beatles again in October, when John and Paul called on him to arrange and notate "Shirley's Wild Accordian," for accordianists Shirley Evans and partner Reg Wale to play at De Lane Lea Music Recording Studios, London, 12 October. It would be featured as incidental music in the *Magical Mystery Tour* TV special, first aired 26 December on BBC-TV. Leander died of cancer in 1996, age fifty-four.)

14.   The photo of Dion seen on the cover of *Sgt. Pepper* first appeared on the cover of Dion's 1963 CBS album, *Donna the Prima Donna*.

15.   The shoes the Beatles wore with their *Sgt. Pepper* uniforms were made by Anello & Davide, where the group had previously gotten their handmade "Chelsea" Cuban heel Beatle boots.

16.   Weaver decorated the roof of John's Rolls-Royce with a representation of the scales of Libra, his zodiac sign.

(Lennon took delivery of his resprayed Rolls on 25 May.)

17.   Race was introducing the Beatles as they prepared to sing "All You Need Is Love," representing Britain in the "Artistic Excellence" segment of the *Our World* television program, the first-ever global satellite linkup, broadcast by BBC1 on 25 June.

18.   The Beatles dubbed Sylvia Nightingale, Beatles Fan Club secretary for Sussex, "Miss Freak-out."

("I had decided to wear hippy gear for the trip and the Beatles constantly reminded me of the fact," wrote Nightingale for *The Beatles Book Monthly*. "They so delicately referred to me as "Zippy-Hippy" and "Miss Freak-out.")

19.   This was the license plate of the blue-and-yellow Panaroma coach, owned by Fox of Hayes, on which the Beatles took their *Magical Mystery Tour*, filmed in various West Country locations beginning 11 September.

20.   Paul's brother Michael met the Bonzos at various venues while performing as Mike McGear with the Scaffold. His recommendation led to their performance of "Death Cab For Cutie" in the strip club sequence for *Magical Mystery Tour*, filmed 18 September at the Raymond Revue Bar, Walker's Court.

21. Both John and Paul were the Walrus.

("In the stills we had taken," McCartney told journalist Robert Yates in 1997, "I was the one with the Walrus head on—in the film it's [John]. So John then immortalized it in "Glass Onion," 'I've got news for you all [sic], the walrus was Paul."

"We've always had fun with the walrus thing," Paul told *Club Sandwich* in the Winter 94/95 edition. "We don't lay many false trails, but the walrus has always been one of them." This means that in still photographs of the four Beatles in costume [most notably John Kelly's *Magical Mystery Tour* EP/LP cover shot] John is the Hippo.)

22. The Beatles' appearance on the cover of the 22 September issue of *Time* was rendered by British illustrator Gerald Scarfe, head and torso in life-sized scale in papier-mâché.

(The Beatles' hair was made from strips of newspaper from the *Daily Mail*, their clothes obtained from London's *In Savita* shop.)

23. Mickey Dolenz refers to the Beatles as ". . . the four kings of EMI" in his lyrics for "Randy Scouse Git" (or "Alternate Title" as it was issued in the UK), included on their *Headquarters* album.

24. Peacock Productions Limited never got beyond submitting a production budget for a full-length *Sgt. Pepper's Lonely Hearts Club Band* TV special.

(The show would have included the film made by Tony Bramwell for "A Day in the Life.")

25. The "Flying" sequence in *Magical Mystery Tour* was created from the hours of unused cloud formation footage director Stanley Kubrick shot for *Dr. Strangelove*.

(O'Dell had purchased the film for Apple, which had become library footage. In an interview with Bob Neverson, O'Dell remembers getting a call from Kubrick shortly after MMT's release asking him what right he had to use the footage. "I was amazed," recalls O'Dell. "I thought, this man is a bloody genius, he'd remembered everything he shot." Kubrick died in Harpenden, Hertfordshire, England, 7 March 1999.)

1968

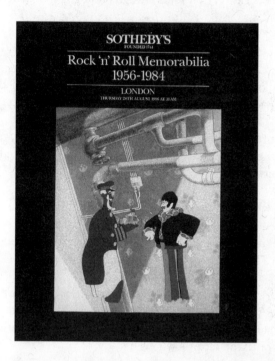

SOTHEBY'S
FOUNDED 1744
Rock 'n' Roll Memorabilia
1956-1984
LONDON
THURSDAY 28TH AUGUST 1986 AT 10 AM

1.   When Wonderwall director Joe Massot undertook the task of re-editing a director's cut of his first feature film in 1996, many months were spent at Abbey Road hunting down George's original stereo recordings for the music to replace the mono-optical soundtrack, including the master-tape with nine music cues (not included on the Wonderwall Music album), which Harrison found at Friar Park. A previously unreleased song, recorded during the January 1968 sessions in London, with a vocal contribution from Harrison, was discovered with the cues—what is its title?

2.   What magazine has Paul said was his initial inspiration for "Lady Madonna"?

3.   "When the truth gets buried deep,/Beneath a thousand years of sleep./Time demands I turn around/And once again the truth is found."
During his stay at the Maharishi's ashram in Rishikesh, India, 15 February–12 April, George Harrison composed the unused verse above for what song?

4.   Used in Richard Hamilton's poster collage for the White Album, what was the occasion that found Ringo photographed dancing with Elizabeth Taylor?

5.   Who is Stocky?

6.   What kind of guitar was Paul playing when he recorded "Blackbird" in Abbey Road's Studio Two, 11 June?

7.   "I want it to replace 'Kilroy was here' on toilet walls," said John, in a quote to the *Daily Mirror*. "It makes more sense." What phrase was he talking about?

8.   From whom did Paul first hear the phrase "Ob-La-Di, Ob-La-Da"?

9.   According to *Yellow Submarine* screenwriter Lee Minoff, who was the Nowhere Man (Jeremy Hillary Boob, Ph.D.) based on?

10.   Though not among the four credited writers of the *Yellow Submarine* screenplay (Al Brodax, Jack Mendelsohn, Lee Minoff, and Eric Segal), this gentleman made substantial contribution adding a distinctive Liverpudlian flavor to the script—who is he?

11.   Originally the Blue Meanies in *Yellow Submarine* weren't supposed to be blue! What color had artistic director Heinz Edelmann intended them to be?

12.   Following their ordeal in the Sea of Time, becoming "senile delinquents" to the strains of "When I'm Sixty-Four," multiple images of a man in a derby holding up a pocket watch are seen. Who is he?

13.   In 1980, Paul McCartney told Vic Garbarini that "Helter Skelter," ". . . came about because I read in the *Melody Maker* that the Who . . . they were talking about a track they made. I don't know what the track was 'cause I never actually heard anything that sounded like the talk. But the track was the loudest, most raucous rock 'n' roll and dirtiest thing we've ever done. But that made me think, 'ooh, gotta do it. I really see that.' " What Who song was it?

14.   On Sunday, 28 July, the Beatles spent the day with several photographers in tow, chief among them Don McCullin. Over the years, the resulting pictures, taken at nine different locations around London, have graced countless publications, book covers, and Beatles record releases, most notably the gatefold photograph taken by McCullin in the *1962–1966* and *1967–1970* collections. Here the Beatles are posed among a small crowd of people behind the railings that divided the St. Pancras Old Church from its gardens. By what name has this day of publicity photo-taking been referred to?

15. "Bow down to the plasticine bananas" was a line included among the original lyrics of which Beatles song?

16. Which Beatles song, recorded during the White Album sessions, mentions the city of Mandalay?

17. At one point, the Beatles had planned to call the White Album *A Doll's House*, but another group beat them to it with their August 1968 release. Who was the group?

18. "Feel so suicidal, just like Dylan's Mr. Jones," John sings in "Yer Blues." Which Bob Dylan song does Mr. Jones show up in?

19. On 20 August, McCartney demoed a ballad in Abbey Road's Studio Two. Titled "Etcetera," Paul took the recording with him; the song remains unreleased. For whom had Paul recorded the demo?

20. What was Beatles press officer and Apple publicist Derek Taylor's lyric contribution to "Savoy Truffle"?

21. What was Richard Cooke III's contribution to the White Album?

22. "Nice to have the time to take this opportunity. Time for me to look at you and you to look at me." What Beatles song includes these lyrics?

23. Derek Taylor describes the cover of *Wonderwall Music* as ". . . a post-Magritte painting of a brick wall with an archetypal member of the mid-twentieth century British bourgeoisie, isolated, loitering, separated by the wall from the Indian maidens at play on the other side . . ." Painted by American designer Bob Gill, Harrison requested one revision to the original work, which Gill didn't want to do. What was it?

24. Paul McCartney did not compose the quote attributed to him on the front cover of John and Yoko's *Unfinished Music No. 1—Two Virgins*, he found it—where?

25. At the suggestion of gallery owner Robert Fraser, English artist Richard Hamilton was asked to design the cover of *The Beatles* and its poster insert. Meeting with McCartney at the group's Apple offices on Savile Row, Hamilton suggested a "plain white album" with each copy numbered to "create the ironic situation of a numbered edition of something like five million copies." Should the group find the all-white sleeve too "clean and empty," Hamilton proposed adding something else to offset the look of the sleeve—what was that?

ANSWERS

1. The cue music mastertape included the song "In the First Place," written by Colin Manley and Tony Ashton of the Remo Four, the group George used on the London *Wonderwall* sessions.

("In the First Place" was inspired in part by the Modern Jazz Quartet's version of Jaoquin Rodrigo's "Adaigio From Concierto De Aranjuez," which Apple first issued in the UK 6 December on the album *Under the Jasmine Tree*.)

2. McCartney took his initial inspiration for "Lady Madonna" from a caption accompanying a photograph in *National Geographic* magazine.

(During John and Paul's business trip to New York City 11–15 May, the pair visited the Salvation Club on 4th Street to catch a show by Jimi Hendrix and the Chamber Brothers. As related by singer Richie Havens, who sat at their table, a young woman from another table approached Paul and asked him if he had written "Lady Madonna" about America. "No. As a matter of fact, it is not about America at all," Paul said. "I was reading *National Geographic* magazine when I saw a photo of an African woman with her baby, and the caption said 'Mountain Madonna,' and I said, 'She looks like a "Lady Madonna."'" That's really what started the song for me.")

3. George's unused verse was for Donovan's song "Hurdy Gurdy Man."

(On the roof of his bungalow in Rishikesh one evening, Donovan composed the song as the Beatles [among others] looked on. Harrison's contribution was eventually dropped when Pye, Donovan's English record label at the time, requested he keep the song under three minutes for release as a single. Donovan performs the song live with the Harrison verse on the CD *Donovan—The Classics Live*, issued on the Great Northwest Arts label in 1991.)

4.   The photo of Ringo dancing with Elizabeth Taylor on the White Album poster was taken at a party at London's Dorchester Hotel, following a private screening, 23 March, of *Around the World in 80 Days* at the Coliseum Cinerama. The event had been hosted by Taylor and Richard Burton.

5.   Stocky McMullen (dubbed the "Office Zombie" by Richard DiLello) arrived from Boston in 1968 with hopes of having his poetry and drawings published by Apple. For several months he was a likable fixture in the Apple Press Office, usually found sitting cross-legged atop the file cabinets.
   (As Derek Taylor noted of him in *Fifty Years Adrift*, "All he wanted to do was be 'cool,' make tea, draw, and write poetry.")

6.   McCartney played a Martin D28 acoustic guitar on "Blackbird."

7.   John wanted the phrase "You Are Here," the name of their art exhibition he staged with Yoko at the Robert Fraser Gallery beginning 1 July, to replace "Kilroy was here" on toilet walls.

8.   Paul heard the phrase "Ob-La-Di, Ob-La-Da" from Jimmy Scott, a Nigerian conga player.
   (McCartney would often meet Scott at London clubs like the Bag o' Nails in Soho. "Ob-La-Di, Ob-La-Da" is a phrase of the Yoruba tribe which means "life goes on." Jimmy Anonmuogharan Scott Emuakpor played congas on the song during an evening session at Abbey Road's Studio Two, 5 July.)

9.   Lee Minoff based the Boob on Jonathan Miller, best known during the sixties as a member of the comedy revue *Beyond the Fringe* (with Alan Bennett, Peter Cook, and Dudley Moore).
   (At the time Lee was writing the *Yellow Submarine* screenplay, Miller was directing *Come Live With Me*, a play Minoff had cowritten with Stanley Price, described in *The Encyclopedia of the American Theatre 1900–1975* as a "leaden farce about the romantic entanglements of an American screenwriter in London." Minoff did not think highly of Miller, calling him "a great intellectualizer [who] really helped to ruin [the play] when it finally got to Broadway.")

10.   Roger McGough.
   (McGough's contributions include Ringo's dialogue at the opening of the film ["Liverpool can be a lonely place on a Saturday night . . . and

this is only Thursday morning"] and the Beatles' banter in the Sea of Monsters.)

11.   Heinz Edelmann had originally envisioned Red Meanies, as a Cold War reference.

(Edelmann believes that it was either an insufficient supply of Dr. Martin's red dye, or a misunderstanding between him and the assistant appointed to color the Meanies that resulted in the blue variety of Meanie. According to Edelmann's assistant, Millicent McMillan, Heinz originally envisioned Purple Meanies. McMillan suggested blue would look better, to which he agreed.)

12.   The man in the derby is Scottish animator/watercolorist Ian Cowan.

(Working with artistic director Heinz Edelmann, Cowan was responsible for many of the backgrounds in *Yellow Submarine*.)

13.   McCartney was inspired to write "Helter Skelter" after reading of the rumbustious merits of the Who's single "I Can See For Miles," released by Track in the UK, 14 October 1967.

14.   McCullin's day photographing the Beatles is known as the "Mad Day."

(Many of the photos taken that day were shot by Beatles aide Tony Bramwell. Artist Richard Hamilton selected three Mad Day photographs for the White Album poster collage: two of Ringo wearing a yellow ruffled shirt under a blue suit jacket, and a smaller black-and-white group shot [just above a shot of Ringo dancing with Elizabeth Taylor] taken atop a concrete block at Old Street Station.)

15.   Included in a spiral notebook compiled at the time by Beatles personal assistant Mal Evans, plasticine bananas figured at one point in McCartney's handwritten lyrics for "Hey Jude."

(Evans' notebook [Lot 56] sold for £111,500 at a rock 'n' roll memorabilia auction held by Sotheby's in London, 15 September 1998.)

16.   A city in central Burma (now called Myanmar), Mandalay is mentioned in George Harrison's "Not Guilty," recorded in August during sessions for the White Album, but ultimately left off.

(In 1979, Harrison remade the song for his *George Harrison* album. The Beatles' version would remain officially unreleased until October 1996, when take 102 was issued on *Anthology 3*.)

17. The Beatles dropped their plans to call the White Album *A Doll's House* when they discovered that the debut album by the Leicester group Family had been titled *Music in a Doll's House.*

18. Dylan mocks Mr. Jones in "Ballad of a Thin Man," from the album *Highway 61 Revisited,* released by Columbia in the U.S., 30 August 1965.

(The identity of Dylan's Mr. Jones is said to be Jeffrey Jones, then a student journalist, on assignment for *Time* magazine at the 1965 Newport Folk Festival. Jones embarrassed himself by attempting to interview Dylan for a piece on the proliferation of the harmonica in contemporary folk music. Jones had the misfortune of bumping into Dylan and his entourage later that day in the hotel dining room. "Mr. Jones!" Dylan shouted. "Getting it all down, Mr. Jones?")

19. Paul had offered "Etcetera" to Marianne Faithfull, who turned it down.

20. Derek's contribution to "Savoy Truffle" was the line, "You know that what you eat you are," a transposition of the title of the 1968 documentary *You Are What You Eat,* starring Tiny Tim, Peter Yarrow, and Barry McGuire.

21. Richard Cooke III was John's inspiration for "The Continuing Story of Bungalow Bill."

(Cooke, then an American college graduate, was studying Transcendental Meditation in Rishikesh, India, with the Marharishi during the same period as the Beatles, beginning 15 February. Accompanied by his mother, Nancy, "he went out tiger hunting with his elephant and gun," at a site three hours by elephant from Rishikesh. The introduction to "Bungalow Bill" is still stored in the memory of the mellotron electric organ John used during sessions for the White Album.)

22. George wrote these lyrics for "It's All Too Much," included in the version heard in the film *Yellow Submarine.*

23. In the liner notes to the 1992 CD release of *Wonderwall Music,* George recalls, "I suggested we take a brick out of the wall to give the fellow on the other side a chance, just as the Jack MacGowran character (played by Oscar Collins) had a chance."

(Though he didn't want to, Gill did remove the brick, the change so irking him that Taylor notes he and the designer "never quite recovered our compatibility.")

24. McCartney selected the lines "When two great saints meet it is a humbling experience. The long battles to prove he was a saint" at random from London's *Sunday Express*.

25. Hamilton suggested "printing a ring of brown stain" on the cover of the White Album "to look as if a coffee cup had been left on it." McCartney rejected the idea as being too flippant.

1969

1. What film was in preproduction during the same time the Beatles were (intermittently) filming *Let It Be* at Twickenham Film Studios, from 2–15 January 1969?

2. During a Twickenham jam, 9 January, the heroine of this song was called Theresa. By 13 January, her Christian name had changed, while her surname continued to evolve, with Paul trying out "Marsh" and "Mary" and John suggesting "Marvin." Who is she?

3. Actress Judy Garland, soul singer Wilson Pickett, Apple employee Peter Brown, John Lennon, English comedian Ronnie Corbett, children's author Enid Blyton, *Mersey Beat* publisher Bill Harry, his wife Virginia, and British Member of Parliament Gerald Nabarro—what do they have in common?

4. Where did Paul McCartney find the word "pataphysical," which he used in "Maxwell's Silver Hammer"?

5. This actor was born George Frederick Joffre Hartree in 1914. What is his connection to *Let It Be*?

6. Whose idea was it for the Beatles to perform live on the roof of Apple?

7. Who bought John the fur coat he is wearing to keep out the lunchtime cold during the Beatles' last public performance on the roof of Apple Corp, 30 January?

8. On the writing of "Something," George has said, "Everybody presumed I wrote it about Pattie, but actually, when I wrote it, I was thinking about . . ." who?

9. Had events proceeded as planned, John and Yoko's wedding anniversary would have been 16 March, four days after Paul and Linda had tied the knot. Arriving at the Southampton Docks, the couple had planned to be married aboard a cross-Channel ferry run by the Thoresen company, when immigration officials turned them away due to "passport irregularities." What was the name of the ferry they had planned to marry on?

10. Which Beatles song did Paul McCartney describe as ". . . a song to rollercoast by"?

11. Prior to its release, "The Ballad of John & Yoko" included a subtitle—what was it?

12. The working title for Paul's "Oh! Darling" also had a subtitle—what was it?

13. What did Señor Bueno de Mesquita, Commissioner for Oaths, do for John and Yoko on 22 April?

14. On 4 May, MacLen, Lennon and McCartney's music publishing company, purchased the seventy-two-acre Tittenhurst estate for £145,000, which John and Yoko moved into 11 August. From their master bedroom, the Lennons enjoyed a view of grounds descending like an enormous green staircase to a sweep of Weeping Blue Atlas cedars. A pair of labeled switches next to the bedroom window turned on the garden lights for night viewing. What did the labels say?

15. Stationery for Apple Corp. Ltd. included a design which read "Words From Apple," the letters in "words" written in the peel coming off a green Granny Smith apple. A variation, "Lies From Apple," appeared later using what fruit?

16. Speculation suggests that the *Get Back* LP was initially circulated by John, who gave a tape or acetate copy to a journalist while in Toronto for the Rock 'n' Roll Revival concert, 13 September. But long before radio stations in New York, Boston, St. Louis and elsewhere began airing the "forthcoming" Beatles album, Ringo had given these songs their first public performance some weeks before—where were they played?

17. The centerpiece, designed and built by Charles Melling of the Newton Instrument Company, Hoylake, consisted of a "quartet" of Perspex containers displaying a mike stand, a record turntable, a speaker cabinet and a Sony tape recorder, along with a closed circuit television set. A collage of black-and-white photographs of Richard Nixon, Dwight Eisenhower, Muhammad Ali, Winston Churchill, Edward Kennedy, Joan Baez, and the Mona Lisa (among others) completed the tableau. What was Melling's creation supposed to represent?

18. What was the working title for "The End"?

19. "I wouldn't mind betting Yoko was in on the writing of that," McCartney mused to Barry Miles of this song, "it's rather her kind of writing." What song on *Abbey Road* is Paul referring to?

20. "Paul is dead" theorists interpret the Beatles' dress on the cover of *Abbey Road* as indicative of Mr. McCartney's demise. Viewed from left to right, they represent a gravedigger, a corpse, an undertaker, and a priest. When Iain Macmillan took this photo, at the intersection of Abbey Road and Grove End Road, 8 August, who were the tailors that had outfitted the Beatles?

21. "I've written with other people as well," John noted in an article in the December 1969 issue of *Hit Parader*. "For instance, there was a mad thing I wrote half with our electronics genius, Alex. It was called [*] and it was meant for the last Beatles album. It was real madness, but we never released it. I'd like to do it again." What song is John referring to?

22. Apple employee Chris O'Dell is the "Miss O'Dell" in question in the song George released as the B-side of his single "Give Me Love (Give

Me Peace on Earth)" in May 1973. But this wasn't the first time Harrison had worked on a song about her. During September and October 1969, he played guitar on sessions at Olympic Sound Studios in London for Leon Russell's first album, which included what song about Chris?

23.   In the 18 October issue of *Rolling Stone*, Greil Marcus, writing as T. M. Christian (The Magic Christian?), fabricated a review for an album by a supergroup called the Masked Marauders. John Lennon, noted the review, was featured singing "I Am the Japanese Sandman," Bob Dylan covered "The Duke of Earl" and Mick Jagger takes the lead on "I Can't Get No Nookie," with Paul McCartney contributing bass and piano. In late November, Deity Records released *The Masked Marauders*, recorded by a Berkeley band following the guidelines of Mr. Christian's "review." Who were the Masked Marauders?

24.   What is the title of the first Beatles bootleg?

25.   When Commonwealth United, the financial backers on *The Magic Christian* took offense at the scene of free money in a vat of excrement and cut off their support, Peter Sellers had to raise the additional money himself to complete the shooting. Ultimately, the film proved a commercial disaster for the comic actor; the only monetary profit Sellers made from *The Magic Christian* came from his association with Ringo Starr. What was it?

ANSWERS

1.   While actual shooting wouldn't commence until February, preproduction activities were well underway on another soundstage for *The Magic Christian*, in which Ringo would play Youngman Grand.

(When it was learned on 14 January that casting for the women was taking place, Paul suggested they should film the auditions. Peter Sellers, Ringo's costar in the film, also visited the Beatles' set on this day.)

2.   Marsh, Mary and Marvin were all early surnames for Loretta Martin, the sweet heroine of "Get Back."

3.   These are some of the people mentioned in "Get Off!" (also known as "White Power"), an improvizational jam captured during filming at Twickenham for *Let It Be*, 9 January.

(Much in the manner of "Dig It" [filmed at Apple, 3 Savile Row, 24 January], the stream of consciousness lyrics of "Get Off!" find Paul and

John simply calling out the names of people that come to mind, to a standard twelve-bar blues. Paul may have been thinking of Judy Garland, for example, as she had just married hairdresser Mickey Deans on 9 January. Similarly, Enid Blyton, who created Noddy, Big Ears, and the Famous Five, had only recently died, 28 November 1968.)

4. Paul discovered the surrealistic science of "pataphyics" in the play *Ubu Cocu* (*Ubu Cuckolded*) by French playwright Alfred Jarry.

(McCartney first heard the work as a radio production by BBC Third Program while driving his Astin Martin to Liverpool in January 1966. Jarry's character, Pere [Pa] Ubu, declares himself at the opening of the play to be ". . . a celebrated pataphysician.")

5. George Hartree is better known to UK audiences as Charles Hawtrey, a comic actor who starred in twenty-three films in the *Carry On* series of comedies. Prefacing a run-through of "Dig A Pony" during the first day of rehearsals at Apple, 22 January, John made his now famous remark, " 'I Dig a Pygmy' by Charles Hawtrey and the Deaf Aids. Phase one, in which Doris gets her oats."

(Phil Spector used this piece of dialogue to open *Let It Be*, added during a stereo mixing session in Room Four at EMI Studios, 27 March 1970. Hawtrey died, aged seventy-three, in October 1988.)

6. *Let It Be* engineer Glyn Johns thought up the idea of a concert on the roof of 3 Savile Row.

(During a lunch in the Apple dining room attended by Johns and director Michael Lindsay-Hogg, 26 January, talk turned to the building, prompting Ringo to remark on what a wonderful roof it had and how the group were planning to turn it into a rooftop garden. "I have an idea," said Glyn looking over at Michael. "We should go up and look at this roof.")

7. John's fur coat was bought by Cynthia Lennon's mother, Lilian Powell.

(Lily bought the coat in April 1968 for £5 in one of the auction salesrooms at Talbot Wilson's in West Kirby, Cheshire.)

8. "When I wrote ["Something"], in my mind I heard Ray Charles singing it, and he did do it some years later."

(Harrison began writing "Something" during a break in sessions for the White Album in Abbey Road's Studio One. Charles included his cover of the song on his album *Volcanic Action of My Soul*, issued by Tangerine/ABC in 1971.)

9. John and Yoko had originally planned to marry on the cross-Channel ferry *Dragon*.

10. Taken from the text of "The Beatles as Nature Intended" ad, McCartney's song to rollercoast by is "Get Back," "a pure spring-time rock number," issued by Apple in the UK backed with "Don't Let Me Down," 11 April.

11. Wisely dropped before its release, "The Ballad of John & Yoko" sported the subtitle, "They're Gonna Crucify Me."

12. The complete working title for "Oh! Darling" included the subtitle "I'll Never Do You No Harm."

13. On 22 April, in a brief ceremony performed by Señor de Mesquita on the roof of Apple, 3 Savile Row, John changed his middle name to Ono.

(While John had adopted his middle name Ono by deed poll, under British law he still had to retain his given middle name of Winston.)

14. The two garden light switches in the master bedroom were labeled "John" and "Yoko," respectively.

15. "Lies From Apple" stationery used a peeling pear.

16. En route to New York aboard the QE2, Ringo gave the *Get Back* album its first public airing in the 736 Club discotheque on the luxury liner, 17 May.

17. Melling's creation represented John and Yoko's "Plastic Ono Band," which the press encountered at a release party for their single "Give Peace A Chance"/"Remember Love," given 3 July at the Chelsea Town Hall, Kings Road.

(Injuries the couple sustained in an auto accident 1 July while vacationing in Golspie, Scotland, prevented them from attending the party. A photo of Melling's sculpture graces the single's picture sleeve, first released by Apple in the UK, 4 July.)

18. The working title for "The End" was "Ending."

19. "Wind, sky and earth are recurring, it's straight out of *Grapefruit*," notes Macca regarding the themes of "Because."

(John composed the lyrics to "Because" on the back of a business letter to the Beatles from John Eastman dated July 1969.)

20. McCartney's suit was made by Savile Row tailor Edward Sexton. George, Ringo and John had obtained their outfits from Tommy Nutter, another Savile Row tailor.

(Paul wore another Edward Sexton suit on the cover of his *Paul Is Live* album, which computer grafted his updated 1993 image onto Macmillan's 1969 photo.)

21. John mentions having written "What's the New Mary Jane" with John Alexis "Magic Alex" Mardas.

(Lennon refers to the song in the *Hit Parader* article as "What a Shame Mary Jane Had a Pain at the Party," recorded 14 August 1968 as a possible track for the White Album ["the last Beatles album" Lennon is referring to]. After some mixing at Abbey Road 26 November 1969, John had planned to release the song as a single by the Plastic Ono Band, with "You Know My Name [Look Up the Number]" as the B-side. Copies were pressed [as APPLES 1002] for rush release 5 December, before being cancelled. After years as a bootleg perennial, the song was finally given an official release when take four was included on disc one of *Anthology 3*, issued by Apple/EMI/Capitol, 29 October 1996.)

22. Leon's song about Chris O'Dell, whom he was dating at the time, is titled "Pisces Apple Lady," included on *Leon Russell*, issued by Shelter Records in the U.S., 23 March 1970.

(Ringo also plays drums on the track.)

23. The Cleanliness and Godliness Band masqueraded as the Masked Marauders.

24. Pressed in Los Angeles, the first "Beatleg" was *Kum Back* (Kum Back #1, WCF), consisting of the eleven songs from sound producer Glyn Johns' initial rough mix for the proposed *Get Back* album, which Johns presented to the group in March 1969.

25. Ringo purchased "Brookfields," Sellers's Elstead, Surrey house for £60,000.

(Remembering Starr during the filming of *The Magic Christian*, Sellers, who also enjoyed playing the drums recalled, "I don't think we spoke about anything else other than drums and drummers.")

1970

1. What is the title of the song the Iveys recorded about Paul McCartney?

2. What does John Lennon have in common with artists Pierre Alechinsky, Roberto Matta and Julian Stanczak?

3. Who did Paul imagine was singing "Let It Be" as he composed it?

4. Who did Paul have in mind when he composed "The Long and Winding Road"?

5. When John needed massed voices to sing and clap on "Instant Karma (We All Shine On)" during its recording in Abbey Road's Studio Three, 27–28 January, what London night club did he recruit patrons from?

6. "We built a fire in the studio but didn't use it," McCartney noted of the recording of which of his songs?

7. What does Paul's song "Suicide" (featured briefly on *McCartney*) have in common with John's "Nobody Loves You (When You're Down and Out)"?

8. Prior to release, which McCartney song sported the subtitle "Rock & Roll Springtime"?

9. "Written in London, at the piano, with the second verse added slightly later, as if you cared." Assuming that we do, what song is Paul referring to?

10. Purchased for $336,000, the Harrisons moved into Friar Park, 12 March. Shortly thereafter, George began an extensive renovation of the grounds, excavating hidden tunnels and adding a few of his own touches, including his own recording studio, FPSHOT (Friar Park Studios, Henley-On-Thames). Outside the main gates, a wooden sign in green and gold was installed in the late seventies declaring "Private: Keep Out" to sight-seers in ten different languages. An American English version offers a slightly different request. What is it?

11. On what project did Ringo collaborate with the Talk of the Town Orchestra, under the direction of George Martin?

12. Ringo contributed liner notes to this prominent jazz band leader's album of Beatles covers released on the Happy Tiger label in 1970. Starr penned them as a way of thanking him for providing an arrangement for one of the songs on his first solo album, *Sentimental Journey*, first issued on Apple, 27 March. Who is he?

13. What title had Ringo originally considered releasing *Sentimental Journey* under?

14. On 23 April, John, George, and Pattie left London on TWA Flight 761 for Los Angeles, where the two Beatles had business to conduct with Capitol Records. What assumed names were the trio traveling under?

15. While in New York, George spent the afternoon with Bob Dylan in Columbia Studio B, 1 May. "Dylan and Harrison hit it off well," reported *Rolling Stone*, "and spent part of the time with Dylan singing Beatles songs and George singing Dylan songs." Which Beatles song did Dylan sing?

16. What do the albums *Postcard* by Mary Hopkin, *Quadrophenia*, by The Who, *Through the Past Darkly* by the Rolling Stones, *Mud Slide Slim* by James Taylor, and *Let It Be* have in common?

17. "All that I can say is not enough. It comforts me to know that we're so much in love."

Bob Dylan wrote these unused lyrics for what Harrison/Dylan collaboration?

18. In "Art of Dying" (included on *All Things Must Pass*), Harrison sings that ". . . nothing 'Sister Mary' can do, will keep me here with you." But in an early draft of this song, it wasn't Sister Mary—who was it?

19. In his book *The Longest Cocktail Party*, Richard DiLello noted that during June, Neil Aspinall could be found on the fourth floor of Apple working on "a massively ambitious cinematic Beatle document that chronicled their rise from the Cavern to Savile Row. With his two assistants, Tony and Graham, he had amassed all existing footage of the Beatles . . . the entire gamut of Beatleological film history . . . to be pruned into 90 comprehensible minutes." Though Aspinall's film was eventually shelved, his idea for a documentary of the band's own history would serve as inspiration for *The Beatles Anthology*, which first ran in the U.S. on ABC-TV, 19, 22 and 23 November 1995, with Aspinall its executive producer. What was the title of Neil's documentary?

20. Who are the Oliver Twists?

21. Before hooking up with Pete Drake to produce *Beaucoups of Blues*, who else had Ringo approached to produce his country album?

22. In a letter sent to *Melody Maker* in August, what did Paul McCartney refer to as "the limping dog of a news story which has been dragging itself across your pages for the past year"?

23. On 26 September, Janis Joplin recorded a sixty-eight-second greeting with the Full Tilt Boogie Band for John's thirtieth birthday, 9 October. The same day, an acetate was made of the recording and (presumably) sent to Lennon. What song did Janis sing?

24. *The Baby Maker* (starring Barbara Hershey), the animated feature *A Boy Named Charlie Brown*, *Darling Lili* (starring Julie Andrews), *Scrooge* (starring Albert Finney) and *Let It Be*—what do these films have in common?

25. ["He] indicated that he is of the opinion that the Beatles laid the groundwork for many of the problems we are having with young people by their filthy unkempt appearances and suggestive music while entertaining in this country during the early and middle 1960s."

The official memo from this entertainer's visit to the FBI Building in Washington, D.C., 31 December, includes this none-too-flattering assessment of the Beatles, which fans might find surprising considering his influence on the group. Whose opinion was this?

ANSWERS

1. Following sessions for the Iveys' contributions to the Commonwealth United soundtrack for *The Magic Christian*, Tom Evans and Pete Ham wrote "Crimson Ship," recounting the group's pleasure at having had the opportunity to record with and learn from Paul McCartney on the sessions.

("Crimson Ship" was first issued by Apple Records in the UK, 9 January on *Magic Christian Music*. By then the Iveys had changed their name, at Neil Aspinall's suggestion, to Badfinger.)

2. All these artists had exhibitions running at the London Arts Gallery, 22 New Bond Street, with Lennon premiering his *Bag One* lithographs there 14 January through the 31st.

(The exhibit was closed briefly on the 16th when eight lithographs were confiscated by Detective-Inspector Patrick Luff by a warrant issued under the Obscene Publications Act. Alechinsky's exhibit followed Lennon's, running from 18 February to 18 March.)

3. Based on a dream he had where his mother Mary came to him with words of reassurance, Paul imagined Aretha Franklin singing "Let It Be" as he wrote it.

(Aretha issued her version of the song in 1970 as the B-side of her Atlantic single "Don't Play That Song.")

4. When Paul was writing "The Long and Winding Road" (in 1968, during sessions for the White Album) he was thinking of Ray Charles.

(McCartney's approach to writing "Road" was to have Charles in his mind "just for an attitude," he told Barry Miles. "[Y]ou place it by thinking, Oh, I love that Ray Charles, and think, Well, what might he do then? So that was in my mind, and would have probably had some bearing on the chord structure of it, which is slightly jazzy.")

5. In addition to Yoko and Mal Evans, the chorale of voices and clapping heard on "Instant Karma" included patrons from the London nightclub Hatchetts.

6. While the fire Paul built at Morgan Studios in London during the recording of "Kreen-Akore" wasn't used, one can hear the sound of the twigs breaking that were used to make it.

7. Lennon and McCartney both wrote these songs with Frank Sinatra in mind.

(Paul actually got a chance to demo "Suicide" for Sinatra's consideration only to have the singer reject the song, thinking McCartney was having a joke at his expense. Sinatra died after suffering an acute heart attack in Los Angeles, California, 14 May 1998. He was eighty-two.)

8. "Momma Miss America."

9. "Maybe I'm Amazed."

10. "Get Your Ass Out'a Here!"

11. On 15 March, the Talk of the Town Orchestra played as Ringo sang and danced in front of an invited audience of friends for filming of a promotional clip for "Sentimental Journey," the title track of his first solo album.

12. Ringo provided liner notes for Count Basie's album *Basie on the Beatles*.

(Ringo requested an arrangement for "Night and Day" from the bandleader, 1 October 1969; a completed score arrived five days later. Starr became the first Beatle to initiate a solo album when he entered Studio Three on 27 October 1969 to record the Cole Porter song, produced by George Martin. The arrangement used, however, was done by Chico O'Farrill, the Latin and Afro-Cuban jazz trumpeter and band leader.)

13. *Sentimental Journey* was originally announced for release under the title *Ringo Stardust*.

14.   John traveled under the name Chambers, while the Harrisons were Mr. and Mrs. Masters.

(One of the earliest entries in John's FBI file is this information on their traveling aliases, supplied to the FBI by the State Department, who in turn obtained it from the American Embassy in London. The FBI's interest in Lennon and the Harrisons stemmed from "their reputations in England as narcotics users," requiring the trio to obtain INS waivers to enter the U.S. The two-page FBI teletype dated 4/23/70 notes that "while Lennon and the Harrisons have shown no propensity to become involved in violent antiwar demonstrations, each recipient must remain alert for any information of such activity on their part or for information indicating they are using narcotics.")

15.   Bob sang a version of "Yesterday," which Dylan authority Clinton Heylin notes was "mangled into yesteryear."

16.   The photographs used on the sleeves of these albums were all taken by photographer Ethan Russell.

17.   Dylan wrote these unused lyrics for "I'd Have You Anytime," which Harrison and Dylan composed together during George's Thanksgiving visit to Dylan's home in Woodstock, New York, in November 1968.

18.   Before "Sister Mary" it was "Mr. Epstein."

19.   Aspinall's Beatles documentary is titled *The Long and Winding Road.*

20.   The Oliver Twists were a fictitious rock group featured in the June 1970 issue of *Batman Comics.* In DC Comics' take on the Paul is Dead rumor, the Caped Crusaders attempt to solve the "death" of Saul Cartwright.

(As the group walk away from a grave on the cover of issue 222, Cartwright is the only member of the Twists who is barefoot. Their album, *Dead Till Proven Alive,* shows the group posed on the front cover à la the Beatles on the back cover of *Sgt. Pepper,* Cartwright has his back to the viewer. Julian Schwartz, the editor of *Batman Comics* at the time, told *Beatlefan* senior correspondent Rick Glover, that that issue "had to be one of the most talked about issues in all of comic history . . . due primarily to the popularity of the figures on the cover." At the time, DC was "blatantly looking for a way to take advantage of the Beatles' popularity." At one point they even considered introducing a group called the "Bat-les."

21. Ringo talked with Bob Johnston, who had produced Bob Dylan's country-influenced *John Wesley Harding* about producing *Beaucoups of Blues*.

(According to Starr, Johnston "wanted too much bread, so I decided not to do it with him.")

22. McCartney viewed the question, "Will the Beatles get together again?" as a limping dog of a news story. In his letter to *Melody Maker* readers, he assured them that the answer was "no."

(Paul's letter [lot 318] sold for £11,000 at a rock 'n' roll memorabilia auction held by Sotheby's in London, 29 August 1985.)

23. Janis sang the Dale Evans song "Happy Trails" at Columbia's West Coast studios in Hollywood.

(On 4 October, Joplin was found dead at the Landmark Hotel in Hollywood of an accidental heroin overdose. Her "Happy Trails" was included on Columbia/Legacy's three-CD retrospective, *Janis* in November 1993.)

24. These films were all nominated for an Oscar for 1970 Best Film Music–Original Film Score by the Academy of Motion Picture Arts and Sciences, with *Let It Be* getting the nod at ceremonies held at the Dorothy Chandler Pavilion in Los Angeles, 15 April 1971. It was the group's only Oscar.

(Beatles-related connections with the other nominees included *Scrooge*, with an appearance by Roy Kinnear [who played Algernon in *Help!*] in the film as a "Portly Gentleman" and the inclusion of Lance Percival [the voice of Paul and Ringo in *The Beatles* cartoon series and Old Fred in *Yellow Submarine*] in the cast of "Darling Lili" as a character named "T. C.")

25. These were Elvis Presley's sentiments regarding the Beatles during a visit to the FBI Building, 31 December, from a memo dated 4 January 1971.

(Elvis expressed similar sentiments during his meeting with Richard Nixon, 21 December. According to a memo submitted by deputy counsel to the president, Egil "Bud" Krogh, Elvis called the Beatles "a focal point for anti-Americanism. They had come to this country, made their money, then gone back to England where they fomented anti-American feeling.")

1971

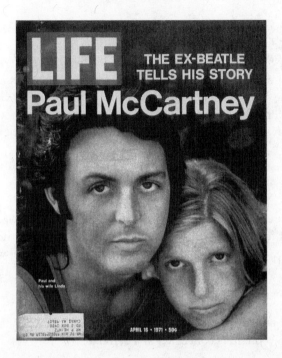

LIFE — THE EX-BEATLE TELLS HIS STORY — Paul McCartney

Paul and his wife Linda

APRIL 16 • 1971 • 50¢

1.   "We got a bit of a reputation from hanging out with the Cambridge Graduate School of Revolutionaries in the UK," wrote John in 1978 of his New Left leanings during this period. Asserting that "they made us feel so guilty about not hating everyone who wasn't poor," what "rather embarrassing" song did Lennon say he "wrote and recorded"?

2.   Frank Zappa was too busy directing *200 Motels* (*Life on the Road*) to actually be in it himself, so the part of Frank Zappa was played by Ringo Starr (billed as Larry the Dwarf). Based on the premise that "touring can make you crazy," the film was fraught with problems from the word go. Halfway through the script readings, Zappa's bassist Jeff Simmons quit the Mothers of Invention and flew back to America. Frank eventually recruited Martin Lickert, Ringo's chauffeur at the time, to replace him in the film (and subsequently in the band). Lickert had been Zappa's second replacement for the departed bassist, the first, who had previously starred in a film with Ringo, quit just before filming was to begin at Pinewood Studios, 23 January. Who was he?

3. Linda McCartney sings, "learning how to do that," on which of her husband's songs?

4. Acting on behalf of John, George and Ringo, Allen Klein began an investigation in February 1969 into the finances of the Beatles to assess their ability to purchase NEMS (which included 237,000 shares in Northern Songs Limited, the public company whose principal assets were the rights to the songs of Lennon and McCartney). In an affidavit submitted to the London High Court 12 February 1971, Klein listed three companies as the "main sources of The Beatles' income"—what were they?

5. In what McCartney song does our lonely heroine "post another letter to the sound of five"?

6. Released on Apple in April, "It Don't Come Easy" would become Ringo's first top-five single. The issued version was actually the song's second remake, recorded 8 March 1970. What was the song's working title when Starr first attempted it in Studio Two at Abbey Road, 18–19 February?

7. In what song do Paul and Linda McCartney write of that "terrible sight of two youngsters concealed in a barrel"?

8. When Apple rejected the first version of the Badfinger album eventually titled *Straight Up*, George stepped in to produce, beginning 31 May, booking the group into Abbey Road's Studio Three. When it came time for Joey Molland to sing his composition "Suitcase," what line did Harrison ask him to change?

9. Starting in June, Ringo could be found in Spain working on his third non-Beatles feature film, *Blindman*, where he played a Mexican bandit named Candy. During the filming, what song did Ringo begin writing?

10. "I expected sort of a grubby maniac with naked women all over the place, you know—sitting on the toilet. The first thing I said was, 'Wow, you look so different. You look great!' " Who was John talking about?

11. John's entire introduction reads: "Rest In Peace. John & Yoko"—what book did he write it for?

12. What song on *Let It Be* did John believe Rod Stewart turned into "Maggie May"?

13. Following the evening Concert for Bangla Desh, 1 August, at Madison Square Garden, a party was thrown at a New York club called Ugano's. What band played a short set at the party?

14. With their return to England following the Concerts for Bangla Desh, Pete Ham found himself on the receiving end of some none too subtle ribbing from Joey Molland and future wife Kathie. The couple were not happy that George had asked Pete rather than Joey to play acoustic guitar with him on "Here Comes the Sun." Ham responded to the inferences that he was putting himself ahead of the group by writing what song, included on Badfinger's Apple album *Straight Up*?

15. Stella McCartney's difficult birth at London's King College Hospital, 13 September, was Paul's inspiration—it might otherwise have been called Turpentine, or the Dazzlers—what?

16. "It was 'Working Class Hero' with chocolate on. I was trying to think of it in terms of children." What song is John talking about?

17. Its soundtrack consists of Yoko making and taking phone calls while John accompanies himself on acoustic guitar, singing early versions of "Aisumasen (I'm Sorry)," "New York City" and an assortment of rock 'n' roll oldies including "Glad All Over," "Wake Up Little Susie," and "Peggy Sue Got Married." What is this film's title?

18. Paul has said that his decision to record *Wild Life* quickly with his new band Wings in September was inspired by the example of another artist. "That kind of rose out of one single factor that we'd heard that [*] had recorded an album in a week."

19. What is "Napoleon's Bladder"?

20. During a party thrown for John's thirty-first birthday, 9 October, this noted poet began by chanting the Padma Sombhava mantra, sitting in a half-lotus position before his harmonium. Lennon grabbed his guitar, as did Klaus Voormann and Phil Spector, with Ringo drumming on an overturned wastebasket. Music was improvised to several mantras followed by a version of William Blake's "Nurse's Song." After about an hour, the group moved to Beatles and Lennon songs, including "Yellow Submarine," "Yesterday," "Crippled Inside," and "Give Peace A Chance." Who was the poet on the harmonium?

21. In October, John and Yoko rented a two-room apartment on Bank Street in Greenwich Village. Who was their landlord?

22. In April 1968, on the balcony of his suite at the Oberoi Hotel in New Delhi, *Wonderwall* director Joe Massot told John and George about his idea for a movie called *Zachariah* (released in 1971). It came to him after "reflecting on the war raging in Vietnam" and from watching John and George doing something—what?

23. "Bring a bag of bread and cheese and find a shady spot beneath the trees." Sounds good—what McCartney song is this from?

24. In December, John and Yoko, Jerry Rubin and David Peel announced the formation of this group, "dedicated to exposing hip capitalist counter-culture ripoffs and politicizing rock music and rock artists." What was the name of their group?

25. Why would Detroit Recorder's Judge Robert J. Columbo be of note to Lennon fans?

ANSWERS

1. "Power to the People."

(Lennon was inspired to write "Power to the People" following an interview for *Red Mole* at Tittenhurst with left wing activists Tarique Ali and Robin Blackburn, 21 January. John recorded the song the following day.)

2. Zappa's first replacement for the Mothers' bassist in *200 Motels* was Wilfred Brambell, who had played John McCartney, Paul's grandfather in *A Hard Day's Night.*

3. Linda sings the backing vocal "learning how to do that" when Paul sings the chorus to "Smile Away," included on *Ram.*

4. Klein's affidavit listed the three main sources of the Beatles' income as United Artists Corporation (which handled the group's films), General Artists Corporation (which handled the band's North American tours) and EMI and its American subsidiary Capitol Records (which released their recordings).

5. Posting letters to the sound of five is part of "Another Day," first issued by Apple as a single in the UK., 19 February.

6. "It Don't Come Easy" had the working title "You Gotta Pay Your Dues."

(Though officially credited as a Richard Starkey composition, Starr admitted in 1997 that he had some help from George. "It was cowritten," Starr told journalist Mark Brown. "I can write two verses and a chorus. In those days you needed three verses. He'd tie up the last verse for me and produce them. 'Back Off Boogaloo,' 'It Don't Come Easy.' He actually produced the first version of 'Photograph.'")

7. Those two youngsters in a barrel were sucking "Monkberry Moon Delight," which Paul sings with amazing gusto on his *Ram* LP, first issued by Apple in the U.S. 17 May.

8. Harrison asked Molland to change the line "Pusher, pusher on the run," a reference to the drug dealers the band encountered at their shows. George felt the drug reference would've hurt the song's chances for airplay.

(Joey would change the words to "butcher, butcher." The first version of "Suitcase," with Molland's drug dealer reference, was one of six bonus tracks included on the CD reissue of *Straight Up*, released by Apple in 1993.)

9. " 'Photograph' was written in Spain," Starr told *Beatlefan* contributing editor, Ken Sharp. "I was doing the movie *Blindman*. And then I finished it on a yacht (the *SS Marala*) in Cannes at the Cannes Film Festival with George."

10. John was talking about his first meeting with Frank Zappa, prior to the Lennon's performance with Zappa and the Mothers of Invention onstage at the Fillmore East in New York City, 6 June.

11. John's brief introduction was written for Jay Thompson's *I Am Also a You*, described by its author as "a book of thoughts with photographs by Jay Thompson."

(Thompson's book includes lyric passages from "I am the Walrus," "Baby You're a Rich Man," and "Tomorrow Never Knows.")

12. "By the way, Rod Stewart turned 'Don't Let Me Down' into (singing) 'Maggie don't go-o-o,' " John told David Sheff in September 1980. "That's one the publishers never noticed."

13.   Badfinger played a short set at the party at Ugano's following the evening Concert for Bangla Desh.

14.   Pete's response to the fall out from his solo spotlight with George at the Concerts for Bangla Desh was the song "Take It All."

15.   The decision to deliver Stella by Caesarean meant McCartney had to leave the delivery room. Paul has said he prayed that she would be delivered "on the wings of an angel" and "Wings" came to him as the name for his new group.

   (Stella Nina McCartney was delivered three weeks premature, weighing in at five pounds, nine ounces. Stella was named after both of Linda's grandmothers, Stella Epstein [her paternal], and Stella Dryfoos Lindner [her maternal].)

16.   "Working Class Hero" with chocolate on is John's assessment of "Imagine," first issued by Apple in the U.S. on the album of the same name, 9 September.

17.   Shot at New York's Regis Hotel 10 September, *Clock* features John's rock oldies soundtrack as the screen shows the hands of their clock marking the passage of an hour.

   (*Clock* premiered 9 October at *This Is Not Here*, an art exhibit by Yoko and friends, which ran at the Everson Art Museum in Syracuse, New York. The film was screened continuously in the museum's foyer during the exhibit's seventeen-day run.)

18.   When Paul went into Abbey Road with Wings in September, recording the nine songs on *Wild Life* in approximately two weeks, he had been inspired by the example of Bob Dylan.

   (Dylan had recorded his *Nashville Skyline* album at Columbia Music Row Studios in Nashville, Tennessee in only four sessions, between 13 February and 18 February 1969.)

19.   "Napoleon's Bladder" was the title of one of the "Water Pieces" John made for Yoko's art retrospective, *This Is Not Here*.

   ("Napoleon's Bladder" consisted of a plastic bag into which John placed a pink sponge which was then displayed inside a small fish tank.)

20.   Allen Ginsberg.

   ("In all, they played for six hours," wrote Michael Schumacher in his biography of Ginsberg, "turning Lennon's hotel suite, as Allen wrote in his journal later, into 'a tiny Madison Square Garden.' " Paul, through *International Times* cofounder Barry Miles, contacted Ginsberg in 1968 with the idea of recording an album for Zapple, Apple's experimental and spoken-word label. For his release, Ginsberg had hoped to make musical notations for all of Blake's *Songs of Innocence* [which includes "Nurse's Song"] and *Songs of Experience*, which he devoted many hours to that autumn.)

21. John and Yoko's apartment at 105 Bank Street was owned by Joe Butler, former drummer with The Lovin' Spoonful.

(A Bob Gruen photograph of this apartment can be seen accompanying the lyrics to "New York City" on the back cover of John and Yoko's *Sometime in New York City* album.)

22. Arriving at the Maharishi's Rishikesh retreat in late March–early April (ostensibly with plans to film the proceedings), Joe Massot got the plot for his "curry Western" *Zachariah* from watching John and George's ongoing meditation "duel."

("George, it seemed, was really studious in his approach to Eastern religion and was locked into some sort of meditational duel with Lennon to see who was the stronger character," Massot told *Mojo* magazine in 1996. "I told them both the plot of *Zachariah* ["A rock Western, ahead of its time"], which I'd come up with watching them dueling together at the meditation centre.")

23. Bread and cheese al fresco is one good way to spend the day in "Tomorrow," included on Wings' first LP *Wild Life*, released by Apple in both the U.S. and the UK 7 December.

24. John and Yoko, Jerry Rubin and David Peel comprised the Rock Liberation Front.

25. In 1969, Judge Columbo gave leftist writer John Sinclair ten years for selling two marijuana cigarettes to an undercover agent. Lennon mentions Columbo in his song "John Sinclair," which he debuted at the concert/political rally to free Sinclair held at the Chrysler Arena in Ann Arbor, Michigan, 10–11 December 1971.

(The lyrics to "John Sinclair" appear in Lennon's FBI files, transcribed as part of the report by agents attending the show. John included the song on his *Sometime in New York City* album released the following June.)

1972

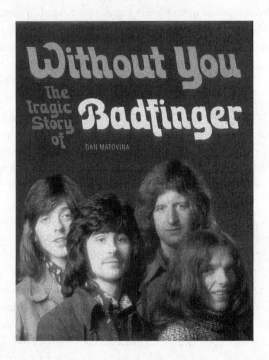

1. George included the song "Sue Me, Sue You Blues," which he'd written "during the big suing period," on his *Living in the Material World* album, first issued by Apple in the U.S., 30 May 1973. But Harrison wasn't the first to record the song—who was?

2. "Sue Me, Sue You Blues" wasn't the only song from *Dark Horse* that Harrison let someone else record before he did. Who recorded "So Sad" (to which Harrison contributed guitar and backing vocals), for an album first released on Chrysalis in the UK, 2 November 1973?

3. "This appears to me to be an important matter, and I think it would be well to be considered at the highest level. As I can see, many headaches might be avoided if appropriate action be taken in time."

The recommendations above were part of a memo forwarded 4 February to Attorney General John Mitchell by this U.S. senator, encouraging the Nixon administration to deport Lennon, whom it was believed had plans to hold a protest concert in Miami Beach in an effort to disrupt Nixon's renomination at the Republican National Convention. Who is the senator?

4. Wings set out in a rented scarlet caravan and an Avis truck, 8 February, embarking on a two-week university tour. Their first show was lunchtime the following day at Nottingham University, but as the troop of six men, two women, three children and three dogs set out from St. John's Wood, where did McCartney want to go first?

5. John and Yoko cohosted the *Mike Douglas Show* the week of 14–18 February (though the shows themselves had been taped one a week for five weeks from early January through early February). Lennon compositions performed by John over the course of the week included "It's So Hard" (on Monday), "Imagine" (Thursday) and "Luck of the Irish" (Friday). Production notes indicate that another Lennon song was considered—which one?

6. By 15 February, FBI director J. Edgar Hoover had instructed his offices to begin monitoring John. FBI records released under the Freedom of Information Act indicate that the agency believed Lennon to be involved in "revolutionary activity," including a $75,000 donation to fund the activities of what "new left" organization?

7. Yoko performed two Ono compositions on the *Mike Douglas Show* that week, "Midsummer New York" (from *Fly*) on Tuesday, and "Sisters, O Sisters" (from *Sometime in New York City*) on Wednesday. On Friday, she sang a traditional Japanese folk song—what was its title?

8. The melody for "Angela," about the imprisonment of black radical and intellectual Angela Davis, was taken from another song Lennon began in September 1971. What was its title?

9. Ringo drew his inspiration for "Back Off Boogaloo" from a dinner guest one evening. "[He] was just an energized guy," Starr would recall in May 1998 during a taping for the VH1 program *Storytellers*. "He used to speak, 'Oh, back off boogaloo! Oooh, you boogaloo!'" Who was Starr referring to?

10. Parodying the front page of the *New York Times*, the front cover of the Late City Edition of *Sometime in New York City*, contains "Ono News That's Fit to Print" by the Joko Press. What "constituted" the weather that day?

11. Whose face is pictured in the apple on the cover of *Sometime in New York City*?

12. In the U.S., John and Yoko's *Sometime in New York City* album included a custom inner sleeve reproducing a British Army recruitment ad taken from the *Sun* newspaper dated 1 April 1970 (April Fool's Day). In addition to filling in his name and date of birth in the coupon, what phrase did John "amend" the face of the ad with?

13. Taken from their appearance with Frank Zappa and the Mothers of Invention at New York's Fillmore East, 6 June 1971, when John and Yoko issued "Scumbag" on their "free live jam LP" included with *Sometime in New York City*, whose vocal contributions did they mix out?

14. Who are Hello, Goodbye, and Maybe?

15. What is Women's Tango Lessons Ltd.?

16. On whose album were George and Ringo credited for their instrumental contributions as George Harrysong and Ritchie Snare?

17. John played his last two full live concerts at New York's Madison Square Garden, 30 August. The One to One Benefit Concerts raised over $1.5 million dollars for what cause?

18. During the One to One evening show, what song did John dramatically punctuate his performance of with the declaration "Stop the War!"?

19. What occasion marked the last time John and Yoko performed in public together?

20. In October 1972, at the same time Paul McCartney and Wings were recording "Live and Let Die" with George Martin at the producer's AIR Studios in London, who was Richard Perry producing in the adjacent studio?

21. Maggie Bell, Richard Harris, Ringo Starr, Rod Stewart and Steve Winwood—what recording project do they have in common?

22. "Bobby lived with Patty" in what song by Wings?

23. What do Fred Astaire, Dick Cavett, George Harrison and Jack Palance have in common?

24. John and Yoko's *Imagine* film includes a sequence to Yoko's "Don't Count the Waves" (from *Fly*) where the couple are seen playing chess with two sets of white pieces. The sets were an art piece created by Ono— what did she title it?

25. In his book *Fear and Loathing in Las Vegas*, what Lennon song does Hunter S. Thompson remark was released "ten years too late"?

ANSWERS

1. Guitarist Jesse "Ed" Davis was the first to release "Sue Me, Sue You Blues" as the A-side of a single issued by Atco in the U.S., 25 January 1972.

(Harrison had given Davis the song in the summer of 1971, prior to doing the Concert for Bangla Desh.)

2. Ten Years After frontman Alvin Lee included a version of "So Sad (No Love of His Own)" on *On the Road to Freedom*, his 1973 album with U.S. gospel singer Mylon LeFevre.

3. Republican senator from South Carolina Strom Thurmond sent the memo to Mitchell.

4. Wings followed the signs to Ashby de la Zouche "because," as Paul remarked shortly afterwords, "we liked the sound of it."

(From there, the entourage proceeded to the village of Heather, where Paul tried without success to buy a pony they saw tied to a post in the village green.)

5. "Gimme Some Truth."

(Bonnie Kent, an assistant for the *John Davidson Show* [which the *Mike Douglas Show* later became], wrote in the fanzine *Instant Karma* that "when the line, '[No] short-haired, yellow-bellied son of tricky dicky' was discovered, a question mark was placed next to the song notes, later replaced by a 'NO!' ")

6. Documents in Lennon's FBI files continually reference Lennon's donation of $75,000 to EYSIC (Election Year Strategy Information Center), also known as the Allamuchy Tribe and the International News Service, headed by "Chicago Seven" defendant Rennie Davis.

7. Yoko sang "Sakura (Cherry Blossoms)."

8. The tune for "Angela" originates with a song Lennon wrote in September 1971 titled "J. J."

9. The dinner guest that inspired Ringo to write "Back Off Boogaloo" was T-Rex singer Marc Bolan.

10. The weather in the Late City Edition of *Sometime in New York City* was the text of Article I of the Bill of Rights in the U.S. Constitution.

("Congress shall make no law respecting an establishment of religion, or prohibiting the free exercise thereof; or abridging the freedom of speech, or of the press; or the right of the people peaceably to assemble, and to petition the Government for a redress of grievances.")

11. The face of Phil Spector, the producer of *Sometime in New York City*, is seen in the apple on the album's cover.

(The caption underneath "To Know Him Is to Love Him," references the hit Spector wrote in 1958 for the Teddy Bears.)

12. "Fit To Die."

(The altered recruitment ad was not included when *Sometime in New York City* was released in the UK, 15 September.)

13. John and Yoko's mix of "Scumbag" on *Sometime in New York City* removed the vocals by Flo and Eddie (Mark Volman and Howard Kaylan).

(Zappa's mix of this show, including Flo and Eddie's vocals, were released on the album *Playground Psychotics*, first issued in the U.S. 3 November 1992 on his Barking Pumpkin label.)

14. Hello, Goodbye, and Maybe were the names Linda McCartney listed as those of her children (Heather, Mary, and Stella) in a lifelines entry for her in the concert program for the 1972 Wings Over Europe tour.

(Listed as Mrs. McCartney's "Pet hates" at the time were "Allen Klien [sic] and Intruders.")

15. Women's Tango Lessons Ltd. is the name of the company Paul and Linda formed with photographer Joe Stevens in 1972 to divide up profits from the sales of photos Stevens took as he documented Wings' first European Tour, which ran from 9 July to 24 August.

(Stevens's photos were credited to "Captain Snaps" to circumvent difficulties he was having securing a British work permit. Photos credited to the captain appear in the booklet accompanying *Red Rose Speedway*.)

16. Harrysong and Snare appeared on Harry Nilsson's *Son of Schmilsson* album, first issued by RCA in the U.S., 10 July.

17. The One to One Benefit Concerts benefitted the Willowbrook Foundation for Retarded Children.

18. John's performance of "Come Together" at the One to One evening show included his declaration to "Stop the War" in Vietnam.

(This performance was included on *New York City* disc 2 of *The John Lennon Anthology*, issued by Capitol in the U.S., 3 November 1998.)

19. John and Yoko's final public performance together was on the Jerry Lewis Muscular Dystrophy Telethon, 6 September.

(Backed by Elephant's Memory, John and Yoko performed "Imagine," "Give Peace a Chance" and "Now or Never." The latter, composed by Ono, was issued by Apple as a single in the U.S., 13 November, backed with "Move On Fast.")

20. At the same time Paul was recording "Live and Let Die," Carly Simon was recording the vocals for her album *No Secrets*, first issued by Elektra in the U.S., 3 November.

(When Paul dropped in on the session, he and Linda ended up contributing backing vocals to the James Taylor composition "Night Owl.")

21. All are guest soloists on Lou Reizner's recording of *Tommy*, performed by the London Symphony Orchestra and Chamber Choir, first issued by Ode in the UK, 24 November.

(As Uncle Ernie, Ringo takes vocal solos on "Fiddle About" and "Tommy's Holiday Camp.")

22. Bobby and Patty live on "C-Moon," first issued by Apple in the UK, 1 December, as the B-side of "Hi Hi Hi."

23. Each man is seen escorting Yoko Ono on their arm in a sequence directed by Jonas Mekas in the Lennons' room at the St. Regis Hotel in New York City, 6 September 1971. It was included in the couple's 70-minute *Imagine* film, which had its world premiere on U.S. television, 23 December 1972.

24. Yoko's chess set in *Imagine* is called *Play It by Trust*.

25. "Power to the People."
("He was turning the cassette tape over. The radio was screaming: 'Power to the People—Right On!' John Lennon's political song, ten years too late.")

1973

1. Produced by Derek Taylor, Harry Nilsson's album of standard ballad revivals, *A Little Touch of Schmilsson in the Night*, was to have included a Beatles song, but arranger/conductor Gordon Jenkins vetoed it as being "too new." What song did Harry want to include?

2. In what Paul McCartney and Wings song do we meet "Jimmy with the big tattoo"?

3. While Pink Floyd was at Abbey Road Studios recording *The Dark Side of the Moon*, Roger Waters devised a series of approximately twenty questions on flash cards. Samples from the responses to such queries as, "What does the dark side of the moon mean to you?" and "When did you last thump someone?" would later be incorporated on several of the tracks. Paul, Linda, and Henry McCulloch of Wings were among those whose responses were recorded. Henry is heard on "Money" and "Us and Them." On what song(s) is Paul heard?

4. What Beatles song can be heard at the conclusion of *The Dark Side of the Moon*?

5. Who are Mike Menarry and J. D. Clover?

6. George's favorite cover of "Something" was released by this artist in 1973 as a B-side. "It should have been the A-side," said Harrison in 1992, "and they should still put it out now. It's incredible." Who is the artist?

7. Before the Lennons moved into their seventh-floor apartment at the Dakota in New York City in late April, a medium was summoned to determine if they were sharing their new home with any spirits of the departed. Whose spirit did the medium contact?

8. While on holiday in Jamaica in late April, Paul dined one evening with actor Dustin Hoffman (who was there filming *Papillon* with Steve McQueen). A discussion of how McCartney wrote songs prompted Hoffman to ask if he could write one on the spot. What did the actor produce to provide Paul with inspiration?

9. A "leaping armadillo"? Yes, in which Paul McCartney and Wings song?

10. In which of George's songs do we hear of ". . . the rice that keeps going astray on its way to Bombay"?

11. Wings played its first scheduled tour of Britain primarily during the month of May, opening the 11th at the Bristol Hippodrome. Who was the opening band on the tour?

12. When George Martin presented producer Harry Saltzman with Paul McCartney and Wings' song for the new James Bond film, Saltzman assumed it was a demo. Who had he suggested should sing "Live and Let Die"?

13. Which Lennon song evolved from two earlier Lennon compositions—"I Promise" (where John took the song's middle eight) and "Make Love, Not War"?

14. "From mystical to magical/To a way to fly/From temple scenes to village green/Let there be light."
This unused verse originates from which Lennon song?

15. Which song on *Mind Games* started out under the working title "Shoeshine"?

16.   What is the title of the book Paul reviewed for the UK magazine *Punch*, dated 8 August?

17.   Considering the trials and traumas Paul went through recording *Band on the Run* at EMI's studio in Lagos, Nigeria—working in a studio still under construction, getting mugged at knifepoint, and fainting one evening due to bronchial spasms—McCartney might have fared better had he recorded the album at the second choice from his list of EMI studios around the world. What country would that have put him in?

18.   Who went on Lagos radio while Paul was in the city recording *Band on the Run* (30 August–22 September) and later confronted McCartney in person, accusing him of visiting the country to exploit and steal African music?

19.   When John sold Tittenhurst estate to Ringo 18 September, it came with an eight-track recording studio, which Lennon had dubbed Ascot Sound. What did Starr rename the facility when he moved in?

20.   What is the title of the book John reviewed in the *New York Times Book Review* dated 30 September?

21.   What were Paul McCartney and Wings doing on the grounds of Osterley House at Osterley Park in West London on 28 October?

22.   First released by Apple in the U.S. 29 October as the B-side of "Mind Games," "Meat City" includes a backward-inserted segment after the line "Just got to give me some rock and roll." Played forwards, the listener is instructed to "check the album." Playing the "Meat City" on *Mind Games*, what does the listener hear?

23.   *Ringo* was first issued on Apple in the U.S., 2 November. What song on first issue copies was incorrectly listed as "Hold On" on the record's label?

24.   According to Dr. Winston O'Boogie, what is "the first sign of dandruff"?

25.   What is the title of the song Badfinger recorded about John Lennon?

ANSWERS

1. Nilsson wanted to include "Hey Jude" on *A Little Touch of Schmilsson in the Night.*

2. Jimmy and his tattoo figure in "The Mess," the B-side of "My Love," first issued by Apple in the UK, 23 March.

("The Mess" was recorded live during Wings' first European tour at the Hague's Congresgebouw, Holland, 21 August 1972.)

3. Paul (and Linda's) responses were not used on *The Dark Side of the Moon.*

(On "Us and Them" McCulloch can be heard responding, "I don't know. I was really drunk at the time! I was just telling him, he couldn't get into number two. He was asking why he wasn't coming up on freely, after I was yelling and screaming and telling him why he wasn't coming up on freely. It came as a heavy blow, but we sorted the matter out.")

4. A sharp increase in volume, following Jerry Driscoll's statement, "There is no dark side of the moon really, matter of fact it's all dark," will reveal an instrumental version of "Ticket To Ride" (particularly evident on CDs remastered in 1992 and 1994).

(Driscoll, or Jerry the Irish Doorman, as he was known, was the Doorman at Abbey Road studios in 1972.)

5. Holiday camp waiter and fairground operator Mike Menarry and camp drummer J. D. Clover are the characters played by Ringo and Keith Moon, respectively, in the film *That'll Be the Day.*

(Moon and Neil Aspinall shared a credit as musical supervisors on the film. Ringo was offered the chance to reprise his role as Mike in the film's 1974 sequel, *Stardust.* "Starr turned it down this time," wrote Tony Fletcher in his biography of Keith Moon, "concerned that Menarry's ousting of a band member just as the Stray Cats were about to break big would remind the public of his own entry into the Beatles at Pete Best's expense." The role of the Stray Cats' first manager would go to Adam Faith.)

6. James Brown released "Something" as the B-side of his third remake of "Think," first issued in the U.S. on Polydor in April 1973.

7. A séance held by the Lennons is said to have contacted the spirit of Jessie Ryan, the wife of actor Robert Ryan, the apartment's previous tenant. Her recent death from cancer had prompted Mr. Ryan to move out of the Dakota.

(Communicating through the medium, Mrs. Ryan indicated her plans to stay in the apartment as a spirit and wouldn't bother the Lennons.)

8. Hoffman related to Paul the events of the last evening of artist Pablo Picasso from an article published in the 23 April issue of *Time* magazine by Robert Hughes, "Pablo Picasso's Last Days and Final Journey."

(To Dustin's amazement, McCartney, guitar in hand, literally composed "Picasso's Last Words [Drink to Me]" on the spot. In an audio interview included with the twenty-fifth anniversary edition of *Band on the Run*, Hoffman still proudly recalls the evening. "It's right under childbirth in terms of great events in my life. I mean, I was at the birth of something." Picasso died in Mougins, France, 8 April 1973 at the age of ninety-one.)

9. A leaping armadillo appears in "Big Barn Bed," included on *Red Rose Speedway*, first issued by Apple in the U.S., 30 April.

10. "Miss O'Dell."
(Released as the B-side of "Give Me Love [Give Me Peace on Earth]," first issued by Apple in the U.S., 7 May.)

11. Wings' British dates were opened by Brinsley Schwarz, featuring twenty-four-year-old Nick Lowe on bass.

12. With Bond songs traditionally sung by women, Harry Saltzman had suggested Thelma Houston to sing "Live and Let Die."

13. "I Promise" and "Make Love, Not War" became "Mind Games."

14. "You Are Here."

15. "Meat City" began in 1971 under the working title "Shoeshine."

16. Paul's review in *Punch* was for the *Paul Simon Song Book*, published by Michael Joseph.

("Splitting hairs, I would say that the book is slightly too heavy for reading on the toilet although on the whole it makes it," wrote McCartney. "As a final word, I'd like to mention the fact that this book costs £2.95 which is 45p dearer than my latest LP. I suggest buying my record and saving 45p.")

17.   McCartney's second choice for recording *Band on the Run* had been EMI's studio in Rio de Janeiro.

("It was going to be either Brazilian percussion or African percussion, and I said African, that would be great, great vibe.")

18.   McCartney was accused of trying to exploit and steal African music by Nigerian singer, multi-instrumentalist and political activist Fela Ransome-Kuti.

(Fela was the inventor of Afro-Beat, a fusion of soul and jazz with African Hi-Life music. Kuti died 2 August 1997 of heart failure brought on by AIDS.)

19.   Ringo renamed Tittenhurst's recording facility Startling Studios.

20.   John reviewed *The Goon Show Scripts* by Spike Milligan.

("Hipper than the Hippest and madder than 'Mad,' a conspiracy against reality," wrote Lennon. "A 'coup d'etat' of the mind! The evidence, for and against, is in this book. A copy of which should be sent to Mr. Nixon and Mr. Ervin.")

21.   On 28 October, Clive Arrowsmith photographed Paul, Linda, Denny, Michael Parkinson, Kenny Lynch, James Coburn, Clement Freud, Christopher Lee, and John Conteh against a brick wall on the grounds of Osterley House for the cover of *Band on the Run.*

22.   "Fuck a pig."

23.   Randy Newman's song "Have You Seen My Baby" was incorrectly listed as "Hold On" on first U.S. pressings of *Ringo.*

24.   "Madness is the first sign of dandruff" is Dr. Winston O'Boogie's pronouncement from the inner sleeve liner notes for *Mind Games.*

25.   "The Winner."

(First issued in the U.S. 26 November on *Ass*, Badfinger's final album for Apple, Joey Molland wrote "The Winner" to express his displeasure with Lennon during this period. "I was so angry that here was this man at the top of the world, who could have anything he wanted. It was at this period when all he seemed to be doing was moaning. He just seemed to be angry about everything, and it just pissed me off.")

1974

Walls and Bridges

1.   Elton John originally thought of calling the new album he was recording in January *Ol' Pink Eyes Is Back*, but it was Ringo who eventually came up with the title it was released under—what was it?

2.   During a visit to Udaipur, India, in February, what did George find on a tin of paint while strolling through the market stalls one day?

3.   This band's name was suggested by their bassist Douglas Colvin, a big fan of Paul McCartney. Who is this group, formed in 1974 in Forest Hills, New York?

4.   At the request of Warner Bros. President Mo Ostin, Derek Taylor was asked to compile a selection of songs for a new concept album for Frank Sinatra. Enlisting George Harrison's assistance, the two compiled an eleven-track song list, 24–25 June. With spoken prefaces to each song by Taylor, the lineup included three songs by Nilsson, and one each by Bob Dylan, Joni Mitchell, and George Harrison. Two reel-to-reel tapes, titled *A very friendly Frank conversation*, were given a professional printing presentation and sent on to Sinatra who, after listening to them, decided to return to "another project previously offered." What Harrison song was proposed for the Sinatra album that never was?

5. While in Los Angeles, Keith Moon, Ringo Starr, and Harry Nilsson frequently held court in a private loft at the Rainbow Bar and Grill on Sunset Boulevard. Management of the Rainbow installed a plaque to identify the loft—what did it say?

6. RCA first issued Nilsson's Lennon-produced album *Pussycats* in the U.S., 19 August. The label had rejected John and Harry's original title for the album—what was it?

7. At 9 P.M. on 23 August, John and May Pang saw a UFO from the terrace of their apartment on East 52nd Street in New York City. What were the couple wearing at the time?

8. What song was at one time scheduled for inclusion on *Walls and Bridges*?

9. Who are the 44th Street Fairies?

10. Photography for *Walls and Bridges* (including the memorable "Listen to This . . ." promotional campaign and the interchangable head shot cover flaps) were taken by Bob Gruen. What noted photographer had art director Roy Kohara originally wanted to use?

11. Capitol's "Listen to This . . ." promotional campaign for *Walls and Bridges* included a "Listen to This Press Kit," featuring two photos of John by Bob Gruen, and a "Listen to This Interview" card, which consisted of Lennon modifying the text of an another interview given by someone else in 1973. Whose interview did John revise?

12. In a letter to *Melody Maker* dated 30 September, John wrote to Todd Rundgren, "I like you, and some of your work, including "I Saw The Light," which is not unlike . . ." what Beatles song "melody wise"?

13. What song did Paul McCartney write and produce for Norma Egstrom in 1974?

14. In what song does Paul sing of the "nightlife" taking him "down to Printer's Alley"?

15. These two Harrison songs were played on the opening night of George's 1974 North American Tour, 2 November, at the Pacific Coliseum in Vancouver, Canada, and then dropped for the remainder of the tour. What were they?

16. What song was the last music to be played over venue PAs before George came out with his group?

17. Opening the show on George's 1974 tour was the Harrison instrumental "Hari's on Tour (Express)," included on the *Dark Horse* album issued by Apple that December. On early dates in the tour, the instrumental sported a different title—what was it?

18. How did the Appalachian Regional Hospitals benefit from The 1974 George Harrison and Friends Tour?

19. The cover of *Goodnight Vienna* was adapted by Roy Kohara from a still from the 1951 sci-fi film *The Day the Earth Stood Still*. Who gave Ringo the idea?

20. After watching this film one day, Bernie Taupin wondered aloud why the Beatles never released "Lucy in the Sky With Diamonds" as a single. Elton John thought that was a good idea and recorded his own version—what movie had Bernie been watching?

21. Which of George's songs draws on the words of British poet Lord Alfred Tennyson for some of its lyrics?

22. First issued by Apple in the U.S., 9 December, the cover of *Dark Horse* displays a section from the Liverpool Institute High School's Lower School class picture from April 1956 sitting atop a large lotus flower. The addition of rugby shirts to the front row of students (spelling out DARK HORSE) and to the row of teachers (whose shirts variously endorse Apple, Dark Horse, Parlophone, and John's Bag Productions) appear the most obvious modifications to the photo, but there is one significant alteration. Three students originally pictured below George (in blue face) have been removed to allow for the inclusion of this man, whose green rugby shirt bears the Capitol logo. Who is he?

23. What was Eric Clapton and Pattie Harrison's contribution to "Bye Bye Love," included on *Dark Horse*?

24. According to George, what "love" is "like the rain, beating on your window brain"?

25. Looking back on the tour, Harrison would comment, "The places (he) played with us, he got 20,000 people. On his own he gets about 1500. A lot of the people who say he stole the show wouldn't write about him if he played on his own." Who was George talking about?

ANSWERS

1. Ringo suggested to Elton John that he call his next album *Caribou*, after Caribou Ranch, the Colorado studio where it was recorded.

(Elton also recorded [possibly as a demo] a version of "Snookeroo" during the *Caribou* sessions. He had written the song with lyricist Bernie Taupin for Ringo's *Goodnight Vienna* album. Bernie has said he had "Yellow Submarine" in mind when he wrote its lyrics, which are about Starr.)

2. Harrison discovered a tin of paint with a white seven-headed horse on its label. George purchased the tin and gave it to an artist who created the black seven-headed version that became the logo for Dark Horse Records.

3. The Ramones.

("When we met [Douglas] he was callin' himself Dee Dee Ramone and he was a big fan of Paul McCartney," recalls lead vocalist Joey Ramone [Jeffrey Hyman]. "Paul used to check into hotel rooms under the alias of, like, Paul Ramon. [McCartney *had actually used the alias as a stage name on the Silver Beetles' tour of Scotland backing Johnny Gentle in May 1960.*] So Dee Dee kind of adapted it from there. Ramone was like kind of a cool-sounding name . . . so we kind of adapted it as our surname to create a sense of unity. Then everyone could have their unique personality within their own thing almost like the Beatles kind of did to some degree.")

4. "Old Brown Shoe."

5. The plaque in the private loft at the Rainbow Bar and Grill read "The Lair of the Hollywood Vampires."

(Ringo references their hangout when he introduces Keith Moon on "Together" [from *Two Sides of the Moon*, recorded September–December 1974] as "the star of stage, screen, and the Rainbow".)

6. John and Harry's original title for the *Pussycats* album was *Strange Pussies*.

7. John and May were naked when they observed their UFO.

(Pang had just stepped out of the shower when John excitedly called her to the terrace where she viewed a large circular object "like a flattened cone" with a "large brilliant red light on top.")

8. A checker proof sheet of the album's lyrics dated 4 September indicates that "Move Over Ms. L" had originally been planned for inclusion on *Walls and Bridges*, sequenced between "Surprise, Surprise (Sweet Bird of Paradox)" and "What You Got."

(John would not release "Move Over Ms. L" until 1975, when it was used as the B-side of "Stand By Me," first issued in the U.S., 10 March.)

9. The 44th Street Fairies is the name given by John in the liner notes for *Walls and Bridges* to the backing vocalists featured on "#9 Dream"— May Pang, Lori Burton, Joey Dambra (at the time fronting a band called Community Apple) and Lennon.

10. Kohara had wanted to use Richard Avedon for the *Walls and Bridges* album.

11. The "Listen to This Interview" consisted of Lennon making playful handwritten revisions to an interview Ringo gave in 1973 to promote his *Ringo* album.

(To the question, "Did you personally develop the album concept?" Lennon crosses out Ringo's response to write in that *Walls and Bridges* is ". . . an unconcept album.")

12. John viewed "I Saw the Light" (the opening cut on *Something/Anything?*) as ". . . not unlike "There's a Place" (Beatles), melody wise."

(John's letter, "AN OPENED LETTUCE TO SODD RUNTLESTUNTLE [from dr. wintston o'boogie]," took Rundgren to task for an interview he gave *Melody Maker*, in which he criticized Lennon and the Beatles, telling Ailan Jones, "John Lennon ain't no revolutionary. He's a fucking idiot, man. Shouting about revolution and acting like an ass.")

13. Paul wrote and produced "Let's Love" for pop vocalist Peggy Lee, born Norma Egstrom, 27 May 1920.

("Let's Love" became the title track of the album Peggy released on Atlantic, first issued in the U.S., 1 October. Lee has said that Paul played uncredited piano and conducted the orchestra on the "Let's Love" session, held at Record Plant West in Los Angeles in June 1974.)

14. Printer's Alley is "where Sally sang a song behind a bar" in "Sally G," the B-side of "Junior's Farm," by Paul McCartney and Wings, first issued in the UK by Apple, 25 October.

15. Harrison only performed "The Lord Loves the One (That Loves the Lord)" and "Who Can See It" (both from *Living in the Material World*) on the opening night of the tour.

16. The last music played over the PA before Harrison would take the stage during his '74 Tour was the "Lumberjack Song," written by Michael Palin and Terry Jones.

(Harrison appeared in the Mountie Chorus during a live rendition of the "Lumberjack Song" performed 20 April 1976 at New York's City Center. An inebriated Harry Nilsson also donned the Mountie costume during Monty Python's three-week run, 14 April–2 May. During a five-city promotional tour for *Thirty-Three & ⅓* in late 1976, Harrison checked into the Copley Plaza Hotel in Boston under the name "Jack Lumbrer.")

17. On the first dozen dates of Harrison's '74 Tour, the opening instrumental was known as "Hari Good Boy Express."

(At the Salt Lake City show, 16 November, the instrumental was retitled "Hari's on Tour [Express].")

18. Proceeds from the sales of the George Harrison and Friends program booklet benefitted Appalachian Regional Hospitals Inc.

19. Ringo got the idea for the cover of *Goodnight Vienna* after seeing color stills from *The Day the Earth Stood Still* on display in Harry Nilsson's home in LA.

("I took one look and said, 'That's the still.' It fit right in with the title *Goodnight Vienna*, which is an old Northern saying that means 'I'm leaving here.' Because when you finish an album, that's just how you feel, like you want to take a trip to Mars just to get away.")

20. Taupin had been watching *Yellow Submarine*.

("Lucy" was recorded at Caribou Ranch in Colorado in late August near the end of sessions for *Captain Fantastic and the Brown Dirt Cowboy*. John flew in with May Pang for three days to assist on the sessions [as Dr. Winston O'Boogie], which also saw Elton record a version of "One Day [At A Time]" for the single's B-side, first released in the UK, 15 November.)

21. Harrison drew the chorus of "Ding Dong, Ding Dong" from verse 106 of the Tennyson poem "In Memoriam A. H. H.," first published in 1850 as a tribute to poet Arthur Henry Hallam.

(George found the lines of the poem painted on one of the walls of his Friar Park home:

Ring out the old, ring in the new,
Ring, happy bells, across the snow,
The Year is going, let him go;
Ring out the false, ring in the true.)

22. The man in the Capitol logo rugby shirt is J. R. Edwards, headmaster of the Liverpool Institute.

(To students of "the Inny" Mr. Edwards was best known as "the Baz." The man with the red sanskrit "Om" on his shirt is Stan Reid, George's art teacher.)

23. Though credited on the inner sleeve as having participated on the track, Eric Clapton and Pattie Harrison actually had no involvement on "Bye Bye Love" beyond being the inspiration for the new verses Harrison wrote for this Everly Brothers song.

("I had to write the credits for that album in about ten minutes because the record company needed it and I was going on tour," George told journalist Mark Ellen in October 1987, "and I put "Bye Bye Love—Pattie and Eric Clapton." And [EMI] saw that and thought they must have appeared and typed "Eric Clapton appears courtesy of RSO Records." And he hadn't appeared on it at all.")

24.   "Maya Love."
(Included on *Dark Horse*, first released by Apple in the U.S., 9 December.)

25.   George was referring to Billy Preston, whose solo showcases during the '74 Tour ("Will It Go Round in Circles?", "Outta Space," and "Nothing From Nothing") were so well-received by the critics, they often felt he upstaged headliner Harrison.

1975

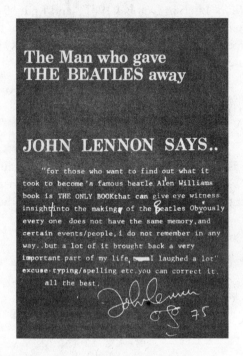

1. Following Geoff Britton's departure in January, Joe English was invited to drum for Wings. On whose recommendation did Paul ask the Georgia resident to come to New Orleans to participate in the recording of *Venus and Mars*?

2. Which Lennon album had but one pressing, comprising 2,444 LPs and 500 eight-track tapes?

3. During February sessions for *Venus and Mars* at Sea Saint Studios in New Orleans, Linda was backed by Wings as she played piano and sang lead on what song?

4. Who is walking past John in the photo on the cover of his *Rock 'N' Roll* album?

5. During the fade of "You Can't Catch Me" (on *Rock 'N' Roll*), what other song does John sing?

6. Which song did John choose for inclusion on *Rock 'N' Roll*, not only because he liked the artist, but because "I remember singing it the only time my mother saw me perform before she died."

7. What was the title of the first album released on Ringo's Ring O' Records label?

8. On 1 March, John acted as a presenter at the Grammy Awards, televised live from New York. Whom did he appear onstage with?

9. In which of Lennon's songs does he note that "they're starving back in China"?

10. Keith Moon's only solo album, *Two Sides of the Moon*, was first issued in the U.S. by Track/MCA, 17 March. Ringo acted as announcer on "Solid Gold" and contributed drums and "rap" to Harry Nilsson's "Together," but Starr made one additional uncredited contribution to the album—what was it?

11. Following the completion of recording on *Venus and Mars* at Wally Heider Studios in Los Angeles, Paul threw a wrap party in Long Beach, 24 March. It was quite a guest list, including George and future wife Olivia, Ella Fitzgerald, Dean Martin, and Michael Jackson, old friends Derek Taylor and Mal Evans—even Bob Dylan made an appearance. Where was the party held?

12. Ringo was a guest on *The Smothers Brothers Comedy Hour*, first broadcast on NBC-TV, 28 April. What song did Starr sing with Tom and Dick?

13. Formed in Zion, Illinois, in 1975, this power-pop group took their name from a flippant remark Paul McCartney once made regarding the origin of the name Beatles. What was their name?

14. Keith Moon's infatuation with English actor Robert Newton (best known for his portrayal of Long John Silver), inspired the Who drummer to meet with this noted director in 1975 with the idea of remaking *Soliders Three*, the story of three army comrades set in nineteenth-century colonial India. Moon envisioned himself, Ringo, and Harry Nilsson in the roles portrayed in the 1951 film by Newton, David Niven, and Stuart Granger. Who was the director Keith approached?

15. "I did the basic track for this in 1971," Harrison said of this song, included on *Extra Texture*. "I remembered we had this track, which was such a good backing track. I thought I'd resurrect it and finish it off." What song is George referring to?

16. What are the names of the concert venues Paul sings about in "Rock Show"?

17. What is 21ZNA9?

18. The last thing one hears on *Venus and Mars*, as Wings' version of the theme from the ITV soap opera *Crossroads* fades, is a voice uttering what phrase?

19. During his last major interview before his five-year seclusion, Pete Hamill asked John if there was anybody he'd like to produce. "I'd like to resurrect [*]," replied Lennon. "But I'd be so scared of him I don't know whether I could *do* it. I'd *like* to do it." Who was John talking about?

20. "I've got to be careful. Whatever I write is going to be quoted on the paperback," declared Paul when this man asked him to sign a copy of his book on the Beatles (published by Macmillan in 1975). McCartney's inscription read: "To [*], Some parts of this book are partially true, Paul McCartney." Whose book was he signing?

21. Aired in the U.S. 13 June, a red-jumpsuited John made his final television appearance as a performing musician on the TV special *A Salute to Sir Lew Grade*, taped 18 April in the Grand Ballroom of New York's Hilton Hotel. His eight-piece band, wearing masks that made them appear two-faced were dubbed "Etcetera" for the occasion, but what was their real name?

22. What was George's original title for "Tired of Midnight Blue"?

23. What song on *Extra Texture—Read All About It*, did Harrison call "a cheap excuse to play a bit of guitar"?

24. George's last album for Apple was once considered for release under a different title—what was it?

25. Harrison proclaims, "He's a cure for whooping cough." Who?

ANSWERS

1. Joe English was asked to join Wings on the recommendation of fellow Georgian Tony Dorsey, leader of the Wings horn section.

2. *John Lennon Sings the Great Rock & Roll Hits (Roots).*

(Mastered from a rough mix of the tapes Capitol would issue as *Rock 'N' Roll*, *Roots* was only available for a brief time from music publisher Morris Levy, via his TV mail-order company, Adam VIII, shipping 7 February, with TV ads running the next day. Capitol's version, issued 17 February, prompted Levy to file a $42 million breach of contract lawsuit. Reportedly, only 1,270 LPs and 175 tapes were sold. Lennon ordered a copy himself, waiting over three weeks to receive it.)

3. Paul and Wings backed Linda McCartney on her composition "New Orleans."

(The song was released on Linda's posthumous solo album *Wide Prairie*, issued by Capitol, 27 October 1998.)

4. From left to right, George, Stuart Sutcliffe, and Paul are walking past John in the photo taken by Jurgen Vollmer on the cover of *Rock 'N' Roll*.

(Taken in the summer of 1961, not far from the Top Ten Club, Vollmer [then nineteen] had the trio walk past John twelve times, shooting an entire roll of film in a two-and-a-quarter-inch Rolleiflex camera he had borrowed from his boss at the time, photographer Reinhart Wolf.)

5. The fade of "You Can't Catch Me" includes a quick quote from Jimmy McCracklin's 1958 song "The Walk."

6. John included Larry Williams' 1957 song "Bony Maronie" on *Rock 'N' Roll* in remembrance of his mother Julia, who had heard him singing it on the one occasion she saw her son perform (with the Quarry Men) before her death, 15 July 1958.

7. The first album released by Ring O' Records was *Star*tling Music*, David Hentschel's synthesizer version of the *Ringo* album, first issued in the U.S., 17 February.

8. John was a Grammy Award presenter for "Records of the Year–Artist and Producer" with Paul Simon and Andy Williams.

9. Lennon mentions starving Chinese in "Move Over Ms. L," the B-side to "Stand By Me" ("They're starving back in China boy, that's what they always said!") and in "Nobody Told Me," first issued as a single in January 1984 ("They're starving back in China, so finish what you got").

10. Ringo suggested Keith Moon call his solo album *Two Sides of the Moon*.

(Moon met with opposition from the label with his original title suggestion, *Like a Rat Up a Pipe*.)

11. Featuring live music by the Meters and Professor Longhair, the *Venus and Mars* wrap party was held aboard the dry-docked ocean liner Queen Elizabeth II.

12. Ringo sang the "No No Song" with the Smothers Brothers.

13. Recording for Elektra, Jeff Murphy, John Murphy, Gary Klebe, and Skip Meyer called themselves the Shoes.

(During an interview conducted in the lobby of the Plaza Hotel, 10 February 1964, a reporter asked, "Who came up with the name Beatles and what does it really mean?" "It means Beatles, doesn't it?" replied John. "That's just a name, like shoe." "The Shoes!" Paul chimes in, "Y'see, we could've been called the Shoes for all you know.")

14. Moon discussed his idea for a remake of *Soldiers Three* with director Samuel Peckinpah.

15. George resurrected the 1971 backing track for "You."

("You" had originally been recorded at Abbey Road studios 2–3 February 1971 as part of a proposed Apple album for Ronnie Spector. When it came time for Harrison to sing to the backing tracks, he found they were too high. "My voice has been dropping over the years, and I had to put it up about three tones for Ronnie!")

16. The lyrics to "Rock Show" mention the Concertgebow in Amsterdam, Holland; Madison Square Garden in New York City; the Hollywood Bowl in Los Angeles; and the Rainbow Theatre in London.

17. 21ZNA9 is the designation of the Starship mentioned in the reprise of *Venus and Mars*.

18. "That's basically it."

19. Interviewed in 1975 for *Rolling Stone*, John told Pete Hamill he'd like to produce Elvis Presley.

("I know what I'd do with Presley. Make a rock and roll album.")

20. Paul's inscription in *The Man Who Gave the Beatles Away* is an accurate assessment of the book *Daily Mirror* writer William Marshall ghosted for Allan Williams, the owner of the Jacaranda Coffee Club responsible for getting the Beatles some of their earliest bookings, including their important Hamburg apprenticeships.

21. The band backing John during his performance for *A Salute to Sir Lew Grade* was actually known by the acronym BOMF, or Band of Motherfuckers.

(BOMF wisely changed their name shortly after their performance to Dog Soldier, taking their name from lyrics Lennon had written for a song titled "Incantation," which John coproduced for the group with Roy Cicala at New York's Record Plant. The song was released in 1998 on a three-track CD included with the book *Beatles Undercover*, by Kristofer K. Engelhardt.)

22. "Tired of Midnight Blue" was originally called "Midnight Blue."

(George modified the title when he discovered that Melissa Manchester had written a song called "Midnight Blue," included on her Arista album, *Melissa*.)

23. "A cheap excuse to play a bit of guitar" is George's assessment of "This Guitar (Can't Keep From Crying)."

24. George had originally considered calling *Extra Texture*, "Ononot himagen."

(As to the origin of the title eventually used, Harrison revealed to journalist Paul Gambaccini that "one of the guys who played bass on some of the tracks was talking to me while we were overdubbing. He said something about the record's texture and I just said 'extra.' At that time, it seemed funny—'Extra Texture, Read All About It.' ")

25. In the lyrics of "His Name Is Legs (Ladies & Gentleman)," George touts former Bonzo Dog Doo-Dah Band member "Legs" Larry Smith as, among other things, the cure for whooping cough.

1976

1. What is the title of the book former Beatles aide Mal Evans was working on with writer John Hoernie at the time of his death?

2. "After all, I'm sure you know, the mayor of Baltimore is here." He is, on what song released by Wings?

3. Where can one hear Paul declare, "Are you rockin' hep cat?"

4. The last time Paul saw John was at the Dakota, 25 April. As they parted company in the hallway of the Dakota, what were the last words John said to Paul?

5. Originally intended for his country album, *Beaucoups of Blues*, the Starkey composition "Band of Steel" was first released by whom?

6. "John and I tried to have it stopped. The cover was disgusting. When we worked, we spent as much time on the cover as on the tracks. We didn't put some crap-house cover on something we'd done." At what album are Ringo's comments directed?

7. George began writing "See Yourself" in 1967 as a commentary on the press' reaction to Paul's admission in a *Life* magazine interview that he had taken LSD. He had forgotten about the song until this man reminded him during sessions for *Thirty-Three & ⅓*. "I remembered it, completed the lyrics to the bridge and the second and third verses and recorded it that year," he wrote in *I Me Mine*. Who had reminded him?

8. Who arranged to have a plane skywrite "Happy Birthday Ringo" above Starr's Sunset Plaza home in Los Angeles for his thirty-sixth birthday, 7 July?

9. Writer Norman Mailer, actress Gloria Swanson, Japanese sculptor Isamu Noguchi, Sam Trust, president of ATV Music, and TV news personality Geraldo Rivera—what is their connection to John Lennon?

10. "I've always thought there's a great woman behind every idiot." Who said this and where?

11. What are A17 597 321 and A19 489 154?

12. Billy Joel noted many historical names and events (including the Beatles) in the lyrics of "We Didn't Start the Fire," which peaked at #1 in the U.S., 9 December 1989. But that wasn't the first song he wrote that mentioned the Beatles—what was?

13. What song do Cilla Black, Ronnie Spector, Leon and Mary Russell, and Ringo have in common?

14. *Ringo's Rotogravure* was first issued by Polydor in the UK, 17 September. From what song written in 1933 did Starr draw the idea for the album's title?

15. Who did Ringo send over to the Dakota to entertain John on his thirty-sixth birthday, 9 October?

16. Issued in October, what Beatles song does Jeff Lynne mention on ELO's Jet/United Artists album *A New World Record*?

17. What Beatles-related release, including a track featuring John on guitar and backing vocals, generated controversy when print ads for the album in the U.S. included a picture of Adolf Hitler wearing headphones?

18. On whose album did Ringo Starr appear credited as "The Voice of Jesus"?

19. A long-time fan of Buck Owens, Ringo twice recorded "Act Naturally," the country artist's theme song, first with the Beatles (for *Help!* in 1965), then with Owens himself (issued as a single in 1989). In November 1976, Starr recorded the Owens composition "Cryin' Time," sharing the vocals with this noted lyricist. Their version remains unreleased. Whom did Ringo record it with?

20. Ex-Zombie Colin Blunstone first released this Elton John/Bernie Taupin song which mentions Mona Best's Casbah Club. What is the song's title?

21. Starring Bing Crosby and Grace Kelly, what does the 1956 film *High Society* have in common with *Thirty-Three & ⅓*?

22. "Now he's been around—with those tears of a clown—through those ups and downs . . ."
George later replaced these lines, included in an early draft from which of his songs?

23. Who lived in the real "Crackerbox Palace," from which George drew his inspiration for the song of the same name?

24. Whom did George originally write "Learning How to Love You" for?

25. What McCartney song includes among its cast of characters an "action painter, Hitler's son, a commie with a tommy gun" and a "cat in satin trousers"?

ANSWERS

1. Mal had been scheduled to deliver the manuscript of his memoirs, *Living with the Beatles Legend,* to Grossett and Dunlap on 12 January when he was shot and killed by Los Angeles police, 4 January.

(Police found a despondent Evans barricaded in the bedroom of the duplex he was renting and opened fire after he refused to lower what turned out to be a Winchester replica air rifle he had pointed at them.)

2. An appearance by "the mayor of Baltimore" is noted in the second verse of "The Note You Never Wrote," sung by Denny Laine on *Wings at the Speed of Sound*, first issued by Capitol in the U.S., 25 March.

3. Preceeded by the sound of the McCartney's chip pan simmering, Paul makes this statement at the start of "Cook of the House," Linda's vocal turn on *Wings at the Speed of Sound*.

(Paul also included the song on Linda's posthumous solo album *Wide Prairie*, issued by Capitol, 27 October 1998.)

4. The last words John spoke to Paul were "Think about me every now and then, old friend," as he patted him on the shoulder.

(In February 1981, Carl Perkins had composed the song "My Old Friend" for Paul as a way of thanking him for the opportunity to visit and record with him on the island of Montserrat. Paul was in tears when Perkins played it for him, unaware until Linda explained that his song had referenced the last thing John had said to him.)

5. Ringo contributed backing vocals and drumming to Guthrie Thomas' recording of Starr's song "Band of Steel," included on his album *Lies & Alibis*, first issued by Capitol, 3 May.

6. Ringo's quoted displeasure was directed at the cover of the double-LP compilation *Rock 'N' Roll Music*, first issued by Capitol in the U.S., 7 June.

("John even said he'd do them a new cover," noted Starr. "It made us look cheap and we were never cheap. We were the sixties. All that Coca-Cola and cars with big fins was the fifties." Paul's reaction to the compilation was a little more philosophical: "I don't mind the *Rock 'N' Roll Music* album," he told Paul Gambaccini. "When it's over, you really don't care what they do with it. If someone comes up to us and says, 'That's a terrible rip-off,' we say, 'It has nothing to do with us!'")

7. It was Kumar Shankar, nephew of sitar master Ravi Shankar, credited as George's second engineer on *Thirty-Three & ⅓*, who reminded him of "See Yourself."

8. Keith Moon arranged for a plane to skywrite "Happy Birthday Ringo."

(Unfortunately, Ringo ended up footing the bill for the display. "In the end I had to stop Keith buying me presents," Starr would say later, "I'd always get the bill.")

9. During his court hearing for permanent resident status in the U.S., 27 July, Mailer, Swanson, Noguchi, and Rivera all spoke as character witnesses for John Lennon on the fourteenth floor of the Immigration and Naturalization Service building in New York City.

10. John made this statement to reporters on the occasion of the successful resolution of his four-and-a-half-year fight to obtain permanent resident status in the U.S., 27 July. He was referring to Yoko, whose support kept him from giving up.

11. These are John and Yoko's respective U.S. alien registration numbers.

(These numbers feature prominently on their green cards, granting them permanent resident status in the United States. Yoko received hers first on 23 March 1973. After enduring a four-year legal battle with an administration bent on his deportation, Judge Ira Fieldsteel finally granted John permanent resident status, 27 July 1976. When John applied for permanent alien resident status, 31 March, his application included his social security number [127-52-1582] and listed his occupation as "self-employed artist.")

12. "Why don't the Beatles get back together?" sings Joel in "All You Wanna Do Is Dance" on his Columbia album, *Turnstiles*.

13. During the seventies, versions of George's song, "I'll Still Love You" were recorded by Cilla Black, Ronnie Spector, Leon and Mary Russell, and Ringo. To date, only Starr's version has been released, which he included on *Ringo's Rotogravure*.

("I always loved it, and I was on the first session it was ever done on," Starr told Lisa Robinson. "So in the end I asked him if instead of writing one could I have that old one. He said fine, it saved him a job." Ringo and Eric Clapton worked with Harrison on Cilla's version in August 1972. Had Cilla released her planned single, it would likely have been titled "When Every Song Is Sung," which was how Harrison had registered the song for copyright, 2 November 1972.)

14. Ringo got the idea for the title of his fifth solo album from the Irving Berlin song "Easter Parade," specifically the version sung by Judy Garland and Fred Astaire in 1948 film *Easter Parade*:

> "On the avenue, Fifth Avenue,
> The photographers will snap us
> And you'll find you're in the rotogravure."

("I thought she was talking Russian or French," said Starr in a 1976 interview for *Circus Magazine*. "What's she saying? I have a book and I write odd things down and that was one of them. It's a great title, *Ringo's Rotogravure*. The tracks are like pictures in their own way. Each track on the album is a visual.")

15.   Ringo arranged to have "porn poet" Cherry Vanilla visit the Dakota 9 October to recite her version of *Romeo and Juliet*.

16.   "Hey Jude" is mentioned in the Electric Light Orchestra song "Shangri-La."

("My Shangri-La has gone away, fading like the Beatles on 'Hey Jude.'")

17.   First issued in the U.S. 25 October on 20th Century Records, the advertising campaign for Lou Reizner's soundtrack for *All This and World War II* drew criticism for using the image of Adolf Hitler wearing headphones.

(John is featured on Elton John's previously issued cover of "Lucy in the Sky With Diamonds." The movie's bizarre concept, a visual documentary of World War II set to Beatles music, first came to Russ Regan, the film's executive producer, in a dream. Regan opted not to include a sequence of submarines being torpedoed to the tune of "Yellow Submarine," as it seemed a little "too obvious." A version of "Yesterday" sung by Leonard Cohen accompanied by the London Symphony Orchestra remains unreleased.)

18.   Improvized on the spot, Ringo is the Voice of Jesus on "Men's Room, L.A.," included on Kinky Friedman's album *Lasso From El Passo*, first issued in the U.S. on Epic, 5 November.

19.   Ringo recorded a duet of "Cryin' Time" with Elton John lyricist, Bernie Taupin.

(The song was to have been included on a solo album Taupin planned to release on Elton's Rocket Record label.)

20.   The Casbah Club is mentioned in "Planes," the title track of Colin Blunstone's November 1976 release on Elton's Rocket Record Company.

(An outtake from the *Captain Fantastic and the Brown Dirt Cowboy* sessions, Elton's version appeared in October 1992 on the *Rare Masters* collection. John appeared at Mona Best's club as a member of Bluesology.)

21.   Both *High Society* and *Thirty Three & ⅓* feature the Cole Porter tune "True Love."

22.   The omitted line, with its reference to the Miracles' hit "The Tears of a Clown," was replaced with one referencing "You've Really Got a Hold on Me" in "Pure Smokey," George's song of appreciation for Motown legend Smokey Robinson.

23.   British comedian Lord Buckley referred to his "beaten-up" house in Los Angeles as "Crackerbox Palace."

(Harrison's reference in the lyrics to "Mr. Greif" was a nod to George Greif, who managed Buckley for eighteen years.)

24.   At his request, George had written "Learning How to Love You" for Herb Alpert. Harrison ended up recording the song himself (for *Thirty-Three & ⅓*), dedicating it to "Herbie Alpert."

25.   McCartney lists some "pretty soily company" in his song "Soily."

(While Wings began playing "Soily" live during their '73 tour of Britain, it would be another three years before the song was given a commercial release on *Wings Over America*, issued by Capitol 10 December 1976 in both the U.S. and UK. "Soily" was the last song to be registered with the U.S.. Copyright Office under the official pseudonym "McCartney," identifying it as a joint composition by Paul and Linda.)

1977

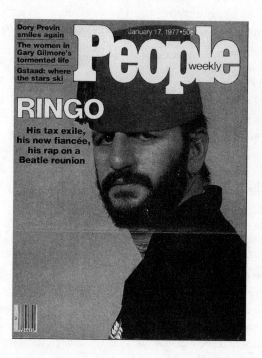

1. When Dark Horse/Warner Bros. issued "Crackerbox Palace" in the U.S. (24 January) and "True Love" in the UK (11 February) as the followup single to "This Song," Jonathan Clyde (younger brother of Jeremy Clyde of the singing duo "Chad and . . .") produced a promotional film to accompany each. Who directed them?

2. Included on *The Beatles Live! at the Star-Club in Hamburg, Germany 1962*, first issued in April on the (West) German Bellaphon label, lead vocals on the Beatle-backed versions of "Be-Bop-A-Lula" and "Hallelujah I Love Her So" were credited to a waiter named Horst Obber. But no one by that name worked at the Star-Club when Adrian Barber recorded the group in December 1962. Who really sang?

3. "A fairy tale is coming true/In the life of the wife of Mr. Montague,/As a fashion photographer closes in./But madam's mind is occupied/When thoughts of horror let defied/Should Misha spot the blackhead on her chin."

First recorded with Wings during sessions for *London Town*, what is the title of this unreleased pimple paean?

4. NBC-TV in the U.S. gave Eric Idle, Neil Innes and *Saturday Night Live* producer Lorne Michaels the green light in April 1977 to produce a ninety-minute documentary on the Rutles. George Harrison began his involvement in the project by showing Idle and Innes something—what did they see?

5. Issued by Capitol in the U.S. and Parlophone in the UK, 6 May, *The Beatles at the Hollywood Bowl* offers highlights from the group's shows at the outdoor venue which Capitol recorded in August 1964 and August 1965. The front cover artwork by Roy Kohara contains a factual error—what is it?

6. Capitol's promotional campaign for *The Beatles at the Hollywood Bowl* included a unique five-song sampler. What made this sampler so distinctive?

7. First issued by Capitol in the U.S., 6 May, Denny Laine's second solo album, *Holly Days*, was recorded at Paul's Rude Studio, a "wood-lined, tin-roofed shack" with a four-track recorder located on the grounds of his farm in Kintyre, Scotland. The album was a trip through the Buddy Holly catalogue recently acquired by Paul, which Macca produced in addition to providing all the instrumental backing. The original plan, however, had been for the album to be recorded in Nashville with local musicians. Who was to have produced it?

8. Wings spent the month of May in the waters off the Virgin Islands on the yacht Fair Carol, recording songs for *London Town*. Several tracks from these sessions remain unissued, including "Running 'Round the Room," "Standing Very Still," and an instrumental titled "El Toro Passing." Who or what was El Toro?

9. Roger Daltrey included Paul's song "Giddy" on his third solo album, *One of the Boys*, first issued by Polydor in the UK, 13 May. "Giddy" had evolved from what unreleased McCartney composition, recorded during the sessions for *Ram*?

10. Tony Palmer's thirteen-part series on the history of rock included an episode devoted to the Beatles titled *Mighty Good*, first aired in Britain on London Weekend Television, 14 May. What was the name of Palmer's series, which borrows a Beatles song as its title?

11. "I feel like writing a song about him," said Paul, "and by the sound of his yell, I think he could sing it." Who is McCartney referring to?

12. On 31 May, Epic in the U.S. released "Seaside Woman"/"B Side to Seaside," by Suzy and the Red Stripes, which were, of course, Linda McCartney and Wings. Linda's nom de plume is said to have originated from the Creedence Clearwater Revival song, "Suzie Q," but what is the origin of the band name?

13. "Someone's driving a six-wheeler," sings George in "It's What You Value," the last single (backed with "Woman Don't You Cry For Me") issued by Dark Horse from *Thirty-Three & ⅓* in the UK, 10 June. What was he referring to?

14. In early 1974, the Residents issued their first album, *Meet the Residents*, collectable among Beatles fans for its cover, which defaces the cover of Capitol's *Meet the Beatles* album. John Lennon is said to have received a copy. In August 1977, a 500-copy limited edition single was offered by mail from Ralph Records. Its A-side, "Beyond the Valley of a Day in the Life," is a well-assembled Beatles song sound collage built around loops from "Tell Me What You See," "Tell Me Why," "She Loves You," John's "God," and a Paul McCartney speech from the Beatles' 1965 Christmas message, "[We certainly tried our best to] please everybody, if we haven't done what we could've done, we've tried . . ." What title did the Residents release this single under?

15. George Martin began work on Robert Stigwood's Beatles musical *Sgt. Pepper's Lonely Hearts Club Band* 1 September at Cherokee Studios in Los Angeles (Stigwood had approached him in November 1976 to arrange and score the film's music soundtrack). In preparing rhythm tracks for the artists to later add lead vocals to, Martin assembled a rhythm quartet, including Max Middleton and Wilbur Bascombe from the Jeff Beck Group. Of special interest was the drummer Martin engaged—who was it?

16. In which song on *Ringo the 4th* does Starr reference one of his former bandmates?

17. John gave his last "public performance" in late September while staying in the immense Presidential Suite at the Hotel Okura in Tokyo. A Japanese couple, arriving in the elevator on what they believed to be the floor of a restaurant, took a seat in the vast living room, smoked cigarettes and chatted as John sang what song, accompanying himself on acoustic guitar?

18. First issued in the U.S. by Atlantic, 26 September, what was Ringo referencing when he titled his disco album *Ringo the 4th*?

19. What single was scheduled to be pulled from the double-LP Beatle ballads compilation *Love Songs*, first issued by Capitol in the U.S., 21 October?

20. "I would like to hear the football crowd at Hampdon Park sing it. That would be nice." What song is Paul referring to?

21. During November and December, John began writing two songs that, unbenownst to him, would one day become new Beatles singles—"Free as a Bird" and "Real Love." The latter song started life under a different theme and with what title?

22. By the end of the year Wings would be back down to a trio, with guitarist Jimmy McCulloch and drummer Joe English departing in September and November, respectively. To what bands did they initially head for?

23. "Only love, catch you up today, take your breath away, make you want to say what you're thinking of."

Paul details some of love's attributes in what unreleased song, recorded during the sessions for *London Town*?

24. During December, Ringo recorded two songs, including one titled "I Love My Suit," for a series of five commercials seen only in Japan for what brand of suit?

25. Written and narrated by actor Donald Pleasence, Ringo Starr provided vocals and dialogue for *Scouse the Mouse*, the little white title mouse of this children's disk issued by Polydor Super in the UK, 16 December. As side one opens, we find Scouse living in a Liverpool pet shop. Among his friends there is another mouse voiced by singer Adam Faith. What is his name?

ANSWERS

1. The promotional films for "Crackerbox Palace" and "True Love" were directed by Eric Idle.

(A third promotional film, made for "This Song," was directed by Harrison.)

2. The lead vocals on "Be-Bop-A-Lula" were sung by a waiter (or Ober) that Christmas night, Star-Club headwaiter Fred Fascher. The vocals on "Hallelujah I Love Her So" were handled by Fred's older brother, Star-Club manager Horst Fascher.

3. "Boil Crisis."

4. Idle and Innes were shown Neil Aspinall's unreleased Beatles documentary, *The Long and Winding Road*.

("We watched this, and it got depressing, because it was real," remembers Innes. "When they broke up, it really was a downer. When Brian Epstein died, it just became a bit too real, the fun definitely stopped. The general feeling was, we could probably tell the story as accurately with the Rutles, but in a more palatable way, because it wasn't really them—it was the Pre-Fab Four, not the Fab Four.")

5. The tickets Kohara created to represent the Beatles' Hollywood Bowl shows list both concert dates as Saturday evenings, when both shows occurred on Sundays.

(Kohara's tickets were patterned primarily after the design of those used at the Beatles' Shea Stadium shows.)

6. Capitol's five-song sampler for *The Beatles at the Hollywood Bowl* was issued on 8-track, the only time the label ever issued a promotional release of Beatles material in this format.

(The sampler featured "Twist and Shout" [from 30 August 1965]; "Dizzie Miss Lizzie" [30 August 1965 until the first guitar solo, when it switches to the 29 August performance]; "Ticket To Ride" [29 August 1965]; and "Things We Said Today" and "She Loves You" [from 23 August 1964].)

7. Plans had originally been made for *Holly Days* to have been produced by Ray Stevens, best known for such novelty songs as "The Streak" and "Spiders and Snakes."

(According to Denny Laine, Stevens hadn't been available when Paul and Denny had wanted him, so Paul ended up doing it himself.)

8. "El Toro" is the name of the yacht that served as the McCartney family's floating home during the *London Town* sessions.

(A third yacht, the "Samala," housed the band and the remainder of Paul's party, which numbered twenty.)

9. "Giddy" evolved from the unreleased McCartney song "Rode All Night."

10. Tony Palmer's thirteen-part rock documentary is titled *All You Need Is Love*.

(Palmer's previous documentary on pop music also bore a Beatles song title, *All My Loving*, first aired on BBC-TV, 31 October 1968.)

11. Paul was referring to his new son, James Louis, born at the Avenue Clinic, St. John's Wood, London, 12 September.

(Weighing in at six pounds, one ounce, the McCartney's son was named James after Paul's father, Jim, and Louis after Linda's grandfather, Louis Eastman.)

12. Red Stripe is a popular brand of Jamaican beer, which Paul and Linda undoubtedly enjoyed many bottles of during their regular holidays on the island.

13. Harrison, a big Formula One racing fan, was referring to the six-wheeled Elf Tyrell racing car that appeared in 1976–77.

14. "Beyond the Valley of a Day in the Life" is the A-side of the single *The Beatles Play the Residents and the Residents Play the Beatles*.

(The Residents' unique arrangement of "Flying" was included as the single's B-side.)

15. Martin engaged New York session drummer Bernard Purdie.

(In an interview published in Max Weinberg's 1984 book, *The Big Beat—Conversations With Rock's Greatest Drummers*, Purdie has claimed that Brian Epstein paid him to play on twenty-one early Beatles songs prior to their release on Capitol. Ringo's response, in an interview from the same book, was basically to ignore it. "Everyone was expecting me to come out and fight it. You don't bother fighting that shit." Purdie is known to have overdubbed Pete Best's drumming on three of the 1961–62 recordings the Beatles made with Tony Sheridan ["Ain't She Sweet," "Take Out Some Insurance On Me, Baby," and "Sweet Georgia Brown"] at a spring 1964 session at Atlantic Recording Studios in New York City prior to their initial release in the U.S. on the Atco label.)

16. The lyrics to "Out on the Streets," which Ringo cowrote with Vini Poncia, name check the Dakota, referring to John and Yoko as "just like two people you'd meet out on the street."

17. As witnessed by Elliot Mintz, John's last public performance, for an unknown Japanese couple, was an acoustic rendition of "Jealous Guy."

18. Even though it was his sixth solo album, *Ringo the 4th* referenced Starr's belief that his solo album output began with his *Ringo* album.

(Talking with Lisa Robinson in 1976, Starr referred to *Sentimental Journey* and *Beaucoups of Blues* as "special" albums, ". . . so I really call the *Ringo* album the first album and *Goodnight Vienna* the second album.")

19. Capitol 4506, "Girl"/"You're Going To Lose That Girl," was planned as a single release from *Love Songs* only to be cancelled at the last minute.

20. Paul thinks it would be nice if football (soccer) crowds, like those at Hampdon Park, sang "Mull of Kintyre," issued as a single by Parlophone in the UK, 11 November, backed with "Girls School."

21. "Real Love" started out as a song titled "Real Life."

22. Jimmy McCulloch left Wings to play in the (short-lived) reunion of the Small Faces. Joe English moved back to Georgia, landing in the jazz-rock band Tall Dogs.

(In 1979, Jimmy's fortunes appeared to be looking up when his new band, the Dukes, were signed by Warner Bros. McCulloch was found dead in his London apartment, 27 September, from an apparent drug overdose. Following the Tall Dogs, Joe played for the Macon band Sea Level. In 1980 he moved to Nashville, forming the Joe English Band to showcase Christian rock.)

23. Recorded during the sessions for *London Town*, "Waterspout" was nearly issued in 1981 on *Cold Cuts*.

24. Ringo recorded "I Love My Suit" and "Simple Life" for Japanese commercials touting Simple Life brand leisure suits.

(Backing vocals for the songs was provided by Monkee Davy Jones.)

25. Adam Faith was the voice of Bonce the Mouse.

1978

1. Who does John refer to as "the 'Mork and Mindy' of the sixties," in his 1978 autobiographical essay, "The Ballad of John and Yoko"?

2. "She's old enough to be my grandmother, so it's sort of embarassing to say, but she's bloody attractive," admitted Ringo to journalist Guy Flatley. Who was he referring to?

3. As the movie was never widely distributed, few people know that *Sextette* is a musical. What Beatles song, for instance, does Dan Turner (Dom DeLuise) sing?

4. Prior to its release on the Warner Bros. LP *The Rutles*, Eric Idle and Neil Innes released a shorter version of "Good Times Roll" under what title?

5. When Rhino Records reissued *The Rutles* soundtrack on CD in 1990, it included six bonus cuts, among them "Goose-Step Mama," from the Silver Rutles' Demo Sessions; "Blue Suede Schubert," a highlight from the Parlourphone LP *Meet the Rutles* (PCS #3045) and "Baby Let Me Be." On what Parlourphone release was this last song "originally" issued?

6. "A love like ours will never die. /Somehow I know, don't ask me why." Which Rutles song included this lyric couplet, sung in rehearsal, but dropped by the time it was recorded?

7. What brand of drums does Rutle Barry Wom play?

8. "Don't Let It Bring You Down" on *London Town* includes passages played on a pair of Irish tin whistles called flageolettes. Who played them?

9. In which of McCartney's songs do we meet "a lead guitarist, who lived in Epping Forest"?

10. What is Ringo's Roadside Attraction?

11. Who are Push-a-lone and Diesel?

12. Whose recommendation to Paul eventually led Laurence Juber to an invitation to join Wings in April?

13. The *Ringo* television special saw Mr. Starr portraying himself and his double Ognir Rrats (Ringo Starr spelt backwards), in Neil Israel's loose adaptation of Mark Twain's *The Prince and the Pauper*, which first aired on NBC-TV in the U.S., 26 April. What did Ognir do for a living?

14. Ognir's girlfriend, Marquine, was played in the special by actress Carrie Fisher. What song did she sing in duet with Ringo?

15. "I think Mick Jagger took (it) and turned it into 'Miss You.' I do hear that lick in it." First issued by Rolling Stones Records/Atlantic as a single, 10 May, which of his songs did John believe Jagger appropriated for "Miss You"?

16. In Robert Stigwood's rock musical *Sgt. Pepper's Lonely Hearts Club Band*, Frankie Howerd plays Mean Mr. Mustard, a demented ex-real estate agent who steals Sgt. Pepper's instruments. Howerd had worked with the four Beatles some years earlier—when was that?

17. Aerosmith was cast in *Sgt. Pepper* in the role of the "FVB" (Future Villian Band), the world's most vicious rock band. Who had Robert Stigwood originally envisioned fronting the FVB?

18. Perhaps best known for his role as Dr. Frankenfurter in *The Rocky Horror Picture Show*, what is the name of the song Tim Curry wrote with Michael Kamen that mentions John and Yoko?

19. The final Rutles release of the seventies was a post-breakup single by Dirk and Stig, "Ging Gang Goolie"/"Mister Sheene," issued only in the UK by EMI, 18 August. Dirk ... er ... Eric Idle directed the promotional video for "Ging Gang Goolie"—where was it filmed?

20. What is "Pneumonia Ceilings"?

21. Who are Zeke and Mary Louise Arias, and what is their relation to George?

22. Paul had recorded this song as the title track for the movie starring Alan Alda and Ellen Burstyn. In the end, it was rejected in favor of Marvin Hamlisch's "The Last Time I Felt Like This." What is the title of McCartney's song?

23. On 3 October, Paul McCartney convened his Rockestra in Abbey Road's Studio Two to record "Rockestra Theme" and "So Glad to See You Here" (released in 1979 on *Back to the Egg*). In addition to new Wings recruit Steve Holley, drumming was handled by Led Zeppelin's John Bonham and former Faces drummer Kenney Jones. Originally, however, what two other drummers had Paul hoped to rockestrate?

24. At a concert by Eric Clapton and Elton John at the Guildford Civic Hall in Surrey, 7 December, George is persuaded to come onstage, where he participates in a performance of "Further On Up The Road." Harrison's surprise appearance is captured on film by Rex Pipe who includes it in what Clapton concert film, released in 1980?

25. George and Ringo were both in attendance when the Star-Club reopened, 15 December. Who was the headliner?

ANSWERS

1. John called Jerry Rubin and Abbie Hoffman "the 'Mork and Mindy' of the sixties."

2. Ringo was referring to Mae West, whom he worked with in *Sextette*, playing one of her ex-husbands, movie director Laslo Karolny.

(*Sextette* was Ms. West's twelfth and final film, based on her 1961 play of the same name.)

3. Dom DeLuise sings "Honey Pie" to Marlo Manners (Mae West).

(*Sextette* first opened for a month at the Cinerama Dome Theater in Hollywood, beginning 2 March.)

4. A forty-five-second version of "Good Times Roll" was first issued in 1976 as "The Children of Rock and Roll" (with Neil Innes singing as Ron Lennon) on the Passport Records LP *The Rutland Weekend Songbook*.

(*The Rutland Weekend Songbook* also includes an early version of "I Must Be In Love," sung by those "fab four Rutland lads, Dirk, Kevin, Stig, and Nasty.")

5. "Baby Let Me Be" was first issued by Parlourphone on the Rutles EP *Twist and Rut* (GEP #8882), 12 July 1963.

6. "Between Us."

7. Barry Wom plays Earwig drums.

8. Paul and Denny played their flageolettes on "Don't Let It Bring You Down" during a session in November 1977 at Abbey Road's Studio Two.

9. The lead guitarist from Epping Forest is one of the musicians who encounter the "Famous Groupies," the song of their exploits included on *London Town*.

10. Ringo's Roadside Attraction, along with Vini Poncia's Peaking Duck Orchestra and Chorus, were the names assigned to the studio musicians who worked on Starr's *Bad Boy* album, recorded late in 1977 at Can Base Studios, Canada, and at Elite Recording Studios in the Bahamas.

(Doctor John, former Apple artist Lon Van Eaton, and guitarist Keith Allison were members of Ringo's Roadside Attraction, which also appeared in the live performance sequence concluding the *Ringo* television special, taped 26 February.)

11. Push-a-lone and Diesel are the pseudonymously credited studio musicians, playing lead guitar and bass, respectively, on *Bad Boy* as part of Ringo's Roadside Attraction.

12. While singing "Go Now" during an appearance on *The David Essex Show*, Denny was suitably impressed by the solo played by Laurence Juber, the guitarist in the show's backup band. The twenty-five-year-old session musician subsequently received an invitation to audition for Wings.

("I came to the basement of the office in Soho Square for an audition and we just had a jam," remembers Juber. "We all had fun, and a couple of days later they asked me if I wanted to play with them.")

13. Ognir sold maps of Hollywood.

14. Ringo and Carrie Fisher sang "You're Sixteen."

15. John believed Mick Jagger turned "Bless You" (from *Walls and Bridges*) into "Miss You."

("The engineer kept wanting me to speed that up," John told David Sheff in September 1980. "He said, 'This is a hit song if you just do it fast.' He was right. 'Cause as 'Miss You' it turned into a hit.")

16. Howerd played drama teacher Sam Ahab in a drama school sequence filmed for *Help!* at Twickenham Film Studios, 28 April 1965, but was ultimately cut from the film.

17. Mick Jagger.

(Stigwood had also wanted to get Fred Astaire to play the mayor of Heartland. Imagine Astaire singing "When I'm 64" rather than George Burns, who got the part.)

18. Tim Curry sings about John and Yoko in "I Do the Rock," included on his A&M album, *Read My Lips*.

("John and Yoko, farming beef,/Raising protein quota./Sometimes they make love and art,/Inside their Dakota." *Read My Lips* also includes a reggae cover of "I Will.")

19. The "Ging Gang Goolie" promotional film was shot at Tittenhurst Park, which Ringo had purchased from John in September 1973.

20. Written at the London Hilton in 1966, "Pneumonia Ceilings" is the unfinished Lennon/McCartney/Dylan song collaboration, lovingly detailed in Mark Shipper's Beatles history spoof *Paperback Writer*.

21. Zeke and Louise became George's in-laws when he married their daughter, Olivia Trinidad Arias, in a civil ceremony at the Henley-on-Thames Register Office, 2 September.

22. Paul's song had been written as the title track for the film *Same Time Next Year*.

(“Same Time Next Year” was finally issued in the UK by Parlophone, 5 February 1990, as a bonus cut on the CD/12" vinyl singles for “Put It There.”)

23. Paul had originally wanted Ringo and Keith Moon to drum in Rockestra.

(Starr was out of the country at the time of the session. On 7 September, Keith Moon died from an overdose of Heminevrin. Ironically, Moon had spent the last night of his life [6th] at a party thrown by McCartney at London's Peppermint Park restaurant prior to a midnight screening of *The Buddy Holly Story*, kicking off that year's Buddy Holly Week, which ran from the seventh [Holly's birthday] through the 14th.)

24. Harrison's appearance is included in Rex Pipe's seventy-minute Angle Films Production, *Eric Clapton and His Rolling Hotel*.

25. Tony Sheridan headlined the reopening of the Star-Club, backed by Elvis Presley's TCB Band (guitarist James Burton, pianist Glen D. Hardin, bassist Emory Gordy, and drummer Ronnie Tutt).

1979

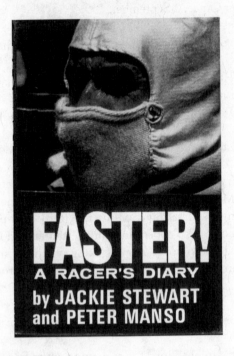

FASTER!
A RACER'S DIARY
by JACKIE STEWART
and PETER MANSO

1. The album *George Harrison* had originally been announced for release under what other title?

2. What song on *George Harrison* drew its initial inspiration from a playful remark made by drummer Jim Keltner about George being an easy mark for a loan?

3. "Worn upon the forehead of the Lord/His devotees worship it—and here it is . . ." George wrote this unused lyric couplet for what song?

4. What song did Harrison call "Son of Deep Blue"?

5. "It is about the circus around it and the feelings people have and the jealousy, all that sort of thing," George said of the song "Faster," during an interview given 4 February in Sao Paulo, Brazil, where he was attending the Interlagos Grand Prix. "The song was really inspired by Jackie Stewart and Niki Lauda." Where did George get the title from?

6. What song, originally intended for inclusion on the *George Harrison* album, was removed at the request of Warner Bros. president Mo Ostin?

7. On 28 March, John and Yoko began their spring break in West Palm Beach, Florida, renting this beachfront mansion, once owned by the Vanderbilts. It was here that Sean met his half-brother Julian for the first time (ironically, this vacation would also be the last time Julian would see his father). What is the name of this villa, built in 1919, which the Lennons would eventually buy for $700,000?

8. Paul McCartney is playing bass, leading the band on the makeshift outdoor stage through Little Richard numbers like "Lawdy Miss Clawdy" and "High School Confidential." And what a band—George Harrison, Eric Clapton and Denny Laine on guitar, with Ringo Starr on drums. When Mick Jagger jumps on stage, the band launches into Eddie Cochran's "Something Else." Sounds like quite a party—what was the occasion?

9. What title had Paul originally considered releasing *Back to the Egg* under?

10. Which song on *Back to the Egg* was originally titled "Radio"?

11. "With tufts of hair, stuck here and there, which Ron liked to tug."
This line of poetry, recited by Diedre Margery, is part of "Reception," the sound collage that opens *Back to the Egg*, Paul's first album for CBS/Columbia and, as it turned out, his last with Wings. From what poem was Diedre reading?

12. Paul had originally written "Baby's Request" at the behest of the Mills Brothers, after having seen them in a cabaret show in the South of France while on holiday the previous summer. Why did Wings end up releasing it first?

13. What song did CBS Records urge McCartney to include on *Back to the Egg*?

14. One of the more puzzling exclusions from *Back to the Egg* was a song titled "Cage." Nearly issued in 1981 as part of the *Cold Cuts* collection, what is notable about the song's title?

15. When EMI got cold feet and withdrew the two million pounds they had agreed to give Monty Python to film *The Life of Brian*, George came to their rescue in 1978, putting up the money with his manager at the time, Denis O'Brien. In addition to being an executive producer on the film, Harrison spent a day on location in Sousse, Tunisia (20 October 1978), filming a brief cameo as Mr. Papadopoulis, "the man who rents Brian's group the mount for the (sermon) next weekend." What was Harrison's only line in *The Life of Brian*, released by his HandMade Films company for Orion Pictures and Warner Bros. in August 1979?

16. "(Just Like) Starting Over" evolved from another song John began demoing in late 1979—what was its title?

17. When John first began writing "Watching the Wheels," what was its working title?

18. "IN WITNESS WHEREOF, I have subscribed and sealed and do publish and declare these presents as and for my Last Will and Testament, this 12th day of November, 1979." Signed "J. Lennon" at the Dakota, who were named as beneficiaries in John's four-page will?

19. Who is Earl Okin and what is his connection to Paul?

20. In late November, John and Yoko purchased a tudor-styled mansion in Cold Spring Harbor, New York, for $450,000. What was it called?

21. On 23 November, ABC-TV premiered Dick Clark's *Birth of the Beatles* in the U.S. on the *ABC Friday Night Movie*. Despite Pete Best's role as technical advisor on the docudrama, the screenplay by John Kurland and Jacob Eskender takes considerable artistic license. An example is the film's depiction of the Beatles' first visit to Hamburg in August 1960, where George Harrison (John Altman) is shown singing "Don't Bother Me." What's wrong with this scene?

22. Here's another scene: The Beatles (actually the Silver Beetles) are shown at Larry Parnes's audition for a backing group for Billy Fury, where they meet Ringo Starr for the first time.

23. One more "Birth" scenario: As Brian Epstein (Brian Jameson) looks on, the Beatles audition for Dick Rowe, Decca's A&R man, singing "Long Tall Sally" and "Love Me Do."

24. Who composed the original score for *Birth of the Beatles*?

25. In 1974, this bootleg label issued their first "Beatleg," *Their Greatest Unreleased*. By the time they called it a day in 1981, their discography comprised 12 LPs, 2 EPs and one 45 by the Beatles, plus one LP by the Move (*Omnibus*). The first label to issue a Ringo Starr bootleg LP (*Down and Out?*), they are perhaps best known among aficionados for their 1979 release, *The Beatles vs. Don Ho*. What was this label's name?

ANSWERS

1. *Faster.*

2. Jim Keltner's remark became George's inspiration for "Soft Touch."
(While it eventually turned into a song about his son Dhani ["As a warm son rises"], Harrison admits "it actually came from a remark Jim Keltner made in one of his lighter moods about me being a soft touch. I had Dark Horse Records at the time, and people think that you're a bank and come to you for money.")

3. George discarded this lyric while writing "Here Comes the Moon."

4. When Warner Bros. staff producer Ted Templeman remarked how much he liked George's "Bangla Desh" B-side, "Deep Blue," Harrison went home and wrote the melody of "Soft Hearted Hana" ". . . in that sort of style . . . a silly sort of Salvation Army thing."
(Hana is located on the Hawaiian island of Maui.)

5. George got the title "Faster" from Jackie Stewart's 1972 book, *Faster! A Racer's Diary*, which he cowrote with Peter Manso.

6. Recorded in 1977, Ostin asked George not to include the song "Mo," which Harrison had written to honor Ostin on the occasion of his fiftieth birthday.
(Harrison tried again in 1989 to release the song on his *Best of Dark Horse 1976–1989* album, but again dropped the song at Ostin's request. It was included as the opening cut on disc one of *Mo's Songs*, a 6-CD promo-only compilation, produced by the artists and staff of Warner Bros. Records. Limited to just over 600 copies, it was presented to Ostin and his guests at his retirement party in December 1994.)

1979

7. John and Yoko's spring break was taken at El Salano.

8. On 19 May, guests at a party at Hurtwood Edge, Eric Clapton's country home in Ewhurst, Surrey, witnessed this impromptu reunion of three Beatles. The occasion was a celebration of Clapton's wedding to Pattie Harrison (George's ex), the ceremony having taken place at Temple Bethel in Tucson, Arizona, 27 March.

9. "It was going to be called "We're Open Tonight," Paul told Capitol Radio DJ Roger Scott, "but we liked 'Back to the Egg' better."

10. "Reception" was originally called "Radio."

11. Mrs. Margery was reading from "The Poodle and the Pug" by A. P. Herbert.
(Diedre's husband, Harold Margery, the owner of Lympne Castle, Kent, where several songs from *Back to the Egg* were recorded, can be heard on "The Broadcast," reading from "The Sport of Kings" by Ian Hay and "The Little Man" by John Galsworthy.)

12. Wings demoed "Baby's Request" at Abbey Road's Studio Two in early October 1978 and sent it along to the Mills Brothers. "But, unfortunately," remembers Paul, "there was a slight cock-up because their manager got the idea that we were going to *pay* them to record it." Paul liked the Wings demo so much, he ended up using it to close *Back to the Egg*.

13. CBS Records had wanted McCartney to include his hit single "Goodnight Tonight" on *Back to the Egg*.
(McCartney refused, reasoning that the song "didn't fit" the album. "I'm making records, I'm not running a record store," he said.)

14. The opening "punky riff" (as guitarist Laurence Juber describes it) of "Cage" is comprised of the chords C-A-G-E.
(Juber related to this author that the calliope sound heard in "Cage" was actually achieved by the members of Wings blowing over the necks of whiskey bottles filled to varying levels, which made for quite a loose session.)

15. Harrison's only line in *The Life of Brian* is "Hello."

16. "(Just Like) Starting Over" began as "My Life."
(A 1980 home demo recording of "My Life" is included on *Dakota*,

disc four of *The John Lennon Anthology*, released by Capitol, 3 November 1998.)

17. "I'm Crazy" was the working title for "Watching the Wheels."

18. Yoko Ono was the only beneficiary named in John's will.

(When John was murdered in December 1980, Ono received one-half of her husband's estate outright. Yoko and Lennon accountant, Eli Garber, were named as Trustees to the remaining half under a Trust Agreement also dated 12 November, the provisions of which were not detailed in the will.)

19. An acoustic guitarist and comedian, Earl Okin opened for Wings on their nineteen-date tour of the UK, which began at the Royal Court Theatre in Liverpool, 23 November, concluding three weeks later at the Glasgow Apollo in Scotland, 17 December.

20. Cannon Hill is John and Yoko's mansion in Cold Spring Harbor, named for the cannon located by the swimming pool.

21. Harrison couldn't have sung "Don't Bother Me" in 1960 as he didn't write the song (his first composition) until 1963.

(George composed "Don't Bother Me" at the Palace Court hotel in Bournemouth during a six-night stand at the city's Gaumont Cinema, 19–24 August.)

22. Ringo was not present at the Larry Parnes audition.

(The only member of Rory Storm and the Hurricanes [who Ringo was drumming for at the time] present at the Larry Parnes audition at the Wyvern Social Club, 10 May 1960, was Storm himself. Rory's purpose for being there was to get his picture taken with Billy Fury. Starr would first meet the Beatles in Hamburg, 4 October 1960, where the two groups shared the bill for eight weeks at the Kaiserkeller.)

23. "Long Tall Sally" and "Love Me Do" were not among the fifteen songs taped at the Beatles' audition for Decca, which was supervised by A&R assistant Mike Smith, not Dick Rowe.

24. The original score for *Birth of the Beatles* was composed and conducted by Carl Davis, who would go on to compose the *Liverpool Oratorio* with Paul McCartney.

25. Melvin Records.

(In 1979, Melvin released a collection of Lennon rarities titled *Come Back Johnny!* Melvin sent John a copy with a note reading "Here's the new album by YOU! When are you going to record again?" "We got a response written in a very familiar hand," Melvin's founders Amos 'n' Isaac recalled for *Beatlefan* magazine in 1992. Lennon's response read: "Don't hold your breath!")

1980

1. Following his arrest at Narita International Airport, 16 January, for possession of 219 grams of marijuana, Paul spent the next ten days at the Metropolitan jail in Tokyo. Awoken every morning at six, McCartney would be required to sit cross-legged for roll call, ". . . like something out of *Bridge on the River Kwai*." What was his prisoner number?

2. What U.S. senator was reportedly instrumental in securing McCartney's release, placing several calls to Tokyo, including the British Embassy?

3. What was the title of the song Denny Laine wrote and recorded that was inspired by Paul's pot bust?

4. In February 1980, Ringo met his future wife Barbara Bach in Durango, Mexico during the filming of *Caveman*, but that wasn't the first time Bach had seen Starr—when was that?

5. When Capitol issued their version of *Rarities* for the U.S. market, 24 March, it seemed more than mere coincidence that nine of the songs on the LP's "tunestack" matched those issued by bootlegger "Richard Ian" on his "Capitol" release from August 1979. Both albums included true stereo mixes of "Penny Lane" (with the extra David Mason trumpet figure from the U.S. mono promo-only 45) and a full-length version of "I Am the Walrus," restored using the extra middle beats from the Capitol single and the longer intro riff from the Parlophone stereo single. What was Richard's "Beatleg" titled?

6. What image of the Beatles had compiler Randall Davis originally wanted for the cover of *Rarities*?

7. For *McCartney II*, Paul essentially made each song up in the studio as he went along, starting with a drum track and building it up ". . . bit by bit without any idea of how the song was going to turn out." Only one song on the album was written beforehand—which one?

8. What was the title of the first song Paul recorded for *McCartney II*?

9. The lyrics of "Temporary Secretary" entreat "Mr. Marks" to find Paul "someone strong and sweet fitting on my knee." Who is Mr. Marks?

10. En route to Bermuda in early June, the forty-three-foot schooner John was on encountered a severe mid-Atlantic storm. While seasickness kept everyone else below, Lennon remained at the wheel for the next two days singing and shouting old sea chanties. What was the name of the schooner?

11. What are "Tippi Tippi Toes," "Sunshine Sometime," and "Nutwood Scene"?

12. What song on *Double Fantasy* drew its inspiration from a phrase spoken to John by Jack Douglas, the album's coproducer?

13. What song by Bob Marley was John's inspiration for "Borrowed Time"?

14. Where did John find the album title *Double Fantasy*?

15. "In excruciating detail, just for you, at a price outside everyday experience, we offer the small change of a short lifetime." What is George referring to?

1980

16. Before going with Jack Douglas, Yoko Ono revealed in 1984 that she and John had considered three other producers for *Double Fantasy*—who were they?

17. Sessions for *Double Fantasy* began at New York's Hit Factory, 7 August. What was the first track recorded?

18. During the second week of sessions for *Double Fantasy*, two members from what noted rock group were invited by the Lennons to play on a version of "I'm Losing You"?

19. In late September, Warner Bros. managing director Derek Taylor acted as liaison between George and the label for the album *Somewhere in England*, personally delivering the master tapes to Warner executive Clyde Bakkemo in Burbank. During an afternoon listening session, the album was rejected along with Basil Pao's sleeve art. George would replace four songs from the original lineup along with the cover art before *England*, originally scheduled for release 2 November, was finally issued in the U.S., 1 June 1981. Ironically, that same morning, whose album had these same executives listened to and approved for release?

20. On 15 and 16 October, Abbey Road conducted their "Sale of the Century" in Studio One, auctioning recording equipment and music memorabilia assembled from EMI studios around the world. One of the most interesting items Phillip's auctioneer Andrew Hilton sold came under the hammer the afternoon of the second day. It had originally been rejected by John Lennon in 1964 as being "too hard and shiny"—what was it?

21. What song recorded during the *Double Fantasy* sessions did John describe as " 'Cold Turkey' rides again"?

22. Lennon considered releasing "I'm Losing You" under a revised title—what was it?

23. Where were Paul, George, and Ringo when they received the news of John's death?

24. "It's a drag, i'n it?" Who said this, and where?

25. On 31 December, the residual rights to *Help!* reverted to Walter Shenson, the film's producer. Shenson had enjoyed a similar windfall

157

when the theatrical, television, and video rights to *A Hard Day's Night* reverted to him, 31 December 1979. Shenson now owned ninety-nine percent of both Beatles films—who did he give the other one percent to?

ANSWERS

1. McCartney was prisoner number twenty-two during his incarceration.

2. Senator Edward Kennedy made several calls to Tokyo regarding McCartney's arrest.

(D. W. F. Warren-Knott, first secretary of the British Embassy, said at the time that senator Kennedy "wanted to inquire about McCartney's case because McCartney and his rock group Wings might be giving a concert in the U.S." Had Paul been convicted, his chances of getting a permit to enter the U.S. might have been compromised.)

3. Denny's song inspired by Paul's Tokyo pot bust is titled "Japanese Tears," recorded at Rock City Studios in London, 28 January.

(Scratch Records first issued the song as a single in the UK, 2 May, backed with "Guess I'm Only Foolin.' ")

4. Barbara was among the 55,600 who attended the Beatles' concert at Shea Stadium, 15 August 1965.

(Bach notes however, that she was never a Beatlemaniac. "When the Beatles were happening, I was too involved in my own life. My sister Marjorie was crazy about the Beatles. I liked Dylan, Ray Charles, and the Rolling Stones.")

5. Richard's "Capitol" bootleg predating *Rarities* was titled *Collector's Items* (SPRO-9462).

6. Davis had hoped to feature an uncropped version of Robert Whitaker's "butcher" shot of the Beatles, used on first issue copies of Capitol's *"Yesterday"* . . . *And Today*.

(The photo was featured inside the album's gatefold cover, along with an unairbrushed version of the "trunk cover" used on subsequent pressings of "Y&T." The photo, showing the Beatles posing in and around a steamer trunk, was taken at Sutherland House, the London Headquarters of NEMS Enterprises, at 5–6 Argyll Street, in the fifth floor office of its director, Geoffrey Ellis.)

7. "Waterfalls" was the only song on *McCartney II* that Paul had written before recording commenced.

8. The first song Paul recorded for *McCartney II* was "Front Parlour," recorded in the front parlor of his Sussex farm house in the summer of 1979.

9. Mr. Marks is a reference to the Alfred Marks Bureau, a well-known employment agency in Britain.

(McCartney refused the Bureau's request to use the song in advertisements.)

10. Lennon piloted the schooner *Megan Jaye*.

11. These are the titles of three of the fourteen songs Paul demoed with Wings as part of a proposed soundtrack to a full-length Rupert the Bear film.

(By June, Paul had approved a script outline for the animated feature, to be produced by MPL. Rupert would eventually emerge as a thirteen-minute featurette, *Rupert and the Frog Song*, shown in theaters in October 1984 preceeding *Give My Regards To Broad Street*. To date, none of the songs from the proposed Rupert feature have been officially released, though fans have noted that "Celebration," from the fourth movement of *Paul McCartney's Standing Stone*, was built around the same melody as the Rupert instrumental "Sea Melody.")

12. "Cleanup Time."

(During John's Bermuda vacation [12 June to 29 July], a phone conversation with Jack Douglas about the Seventies and people changing their habits—"cleanin' up and gettin' out of drugs and alcohol"—concluded with Douglas making the remark, "Well, it's cleanup time, right?" Lennon hung up the phone, went immediately to a piano and began composing the song.)

13. "Borrowed Time" drew its inspiration from Bob Marley's song "Hallelujah Time."

(Featured on the album *Burnin'*, the song includes the lines "We got to keep on living,/Living on borrowed time." Lennon played the album in June during his Bermuda holiday.)

14. While visiting the Bermuda Botanical Gardens, 24 June, a freesia hybrid caught John's eye. Engraved in white letters against a black background, the small rectangular card read: "Double Fantasy."

15. This quote was taken from George's forward for his autobiography, *I Me Mine*.

(Harrison drew sharp criticism when he allowed Genesis Publications to publish the 450-page book in July as a leather-bound, 2,000-copy signed limited edition priced at £148, with critics decrying such things as "Now who's living in the material world?" A more affordable 400-page hardcover edition [priced at $12.95], was published in November 1981 by Simon and Schuster.)

16. In testimony in a New York Supreme Court during a breach of contract suit brought by record producer Jack Douglas over unpaid royalties, Yoko revealed that she and John had originally considered George Martin, Phil Spector, and Richard Perry for the job of producing *Double Fantasy*.

17. "(Just Like) Starting Over" was the first song recorded at the *Double Fantasy* sessions.

18. Guitarist Rick Nielsen and drummer Bun E. Carlos of Cheap Trick were invited to the Hit Factory 12 August, where they played on a harder rocking version of "I'm Losing You."

(Rick and Bun E. also played on a version of Yoko's "I'm Moving On." The session had been arranged as a favor to coproducer Jack Douglas, who had produced the group's debut album *Cheap Trick*. This version of "I'm Losing You" was not officially released until November 1998, where it opens *Dakota*, disc four of the *John Lennon Anthology* box set. Though the booklet notes on first pressing copies of *Anthology* also place Cheap Trick bassist Tom Petersson at this session, it was actually Tony Levin who played bass.)

19. That morning Warner Bros. executives had approved John and Yoko's *Double Fantasy*, which the label distributed for (David) Geffen Records.

20. Jokingly described as "the star item of the auction," an (unused) roll of toilet paper, stamped the property of EMI sold for £85 on its merit of having been rejected by John as "too hard and shiny."

(A Mellotron tape organ used by the group on *Magical Mystery Tour* [with the original tapes still in place] went for £1000 to *Tubular Bells* composer Mike Oldfield.)

21.   " 'Cold Turkey' rides again" is how John described "I'm Losing You."

22.   Early into David Sheff's three weeks of interviews with the Lennons for *Playboy*, John had considered titling "Losing You"—as it was known at the time—"(Afraid I'm) Losing You," his reasoning being that leaving the title unqualified might work as a self-fulfilling prophecy.

("I'm Losing You" began under the working title "Stranger's Room.")

23.   On the morning of 9 December, Paul was at his London home when he received the call from Stephen Shrimpton, managing director of MPL Communications. George was at his Friar Park estate when he got the news from his brother, Harry, who had received a call from their sister Louise in the U.S. While on vacation in the Bahamas with future wife Barbara Bach, Ringo got the call from Barbara's daughter, Francesca Gregorini.

("Barbara and I are sitting in the Bahamas," Starr told *People* magazine, "and we get these calls. He's been shot. And then . . . he's dead.")

24.   This was Paul's comment on John's death, given to a reporter as he left AIR Studios in London, 9 December. His remark was widely interpreted and criticized as flippant.

("It looked so callous in print," said McCartney. "I should have said, 'It's the most unholiest of drags,' and it might have been better. What I meant was, 'Fuck off! Don't invade my privacy.' ")

25.   Shenson gave one percent of the residual rights for A *Hard Day's Night* and *Help!* to the films' director Richard Lester as a bonus.

1981

Somewhere
in
Utopia

1. In early 1981, it was announced that Ringo's next album, *Can't Fight Lightning*, was tentatively scheduled for the second week of April. "It was a phrase I'd had in my notebook for some time," he said. "Then I met Barbara and it made the point very clear—you *can't* fight lightning. That's how we got together." Before John's death, however, what title had Starr been planning to use?

2. "Getting this together after what happened was hard. But I knew John would not rest his mind if I hadn't. I hope you like it, John. I did my best." What is Yoko Ono referring to?

3. At the same time George Martin was producing Paul's *Tug of War* at AIR Studios in Montserrat, what artist was Geoff Emerick there producing an album for in an adjacent studio?

4. This group scored their only UK number one when their cover of "Jealous Guy," recorded as a tribute to John, topped the charts, 14 March. Who are they?

5. "I read that one in three hours or something, and it drained me," Paul told journalist James Henke. "And I said 'God, what am I going to do? I'm not like *that*.' That guy is a John fan, and kept saying, 'John was it. John was it. Paul's a bastard.' And that kind of got the myth going." What book is McCartney referring to?

6. It was reported in 1981 that Yoko was considering whether or not to publish a magazine dedicated to keeping alive the ideals of her late husband. What was this magazine to have been called?

7. What were the taglines featured on posters and print ads for *Caveman*?

8. Ringo married actress Barbara Bach at Marylebone Registry Office in London, 27 April, the ceremony conducted by senior superintendant registrar Joseph Jevans. Wedding guests, including Paul and Linda and George and Olivia, all received a memento of the occasion— what was it?

9. Who were the two men who signed the register as witnesses to Ringo and Barbara's wedding? Also, who were Barbara's bridesmaids?

10. In which of his songs does George mention Frank Zappa?

11. "Hong Kong Blues" was one of two songs by Hoagland Howard "Hoagy" Carmichael covered by Harrison on *Somewhere In England* ("Baltimore Oriole" being the other). The song has a special significance for George which might explain its inclusion—what is it?

12. What had been Dundee University's contribution to *Somewhere In England*?

13. George's new album may have found him "Somewhere In England," but who was credited as being "Somewhere in Yin Yang"?

14. "There was never a time when I did not exist, nor you. Nor will there be any future where we cease to be." What is the significance of this quote from the *Bhagavadgita*?

15. Yoko garnered mostly positive reviews for her album length carharsis, *Seasons of Glass*, first issued by Polydor in the U.S., 8 June. "I Don't Know Why," written less than two weeks after John's death, came to Ono as a result of well-meaning fans continuing to do something outside the Dakota—what were they doing?

16. What was the Harrison song WEA Records in the UK planned to release in July as part of an EP, but were refused permission by HandMade Films, George's production company?

17. Who are the Monarchists?

18. What is the title of the song by Prince that mentions John Lennon?

19. Stephanie LaMotta, who dated Ringo in the late seventies, wrote a film script based on their time together, with filming reportedly set for the fall of 1981. What was the screenplay's title?

20. In which of Harrison's songs does he lament of "coming up with something you'd enjoy as much as TV"?

21. "You're only here once, and I've been here longer than most of you!" Who said this, and where?

22. In what song does Ringo name check actress Betty Grable?

23. At one point, *Stop and Smell the Roses* was proposed to Boardwalk Records with a cover shot of Ringo posing in front of a device that gave him the appearance of having electricity coming out of his ears. Based on this photo by Tom Wilkes, what had Ringo wanted to title the album?

24. What are "Brandy" and "Waking Up"?

25. Why would Kensington Fields Estates, located about two miles from Liverpool city center, be of interest to Beatle fans?

ANSWERS

1. Before John's assassination, Ringo had planned to call his eighth solo album *Dead Giveaway*, after the song he'd cowritten for the project with Ron Wood.

2. Yoko's comments are in reference to the release of her single "Walking On Thin Ice"/"It Happened," first issued by Geffen in the U.S., 1 February.

(John had been working on the final mix of "Walking On Thin Ice" with Yoko and Jack Douglas the night he died.)

3. During February, while Geoff Emerick was producing Elvis Costello's *Imperial Bedroom* at AIR Studios, McCartney was recording *Tug of War* with George Martin.

4. Roxy Music spent two weeks at the top of the UK charts with their cover of "Jealous Guy."

5. McCartney was referring to *Shout! The True Story of the Beatles*, by the *London Sunday Times* correspondent Philip Norman, published in the UK 30 March by Elm Tree Books.

(Or, as Paul told journalist Steve Grant, "I call him Norma Philips and the book '*Shite!!!*.'")

6. Yoko considered publishing a magazine called *Imagine*.

7. *Caveman* had two taglines, "Back when women were women, and men were animals . . ." and "Back when you had to beat it before you could eat it . . ."

8. Guests at Ringo and Barbara's wedding all received a five-pointed star engraved "R" and "B" along with the wedding date.

(The couple first met in February 1980 during the filming of *Caveman*, which might explain the day they chose to wed. In an interview for *People* magazine Bach remembers, "On April 27 he told me he loved me." Joseph Jevans was the same registrar who conducted Paul and Linda's ceremony at Marylebone—in the same room—12 March 1969.)

9. The witnesses at Ringo and Barbara's wedding were Hilary Gerrard, Starr's business manager, and Roger Shine, a property developer friend. Barbara's bridesmaids were her daughter, Francesca, and Ringo's daughter, Lee.

10. Frank Zappa is mentioned in "Blood From a Clone," included on the *Somewhere In England* album, first issued by Dark Horse/Warner Bros. in the U.S., 1 June.

("You need some oomph-papa, nothing like Frank Zappa.")

11. George cites "Hong Kong Blues" as one of the earliest songs he can remember, from about the age of four.

(Harrison is known to have reviewed Hoagy's performance of the song in the 1944 Humphrey Bogart film *To Have and Have Not*; a 16mm print of the Warner Bros. film was delivered to Friar Park 4 July 1980 and returned to London four days later. Carmichael, living at the time in California, died of a heart attack 27 December at the age of eighty-two.)

12. Dundee University in Nethergate, Dundee, Scotland, supplied the black and white satellite photographs of the United Kingdom that Basil Pao used for the original cover of *Somewhere In England*.

13. The custom inner sleeve of *Somewhere In England* includes a black and white photograph of George, his face covered with acupuncture needles. The caption beneath the photo, "Needles by Zion Yu (Somewhere in Yin Yang)," is a thank you from Harrison to the Los Angeles acupuncturist.

(Harrison also thanked Yu in the liner notes on *Thirty-Three & ⅓*.)

14. George dedicated *Somewhere In England* to John with this quote, attributed to Sri Krishna, from the *Bhagavadgita*, included in the album's custom inner sleeve.

15. "I Don't Know Why" came to Ono after ten days of listening to fans outside the Dakota continuously play John's "Imagine."

("My bedroom is right on 72nd Street," Ono told John Palmer of the *New York Times*. "I was like a zombie, just lying there and hearing him sing 'Imagine' over and over and over. For about ten days it went on like that, and then one night I started to wonder why, why it was like that, and suddenly that wondering became a song.")

16. HandMade Films blocked WEA Records' plans to release "Dream Away" as part of a four-cut *Time Bandits* soundtrack EP.

(Harrison would eventually include the song on his *Gone Troppo* album, released in 1982.)

17. The Monarchists were the backing group on Mike (McCartney) McGear's single "No Lar Di Dar (Is Lady Di)"/"God Bless the Gracious Queen," released by Conn Records in the UK, 27 July in observance of the Royal Wedding, 29 July. The group consisted of Mike's three daughters, Benna, Theran, and Abbi.

18. Lennon is mentioned in the lyrics of "Annie Christian," included on Prince's Warner Bros. album *Controversy*.

("Being good was such a bore, so she bought a gun. She killed John Lennon, shot him down cold.")

19. LaMotta's film script was titled *Goodnight Vienna*.

20. Harrison expresses these sentiments in "Wrack My Brain," the song he wrote and produced for Ringo's album *Stop and Smell the Roses*.

21. Ringo makes this declaration during the song "Drumming Is My Madness," included on *Stop and Smell the Roses*.

22. "Stop, you must remember Clark and Betty Grable," sings Ringo in "Stop and Take the Time to Smell the Roses."

23. Tom Wilkes's photograph of Ringo, taken at the Griffith Observatory in Los Angeles, inspired Starr at one point to consider titling his album *Ringostein*.

(Boardwalk Records rejected the title as well as Wilkes's photo.)

24. "Brandy" and "Waking Up" are the titles of two of the three songs rejected by Boardwalk for the album first issued in the U.S. 27 October as *Stop and Smell the Roses*.

(The third song was the album's proposed title cut, "Can't Fight Lightning," an instrumental jam written by Starr and produced by Paul McCartney during sessions in July 1980 at Superbear Studios in Nice, France.)

25. On 27 November, Michael Heseltine, Britain's Environmental Secretary, opened Kensington Fields Estate, a new housing development (off Farnworth Street) whose four main streets were to be named after the Beatles: John Lennon Drive, Paul McCartney Way, George Harrison Close, and Ringo Starr Drive. The signs were officially put up 16 August 1982.

(Approved in June by a reluctant Liverpool City Council, the street designations at the 163-home estate were the city's first tangible tribute to its famous sons. In 1980, the Liverpool City Council had voted down a motion to name four streets in a new subdivision John Lennon Lane, Paul McCartney Avenue, George Harrison Heights, and Ringo Starr Drive.)

1982

RINGO STARR

HIT PARADER

1. "You get it from the shop, put it in the machine, push the button and it sounds like that," says Paul at the conclusion of a TV commercial shown in Britain in January for what home video release?

2. Beyond the obvious musical connection, what do the following people have in common: Chuck Berry, Julian Bream, the Coasters, John Lennon, Little Richard, Jim McCartney, Elvis Presley, and Gene Vincent?

3. Paul composed "Ebony and Ivory" in his home studio in Scotland after recalling the time he'd heard this comedian on a television talk show make the analogy of racial harmony being like the black and white notes on a piano keyboard. "He'd said, 'You know, it's a funny kind of thing—black notes, white notes, and you need to play the two to make harmony folks!' " Who was McCartney referring to?

4. What is the title of the last Beatles album issued on 8-track tape?

5. "Take It Away" hadn't been McCartney's first choice to follow the *Tug of War* title cut. What song had?

6. What song on *Tug of War* had Paul originally composed with Ringo in mind?

7. Which noted guitarist did Paul ask without success to add a guitar line to "Wanderlust"?

8. In which song do we hear of the Lady Demure?

9. What distinction does *Tug of War* share with *Red Rose Speedway*?

10. MPL Communications entered what it described as "a surrealist musical film" as the official British entry in the Best Short Subject category at this year's Cannes Film Festival. Directed by Kevin Godley and Lol Creme (late of 10cc), what was the title of the eleven-minute short, screened at the Palais de Festivals, 24 May?

11. When Parlophone first issued "Take It Away" in the UK 21 June as the second single from *Tug of War*, it included the non-album B-side "I'll Give You a Ring." Hardcore Macca fans recognized this song from its earlier appearance in what film?

12. During the shooting of the "Take It Away" video, 23 June, Paul and his band treated the 600 members of his Fun Club (invited to act as the audience) to frequent jams during the four hour shoot. During one such jam, Macca played Mike Post's "Hill Street Blues Theme," which he retitled for the occasion. What was the new title?

13. Directed by John McKenzie (director of the HandMade film *The Long Good Friday*), the "Take It Away" video debuted on BBC's *Top of the Pops*, 15 July. Who was the actor who portrayed the important impresario "watching the show with a paper in his hand"?

14. What is the title of the novel by Philip K. Dick that begins the day after the assassination of John Lennon?

15. McCartney's first directorial work since 1967 was the promotional video for this group's version of Crewe & Gaudio's "Big Girls Don't Cry," released on Safari Records in the UK, 3 September. Who is the group?

16. Columbia issued the title song from *Tug of War* as the album's third single, 26 September. In an interview with *Billboard* in 1983, George Martin said he "didn't really approve of 'Tug of War' as the third single." What song would Martin have released?

17. What is the Shorrock Starr Band?

18. When Liverpudlian Bob Eaton brought his musical play *Lennon* to the Entermedia Theatre in New York City, 5 October, his off-Broadway cast of seven men and two women for the sixty-three different roles only included one British actor, but one with a strong Beatles connection. Who was it?

19. *Gone Troppo*, the title of George's tenth solo album, is an Australian term—what does it mean?

20. *Gone Troppo* includes a very credible doo-wop remake of "I Really Love You." Who first had a hit with the song in 1961?

21. It's likely to be the only song by a Beatle to include a reference to the "fruit bat"—what Harrison song is it?

22. Joanie Cunningham (Erin Moran) believes she's seen Paul McCartney (Mitch Weissman) recovering from exhaustion in the hospital where she works, using the name Marvin O. Pizika. What is the name of this episode of *Joanie Loves Chachi*, the short-lived spin-off of *Happy Days*, which first aired on ABC-TV in the U.S., 11 November?

23. John makes a posthumous appearance on Yoko's album *It's Alright*, first issued by Polydor in the U.S., 29 November. What is he shouting on the cut "Never Say Goodbye"?

24. In December, Epic issued the Michael Jackson/Paul McCartney duet *"The Girl is Mine"* in Israel. The yellow vinyl 45 was the first to be released in that country by any manufacturer in five years. What song was on the last one?

25. During an interview with *Beatlefan* publisher Bill King in December, Cynthia Lennon said she had been working on a book of drawings about the Beatles (similar to the ones she included in her 1978 autobiography, *A Twist of Lennon*). The book, which she had hoped would be published by the end of the year, never materialized. What was to have been its title?

ANSWERS

1. Paul's TV ad was for the home video release of *Rockshow*, the documentary of Wings' 1976 American Tour, issued by Thorn-EMI in the UK, 12 October 1981.

(The majority of *Rockshow* was filmed at Wings' concert at the Seattle Kingdome, 10 June. McCartney hosted the first concert at the venue, setting a new world indoor attendance record when he played before 67,100 paying customers. The Kingdome was torn down in a controlled implosion at 8:30 A.M. on 26 March 2000.)

2. These were the artists who performed on the eight records Paul McCartney would take with him were he to become stranded on a desert island, as related to Roy Plomley on the 40th anniversary edition of his BBC Radio Four show *Desert Island Discs*, broadcast 30 January.

(McCartney's eight Desert Island discs were: "Sweet Little Sixteen" [Chuck Berry]; "Dances From Gloriana" [written by Benjamin Brittan as played by Julian Bream]; "Searching" [The Coasters]; "Beautiful Boy" [John Lennon]; "Tutti Frutti" [Little Richard]; "Walking In the Park with Eloise" [Jim McCartney] and "Be-Bop-A-Lula" [Gene Vincent].)

3. Paul first heard the "ebony and ivory" analogy from Goon Spike Milligan during an interview on a television talk show.

("He just made a little joke out of it, said McCartney in an interview for the *Daily Mirror*, "but I thought, 'Yes, this is a good analogy for harmony between people.' " "The trouble is the image is inaccurate," writes Robert Palmer in his review of *Tug of War* for the *New York Times*. "The notes on a piano keyboard are not in acoustically perfect harmony at all, far from it. The simple, acoustically pure intervals one hears in much of the world's folk music have been compressed or stretched to fit into an arbitrary subdivision of twelve tones to the octave.")

4. The last Beatles album issued on 8-track was the movie compilation *Reel Music* (Capitol 8XV-12199), issued in the spring of 1982.

(The first Beatles 8-track was *Rubber Soul* [Capitol 8XT-2442], issued in December 1965.)

5. "Average Person" was originally planned as the second cut on *Tug of War*.

(The song would be held back until October 1983 when it was included on *Pipes of Peace*.)

6. Paul originally composed "Take It Away" with Ringo in mind.

("I was writing some songs for Ringo and "Take It Away" was in amongst those songs. I thought it would suit me better the way it went into the chorus and stuff; I didn't think it was very Ringo.")

7. McCartney had asked George if he would do a guitar overdub for "Wanderlust," which Harrison never contributed.

("Wanderlust" was the name of the trimaran Paul and Wings used in the Virgin Islands during the recording of *London Town*.)

8. The Lady Demure appears in "Get It," which Paul sings with Carl Perkins on *Tug of War*.

("The life of Cadillac and ultra for sure/Is automatic for the Lady Demure.")

9. McCartney had originally planned both albums as double LPs.

(Owing to the economic slump prevalent in the recording industry at the time, McCartney was discouraged by Columbia from releasing *Tug of War* as a more expensive double album.)

10. MPL entered *The Cooler* at Cannes, starring Ringo Starr and Barbara Bach, with cameos by Paul and Linda McCartney.

(*The Cooler* featured three songs from Ringo's recent album *Stop and Smell the Roses*: "Private Property," "Attention," and "Sure to Fall." While the film failed to win, the McCartneys haven't always gone away empty-handed at Cannes. In 1980, the five-minute animated short *Seaside Woman*, produced by Linda and directed by cartoonist Oscar Grillo won the festival's Palme d'Or [Golden Palm] award.)

11. Dressed in a tuxedo, McCartney performs "I'll Give You a Ring" solo on piano in David Litchfield's Wings film *One Hand Clapping*, shot at Abbey Road studios in the fall of 1974. The film has never been released commercially.

12. "Hill Street Blues" became "Elstree Blues," in reference to EMI's Elstree Studios in Boreham Wood, where a band performance sequence for the video was being filmed in Studio Four.

13. The important impresario was played by actor John Hurt, notable for his roles in such films as *The Elephant Man*, *Midnight Express*, and the TV series *I Claudius*.

14. Published posthumously, *The Transmigration of Timothy Archer*, the third novel in P. K. Dick's VALIS trilogy, opens the day after John Lennon's assassination.

(As the story opens, Angel Archer is arriving to attend a seminar conducted by Edgar Barefoot on his houseboat in Sausalito. "It costs a hundred dollars to find out why we are on this Earth. You also get a sandwich, but I wasn't hungry that day. John Lennon had just been killed and I think I know why we are on this Earth; it's to find out that what you love the most will be taken away from you, probably due to an error in high places rather than by design.")

15. McCartney's first directorial work since *Magical Mystery Tour* and the "Hello Goodbye" promotional films in 1967 was the promotional video for The Cimarons' reggae interpretation of the Four Seasons hit "Big Girls Don't Cry."

16. Martin believed *Tug of War* might have had more "staying power in the States" if "What's That You're Doing," the McCartney/Wonder composition/duet had been the third single release.

17. When Ringo flew to Sydney 28 September to tape an appearance for *Parkinson In Australia*, host Michael Parkinson managed to coax him over to a drum kit, introducing the band, featuring former Little River Band leader Glenn Shorrock, as the "Shorrock Starr Band."

(Starr drummed on a version of "Honey Don't," adding the occasional vocal on an encore medley of "Honey Don't"/"Blue Suede Shoes" sung by Shorrock. The performance aired in Australia 9 October.)

18. The only Brit in the off-Broadway version of *Lennon* was Greg Martyn [sic], the son of Beatles producer George Martin.

("I told them who I was when I walked in," Greg told *Rolling Stone*, "but no one believed me." George visited the rehearsals in July, reportedly "entrancing" the cast with his stories.)

19. In Australia, if someone has "gone troppo," it means they've "gone soft in the head from too much exposure to the tropical sun."

20. Issued in 1961 on the Cub Records label, "I Really Love You" was a hit for the Stereos.

21. Harrison mentions the fruit bat in "Gone Troppo."
("Night life, counting de fruit bat.")

22. Marvin O. Pizika recovers from exhaustion in "Beatlemania," the eleventh in the seventeen-episode run of *Joanie Loves Chachi*.

23. John shouts "Yoko!" on "Never Say Goodbye."

24. The last single issued in Israel before the "Girl Is Mine" was "Mull Of Kintyre" by Paul McCartney and Wings in 1977.

25. Cynthia Lennon's book, which she described as "a fairy tale of the story of the Beatles" was to have been titled *Fairy Tales*.

1983

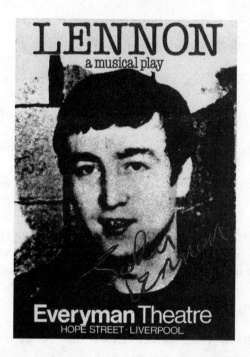

LENNON
a musical play

Everyman Theatre
HOPE STREET · LIVERPOOL

1. Set on the corner of 72nd Street and Central Park West in the early hours of 9 December 1980, this one-act play examines the reactions of a group of nine people to John's death. What is the title of this play, written by James McClure, which had its world premiere in Princeton, New Jersey, 19 January, by the McCarter Theatre Company?

2. In an interview for the *London Sun* published 27 January, George commented on his involvement with this group, "Let's face it, there are certain things in life which make it worth living and one of those things is . . ." who?

3. The Ringo Starr bootleg *Richie & His Pals*, released in the spring of 1983 on Wibble Records, was a decent compilation of film, television and record appearances, including Starr's vocals from the hard-to-find *Scouse the Mouse* LP. But it was the way Wibble packaged this release that made it so unique. What did they do?

4.   Which Beatles song, whistled by a time traveler in 1810 London, figures prominently in Tim Powers's science fiction novel, *The Anubis Gates*?

5.   What is the "Rock & Rock Review"?

6.   Who inspired Ringo to title his 1983 album *Old Wave*?

7.   What song on *Old Wave* did Ringo write for wife Barbara Bach?

8.   In what country was Ringo's album *Old Wave* first released?

9.   When Sam Havadtoy announced in June that he was in charge of coordinating an album featuring artists covering the songs of Yoko Ono, he was putting into motion a project John had hoped to present to Yoko in 1983 as a fiftieth birthday present. Among those initially announced as planning to contribute were Roberta Flack, covering "Goodbye Sadness," and Eddie Money, with a heavy metal arrangement of "I'm Moving On." Carly Simon and Elton John were also going to participate—what songs were they going to cover?

10.   From 18 July to 11 September, more than 20,000 fans from around the world got a rare opportunity to tour Abbey Road Studio Number Two when EMI presented *The Beatles at Abbey Road*, a ninety-minute film, video and slide documentary, written and narrated by Capitol Radio DJ Roger Scott. Why would a busy studio complex like Abbey Road suddenly decide to allow visitors inside?

11.   What kind of car is Paul driving during his cameo in Tracy Ullman's video for "They Don't Know"?

12.   The Peace Museum in Chicago opened their exhibit on the contributions made by music and musicians through the decades toward the effort to achieve peace, 11 September. *Give Peace a Chance: Music and the Struggle for Peace*, which ran through 31 January 1984, included many items loaned by Yoko Ono documenting the Lennons' peace efforts, including box #246 of what?

13.   On 21 September, this one-man play portraying "scenes from the life of Stuart Sutcliffe" opened at the Bromley Little Theatre in Bromley, Kent. What was its title?

14. *Pipes of Peace*, Paul's follow-up to *Tug of War*, was issued simultaneously in the U.S. and the UK, 31 October. What title had McCartney initially considered using?

15. What is the connection between Paul and the Pestalozzi Children's Village Choir in Sedelscombe?

16. John and Paul have done the math before, writing "One and One Is Two" for Mike Shannon and The Strangers in 1964, upping the ante in 1969—"one and one and one is three"—in "Come Together." In 1983, McCartney was again telling us, "I know that one and one makes two"—where?

17. The former engine driver in McCartney's "Average Person" kept his engine "spit and polished up" (much like a certain fireman on Penny Lane), but what was this man's "only great ambition"?

18. For the opening of "Tug of Peace," Paul envisioned "having a kind of Zulu sound. I wanted to get the noise of thumping assegais (a light African spear) on the ground." How did McCartney and producer George Martin achieve this?

19. First aired in the UK on Channel Four's *The Tube*, 28 October, the video for "Say Say Say" finds Paul McCartney and Michael Jackson playing a couple of con-men traveling through the southwestern U.S., circa 1920. In one scene, Paul is shown hustling a game of pool—who played his opponent?

20. "I thought just over a million dollars would see us through," said Paul in an interview in the British Airways magazine *High Life*. "In the third week alone, we'd spent nearly all that and I was ordering new check books." What was McCartney spending so much money on?

21. Who are Mr. Manley and Mr. Newbury?

22. "I guess if I had gone too far, the gay community could have been easily offended," said Ringo. "I don't think that will happen though." What was Starr talking about?

23. Australian guitarist John Williams of the instrumental group Sky played guitar with Paul on what McCartney composition, first issued as a single by Island in the UK, 19 December?

1983

24. In December, Ringo agreed to narrate twenty-six five-minute episodes of *Thomas the Tank Engine and Friends* for Central Television in the UK. What has Ringo said was his favorite train to voice?

25. In the U.S., these animated episodes were incorporated into a half-hour children's show which debuted the weekend of 28 January 1989 on the Public Broadcasting System. What was the name of this PBS show, in which Ringo also appeared as the 18-inch tall Mr. Conductor?

ANSWERS

1. James McClure's play is titled *The Day They Shot John Lennon*.

(McClure was living across from the Dakota the night John was shot. Much of the dialogue heard in the play McClure said he overheard while mingling with the mourners in front of the apartment house in the days that followed.)

2. ". . . one of those things is (Monty) Python . . . laughter is the great release."

3. *Richie & His Pals* was the first bootleg ever issued with a 3-D cover design.

178

4. "Yesterday."

While accompanying a time traveling party back to 1810 London to hear a lecture by the British poet Samuel Taylor Coleridge, Professor Brendan Doyle is kidnapped before he can rejoin his party for their return to 1983. Walking its streets one evening, Doyle hears whistling from somebody crossing a rooftop bridge:

> He froze and his eyes widened in shock. It was *Yesterday*, the Beatles song by John Lennon and Paul McCartney.
>
> "Hey, come back! I'm from the twentieth century, too! Damn, it," Doyle yelled desparingly, "Coca-Cola, Clint Eastwood, Cadillac!"
>
> He crossed the little bridge and then descended through the other building, panting, but singing *Yesterday* as loudly as he could, and shouting the lyrics down all cross corridors. He drew many complaints but didn't get anyone who seemed to know what the song was.
>
> "I'll give you a place to hide away, mate," shouted one furious old man who seemed to think Doyle's behavior had been specifically calculated to upset him, "if you don't get out of here this instant!"

5. The "Rock & Rock Review" were the quartet of studio musicians responsible for most of the playing on *Old Wave*, recorded during the summer of 1982 at Startling Studios, Ringo's recording facility at Tittenhurst Park.

(The "Rock & Rock Review" were: Ringo [drums], Joe Walsh [guitars, in addition to producing], Gary Brooker and Chris Stainton [keyboards] and Mo Foster [bass].)

6. Ringo named his album *Old Wave* after Barbara Bach's daughter, Francesca Gregorini, had asked him if he was "old wave."

(At one point Starr had considered using the title *It Beats Sleep*.)

7. Cowritten with Joe Walsh, Ringo wrote "Alibi" for Barbara.

8. *Old Wave* was first issued by Bellaphon in West Germany, 16 June.

9. During an interview with *Rolling Stone*, Havadtoy announced that Carly Simon was planning to cover "Men, Men, Men" (from *Feeling the Space*), while Elton John would contribute "Winter Song" (from *Approximately Infinite Universe*).

(Neither artist appeared on the final album, first issued by Polydor in the U.S., 13 September 1984 as *Every Man has a Woman*.)

10. EMI needed to close Studio Two to install a new mixing console in the upstairs control room.

(It was Ken Townsend, then Abbey Road's Manager, who came up with the idea of opening up the studio during the refurbishment with a presentation based on the Beatles at Abbey Road.)

11. Paul is driving a Robin Reliant in "They Don't Know."

(McCartney was paid £43 and luncheon vouchers for his afternoon's work in Ullman's video, his first cameo in another artist's video.)

12. Among the items Yoko loaned the Peace Musem was her last box of peace acorns (#246), from the Lennons' April 1969 "Acorns For Peace" campaign.

(World leaders were each sent two acorns that they were encouraged to plant for peace. "Perhaps if they plant them and watch them grow, they might get the idea into their heads," John said at the time. Golda Meir in Israel and Pierre Trudeau in Canada were the only leaders known to have planted theirs.)

13. *Stu.*

(Written by Jeremy Stockwell and Hugh O'Neil, the part of Sutcliffe in the production was played by Paul Almond.)

14. Speaking to Simon Bates for London's Radio One 16 June, McCartney said he had considered calling his upcoming album *Tug of War II*.

("It's a sequel to *Tug of War* and I was going to call it *Tug of War II*, but I thought the Rocky thing of *Rocky I*, *Rocky II*, and *Rocky III* was really boring, so I've called it *Pipes of Peace*, y'see.")

15. Paul featured the singing of the Pestalozzi Children's Village Choir on the title track for *Pipes of Peace*.

16. "Well I know that one and one makes two" is a line from "The Other Me," included on *Pipes of Peace*.

17. In "Average Person" (included on *Pipes of Peace*), the former engine driver's only great ambition "was to work with lions in a zoo."

18. Wielding approximately thirty garden canes between them, McCartney and Martin produced the desired rhythm heard at the start of "Tug of Peace" by thumping them on the floor of the studio.

19. Paul's opponent in his pool hustle is Bob Giraldi, the director of "Say Say Say."

20. McCartney told British film critic Alexander Walker that when filming began on *Give My Regards to Broad Street* at West Wycombe Park, London, 5 November 1982, he was covering the initial production costs with his own money.

(Paul subsequently signed a deal with 20th Century Fox, who then financed the film, believed to have run $6–8 million.)

21. Mr. Manley and Mr. Newbury were the names Paul and Ringo used to book themselves in at studios during the filming of *Give My Regards to Broad Street*.

22. Ringo was referring to the roles of Robin and Vanessa Valarian, the gay dress designers which he and Barbara Bach played in part two of NBC-TV's adaptation of Judith Krantz's 1980 novel *Princess Daisy*, first aired 6–7 November.

("We wanted to go to town," said Starr, "but we were urged [by director Waris Hussein] not to push the point.")

23. John Williams and Paul played guitar on McCartney's composition "Theme From 'The Honorary Consul,'" the signature theme from the 1984 film directed by John McKenzie.

24. Ringo told *Q* magazine in 1998 that his favorite train to voice was Gordon, the blue Tender Engine.

("I like Gordon with his big Gordon attitude," said Starr, "and he allowed me to do a deep voice—Thomas and Gordon." "Thomas" coproducer Britt Allcroft picked Starr after hearing his voice on a talk show playing on her television as she walked through her home.)

25. Ringo appeared as Mr. Conductor on *Shining Time Station*.

1984

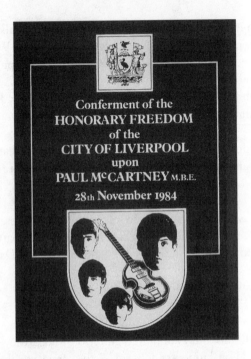

Conferment of the
HONORARY FREEDOM
of the
CITY OF LIVERPOOL
upon
PAUL McCARTNEY M.B.E.

28th November 1984

1. In Britain, Polydor's promotional campaign for the single "Nobody Told Me" (issued 9 January with "O'Sanity") included billboards in London picturing John and Yoko with what tagline?

2. What song on *Milk and Honey* is John said to have written for May Pang?

3. While vacationing in St. James Parish, Barbados, police raided Porter House, the private home where Paul and Linda were staying, 15 January. Both were charged and later pled guilty in court, paying a $100 fine each. What did Mr. and Mrs. Mac do?

4. Parlophone's plan to issue the McCartney/Jackson duet "The Man" as a single, 13 February, was subsequently canceled. What unreleased song was to have been on the B-side?

5. Who was the singer reported to have been reduced to tears at his wedding, 14 February, when he received a telegram from Sean Lennon which read, "My Daddy would (have) loved to have been there"?

6. What is the title of the song Pink Floyd member David Gilmour wrote in response to the assassination of John Lennon?

7. What is the title of the song Pink Floyd member Roger Waters wrote that mentions Yoko Ono?

8. When Ringo agreed to make an appearance on ITV's *What's My Line*, 14 May, it was on condition that a TV set be made available to him immediately after the show so he could watch his favorite soap opera—which one?

9. Sotheby's in New York held a "Collector's Carrousel" auction, 23 June, highlighted by the auctioning of 123 lots of personal possessions submitted by Yoko Ono, including the Lennons' 1965 Rolls Royce Phantom V, which sold for $184,250. Lucy McConaghie, a musicologist from St. Augustine, Florida, purchased John's Brambach Baby Grand piano for $8,800. What song had Lennon composed on the instrument?

10. Alvin Stardust had a hit in the UK in 1984 with what song that mentions Paul McCartney?

11. At a Sotheby's rock and roll memorabilia auction conducted in London, 30 August, a sixteen-page, handwritten manuscript of unpublished poetry, prose, and drawings by John was sold by Rod Murray, Lennon's former flatmate from Gambier Terrace. What did John title the work, which sold for $22,880?

12. In what song does Paul declare that ". . . the summertime never seems to last when you're riding on a rocket"?

13. "I think it's a better track than the original," declared *Broad Street* producer George Martin of this Beatles song remake. "I like Dick Morrisey's sax playing. It fit the mood." What is the song?

14. Paul has tried several times to get solo movie projects off the ground. In 1979, Willy Russell (who wrote the stage show *John, Paul, George, Ringo . . . and Bert*) was commissioned to write *Band On the Run*, in which Paul would have played a rock star named Jet. EMI Films even announced plans to produce the project before it was eventually shelved. *Give My Regards to Broad Street* came about when McCartney found himself struck in a traffic jam and began writing the screenplay. But *Broad Street* might never have been written had this noted British playwright been able to complete his screenplay based on one of McCartney's songs. Who is the playwright and which song was he inspired by?

15. When Paul originally wrote his screenplay for *Broad Street*, what part did he write for Linda?

16. Who did Paul McCartney first propose for the role of Jim in *Give My Regards to Broad Street*?

17. Who is Martin Ruane and what was his contribution to *Give My Regards to Broad Street*?

18. What song was nearly dropped from *Give My Regards to Broad Street* but for Ringo and Linda's insistence that it be kept it?

19. *Rupert and the Frog Song* had its world premiere with *Give My Regards to Broad Street*, 25 October at New York's Gotham Theater. Voices in the featurette were handled by June Whitfield and Winsdor Davis, save Rupert, who was done by Paul. Originally McCartney had planned the character to be voiced by a child—what was the problem?

20. Where can you find the "Broad Street Escape Kit"?

21. Prior to the Liverpool premiere of *Give My Regards to Broad Street* at the Odeon Cinema, 28 November, Paul McCartney accepted the city's conferment as Honorary Freeman, in a ceremony held at the Picton Library. In his acceptance speech, McCartney noted, "The last time I was in this place was 1953, and I was shaking like a jelly and my legs were all rubbery." What was the occasion?

22. George did not attend the London premiere of *Give My Regards to Broad Street* at the Empire Theater in Leicester Square, 29 November. Who did he send in his place?

23. Harry Nilsson and Ringo Starr had planned to spend the winter filming down under in their updated version of the Bing Crosby/Bob Hope "Road" pictures. Barbara Bach was to costar, Harry Nilsson was set to write the music and Norman Panama (who had cowritten 1962's *Road to Hong Kong*) was set to do the script. The $8 million film, which Starr, Nilsson and Bob Levinson of Levinson Entertainment Ventures were to bankroll, was never made. What was to have been its title?

24. On 6 December, Michael Jackson was in the Chicago courtroom of U.S. district judge Marvin E. Aspen to testify that his song "The Girl is Mine" was not stolen from what song, written by Fred Sanford, a musician from Schaumberg, Illinois?

25. What was the name of the group whose song, issued 7 December, toppled Paul McCartney's record (with "Mull of Kintyre") for the best selling UK single ever?

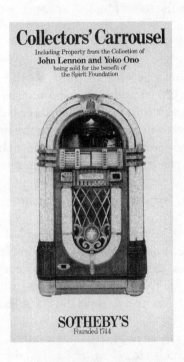

Collectors' Carrousel
Including Property from the Collection of
John Lennon and Yoko Ono
being sold for the benefit of
the Spirit Foundation

SOTHEBY'S
Founded 1744

ANSWERS

1. The tagline on Polydor's billboards was "Strange Days Indeed."

2. "(Forgive Me) My Little Flower Princess."

3. Paul and Linda pled guilty to possession of ten and seven grams, respectively, of marijuana.

(Arriving back in London, 17 January, customs officials at Heathrow Airport arrested Linda when more marijuana was found in an empty film cannister in her handbag. On 24 January, she pled guilty to possession of five grams of "herbal cannabis" and was fined $105.)

4. The B-side of the canceled single for "The Man" (Parlophone R6066), was to have been the unreleased McCartney composition "Blackpool."

5. Sean's telegram was to his godfather, Elton John, who married studio engineer Renate Blauer in Darling Point, Sydney, Australia on Valentine's Day.

6. Gilmour wrote the song "Murder" in response to John's death.
("Murder" is included on *About Face*, Gilmour's second solo album, released 5 March.)

7. Yoko is mentioned in the third verse of "5:01 A.M. (The Pros and Cons of Hitchhiking)," included on Waters's first solo album *The Pros and Cons of Hitch Hiking*, first issued by Harvest Records in the UK, 30 April.
(Ono's inclusion was based on a dream drummer Andy Newmark related to Waters over lunch in a pub. In the dream he saw himself standing on the wing of a plane with Yoko telling him to jump.)

8. Ringo's favorite soap opera is *Coronation Street*.

9. John wrote the *Double Fantasy* song "Dear Yoko" on the Brambach Baby Grand piano Yoko auctioned at Sotheby's in New York, 23 June.
(It was also at this piano where Yoko composed "Wake Up," included on *It's Alright*. Yoko's proceeds from the auction, $430,936, was donated to various children's causes via the Spirit Foundation.)

10. Issued on Ariola/Chrysalis, Alvin Stardust's UK hit that mentions Paul is "I Feel Like Buddy Holly," written and produced by Mike Batt.
("Now I know how Paul McCartney felt, when he got up to say, "I wish it was yesterday.")

11. When John vacated the Gambier Terrace flat he shared with Rod Murray in the summer of 1960, one of the things he left behind was a manuscript titled *A Treasury of Art and Poetry*.

12. This summertime reference is included in an additional verse exclusive to Paul's remake of "Ballroom Dancing," included on *Give My Regards to Broad Street*, released 22 October.

13. Not surprisingly, George Martin prefers the version of "The Long and Winding Road" he produced for *Give My Regards to Broad Street* to the original Beatles version, noted for its choral and orchestral score by Richard Hewson that Phil Spector produced for *Let It Be*, 1 April 1970 in Abbey Road's Studio One.

14.   Playwright Tom Stoppard (*Rosencrantz & Guildenstern Are Dead*) wanted to base his screenplay around the song "Tug of War." Time constraints from prior commitments Stoppard had made ultimately stalled the project.

("The thing was gonna be something like young cocky kid, who's very military . . . goes off to war with these wonderful dreams and gets a leg blown off. So I was trying to do this "Tug of War" thing with [director Peter Webb] and Tom Stoppard and it was falling down. And I was stuck in a traffic jam, so I said I'll write something then.")

15.   Originally, Paul *did not* include a part in *Give My Regards to Broad Street* for Linda.

(A part for Mrs. Mac was added after she protested the oversight.)

16.   "Alec Guinness was my first suggestion, but we (McCartney and director Peter Webb) felt he didn't have the twinkle that Ralph's (Sir Ralph Richardson) got."

17.   Martin Ruane (a.k.a. Luke McMasters) is better known to British wrestling fans as Giant Haystacks. The 6' 7", 588-pound "grappler" played Big Bob, a bootlegger whom Paul confers with during *Broad Street's* rehearsal sequence in a riverside warehouse.

(McCartney and son James would often go to wrestling shows in Sussex when Haystacks was top of the bill. In 1996, Martin wrestled in the U.S. for the WCW as "The Loch Ness Monster." Ruane was fifty-five when he died of stomach cancer, 29 November 1998.)

18.   "Not Such A Bad Boy."

("Ringo and Linda demanded that got in the film, 'cause they really liked that one," McCartney told *Beatlefan* publisher Bill King in October 1984. "It was teetering for a minute there. But they said, 'It will be in. We demand it.")

19.   "I'm Rupert in The Frog Song," Paul told *Q* magazine in 1993, "on account of us auditioning every kid at every stage school in London and them all having one problem—couldn't say "frogs." Said "fwogs." Which was a bit of a disadvantage when the film's about frogs."

20.   The "Broad Street Escape Kit" was a booklet of clues and answers included with Mastertronic's *Give My Regards to Broad Street Computer Game.*

21.   In 1953, eleven-year-old Paul McCartney was at the Picton Library to receive a Coronation Day essay prize.

("Out of two hundred entries from the City of Liverpool, I was the triumphant winner who walked wobbly-kneed to accept his prize from the Lord Mayor himself," remembered Paul in a 1973 review for *Punch* magazine. "The prize was two books about the Queen [including *Seven Queens of England*, by Geoffrey Trease] which are treasured to this day." The Liverpool City Council passed a resolution conferring the status of Honorary Freeman on all four Beatles, 7 March 1984.)

22.   George sent his wife Olivia in his place to attend the London premiere of *Give My Regards to Broad Street.*

(Harrison was in Auckland, New Zealand 28 November and in Sydney, Australia on the 30th promoting Derek Taylor's autobiography for Genesis Publications, *Fifty Years Adrift*, for which he served as editor.)

23.   Ringo and Harry's film would have been titled *Road to Australia.*

24.   Sanford's song is titled "Please Love Me Now."

(Under oath, Jackson testified that he began composing "The Girl is Mine" [at producer Quincy Jones' request] in 1981, sometime before a Thanksgiving trip to England to work with Paul. Jackson and McCartney recorded a demo of the song 29 March 1982. Sanford claimed his song, which he passed along to a CBS employee 10 March 1982, was written in the summer of 1981. On 14 December 1984, a federal court jury rejected Sanford's $5 million copyright infringement suit, ruling that CBS Records was not liable for the similarities between the two songs.)

25.   The thirty-six artists comprising Band Aid, the trust organized by Bob Geldof to assist famine-stricken Africa, broke McCartney's record for the best selling UK single ever with "Do They Know it's Christmas?"

(Debuting at number one the day of its release, "Christmas" sold more than three million copies during its five-week reign at the top of the charts.)

1985

1.   The world premiere of the HandMade Film *Water,* starring Michael Caine and Valerie Perrine, was held at the Odeon Cinema in London, 18 January. Its soundtrack featured two songs cowritten by George, "Celebration" and "Focus of Attention," both sung by Jimmy Helms. Harrison makes a cameo appearance in the film as a member of a band performing at a UN function. What was the name of this band that also included Ringo, Eric Clapton, and Billy Connolly?

2.   Who is Sarah Menikides and what is her relationship to Ringo Starr?

3.   First slated for release in November 1984, *Sessions,* EMI/Capitol's collection of unreleased Beatles tracks, was rescheduled for 25 February 1985 when McCartney's objections to the format tabled the project. As late as the summer of 1984, the collection had been planned for release under a different title—what was it?

4.   What was Capitol Records' in-house code name for the *Sessions* album project?

5. Harrison demoed Bob Dylan's song "I Don't Want to Do It" for possible inclusion on his *All Things Must Pass* album. It is said to have been among the songs on a tape Harrison received when he visited Dylan at his home in upstate New York in late November 1968. While Bob has yet to commercially issue the song himself, in November 1984 Harrison finally recorded his version, which was first released in the U.S. 14 March as part of what soundtrack album?

6. What is the title of the unreleased song George cowrote and recorded in March with Alvin Lee of Ten Years After?

7. Recorded between March and May with producer Hugh Padgham, sessions for McCartney's *Press to Play* included several collaborations with 10cc's Eric Stewart. What is the title of the song they wrote together, inspired by a postcard Stewart had received from Pink Floyd drummer Nick Mason?

8. Ringo made a non-musical cameo on what Stones-related video project, which premiered on MTV, 22 April?

9. On 13 May, British Rail held a ceremony at Liverpool's Lime Street Station to dedicate one of their new Merseyside Pullman carriages, named in a contest sponsored by the *Liverpool Echo*. What was the winning name, suggested by Beatle fan Madeleine Schatz?

10. Gerry Marsden organized an all-star remake of the Pacemakers' hit "You'll Never Walk Alone" for a single benefiting the victims and families of a soccer stadium fire in Bradford City that killed fifty-five people and injured hundreds more, 11 May. Unable to attend the recording session, Paul was among the dozen celebrities who recorded a message of sympathy on the 15th for the "Messages" B-side. Under what group name was the single issued by Spartan Records in the UK, 24 May?

11. What is "Lennon Circle"?

12. Julian Lennon's announced appearance at Live Aid, 13 July, only added fuel to the rumor that the Beatles were going to reunite during the concert, with Lennon standing in for his father. Instead he was a no show, some speculating that the pressure caused by a reunion rumor in the press may have unnerved him. Who had Jules been planning to perform with?

13. What Beatles song did McCartney's future songwriting partner, Elvis Costello, sing at Live Aid?

14. What is the title of the song about John's murder written by folk singer Louden Wainwright III?

15. At 2:45 A.M. on 10 August, contracts were signed in London giving Michael Jackson ATV Music, a catalogue of neary 4,000 songs, including the rights to the nearly 270 Lennon/McCartney compositions published by Northern Songs. Who did Jackson purchase ATV from?

16. Recorded in September, the title song for the John Landis comedy *Spies Like Us* (issued 18 November), marked a recording first for McCartney—what was it?

17. How does the UK version of the *Spies Like Us* video, directed by Landis, differ from the U.S. version?

18. On 20 September, Yoko registered more than two dozen unreleased Lennon compositions with the U.S. copyright office in Washington, D.C. Included were future Beatles singles "Free as a Bird" and "Real Love" (registered as "Girls and Boys"); "Life Begins at Forty," and "Lullaby for a Lazy Day." Ono jumped the gun on the last song however, as "Lullaby" (its actual title) belonged to whom?

19. Yoko Ono and son Sean joined New York mayor Ed Koch in dedicating Strawberry Fields, a 2.5 acre tear-shaped park within the city's Central Park, 9 October. Located one hundred yards from the Dakota, the "growing monument" to John comprised one hundred and sixty-one species from one hundred and twenty-three countries, including dogwoods from the late Princess Grace of Monaco, birches from the Soviet Union, maples from Canada, daffodil bulbs from the Netherlands and a cedar from Israel. What did the U.S. contribute?

20. When Carl Perkins sent out invitations to join him in the taping of his Cinemax TV special celebrating the thirtieth anniversary of his song "Blue Suede Shoes," George was said to be the first to sign and return the card Perkins had enclosed. What form did Carl's invitation take?

21. Victor Spinetti and Roy Kinnear (Foot and Algernon in *Help!*) appeared together in the video for what song from Genesis guitarist Mike Rutherford's group, Mike and the Mechanics?

22. Paul found himself in hot water when a quote from a 1981 phone interview he gave Hunter Davies about his former songwriting partner was seized upon by the world press, 5 November. Yoko was quoted as being "stunned" by McCartney's remarks. What did he say?

23. Ringo's eldest son, Zak, has earned a reputation as a talented drummer in his own right. Starkey toured with his father as part of the 1992 All Starr Band featured on the subsequent commercial release, *Volume Two: Live from Montreaux*, issued by Rykodisc, 14 September 1993. But this wasn't the first time father and son appeared together on a commercial release—what was?

24. What do Telly Savalas, Jonathan Winters, Anthony Newley, and Ringo Starr have in common?

25. "I was pretty skeptical when it all began, but it's fun when you come down to it," said Ringo, who was in Nepal with wife Barbara, 15 December. The couple were part of the Cartier of Paris celebrity team playing what sport?

ANSWERS

1. Harrison made a cameo in *Water* as a part of The Singing Rebels Band performing the song "Freedom."

2. Sarah became Ringo's daughter-in-law when she married Ringo's son Zak in a private civil ceremony in Bracknell, Berkshire, 22 January.

3. *One Two Three Four.*
   (Another title suggested was *Boots*, linking the album to the Robert Freeman photo of the Beatles' cuban-heeled footwear that was to have graced the album's back cover. EMI rejected this because of its reference to bootlegs. *Goodbye* was also a title contender when McCartney's demo of "Goodbye" was considered for inclusion on the album, but EMI nixed this as too depressing.)

4. Capitol's code name for *Sessions* was "Mary Jane."

5. Columbia Records included George's version of "I Don't Want To Do It" on the *Porky's Revenge* soundtrack album.

6. George and Alvin Lee's unreleased song collaboration is titled "Shelter In Your Love."

7. The McCartney/Stewart song "Yvonne's the One" was inspired by a postcard from Nick Mason.

(Though McCartney has yet to issue a version of the song commercially, in 1993 Stewart recorded his version, included on UK and Japanese editions of the 10cc collection *Mirror Mirror*, issued in 1995.)

8. Ringo made a non-musical cameo appearance (as a caretaker sweeping up after the show), during filming 11 May for the 30-minute *Willie and the Poor Boys—The Video*, issued by PolyGram Music Video, 25 May.

(Benefitting multiple sclerosis research, the charity video, organized by Rolling Stones bassist Bill Wyman, was touted as the first to assemble members of the Stones [Wyman and Charlie Watts], the Beatles and the Who [Kenney Jones].)

9. Madeleine's winning name for the Merseyside Pullman carriage was the *John Lennon*.

10. The Bradford City soccer fire benefit single is credited to the Crowd.

(Denny Laine and Zak Starkey were among those singing in the chorus on "You'll Never Walk Alone.")

11. "Lennon Circle" is the name of the sunburst design mosaic featuring the word "Imagine" that is the centerpiece of Strawberry Fields, New York Central Park's tear-shaped, two-and-half acre garden tribute to John.

(The ten-foot diameter, black-and-white mosaic, a gift from the Italian government, was dedicated by Yoko Ono, 11 July.)

12. Julian had planned to sing a duet with Phil Collins at Live Aid.

(When Lennon was made aware of the reunion rumor, he composed a statement for the press, which he never issued: "I love the Beatles but I have no intention of working with any of them. I don't want to confuse the world with rumors of something that is not a possibility.")

13. Singing what he prefaced to the Wembley Stadium crowd as an "old Northern English folk song," Costello sang "All You Need Is Love" at Live Aid.

14. Louden Wainwright III's song about Lennon's assassination is titled "Not John," included on his Rounder album, *I'm Alright*.

15. Jackson purchased ATV Music for $47.5 million from Australian tycoon Rupert Holmes a Court.

(Jackson's bid was not the highest Holmes a Court received. Charles Koppelman and Marty Bandier's Entertainment Co. had submitted a bid for $50 million. Holmes a Court went with Jackson because he could close the deal faster.)

16. "Spies Like Us" was the first release McCartney recorded at The Mill, his 48-track home studio in Sussex.

17. Scenes shot at Abbey Road studios of Dan Aykroyd and Chevy Chase miming with musical instruments had to be reedited in the version of the *Spies Like Us* video broadcast in the UK to keep the clip from running afoul of British Musician's Union rules.

(Aykroyd and Chase are shown from the chest up in the UK version so that no one can tell they're miming.)

18. "Lullaby" is a composition by Grapefruit, the first group signed by Apple (publishing only) in 1968.

(Yoko also inadvertently registered John as the composer of "Have You Heard the Word," frequently passed off on early Beatles bootlegs as a collaboration between Lennon and the Bee Gees, but actually written by Steve Kipner and Steve Groves, members of the Australian group Tin Tin.)

19. The U.S. was not represented at the dedication of Strawberry Fields; the Reagan White House did not respond to Yoko's request for a donation.

20. Carl's invitation to participate in his TV special was on videotape.

("Hello, I'm Carl Perkins. A lot older, a lot fatter than when you last saw me. I would certainly love to do a TV special one time in my life, something I never have done. I would certainly love to have you be a part of it. If you're interested, sign the enclosed card and I'll put it together." Among those sending their regrets were Bob Dylan, John Fogerty, and Paul McCartney. Taped 21 October at Limehouse Studios in London, the one-hour show was first aired in the UK on BBC Channel 4, 1 January 1986 as *Blue Suede Shoes: A Rockabilly Session*.)

21. Spinetti and Kinnear appeared together in the video for "All I Need is a Miracle," included on Mike and the Mechanics' Atlantic album debut *Mike and the Mechanics*.

("They are my idols," said Rutherford in the December 1986 issue of *Inside Tracks* magazine. "Without any doubt, it was the Beatles who had the greatest influence on me musically. In some fundamental ways, it has been sort of downhill ever since they split up.")

22. During his interview with Davies, which was to be incorporated into an updated edition of *The Beatles* authorized biography, McCartney stated that John "could be a maneuvering swine, which no one ever realized. Now since the death he's become Martin Luther Lennon."

(In his defense, Davies explained that Paul had been upset at the time of the interview [conducted 3 May 1981] over a comment made by Yoko that he had hurt John "more than any other person.")

23. Ringo and Zak both drummed as part of Artists United Against Apartheid on the song "Sun City," released by Manhattan, 11 November.

24. All appeared in Irwin Allen's musical version of *Alice In Wonderland*, first screened on CBS-TV in the U.S., 9–10 December.

(Ringo appeared as the Mock Turtle in part one, singing a song written by Steve Allen titled "Nonsense." Filmed in May, the cast included Telly Savalas as the Cheshire Cat, Jonathan Winters as the Dodo, and Anthony Newley as the Mad Hatter.)

25. Ringo and Barbara were among the ten teams in Nepal playing for charity in the World Elephant Polo Championship.

(Also playing on the Cartier team were comedian (and *Water* costar) Billy Connolly and Max Boyce.)

1986

1.   At the first Rock and Roll Hall of Fame induction ceremony, held at New York's Waldorf-Astoria Hotel, 23 January, who did Julian and Sean Lennon induct into the Hall of Fame in memory of their father?

2.   What is the title of the song written by Carl Perkins that mentions the Beatles?

3.   Yoko's Starpeace Tour kicked off 28 February in Brussels, Belgium. What two songs by John did she include in her set?

4.   During a London press conference at the Roof Gardens club, 6 March, George stated, "There are no naked women in it. There are lots of naked men." What was he referring to?

5.   When Parlophone wanted to issue " 'Til There Was You" as the Beatles' follow-up to "Love Me Do," John, George, and Ringo walked out on Brian Epstein; the group never became famous. Thirty years later, Paul enjoys a successful career singing in Las Vegas as Paul Montana. Ringo still drums (for Gerry and the Pacemakers), living off wife Maureen's income as a hairdresser. George became a Jesuit priest, while John amounted to nothing. These were the fates that befell the Fabs in Irish playwright Larry Kirwan's off-Broadway production by Theaterworkers, which opened at the Charas Theatro La Terraza in New York City, 1 May. What is the play's title?

6. A series of limited edition serigraphs and lithographs, along with three crystal etchings which Yoko had commissioned based on seventeen of John's sketches, debuted in May at galleries in San Francisco and Beverly Hills. What was the name of the exhibit?

7. What does John Lennon have in common with choreographer George Balanchine, architect Walter Gropius and writer Franz Werfel?

8. Julian Lennon opened a forty-city North American tour in Miami, 28 May, supporting his second solo album, *The Secret Value of Daydreaming*. During the second of three nights at New York's Radio City Music Hall, Julian was joined onstage by his ten-year-old half-brother Sean to sing one of their father's Beatle songs—which one?

9. Available only in the UK by mail order beginning 1 July, the cassette release *Only the Beatles . . .* (Parlophone SMMC 151) marked the first (and last) time EMI issued a special release of Beatles songs promoting a commercial product. What was the product?

10. What is "Liberty and Strawberries"?

11. Where was the promotional video for "Press" filmed, which had its world television premiere on a Channel 4 *Eurotube* special, 5 July?

12. What is the title of the Beatles song the Beastie Boys had planned to include on their 1986 Def Jam/Columbia album, *Licensed to Ill*?

13. Published in Japan in 1986, what is the title of Yoko Ono's autobiography?

14. "The widow was open, outside was a spaceship, it took off into the sky leaving a trail of smoke behind it." What is the significance of this phrase?

15. How does Tom Waits figure in the creation of *Press to Play*?

16.   What is "12 Bar Bali"?

17.   For Linda's forty-fifth birthday, 24 September, Paul presented her with a recording he'd made performing a cover of what song?

18.   At a press conference in Atlanta 6 October, Ringo confirmed his interest in starring in a comedy special for the Showtime cable network in which he plays a rock club promoter. While the project was eventually shelved, what was the special to have been called?

19.   Intended for a compilation album to benefit Costa Rica's University for Peace, what is the title of the song Paul wrote and demoed with Peter Gabriel?

20.   Who played the runaway in the video directed by Steve Barron for "Pretty Little Head," the second UK single from *Press to Play*, issued by Parlophone, 27 October?

21.   Work on a *Cold Cuts* mastertape was one of the last projects Wings completed in the Fall of 1980 before the group folded. For a week at the beginning of November 1986, Paul returned to the project, preparing a fourteen-song lineup at AIR Studios in London. While the project was once again shelved, probably for good, McCartney later revealed that he had gotten this noted cartoonist to draw the cover art—who?

22.   Paul made his first appearance as a solo artist at the Royal Variety Show, 24 November, at London's Theatre Royal, Drury Lane. Unlike his last appearance (at the Prince of Wales Theatre, 4 November 1963), when some upstart told the royals to "rattle your jewelry," McCartney only sang one song—what was it?

23.   What is "You Know It Makes Sense?"

24.   What is the title of choreographer Christopher Bruce's ballet interpretation of John's *Plastic Ono Band* album, first aired in the UK 30 November on London Weekend Television's *South Bank Show*?

25.   "How come I'm not going to be in the bear suit?" Ringo asked disappointedly at his first meeting with members of this firm. What was he talking about?

ANSWERS

1. Julian and Sean inducted Elvis Presley into the Rock and Roll Hall of Fame, reading a letter written by John praising the King.

("Elvis was the thing," said Julian quoting his father, "Whatever people say, he was it. I wanted to be Elvis.")

2. Perkins mentions the Beatles in "Birth of Rock and Roll," included on *Class of '55*, an album he recorded with Johnny Cash, Roy Orbison and Jerry Lee Lewis.

("Sixty-four the Beatles were the four/That was rock 'n' roll's best friend./The Beatles and the Stones took the ol' beat home/And the world went crazy again.")

3. Yoko sang "Imagine" and "Give Peace a Chance" on her Starpeace Tour.

4. Harrison was talking about the HandMade Films production *Shanghai Surprise*, starring Madonna and Sean Penn, which opened in the U.S., 29 August.

(Specifically, George was elaborating on Madonna's response when asked if the movie had any sexy scenes.)

5. Larry Kirwan's Beatles play is titled *Liverpool Fantasy*.

6. Yoko's exhibit of John's sketches was titled *This Is My Story Both Humble and True*.

(The exhibit took its title from a line of an alphabet John composed in February 1969 to accompany his *Bag One* lithographs: "This is my story both humble and true. Take it to pieces and mend it with glue.")

7. British-born Lennon, Russian-born Balanchine, German-born Gropius, and Austrian-born Werfel were all honored by the Republic of Maldives as famous people who immigrated to the U.S. on a series of four stamps commemorating the centennial of the Statue of Liberty, issued 5 May.

(Lennon's appearance on the seventy-laree stamp, based on John Kelly's photo included with the White Album, marked the first appearance of a Beatle on a postage stamp.)

8. Julian and Sean sang "Day Tripper."

9. Heineken Beer.

(The 12-track compilation of Beatles songs from 1962–1967 [including the first appearance of "Yes It is" in a true stereo mix], could be obtained by sending four Heineken pull tabs along with £2.99. On 18 July, the Beatles and Apple Corp. Ltd. sued EMI and Whitbread Brewery [who make Heineken Beer in the UK] to have the cassette withdrawn.)

10. Located in the Strawberry Fields section of New York City's Central Park, artist Peter Max created the mural "Liberty and Strawberries," which he dedicated to John in a ceremony attended by Yoko and Sean, 4 July.

11. The video for "Press" was shot in London's subway, mostly in the Bond Street tube station.

("We filmed on the Central and Jubilee Lines, going as far as Mile End and North Finchley," recalls director Phillip Davie. "It took about four hours, so we got our 60p's worth.")

12. The Beastie Boys were denied clearance to include their rewritten rap version of "I'm Down" on *Licensed to Ill*, reportedly by Michael Jackson himself.

13. Published only in Japan, Yoko's autobiography is titled *Just Me!* (*Tada no atashi*).

14. Recited by Paul's son James, this is the spoken-word introduction to "Talk More Talk," the third cut on *Press to Play*, first issued by Capitol in the U.S., 22 August.

15. A quote McCartney pulled from an interview by Tom Waits figures among the lyrics in "Talk More Talk."

("I don't actually like sitting down music. Music is ideas.")

16. "12 Bar Bali" is the title of a piece of incidental music composed by George for the film soundtrack of *Shanghai Surprise*.

17. With the help of fifteen studio musicians, Paul gifted his wife with a privately pressed single containing two versions (in Latin and Big Band arrangements) of the Jack Lawrence song "Linda."

(Lawrence wrote the song, which he dedicated to Linda, in 1946, signing over the copyright to her father, attorney Lee Eastman, in exchange for legal services. It was first recorded by Buddy Clark [with Ray Noble and His Orchestra] in 1947. In February 1963, Jan and Dean had a moderate hit with their cover for Capitol, which peaked at #28. They included the song on their album *Jan and Dean Take Linda Surfin'*.)

18. Starr's Showtime comedy special was to have been called *Ringo's Rock Riot*.

19. Visiting each other's homes to rehearse, Paul and Peter Gabriel wrote and recorded a demo for "The Politics of Love" in October 1986.

(Gabriel had been enlisted that August to recruit artists for an album to fund the University's efforts to establish a Global Computer Network. The album project went into limbo when funding was achieved instead via The Hurricane Irene concerts, featuring Gabriel, held in Tokyo's Jingu baseball stadium, 20–21 December.)

20. Sixteen-year-old Gabrielle Anwar played the runaway in Steve Barron's video for "Pretty Little Head."

(Anwar's subsequent film work includes *Scent of a Woman* [with Al Pacino, 1992]; *The Three Musketeers* [with Charlie Sheen and Keifer Sutherland, 1993] and *Things to Do in Denver When You're Dead* [1995].)

21. Cover art for *Cold Cuts* was drawn by *New Yorker* cartoonist Saul Steinberg.

(Combining elements of cubism and pointalism, Steinberg is best known for his oft-imitated 29 March 1976 *New Yorker* cover, "View of the World from 9th Avenue." Steinberg died 12 May 1999 at the age of eighty-four. In 1994, McCartney admitted in *Club Sandwich* that the appearance of *Cold Cuts* bootlegs [starting in 1986], "put me off the idea" of an official release.)

22. Paul sang "Only Love Remains" at the Royal Variety Show, a great plug for the third single Parlophone would release from *Press to Play*, 1 December.

23. "You Know It Makes Sense" is the title of Ringo Starr's anti-heroin message, recorded for the Anti-Heroin Project album *It's a Live In World*, issued by EMI in the UK, 24 November.

24. Performed by New York's Cullberg Ballet, Christopher Bruce's Lennon ballet is titled *The Dream Is Over*.

25.   During the first week of December, Starr filmed and recorded several TV and radio spots in the Bahamas to promote Sun Country's new Classic wine cooler line. At his first meeting with Canandaigua Wine Company executives, Ringo expressed his disappointment that the $20 million campaign would not give him the opportunity to wear the polar bear suit worn by several celebrities in previous Sun Country ads.

(Starr's seven-figure deal with Sun Country marked the first time a Beatle had endorsed a commercial product in the U.S.)

1987

1. From 4–10 February (and again from 25–30 April), Ringo laid down tracks at Three Alarm Studios in Memphis on what was to have been his next album. Eric Clapton, Bob Dylan, Dave Edmunds, and Carl Perkins variously participated. Unhappy with the results, Starr would shelve the project, which at one point had been scheduled for a July 1989 release on CBS. Who was the album's producer, who attempted to issue the material that August to coincide with Ringo's successful All-Starr tour?

2. When the passenger ferry boat, *Herald of Free Enterprise* capsized 6 March following its departure from Zeebrugge, Belgium, an all-star benefit recording was quickly recorded to aid the families of the 188 people killed. While McCartney couldn't attend the sessions for *Ferry Aid*, held 14–16 March at PWL Studios in London, he did give permission for his vocal from which Beatles song to be sampled to open the song?

3. What is the title of the Canadian film set in 1964 that tells the story of the Beatles' upcoming concerts in Toronto and the rock group one young man forms with his friends to win a competition to see them?

4. Julian Lennon appeared at the Royal Albert Hall, 1 April, to reprise his role on Mike Batt's musical concept album, *The Hunting of the Snark* (issued by Epic/Adventure in the UK, 24 November 1986). Based on Lewis Carroll's 1874 poem "Snark," the one-time performance was in aid of the British Deaf Association. What role did Julian play?

5. On 30 May, a four-acre section of Griffith Park in Los Angeles was dedicated to the Beatles, featuring a grove of twenty-nine blossoming Cassia, Tipu and, appropriately, Tangerine trees. What is the name of the site, commemorated with a plaque mounted on a stone donated by Capitol Records?

6. At a party held at Abbey Road studios 1 June to celebrate the twentieth anniversary of the release of *Sgt. Pepper*, Roy Orbison proposed the idea to Paul of producing him on a cover of what Beatles song?

7. Produced by Phil Ramone during sessions in June, Paul's tribute to *Sgt. Pepper* was at one point said to have been planned for September release as a single, backed by "Love Come Tumbling Down." While the proposed B-side eventually surfaced in 1997 on one of the "Beautiful Night" CD singles, what was the title of the unreleased A-side?

8. Assisted by both Paul and George, a suggested title for this guitarist's album had been *Rockestra*. Who is he?

9. What songs comprised the first Beatles cassette single?

10. When disc jockey Alan Freeman observed his sixtieth birthday in July, Paul recorded a special gift for him. Aired 6 July on London's Capitol Radio, what Beatles song did McCartney remake for the occasion?

11. How had Paul originally envisioned releasing selections from the rock oldies he covered with various musicians, 20–21 July 1987?

12. Who was the only member of The Paul McCartney Band to work on the sessions that produced *CHOBA b CCCP*?

13. Paul called up Elvis Costello during the summer of 1987 to ask if he would like to write and record with him. They started by finishing off two songs, one each, begun individually—what were they?

14.   For their first true collaboration from scratch, Paul suggested to Elvis that they should sound like "Smokey (Robinson) & The Miracles." What is the title of the song that resulted?

15.   Rappers the Fat Boys (Mark "Prince Markie Dee" Morales, Darren "The Human Beat Box" Robinson, and Damon "Kool Rockski" Wimbley) play three bumbling orderlies hired to take care of a rich old man (Ralph Bellamy) in *Disorderlies*, first screened in U.S. theaters in August. What Beatles song did the film's producers get permission from Michael Jackson to cover in the film?

16.   What is the name of the Manchester band who issued a single on the Remorse label, 24 August, titled "Paul McCartney"?

17.   What is the title of the first Beatles bootleg CD?

18.   Jeff Lynne's coproduction of *Cloud Nine* opened a great many doors for the ELO founder, including membership in the Traveling Wilburys and the opportunity to coproduce the Beatles' reunion singles "Free As A Bird" and "Real Love." Who introduced Jeff to George?

19.   What is the title of the first song Jeff Lynne produced with George?

20.   Before coming up with *Cloud Nine*, what had George been thinking of calling his 1987 release?

21.   Harrison wasn't the first Beatle to reference "cloud nine" in his lyrics. In which of his songs did John mention this elative state?

22.   What song on *Cloud Nine* takes its title from an Alcoholics Anonymous brochure?

23.   What was the working title for "When We Was Fab"?

24.   Harrison came by the inspiration for what song while driving past "a church in a little country town in England"?

25.   In what song does George mention country blues singer/guitarist Big Bill Broonzy?

ANSWERS

1. Ringo received an injunction from an Atlanta court in November 1989 to block Lincoln "Chips" Moman (owner of Three Alarm Studios), from issuing the 1987 sessions he produced for Starr on his own CRS Records label.

(In January 1990, Moman was ordered to turn over the master tapes, which included the '50s classic "Ain't That A Shame." Ironically, the same year Ringo recorded his version, McCartney also covered the song 21 July, including it on his Russian album, *CHOBA b CCCP*. Had Starr released his version, it would have given the Antoine "Fats" Domino/Dave Bartholomew composition the unique distinction of having been covered by three of the four Beatles—John's version was included on his *Rock 'N' Roll* album).

2. Paul allowed his vocal from the Beatles' version of "Let It Be" to be used to open the Zeebrugge Ferry Disaster single, first issued by the *London Sun* in the UK, 23 March.

3. *Concrete Angels*.

(In 1964, the Beatles played two shows at Toronto's Maple Leaf Gardens the evening of 7 September. Beatles songs heard in the film were performed by the soundalike band 1964.)

4. Julian played the Baker in *The Hunting of the Snark*.

5. The Griffith Park site dedicated to the Beatles is called "Pepperland."

6. When Paul related to Roy how "Please Please Me" had originally been recorded and rejected by George Martin for sounding too much like an Orbison number (in Studio Two, 11 September 1962), Roy suggested McCartney produce him recording the song in that tempo.

(Roy had even hoped to get fellow Wilbury George Harrison to help out. Sadly, before the project ever got off the ground, Orbison died of a heart attack, 6 December 1988.)

7. McCartney titled his unreleased tribute to *Sgt. Pepper* "Return to Pepperland."

8. *Rockestra* was suggested at one point for the title of the album *Duane Eddy*, released by the guitar instrumentalist on Capitol, 19 June.

(With Paul contributing bass and backing vocals, Eddy recorded the "Rockestra Theme" at McCartney's Sussex studio, The Mill, 4 February. Moving to Harrison's Friar Park Studio, 10–11 February, Duane recorded the "The Trembler" and "Theme for Something Really Important" with George contributing his trademark slide guitar.)

9.   The first Beatles cassingle contained "All You Need Is Love" and "Baby You're a Rich Man," issued by EMI/Parlophone 6 July as part of the label's twentieth anniversary reissue campaign for the single.

(The first McCartney cassingle was a 2,000 copy limited edition release comprising "Pretty Little Head"/"Write Away"/"Angry," issued by Parlophone in the UK, 17 November 1986.)

10.   McCartney recorded an elaborate remake of "Sgt. Pepper's Lonely Heart's Club Band" for DJ Alan Freeman's sixtieth birthday.

(Opening lines: "It was sixty years ago today/Alan Freeman saw the light of day.")

11.   Paul originally wanted to package an album that made it appear that the Soviets had bootlegged some secret McCartney tapes and smuggled copies into England.

(When McCartney's personal manager, Richard Ogden, approached EMI with the idea they rejected it. "I was not pleased at all," Paul told journalist James Henke. "I said, 'We're boring these days, aren't we? We can't do that kind of shit. We're too elevated to have that kind of fun.' ")

12.   Drummer Chris Whitten was the only member of The Paul McCartney Band to also play on *CHOBA b CCCP*.

13.   McCartney would help Costello finish "Veronica," while Elvis helped Paul complete "Back On My Feet."

(Costello included "Veronica" on his album *Spike*, first issued by Warner Bros. in the U.S., 7 February 1989. McCartney issued "Back On My Feet" as the B-side of "Once Upon A Long Ago," released by Parlophone in the UK, 16 November 1987.)

14.   The first McCartney/MacManus collaboration from scratch was "The Lovers that Never Were," which Paul included on his 1993 album *Off the Ground*.

15.   In *Disorderlies*, the Fat Boys are seen making a video of themselves performing "Baby You're a Rich Man."

16. The Remorse single "Paul McCartney" (LOSS 5) was released by a Manchester band called Laugh.

17. A Beatles collector from the Northwestern part of the U.S. released the first *three* Beatles bootleg CDs simultaneously. Issued on the "EMI/Parlophone" label, they were vinyl mastered copies of the "Beatleg" LPs *Sessions* (CDP 7 48001), *At The Beeb Vol. 1* (CDP 7 48002) and *Get Back with Don't Let Me Down and 9 Other Songs* (CDP 7 48003).

(Manufactured by an unwitting US. East Coast pressing plant, each disc was limited to five hundred copies.)

18. Lynne was introduced to Harrison by Dave Edmunds.

19. Lynne's first production collaboration with Harrison was the instrumental "Zig Zag," recorded 18 July 1986 for the film soundtrack of *Shanghai Surprise* and released 25 January 1988 as the B-side of "When We Was Fab."

20. As a way of joking about his Beatle past, Harrison originally considered calling his 1987 album *Fab*.

21. "Nobody Loves You (When You're Down and Out)."
("Nobody knows you when you're on cloud nine.")

22. Harrison took not only the title, but adapted the first lines of "Just for Today" from a credo published by Alcoholics Anonymous.

("Just for today I will try to live through this day only, and not tackle all my problems at once." One of Harrison's favorite songs on *Cloud Nine*, George wrote "Just for Today" in 1984 "after I had some alcoholic friends over to the house. It was trying to tell people to relax, to not try and deal with everything at once, which I think is good advice for everyone. You don't need to be an alcoholic to be reminded to stay cool for one day.")

23. "When We Was Fab" first went by the working title "Aussie Fab."
(While vacationing in Australia with Jeff Lynne [to attend the Adelaide Grand Prix], Harrison decided he wanted to write a song evocative of the Beatles period. The Antipodian locale prompted the working title.)

24. George drew his inspiration for "The Devil's Radio" from a billboard outside a church he was driving past.

(The billboard read: GOSSIP—THE DEVIL'S RADIO. DON'T BE A BROAD-CASTER.)

25. George mentions Big Bill Broonzy in "Wreck of the Hesperus," included on *Cloud Nine*.

("I'm not the wreck of the Hesperus./Feel more like Big Bill Broonzy.")

1988

1. Which Beatles song title does Sir Arthur C. Clarke make reference to in his 1988 novel, *2061: odyssey three*?

2. Who inducted the Beatles at the third annual Rock and Roll Hall of Fame awards dinner at New York's Waldorf-Astoria Hotel, 20 January?

3. What marred the Beatles' induction into the Hall?

4. Which Beatles song does Joey "The Lips" Fagan claim to have played trumpet on, in Roddy Doyle's 1988 novel, *The Commitments*?

5. What is the title of Weird Al Yankovich's takeoff of "Got My Mind Set On You"?

6. This group's *Abbey Road* EP (released by EMI/Manhattan in May), shows them making the famous zebra-striped crossing nude, save for some strategically placed tube socks—who are they?

7. On 21 June, Australia jointly issued a series of four stamps with Great Britain commemorating the Australian Bicentenary. On one of the stamps, John Lennon is featured, sharing the honor with what prominent English writer?

8. What Beatles song does Raymond Babbitt sing with his brother Charlie in the 1988 film *Rain Man*?

9. What is the name of the song by U2 in which Bono comments on Albert Goldman's Lennon biography *The Lives of John Lennon*, published by William Morrow in the U.S, 22 August?

10. What Beatles song served as the opening theme song for *The Wonder Years*, which ran on ABC-TV in the U.S. from 1988 to 1993?

11. What is the connection between *The Wonder Years* and *A Hard Day's Night*?

12. David L. Wolper and Andrew Solt's documentary *Imagine: John Lennon*, had its world premiere 3 October in Los Angeles, attended by both Cynthia Lennon and Yoko Ono. When production of the film was made public in early 1987, what Beatles song was announced as the documentary's title?

13. During the recording of *Cloud Nine*, George and producer Jeff Lynne would fantasize about their ultimate rock 'n' roll band, which they called the "Trembling Wilburys." While the trembling evolved into traveling, what is the origin of the name "Wilbury"?

14. What is the title of the first song recorded for *Volume 1*? Where was this song recorded?

15. Where did George Harrison first meet his future Wilbury mates Roy Orbison, Bob Dylan, and Jeff Lynne?

16. What is the origin of Roy Orbison's Wilbury name, Lefty?

17. "Some people said Daddy was a cad and a bounder," recalled Lefty Wilbury. "I remember him as a Baptist minister." The Wilburys' dad is said to have fathered each of his five sons by as many mothers. What was his name?

18. Which Wilbury song derived some of its lyrics from random words selected from such magazines as *Vogue* and *Autosport*?

19. Who is Hugh Jampton?

20. *Stay Awake*, A&M Records collection of Disney movie song covers, was first issued in the U.S., 18 October. What song did Ringo contribute?

21. Paul McCartney and Andrei Gavrilov's comments are both featured here—where?

22. Returning to England following five weeks treatment for alcoholism at the Sierre Tucson clinic near Tucson, Arizona, 25 November, Ringo told journalist Robert Sandall that he wondered "what I was gonna do now that I don't drink and don't take stuff any more." What he did was form his first All-Starr Band. Who was the first person he called?

23. Late in 1988, two landmark Beatles CD bootlegs appeared sporting the Swingin' Pig label. Comprising a dozen cuts copied from EMI's vaults, another six from acetates and three further selections from a pristine copy of the *Sessions* tape, these two thirty-minute CDs stunned collectors—and EMI/Capitol—with their quality, inaugurating a new era of Beatlegs. What are the titles of these CDs?

24. The Wilburys had been planning to make a promotional video in Los Angeles, 10 December for what song, when Roy Orbison died of a heart attack, 6 December?

25. What is the title of the film in which thirteen-year-old Sean Lennon made his acting debut?

ANSWERS

1. *2061* mentions "Lucy In the Sky with Diamonds."

(Confirming that the composition of Mount Zeus on the planet Europa is a single diamond bigger than Mount Everest, Dr. Rolf van der Berg contacts Ganymede Central with the message "LUCY IS HERE. LUCY IS HERE." When Dr. Heywood Floyd later asks van der Berg if the code word Lucy was "anybody in particular," van der Berg responds that they "came across her in a computer search":

"I'd never heard of them, but a hundred years ago there was a group of popular musicians with a very strange name—the Beatles—spelled B-E-A-T-L-E-S, don't ask me why. And they wrote a song with an equally strange title: 'Lucy in the Sky with Diamonds.' Weird, isn't it? Almost as if they knew . . .")

2. The Beatles were inducted into the Rock and Roll Hall of Fame by Mick Jagger.

3. Calling it a "fake reunion," Paul McCartney refused to attend the induction.

(In a statement issued prior to the awards dinner, McCartney said, "The Beatles still have some business differences, which I had hoped would be settled by now. Unfortunately, they haven't been." Paul was referring to a lawsuit Harrison, Starr, and Yoko Ono filed against him in February 1985, accusing him of negotiating a higher royalty rate with EMI for himself on Beatles recordings without informing the others.)

4. "All You Need is Love."

(Naming off some of the people he's played with for Commitments manager Jimmy Rabbitte Jr., Joey recalls the time he played with the Beatles:

—The Beatles, said Jimmy.

—Money for jam, said Joey the Lips.—ALL YOU NEED IS LOVE—DOO DUH DOO DUH DOO.

—Was tha' you?

—Indeed it was me, Brother. Five pounds, three and six pence. A fair whack in those days.——I couldn't stand Paul, couldn't take to him. I was up on the roof for Let It Be. But I stayed well back. I'm not a very photogenic Brother. I take a shocking photograph.

With all due respect to Mr. Fagan, the real trumpet player on "All You Need is Love" was David Mason, who played the same trumpet he used for "Penny Lane," an 18-inch B-flat piccolo trumpet made by Couesnon of Paris.)

5. Weird Al's parody of "Got My Mind Set on You" is titled "(This Song's Just) Six Words Long," first released in the US in April on the Way Moby/Volcano album *Even Worse*.

6. The Red Hot Chili Peppers (Anthony Kiedis, Flea [Michael Balzary], Hillel Slovak, and Jack Irons) made the crossing one chilly morning in May 1988.

7. Designed by Gary Emery of Melbourne, John shares a 34 pence stamp (in Great Britain) and a $1 stamp (in Australia) with William Shakespeare, along with images of Sydney's Harbour Bridge and Opera House.

8. Raymond (Dustin Hoffman) and Charlie (Tom Cruise) sing "I Saw Her Standing There" in *Rain Man*.

9. In "God II," issued on the Island album *Rattle and Hum*, Bono has nothing good to say about Goldman's Lennon biography.

("Don't believe in Goldman. His type like a curse. Instant karma's gonna get him, if I don't get him first." Albert Goldman died of a heart attack, 28 March 1994.)

10. The opening credits to *The Wonder Years* played to Joe Cocker's version of "With a Little Help from My Friends."

(Beatles songs figured prominently in several episodes in the series, including "Blackbird" [episode 3, "My Father's Office"]; "I Want to Hold Your Hand" [episode 33, "Rock 'n' Roll"] and "All You Need is Love" [episode 37, "St. Valentine's Day Massacre"].)

11. Actress Olivia d'Abo (who played Karen Arnold on the show), is the daughter of Maggie London. In 1964, London had a small role as a showgirl in *A Hard Day's Night*.

(Olivia dated Julian Lennon for a time, after the two were introduced by mutual friends at d'Abo's twenty-first birthday party, 22 January 1988.)

12. "In My Life" was first announced as the working title of the *Imagine: John Lennon* documentary.

13. Harrison and Lynne had a habit of calling troublesome recording glitches "wilburys."

14. "Handle With Care" was the first song recorded for *Volume 1* in April at Bob Dylan's Malibu home studio, dubbed "Lucky Studios" for the occasion.

("Handle" was originally envisioned as the B-side of a German 12" single for "This Is Love," but Harrison deemed the end result too good to simply hide on a B-side and the Wilburys grew from there.)

15. George (and the other Beatles) first met Roy Orbison in 1963 as part of a UK package tour, which ran from 18 May to 9 June. The Beatles were introduced to Bob Dylan by journalist Al Aronowitz at New York's Delmonico Hotel, 28 August 1964, during the group's twenty-five-date tour of America and Canada. (Adjourning to a bedroom in their suite, Dylan then introduced the group to marijuana.) While a member of the Idle Race, Lynne was invited 10 October 1968 to Abbey Road to watch George and John add strings to "Glass Onion" in Studio Two and watched Paul and Ringo record "Why Don't We Do It in the Road" in Studio Three.

16. "My (Wilbury) name," remarked Orbison, "came from Lefty Frizzell, the country singer of the '50s who was a great inspiration to me and still is a favorite singer."

(Roy was backstage before a concert in Anaheim, California when George, Jeff, and Tom Petty asked him to complete the Wilburys' lineup.)

17. The Wilbury's Dad was Charles Truscott Wilbury, Sr.

18. In "Dirty World," the items denoted after each singing of the phrase "he loves your . . ." were compiled from a list of words read out of magazines each Wilbury was given. Bob Dylan was reading from a copy of *Autosport*, while Roy Orbison pored over an issue of *Vogue*.

19. Hugh Jampton, E. F. Norti-Bitz Reader In Applied Jacket, Faculty of Sleeve Notes, University of Krakatoa (East of Java) is in reality Monty Python alum Michael Palin, whose history of the original Wilburys graces *Volume 1*.

(Harrison once toyed with the idea of basing a full-length movie around Palin's sleeve notes. Hugh Jampton's origins date back to 1956, portrayed by Peter Sellers on the TV version of the *Goon Show, Idiot Weekly, Price 2d.*)

20. Featuring a trumpet solo by Herb Alpert, Ringo sang "When You Wish Upon A Star."

(Starr's cover was part of a medley following an instrumental titled "Desolation Theme.")

21. The liner notes on the back of the eleven-song first pressing of *CHOBA b CCCP*, released in the Soviet Union 31 October, were written by McCartney and Russian music journalist Andrei Gavrilov.

(Pronounced *Sno* va v'ess ess ess *ehr*, *CHOBA b CCCP* translates in English as *Again in the USSR* or *Back in the USSR*.)

22. Ringo's first call went to Joe Walsh.

("... a great guitarist and a good pal and he also produced my last album, Old Wave.")

23. Including alternate takes (in stereo) of "I Saw Her Standing There," "She's A Woman," and "Norwegian Wood," Swingin' Pig's CDs were titled *Ultra Rare Trax* Vols. 1 and 2.

24. At the time of Orbison's death, the Wilburys were preparing to shoot a video for "Last Night."

(The promo clip [and the single it was presumably intended to promote] were subsequently shelved, though not before a five-inch promo CD of "Last Night" was issued by Wilbury/Warner Bros. in the U.S. [PRO-CD-3337]. "End of the Line" was eventually selected as the second single from *Volume 1*, first issued in the U.S., 23 January 1989. The accompanying video [which debuted on MTV, 30 January], included a tribute to Orbison. While several prominent rockers were tapped in the press as Lefty's successor, including Eric Clapton, Roger McGuinn, Randy Newman, Carl Perkins, Del Shannon, and Bruce Springsteen, Roy was not replaced when the Wilburys assembled in 1990 to record their follow-up, *Vol. 3*.)

25. Sean made his acting debut in Michael Jackson's film *Moonwalker*.

(*Moonwalker* also features Jackson's cover of "Come Together.")

1989

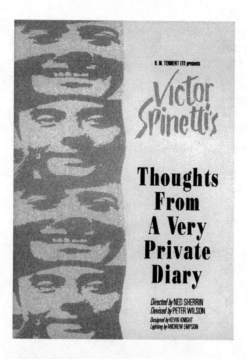

1. On 24 February, Rhino Records issued *Starr Struck: Best of Ringo Starr Vol. 2*, a compilation of post-EMI Ringo recordings. Its cover resurrected a Tom Wilkes photo of Starr taken at the Griffith Observatory in Los Angeles, originally intended for the cover of the 1981 album *Can't Fight Lightning*. Before Rhino could use the shot, they had to airbrush something out. What was it?

2. When producer Risty first got the go ahead from Rhino Records President Harold Bronson to compile the album that became *Starr Struck*, what was its working title?

3. Victor Spinetti opened a one-man show at the Donmar Warehouse Theatre in London's Covent Gardens, 27 February, the two-hour performance of recollections from the actor's life being what he called a substitute for writing a book. Naturally, anecdotes involving the Beatles figured prominently, including a recreation of the drill sergeant routine from *Magical Mystery Tour*, requiring volunteers from the audience to participate. What was the name of the show?

4. Debuting on MTV in the U.S., 10 April, whose video featured George playing guitar, Ringo behind the drums and Jeff Lynne on bass?

5. What song on *Flowers in the Dirt* did Paul describe as "me trying to be Big Bill Broonzy"?

6. "We imagined a Tom and Jerry cartoon, where there's an angel and a devil above, and one says, 'Go ahead, do it,' and the other says, 'No, don't do it.'" What song collaboration with Elvis Costello is Paul referring to?

7. In this McCartney song, what are like "butterflies . . . buzzing 'round my head"?

8. "The first verse is very John and Cyn," noted Paul of which song on *Flowers in the Dirt*?

9. Which song on *Flowers in the Dirt* was written in two thirty-minute sessions during a skiing holiday McCartney took in Zermatt, a village in southern Switzerland?

10. "Where is the sun? In the head. Work." Interesting . . . what does it mean?

11. What did EMI give Paul McCartney as a gift in honor of his forty-seventh birthday, 18 June?

12. Though he wouldn't provide a name, what song, recorded during the sessions for *Flowers in the Dirt*, did McCartney reveal was inspired by an American TV evangelist?

13. Kicking off at the Park Central Amphitheatre in Dallas, Texas, 23 July, who was in Ringo Starr's 1989 "All-Starr Band"?

14. What is the title of the Beastie Boys rap that samples *Sgt. Pepper* and *Abbey Road*?

15. When Ringo's All-Starrs played the Garden Arts Center in Holmdel, New Jersey, 11 August, Bruce Springsteen made a surprise appearance onstage, joining the band for the last four songs of the evening. On what Beatles song did the Boss share lead vocals with Billy Preston?

16. At a press conference at New York's Lyceum Theatre, 24 August, Paul announced the first round of U.S. dates on his World Tour. While noting the summer tours of Ringo's All-Starrs and the Who, these groups weren't what prompted him to hit the road—what group did?

17. What Beatles song served as the opening theme of *Life Goes On*, which ran in the U.S. on ABC-TV from 1989–1993?

18. Discussing his World Tour with David Fricke, Paul recalled that "Originally we were going to open with (this Beatles song). But I really got upset by the idea. I was going home one night and I thought, "That's really betraying our new material . . ." What song had McCartney initially considered opening his shows with?

19. What are "The Flowers in the Dirt," "Game Plan," "Lumpy Trousers," and "Paul McCartney's Think Tank"?

20. Who are the Three Degrees?

21. "Found my chops on Eel Pie Island" notes Harrison—in what song?

22. In 1989, First Maxi marketed a line of condoms with computer chips in their rims, programmed to play thirty-second samples of hit songs when body movements reach the desired pitch. Among the condoms initially offered by the London firm was one that played which Beatles tune?

23. What are "Woman" and "Morning, Noon and Night"?

24. What song from *Flowers in the Dirt* was issued in the UK in a "Club Lovejoys Mix"?

25. McCartney raised a few eyebrows at a Los Angeles press conference 27 November when he announced this corporate sponsor would be underwriting part of the 1990 American tour dates. Who had Macca signed on with?

ANSWERS

1. The eyes and the top of Barbara Bach's head can be seen in front of Starr in Tom Wilkes's original photo. According to Rhino Records producer Risty, Barbara insisted that she be airbrushed out before they used it.

(Previously, Tom Wilkes had taken the photographs for the booklet included in *The Concert for Bangla Desh* album.)

2. When Risty made his first proposed track list for *Starr Struck* in February 1988, its working title was *Starrdust*.

(Ringo didn't care for the title *Starrdust*, saying it sounded "too fruity" and "non-heavy." It was Ringo who came up with the title *Starr Struck* at a meeting at a Beverly Hills hotel Risty attended with Harold Bronson, 2 September 1988.)

3. Spinetti's two-act show (which ran through 1 April), was titled *Thoughts from a Very Private Diary*.

4. Harrison, Starr, and Lynne were featured players in Tom Petty's video for "I Won't Back Down."

(The first single from Petty's solo album, *Full Moon Fever*, the video was filmed at Pinewood Studios, London, 22–23 March.)

5. "Me trying to be Big Bill Broonzy" is Paul's description of "Rough Ride," included on *Flowers in the Dirt*, first issued by Parlophone in the UK, 5 June.

("I'd seen a blues program, and I thought, well these guys do a song and it's all one chord, two verses and a little guitar riff. That's all I had [when he brought the song to producers Trevor Horn and Steve Lipson], and it grew from nothing, (a) little 12-bar . . .")

6. Paul is referring to "You Want Her Too," included on *Flowers in the Dirt*.

7. Distractions.
(From "Distractions," released on *Flowers in the Dirt*.)

8. Paul was referencing John and first wife Cynthia Lennon in the first verse of "We Got Married."

("[T]hey were like art students and it was the first time I'd ever heard of anyone making love in the afternoon. I was about sixteen, and fairly 'Whaaat! In the afternoon? Whoo! It's like a French film!' I was fairly naive.")

9.   Paul wrote "Put It There" while on vacation in Zermatt, Switzerland.

   ("Put It There" is based on an old McCartney family saying, used "as a welcome," notes Mike McCartney in his 1981 autobiography *The Macs*—" 'put it there if it weighs a . . . ton,' to be announced on the full extent and a tight squeeze of the hand.")

10.   "Where is the sun? In the head. Work," is the English translation of Paul's French lyrics to the song "Ou est le Soleil," included as a bonus track on the CD and cassette versions of *Flowers in the Dirt* ("Ou est le soleil/Dan la tete/Travaillez.").

11.   As a special gift for his forty-seventh birthday, EMI arranged to have a medium pink hybrid tea rose grown in the South of France named The Paul McCartney (Meizeli).

   (EMI "picked" an excellent rose; in 1988 the bush hybrid tea, described as a "vibrant pink, with a strong fragrance," was awarded gold medals at competitions in Geneva, LeRoeix and Monza. The Paul McCartney was officially registered in Meillard, France in 1995.)

12.   At a press conference in Chicago, 3 December, McCartney stated that the inspiration for "The First Stone" (cowritten with Hamish Stuart) was a noted American TV evangelist (most likely Jimmy Swaggart).

   ("The First Stone" was first issued by Parlophone in the UK 17 July as the B-side of "This One.")

13.   The All-Starr band for Ringo's 1989 "Tour for All Generations" included Clarence Clemons (sax), Rick Danko (bass), Levon Helm (percussion), Mac Rebennack, aka Dr. John (keyboards), Jim Keltner (drums), Nils Lofgren (guitar), Billy Preston (keyboards and music director) and Joe Walsh (guitar).

14.   "The Sounds of Science," from the Beastie Boys' Capitol album *Paul's Boutique*, samples the orchestral warm-up and expectant audience from "Sgt. Pepper's Lonely Hearts Club Band," Ringo's drum opening from "Sgt. Pepper's Lonely Hearts Club Band (Reprise)," and the guitar riff and Ringo's drum solo from "The End."

15.   Springsteen and Preston sang "Get Back."

16. The Grateful Dead.

("Listen, you know, if Jerry [Garcia] can still do it that good . . . there's hope for us all.")

17. The opening credits to *Life Goes On* were accompanied by a version of "Ob-La-Di, Ob-La-Da" sung by the show's cast, featuring Patti DuPone, who played mother Elizabeth "Libby" Thatcher.

18. Paul had first considered opening his shows with "I Saw Her Standing There."

("[It was] like saying, 'Hey, I haven't been around for thirteen years and I haven't done anything worthwhile. Here's the Beatles stuff." McCartney opted instead to open with "Figure Of Eight," his current single from *Flowers in the Dirt* as the tour began.)

19. These were all vetted as possible names for the band who backed Paul on his 1989–1990 World Tour.

(Hamish Stuart, Robbie McIntosh, Chris Whitten, Wix [Paul Wickens], and Linda McCartney were eventually billed as The Paul McCartney Band.)

20. The Three Degrees (which included L.A. policeman Clay Tave) was the name given to the three black gentlemen in charge of security during the 1989–1990 Paul McCartney World Tour.

21. George mentions Eel Pie Island in "Cockamamie Business"—one of two new songs Harrison included as bonus tracks on his *Best of Dark Horse 1976–1989* album, first issued by Dark Horse/Warner Bros. in the U.S., 17 October.

(Junk shop worker Arthur Chisnall first opened the Eel Pie Island Hotel in Twickenham in April 1956 to host traditional jazz acts, but its glory days came after it switched to R&B beginning in 1964. The club was destroyed by fire in March 1971.)

22. First Maxi's Beatles condom played "Love Me Do."

23. "Woman" and "Morning, Noon and Night" are the names of the Cynthia Lennon line of herbal-based perfumes and colognes, produced by the Isle of Man perfumery Pierre de St. Jean.

24. "This One" was issued in a 6:10 "Club Lovejoys Mix."

(This mix was issued by Parlophone 13 November as the B-side of a

"Figure of Eight" twelve-inch, one of eight different formats released for the song, including two more on twelve-inch, three on CD and one each on seven-inch 45 and cassette. In October 1990, McCartney admitted to *New York Times* music critic Allan Kozinn that he really didn't like the multiple format release campaign used on *Flowers*. "It's actually gone mad, the whole business," he said. "Now what you get is groups of marketing people, you get your manager, with ideas. We do make some cool decisions, and like everyone, we make some uncool decisions.")

25. The Visa credit card company signed a tour-sponsorship deal with McCartney for the 1990 American dates, which started at the Palace of Auburn Hills in Detroit, 1–2 February.

(Visa began running its McCartney Tour TV commercial 14 January 1990. Trade magazine *Ad Age* reported that American Express had also tried unsuccessfully to sign McCartney. Paul noted in a *Rolling Stone* interview a few weeks later that the deal basically covered the cost of transport for the tour.)

1990

1. When Paul played bass on his World Tour, he alternated between his trademark Hofner violin-shaped "Beatle" bass, a customized Rickenbacker 4001, and a new axe, a Wal five-string. On whose recommendation did Paul invest in a Wal?

2. Who is Gertrude Higgins?

3. In whose novel does Paul McCartney appear portraying Kevin McHale in a docudrama on the L.A. Lakers?

4. At the Grammy Awards ceremony televised from Los Angeles' Shrine Auditorium, 21 February, McCartney made an appearance to accept a Lifetime Achievement Award. Following performances of "Eleanor Rigby" by Ray Charles and "We Can Work It Out" by Stevie Wonder, who presented Paul his Grammy?

5. In March, EMI Odeon in Japan issued a double CD version of *Flowers in the Dirt*. In addition to collecting many of the bonus tracks previously issued on twelve-inch and CD singles, the second disc included the only official release of "P.S. Love Me Do," a new studio arrangement of one of the only two Beatles songs controlled by McCartney's publishing company, MPL Communications. Who produced the new medley?

6. On 16 March, HandMade Films, the company George created with his (then) partner/manager Denis O'Brien in 1978, released what turned out to be its final film—*Nuns on the Run*, starring Eric Idle and Robbie Coltrane. What Harrison song is included in the film's soundtrack?

7. While McCartney's favorite British children's bear is Rupert, George made his preference known when he wrote the forward for a book about this black-and-white teddy in 1990. "[He] is a subtle character who, if you missed him in your own childhood, you may discover with your own child, as I did with my son." What is this bear's name?

8. This Paul McCartney Band composition was only issued commercially with the *Flowers in the Dirt World Tour Pack* and on the two-CD *Flowers in the Dirt* special Package released in Japan. What is the song?

9. With proceeds benefiting the Nordoff-Robbins Music Therapy Charity, over two dozen artists contributed covers to *The Last Temptation of Elvis*, first made available in the UK by mail from the *New Musical Express* starting 24 March. Bruce Springsteen covered "Viva Las Vegas," Vivian Stanshall took on "[There's] No Room to Rhumba In a Sports Car," while Robert Plant sang "Let's Have A Party." What song did Paul McCartney contribute?

10. First issued by Virgin in the UK 26 March, Gary Moore's album *Still Got the Blues* includes the Harrison composition "That Kind of Woman." Although Moore was the first to release the song (which George also produced), he wasn't the first to record it—who was?

11. Recorded in April during sessions for *Vol. 3*, "Nobody's Child" was issued by the Wilburys as the title track of a star-studded charity album benefitting the Romanian Angel's Appeal Fund. "I remembered that old song from the late '50s . . . Lonnie Donegan had it on one of his albums," Harrison told *Q* magazine. "I could remember a bit of how the tune went but I didn't know the words." What did George do?

12. No stranger to *The Guinness Book of World Records*, Paul added another entry, playing to the "largest paying audience ever attracted by a solo performer," with his stop on the World Tour in what city?

13. Yoko Ono staged an all-star tribute to John Lennon, 5 May, at the Pier Head in Liverpool to raise money for her Greening of the World John Lennon Scholarship Fund, with covers of Lennon's songs attempted by a varied field of performers during the 3½ hour show. While none of the surviving Beatles made an appearance, Ringo sent a video greeting which included a studio performance of "I Call Your Name," backed by Tom Petty, Jeff Lynne, and Jim Keltner. Paul did likewise, enclosing a concert performance with his band of "P.S. Love Me Do." What did George send?

14. Featuring George on acoustic guitar and backing vocals, what is the title of the Beatles song covered by The Jeff Healey Band?

15. McCartney saved his appearance at the Scottish Exhibition and Conference Centre arena in Glasgow, 23 June, for his only performance on The Paul McCartney World Tour of what song?

16. Paul had something special planned for the hometown crowd when he played the King's Dock in Liverpool, 28 June. "This is just a little tribute to someone we loved dearly," he announced before launching into his first public performance of John's songs, a medley consisting of "Strawberry Fields Forever," "Help!" and "Give Peace a Chance." McCartney only performed the piece once more—where?

17. The weekend of 7–8 July, Yoko took Sean to the Amsterdam Hilton to see the Presidential Suite, where John and Yoko conducted their seven-day bed-in for peace, 25–31 March 1969. While Yoko would not sleep in Room 902, she wanted Sean to do so, "he can then understand better how his father and mother felt in those days." What had the Hilton renamed the suite?

18. "My role in this is much different to the concert for Bangla Desh," George told Q of *Nobody's Child*, the Romanian Angel's Appeal album, first released by Warner Bros. in the UK 23 July. "This was more rallying 'round the troops and getting out the best record as possible that will get the appeal as much money as possible." To that end, George performed his job admirably, securing contributions from Eric Clapton, Billy Joel, Elton John, Van Morrison, and Stevie Wonder. While Harrison tried without success to get Michael Jackson and Bruce Springsteen to donate tracks, what two acts came up with songs too late to be included?

19. "I think I'd like to play guitar and be a beatle that would be so swell." What group sang this line in "All I Want Is Everything," included on their August 1990 debut on Charisma Records?

20. What are "Andy In the Garden," "Beach Towels," "Bowie Spewing," and "John's Room"?

21. Basic tracks exist for fourteen songs recorded by the Traveling Wilburys for *Vol. 3*, their follow-up to *Volume 1*, first released in the UK, 29 October. Of these, eleven appear on the album. Of the three held back, the first was a Jeff Lynne cover of "Runaway," which would surface as a bonus track in the UK on the CD single for "She's My Baby." What were the titles of the other two?

22. What song on *Vol. 3* makes reference to a band from Clayton Wilbury's past?

23. The liner notes for *Vol. 3* include a dissertation by Professor "Tiny" Hampton on the "etymological origins of the Traveling Wilburys" that's very silly. Who really wrote it?

24. What is ". . . plucked from the walls of damp caverns with ancient wooden tongs and dried by the breath of a young marsupial named 'Red,' " and combined with "lynneseed oil, savoy truffles, gator juice," and "absolutely sweet marie"?

25. In December, George filed suit against the *Globe*, seeking more than $200 million in damages, after the Florida-based tabloid paper refused to print a retraction to a story they ran in September stating that Harrison was an "admirer and fan" of whom?

ANSWERS

1. McCartney bought a Wal five-string on the recommendation of producer Trevor Horn.

("We had these jams in Docklands in London that turned into the Russian Album, and Trevor Horn showed up one time," McCartney told journalist Tony Bacon, "[A]nd he had a Wal five-string bass. I said, 'Oh, that's cool: low B, great.' So I got one too . . ." McCartney featured his Wal on "Free As Bird." "There's one lovely moment when it modulates to C, so I was able to use the low C of the five-string—and that's it, the only time I use the low one, which I like . . . it's a real cool moment that I'm proud of. That's my Wal moment.")

2. During the Paul McCartney World Tour, Paul would often introduce wife Linda to the audience as Gertrude Higgins.

(As to why the nom de plume, Paul told journalist Allan Kozinn, "It's difficult to know how to . . . introduce Linda with the history of it all. Because you don't want the wag in the crowd to boo her. And there's one in every crowd.")

3. Paul McCartney makes an appearance "in his first acting role, as Kevin McHale" in Thomas Pynchon's 1990 novel, *Vineland*.

(Other noted actors in this docudrama, "a story of transcendent courage on the part of the gallant but doomed L.A. Lakers, as they struggled under hellish and subhuman conditions at Boston Garden" include Sidney Poitier as K. C. Jones and Sean Penn as Larry Bird.)

4. Paul received his Lifetime Achievement Award from actress Meryl Streep.

(In her presentation speech Streep recalled being among the 55,600 screaming fans at the Beatles' first Shea Stadium concert, 15 August 1965, holding a sign that read "I Love You Forever Paul.")

5. Recorded in June 1987, the studio medley of "P.S. Love Me Do" was produced by Phil Ramone.

6. The soundtrack of *Nuns on the Run* includes "Blow Away," from George's 1979 album *George Harrison*.

(In May 1994, HandMade was acquired for $8.5 million by the Toronto-based Paragon Entertainment Corp.)

7. Sooty the Bear.

(Harrison's quote is from his forward for *The Secret Life of Sooty*, by Geoff Tibballs. In 1980 Harrison wrote and demoed the song "Sooty Goes to Hawaii," which remains unreleased.)

8. Credited to P. McCartney/L. McCartney/McIntosh/Stuart/Whitten/Wickens, "Party Party" was only included (as a bonus 45/CD3) on the *Flowers in the Dirt World Tour Pack* and as part of a second bonus tracks compilation CD included in the *Flowers in the Dirt* special package issued in March by EMI/Odeon in Japan.

9. *The Last Temptation of Elvis* includes Paul's cover of Presley's 1960 hit "It's Now or Never" (an adaptation of Eduardo di Capua's 1899 Italian song "O Sole Mio").

(The first artist approached by Roy Carr, the *NME's* Special Projects editor, McCartney had recorded his contribution during the 20–21 July 1987 sessions in London that had produced *CHOBA b CCCP*.)

10. Eric Clapton recorded a version of "That Kind of Woman" during sessions for his *Journeyman* album in 1989, but opted not to include it in the release.

(Clapton's version eventually surfaced on the charity album *Nobody's Child: Romanian Angel Appeal*, first issued by Warner Bros. in the UK, 23 July.)

11. Harrison phoned Joe Brown in London, who remembered the first verse. Unable to secure the second verse, George wrote a new one relevant to the Romanian orphans.

(The Beatles backed Tony Sheridan on a version of "Nobody's Child" recorded at the Friedrich Ebert Halle, Hamburg, 22–33 June 1961. "Nobody's Child" was first issued in [West] Germany on *The Beatles' First* by Polydor, in April/August 1964.)

12. Attendance at McCartney's second show at the Maracana Stadium in Rio de Janeiro, 21 April, was estimated between 180,000 and 184,000.

(McCartney received an award from *The Guinness Book of World Records* for the record-breaking show at a presentation during the End of the World Tour Party at *Boardwalk*, a restaurant in London's Soho district, 12 December.)

13. George did not participate in Yoko's tribute concert, saying that he found the whole show in bad taste.

14. The Jeff Healey Band's cover of "While My Guitar Gently Weeps" includes overdubbed acoustic guitar and backing vocals from George and Jeff Lynne.

(A popular number in their live sets, Healey's "Guitar" was included on *Hell to Pay*, issued by Arista in May 1990. Harrison's overdubs were done at Rumbo Recorders in Los Angeles in February during sessions for Lynne's *Armchair Theatre* album.)

15. Accompanied by the Power of Scotland Pipe Band, Paul performed "Mull of Kintyre" for 11,000 appreciative Scots during his encore at the SECC in Glasgow.

16. Paul performed his Lennon medley once more during his forty-five-minute set for the 120,000 people gathered 30 June in Knebworth Park for Knebworth '90, a day-long benefit for the Nordoff-Robbins Centre in London and the British Recording Industry Trust (BRIT) Performing Arts and Technical School.

17. The Amsterdam Hilton had renamed the Presidential Suite on the seventh floor the "John and Yoko Suite."

18. Both Steve Winwood and Queen had tracks to donate to *Nobody's Child*, but delivered them too late to be included.

19. Sung by Andy Sturmer, "All I Want is Everything" is on *Bellybutton*, the debut album by Jellyfish.

20. These are all titles of paintings Paul did in 1990.

(These titles were among the seventy-three oil and acrylic works in *The Paintings of Paul McCartney*, an exhibit which ran at the Lyz Art Forum in Siegen, Germany from 1 May to 25 July 1999. Describing "John's Room" as "a new encounter with familiar faces, like in a dream," McCartney identifies the figure crouching in a red robe as John Lennon along with a profile of former manager Brian Brolly.)

21. In addition to "Runaway," the songs left off *Vol. 3* include "Maxine," sung by George, and "Like A Ship," sung by Bob Dylan.

(Lynne's cover of the Del Shannon hit was likely a nod to an early influence. Jeff was turned on to music at the age of thirteen after his father bought him a ticket to a Del Shannon concert.)

22. "Cool Dry Place" makes reference to Jeff Lynne's late sixties outfit The Idle Race.

("I paid my first subscription/Then I joined the Idle Race/And they said 'store it in a cool dry place.' " In 1966, nineteen-year-old Lynne joined a Birmingham band called The Nightriders as a guitarist. The group changed their name to the Idle Race, with Lynne fronting the band and writing most of the material on their two LPs. Lynne left the group in 1970 to join the Move.)

23. Tiny Hampton was the pseudonym for Eric Idle, who is among those thanked in the album's credits for *Vol. 3*.

24. "Wil-Berries" plucked in the manner prescribed from the walls of damp caverns and combined with the aforementioned ingredients produces *Genuine Wil-Berry Jam*.

25. George sued the *Globe* after they ran a story calling him an "admirer and a fan of Adolf Hitler and Nazism."

1991

1.   Issued by Virgin 15 January, the Peace Choir's version of "Give Peace a Chance" included new lyrics, updating the song to comment on events and issues of the new decade and the new war (the Iraq invasion of Kuwait). Who wrote the revised lyrics?

2.   With new drummer Blair Cunningham, McCartney and his band were taped at Wembley's Limehouse Studios, 25 January, for the MTV series *Unplugged*, first aired in the U.S., 3 April. Beating bootleggers to the punch, Paul issued a numbered, limited edition album, *Unplugged: The Official Bootleg*, first released in the UK, 20 May. What had been McCartney's initial choice for the album's title?

3.   John Lennon was posthumously presented with a Lifetime Achievement Award at the Grammy Awards ceremony held at Radio City Music Hall in New York, 20 February. Musical tributes included Tracy Chapman singing "Imagine" and Aerosmith singing what song?

4. George appeared onstage at the Winter Gardens in Blackpool, 3 March at a convention of fans of British music hall star George Formby. What song did Harrison sing, accompanying himself on ukulele?

5. Who did Sean Lennon write his first credited song with, included on this artist's album released by Virgin America, 2 April?

6. Ringo Starr was the first Beatle to do a guest voice (as himself) for *The Simpsons*, during the show's second season. What was the episode's title, first aired on FOX-TV in the U.S., 11 April?

7. At a news conference hosted by the McCartneys at London's Savoy Hotel, Linda's line of frozen veggie convenience foods was launched in the UK, 29 April. What Wings song was used in commercials?

8. In May, Yoko Ono took exception to a recitation of the opening lines of "Watching The Wheels" heard at the start of "Lies," a track on *Schubert Dip*, the Parlophone/EMI debut album by the Cinderford, England band EMF. While Yoko's lawyers cited breach of copyright on the words, her displeasure is likely to have originated with the identity of the person EMF sampled reciting "Wheels"—who was it?

9. During May, June, and July, Paul played a half dozen "secret gigs" with his band at intimate venues in Spain, Italy, Denmark, and the UK. What band did McCartney make arrangements to switch dates with for the opening show at the Zeleste club in Barcelona, 8 May?

10. Who sang "Good Day Sunshine" for a commercial advertising Frito-Lay's *Sun Chips*?

11. What two McCartney/MacManus compositions did Elvis Costello include on his album *Mighty Like A Rose*, issued by Warner Bros. in the U.S., 14 May?

12. On 28 May, Walt Disney Records issued *For Our Children*, a charity album benefiting the Pediatric AIDS Foundation. The CD includes Paul's "Mary had a Little Lamb" from 1972, plus a cover of "Golden Slumbers"— who sings this?

13. In June, Barbara accompanied Ringo at the opening of daughter Lee Starkey's Los Angeles clothing boutique. Regular customers might even have seen mother Maureen helping out in the Melrose Avenue shop. What was it called?

14. George used the Japanese tour "as a motive" to quit doing something—what was it?

15. Who are Shanty and Mary Dee?

16. "War," the first movement of *Paul McCartney's Liverpool Oratorio*, opens with the singing of the Latin motto *"Non Nobis Solum Sed Toti Mundo"* by a boy soloist and boy's choir. What is the significance of the phrase to McCartney?

17. First released in July 1991, what is the name of the five-man Toronto folk-pop band who came to prominence with the song "Be My Yoko Ono"?

18. At his 19 July show at the Cliffs Pavilion in Westcliff-on-Sea, near Southend England, Paul's special guest between sets was poet Adrian Mitchell. Mitchell read four poems, three backed by Macca and the band. For the poem "Maybe Maytime," what McCartney composition was played?

19. In this 1991 Australian film, viewers regard the lives of five Australian teenagers trapped in the basement of the Melbourne hotel where the Beatles are staying in 1964. What is the title of this film, directed by Michael Pattinson?

20. During the recording of *Help Yourself*, Julian Lennon's fourth album, Jules asked George if he could provide one of his distinctive slide guitar solos to this cut. What song did George receive tapes for?

21. In 1991, Epic released *The Greatest Hits* compilation for Cheap Trick, which includes a previously unreleased cover of "Magical Mystery Tour." What Beatles song is sampled on the cut?

22. Produced by Steve Dorff in Los Angeles 14 September at the conclusion of sessions with Peter Asher for his *Time Takes Time* album, Ringo recorded "You Never Know," heard over the closing credits of what film?

23. *Get Back*, Paul McCartney's feature film of his 1989–90 World Tour had its world premiere 18 September at the Passage Kino in Hamburg,

Germany. According to director Richard Lester, how had Paul originally envisioned opening the film?

24. George toured Japan for the first time in December, playing twelve dates in six cities with Eric Clapton and his band. What two songs did Harrison play opening night at the Yokohama Arena, Yokohama, 1 December, and no where else?

25. During shows in Osaka (12 December) and Tokyo (15, 17 December), what did drummer Steve Farrone do to augment George's performance of "Piggies"?

ANSWERS

1. The Peace Choir's version of "Give Peace a Chance" included new lyrics credited to Sean Lennon.

2. The *International CD Exchange* (ICE) reported that Paul had initially planned to call his *Unplugged* album *Bootleg*.

3. The Future Villain Band returns! Aerosmith performed "Come Together" at the Grammy Awards.

4. George sang "In My Little Snapshot Album."
(Harrison also joined in an ensemble singalong that included "Mr. Woo" and "With My Little Stick of Blackpool Rock." George's comments on Formby [recorded during the Blackpool convention] were included in *The Emperor of Lancashire*, a documentary aired on BBC Radio Two, 26 May. John can be heard uttering the George Formby catchphrase, "Turned out nice again" [which the performer used to end to his act], when the backwards vocals heard at the end of the Beatles' 1995 reunion single "Free as a Bird" are played forwards. Harrison called the ukulele "one instrument you can't play and not laugh," in an introduction he penned 2 February 1999 for the songbook *Jumpin' Jim's '60s Uke-In*. "I love them— the more the merrier—everyone I know who is into the ukulele is 'crackers' so get yourself a few and enjoy yourselves.")

5. Lenny Kravitz included "All I Ever Wanted," his collaboration with Sean Lennon, on his second album, *Mama Said*.
(Sean also plays piano on the song.)

6. Ringo's guest voice for *The Simpsons* was for episode #7F18, "Brush with Greatness."

(Starr felt honored to be asked, telling *Q* magazine in 1998 "I thought the storyline was cute—I'm still in my room signing the fan mail, which I am of course. So if you're out there and I haven't answered yet, just hold on! I'll get round to it." Obviously big Beatles fans, the producers of *The Simpsons* have frequently referenced the group. In "Last Exit to Springfield" [#9F15, first aired 11 March 1993], Lisa's hallucinations while under gas in an orthodontist's office parody *Yellow Submarine*. A "couch gag" from season eight [first shown in "Bart After Dark," #4F06, 24 November 1996], has the Simpsons converging on their couch dressed in "Sgt. Pepper" uniforms. Their living room, filled with the citizens of Springfield, becomes a version of the album cover, including donuts that spell out "Simpsons." Homer, dressed as Paul, completes the gag by turning his back to face the viewers.)

7. Commercials introducing Linda's frozen vegetarian dishes featured "Cook of the House."

(Interviewed for the June 1998 issue of *VIVA! Life* magazine, Paul revealed to Juliet Gellatley that McCartney's advisors had originally suggested the veggie line be called "Paul McCartney Foods" ". . . but that sounded too Beatley. It didn't ring true. So it was Linda McCartney, mother and cook.")

8. EMF (Epson Mad Funkers) had sampled John's killer, Mark David Chapman, reciting the opening lines of "Watching The Wheels."

(To avoid an injunction against sales of the album, which had already sold a half million copies in the U.S. three weeks after its release, EMF agreed to cut the sample from all future pressings of *Schubert Dip* and pay a royalty on all copies sold that included it.)

9. McCartney made arrangements with British band The Godfathers to switch dates so he could play Barcelona's Zeleste club on Wednesday, 8 May.

10. Carly Simon sang "Good Day Sunshine" for a Frito-Lay's Sun Chips commercial.

11. *Mighty Like a Rose* includes two McCartney/MacManus collaborations, "So Like Candy" and "Playboy to a Man."

(Elvis also mentions Paul's former writing partner on *Mighty* in the song "The Other Side of Summer," its lyrics at one point asking, "Was it a millionaire who said 'imagine no possessions'?")

12. Jackson Browne and Jennifer Warnes duet on "Golden Slumbers."

13. Lee's shop (which she coowned with Christian Paris) was called Planet Alice.

14. Beginning in June, Harrison used the tour (then in the planning stages), as his motive to quit smoking, which he successfully did.

15. Shanty is the name of the protagonist in *The Paul McCartney Liverpool Oratorio*, first sung by tenor Jerry Hadley at the composition's world premiere, 28 June, at the Anglican Cathedral in Liverpool. Mary Dee, who becomes Shanty's wife, was first sung by soprano Dame Kiri Te Kanawa.

16. *"Non Nobis Solum Sed Toti Mundo Nati"* ("Not for ourselves, but for the whole world were we born") was the Latin motto of the Liverpool Institute, a feature of the patches sewn onto the black uniform blazers of boys (Paul and George among them) attending "the Inny."

(The motto was subsequently retained by the Liverpool Institute's successor, the Liverpool Institute for the Performing Arts, which opened in 1996.)

17. The Barenaked Ladies got their big break when "Be My Yoko Ono," on their eponymously titled cassette EP (also known as *The Yellow Tape*), became the first independent release in Canadian music history to go gold.

(The pro-Ono song, sung by cowriter Steven Page, was also included on the group's major label debut, *Gordon*, released by Sire/Reprise, 28 July 1992.)

18. Mitchell read "Maybe Maytime" as Paul and his band played "Singalong Junk."

19. *One Crazy Night.*

(The Beatles performed six shows over three nights at the Festival Hall in Melbourne, 15–17 June 1964, staying at the Southern Cross Hotel in Swanston Street.)

20. Julian asked George if he would contribute a guitar solo to "Salt-water."

(While the resulting tape contributed a few ideas, Lennon told *Beatlefan* contributing editor Ken Sharp that "George was not that focused," which he attributed to the recent death of Eric Clapton's four-year-old son, Conor [20 March]. The final solo, played by guitarist Steve Hunter, while including some of Harrison's input, was mostly Julian's.)

21. Cheap Trick's great cover of "Magical Mystery Tour" includes two samples from "I Am the Walrus."

22. Cowritten by Steve Dorff and John Bettis, "You Never Know" is heard over the closing credits of *Curly Sue*, included on the soundtrack album, first issued by Giant Records in the U.S., 26 November.

23. Having given Friends of the Earth access to his 1989–90 concerts to distribute information about their work, Paul had wanted to open *Get Back* with a sequence where he is seen walking through a rainforest talking about ecology and conservation, an idea Lester was not keen on.

24. George played "Fish On the Sand" (from *Cloud Nine*) and "Love Comes to Everyone" (from *George Harrison*) in Yokohama then dropped them for the remainder of the tour, which concluded at the Tokyo Dome Stadium, 17 December.

25. During "Piggies," drummer Steve Farrone danced about the stage wearing a pig mask.

1992

1. Who was nominated for a Grammy for Best Hard Rock Performance With Vocal for their cover of "Live and Let Die"?

2. On 2 March, Rykodisc issued *Onobox*, a six-CD, 105-track Yoko Ono retrospective, featuring *A Story*, a previously unreleased album Yoko recorded during her separation from John in 1973–74. A 300-copy signed limited edition version of the set, *Onobox Ultracase*, was also available. Each copy included a sculpture—what was the title of the piece?

3. In March, comedian Eddie Murphy flew to London to record Paul's vocal for "Yeah," included on Murphy's *Love's Alright* album, released on Motown Records, 23 February 1993. McCartney agreed to contribute to the all-star track (which also features Jon Bon Jovi, Garth Brooks, Michael and Janet Jackson, Elton John, and Stevie Wonder) if Murphy agreed to do something for one week. What did Eddie agree to do?

4. Three days before the British National Election, George staged a benefit concert for this new political party at the Royal Albert Hall, 6 April. "I believe this party offers the only option to get out of our problems

and create the beautiful nation we would all like to have," stated Harrison in a flyer promoting the show. What party was George endorsing?

5. When director Christopher Munch wrote the screenplay for his fictionalized account of Brian's Spanish holiday with John in 1988, he had originally considered not naming his characters Epstein and Lennon, "but in the end the power of the story seemed diminished by not being about them." What is the title of Munch's film, screened at London's gay film festival in April?

6. What Lennon song did Nike use in commercials for its running shoes, which began airing 1 May?

7. Who did Ringo Starr get to produce *Time Takes Time*, first issued on Private Music in the U.S., 12 May?

8. The first song credited to McCartney/Starkey is "Really Love You," included on Paul's 1997 album *Flaming Pie*. Had things gone differently, *Time Takes Time* might've had that distinction had what song been included on the album?

9. What is Ringo saying at the end of "What Goes Around," the closing cut on *Time Takes Time*?

10. What are "Right," "Wrong," "Justice," "Punishment," "Payment," and "Release"?

11. Sweden's King Carl Gustav conferred on Paul his country's first award of this prize, having been cited by the Royal Swedish Academy of Music "for his creativity and imagination as a composer and artist which has revitalized popular music worldwide over the last thirty years." What is the name of the prize McCartney received?

12. Opening night of the 1992 version of Ringo's "All-Starr Band" saw the tour at the Sunrise Pavilion in Fort Lauderdale, Florida, 2 June. Who was in Ritchie's band this time around?

13. First aired in the UK on Channel 4, 6 June, the music documentary *Mr. Roadrunner* includes a 1991 film clip of George performing what song?

14. A time capsule was buried on the grounds of Capitol Records' Tower headquarters, 11 June. What of Beatle note was included in it?

15. In a commercial seen only in Japan, Sean Lennon is shown rinsing his hair with a product from the Shiseido Dungaree line of male cosmetics. What John Lennon song accompanied the ad?

16. Harrison's two-CD *Live in Japan* (first issued in the U.S. by Dark Horse/Warner Bros., 13 July) includes a version of "Taxman," recorded 15 December at the Tokyo Dome Stadium. Harrison's revised lyrics no longer referred to Mr. (Harold) Wilson and Mr. (Edward) Heath. Who is mentioned instead?

17. Speculating on the destinies of the Kennedy family, the science fiction anthology *Alternate Kennedys* features cover art by Barclay Shaw of note for being a parody of what Beatles album?

18. In this short story by Ian R. MacLeod, John leaves the Beatles (Paul, George, Stu and Ringo) in 1962, refusing to go along with the group when George Martin offers them the chance to record "How Do You Do It." The single (sporting "Love Me Do" as its B-side) takes off and the Beatles are on their way. Now fifty, "Dr. Winston O'Boogie" lives in Birmingham working for the Civil Service when the Beatles' "Greatest Hits Tour" comes to the NEC. What is the title of MacLeod's short story?

19. As this novel opens, it is twenty years after Nazi Germany's victory in World War II. Reading through the arts pages of the *Berliner Tageblatt* for April 13, 1964, Berlin detective Xavier March comes across "a piece by the music critic attacking the 'pernicious Negroid wailings' of a group of young Englishmen from Liverpool who were playing to packed houses of German youths in Hamburg." What is the title of this book where this alternate time line finds the Beatles still paying their dues in Hamburg?

20. In addition to singing "Girls Talk" and "I Hear You Knocking," what Beatles song did Dave Edmunds frequently feature as a guitar instrumental during Ringo Starr and His All-Starr Band's summer tour?

21. Ringo wound up the tour with four shows at Caesar's Palace in Las Vegas, Nevada, 4–6 September. A highlight the first night was a rare onstage appearance by Harry Nilsson. What song did he sing with the All-Starrs?

22. On 16 October, Harrison appeared at an all-star salute to Bob Dylan at Madison Square Garden, his first U.S. concert appearance in eighteen years. What two Dylan songs did he perform?

23. When Frank Zappa released his version 3 November, it was titled "A Small Eternity with Yoko Ono." What had John and Yoko called it?

24. During an interview included in the 5 December issue of *Billboard* magazine, George stated that for the last forty-nine years, he's been doing this on the wrong day—what was it?

25. Paul and his band spent the evening of 10–11 December in New York City taping an *Up Close* program for MTV. Following a run through of "Twenty Flight Rock," Macca told the audience, "I got the strangest feeling of deja vu. I feel like I've been here, I don't know what it was. Some previous life, probably." Where was the program taped?

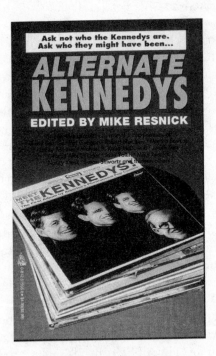

ANSWERS

1. Guns N' Roses were nominated for a Grammy in the Best Hard Rock Performance With Vocal category for their cover of "Live and Let Die."

(The Gunners lost out to Van Halen at the 34th annual Grammy Awards, held 25 February at New York's Radio City Music Hall in New York City. "Live and Let Die" was included on *Use Your Illusion I*, issued by Warner Bros., 17 September 1991.)

2. The *Onobox Ultracase* sculpture was titled "A Key to Open the Universe."

3. McCartney agreed to sing on "Yeah" if Murphy would become a vegetarian for one week.

(*Love's Alright* also includes a cover of "Good Day Sunshine.")

4. Founded in mid-March by the Maharishi Mahesh Yogi(!), George's Albert Hall concert 6 April was a benefit for the Natural Law Party.

(Ringo joined George onstage, taking his place behind a second drum kit for encores of "While My Guitar Gently Weeps" [featuring Gary Moore] and "Roll Over Beethoven" [with Joe Walsh].)

5. Starring Ian Hart as John and David Angus as Brian, *The Hours and Times* is director Christopher Munch's fictionalized account of their holiday in Spain, from 28 April to 9 May 1963.

(Munch acknowledges the visual influence of D. A. [Donn Alan] Pennebaker's 1967 Dylan documentary *Don't Look Back* on "Hours." "It's utterly specific to that time. Those images recall that period.")

6. Nike's running shoe commercials used "Instant Karma!"

(The $800,000 Yoko Ono received to approve its use was donated to the United Negro College Fund.)

7. Ringo used *four* people to produce the tracks on *Time Takes Time*—Peter Asher, Jeff Lynne, Phil Ramone, and Don Was.

8. Paul contributed "Angel in Disguise" to the *Time Takes Time* sessions, to which Ringo added a third verse.

(Recorded during sessions in 1991, the song remains in the can. "It just didn't fill the space on the album," Starr explained to journalist Allan Kozinn in April 1992.)

9. Ringo says "We're all the same," at the end of "What Goes Around."

10. These are the titles of the six instrumental pieces Paul composed for *Daumier's Law*, the fifteen-minute animated film created by Paul, Linda, and animator Geoff Dunbar, based on the drawings of nineteenth century French artist Honore Daumier.

(Begun in mid-1989 at Dunbar's London-based Grand Slamm Productions company, the film was finished just before Christmas 1991. *Daumier's Law* had its world premiere in May 1992 at the Cannes Film Festival. A Daumier drawing is featured on the sleeve for the etched disk 12" single "Figure of Eight"/"Ou est le Soleil?" issued by Parlophone in the UK, 20 November 1989.)

11. On 18 May, Paul McCartney, along with the Baltic States of Estonia, Latvia, and Lithuania, became the premiere recipients of Sweden's Polar Music Prize.

(McCartney divided the prize money, 1 million Kronar [$172,000], between donations to his local hospital and toward establishing the Liverpool Institute of the Performing Arts. Other musicians of Beatle note who have won the Polar in the years ensuing include Elton John [1995], Ravi Shankar and Ray Charles [1998], Stevie Wonder [1999], and Bob Dylan [2000].)

12. In addition to 1989 "All-Starr Band" alumni Joe Walsh (guitar) and Nils Lofgren (guitar), the 1992 band included Tim Capello (sax, percussion, keyboards), Burton Cummings (keyboards, guitars), Dave Edmunds (guitar), Todd Rundgren (guitar, keyboards), Timothy B. Schmit (bass) and Ringo's son, Zak Starkey (drums).

13. Accompanying himself on ukulele, Harrison is seen performing "Between The Devil and the Deep Blue Sea" on *Mr. Roadrunner*.

14. A letter from Paul McCartney was included in Capitol's time capsule.

15. "Beautiful Boy" was used in Sean Lennon's commercial for Shiseido Dungaree.

(Sean has also done a commercial in Japan for Seiko watches.)

16. Harrison's revised "Taxman" mentions Mr. Major, (John Major, leader of Britain's Conservative Party) and Mr. Kinnock (Neil Kinnock, leader of the Labour Party).

(A new verse about V.A.T.s [value-added tax], also mentions Boris Yeltsin [then president of the USSR] and Mr. Bush [U.S. president George Bush].)

17. Barclay Shaw's *Alternate Kennedys* cover art, *Meet the Kennedys!* is a takeoff on the cover of Capitol's *Meet the Beatles!*

(Shaw's cover most closely relates to Judith Tarr's short story "Them Old Hyannis Blues," where the singing Kennedy Brothers are seen performing at President Presley's Inaugural Ball, being held at the Richie Valens Center for the Performing Arts. Among those in attendance is Secretary Lennon.)

18. MacLeod's short story is titled "Snodgrass."

(While attending the Liverpool College of Art, John Lennon was remembered by fellow student Helen Anderson for "pick [ing] on all kinds of characters in school, whatever their backgrounds, and try[ing] to find some way of laughing at them. There was one, awfully nice well brought-up fellow with frizzy red hair, whom John persisted in annoying by calling him Snodgrass and making everyone laugh. [It was] 'Snoddy' this and 'Snoddy' that, to the annoyance of this very straight student.")

19. In the April 1964 of Robert Harris's first novel *Fatherland*, the Beatles are still playing the clubs of Hamburg.

(In the real Beatles time line, the boys were in the midst of filming *A Hard Day's Night* during this period. Having completed their final thirteen-night stint at the Star-Club, 31 December 1962, the group would not return to Hamburg until their final concert tour in 1966, playing two shows at the Ernst Merck Halle, 26 June.)

20. During many of the shows on the All-Starr Band's summer tour, Dave Edmunds was featured in a solo spot playing an instrumental version of "Lady Madonna."

(During the All-Starrs' show at Liverpool's Empire Theatre, 6 July, Todd Rundgren sang "You've Got to Hide Your Love Away" during his solo spot.)

21. Harry joined Ringo and the All-Starrs to sing "Without You" in the Circus Maximus Showroom at Caesar's Palace, 4 September.

22. George performed "If Not for You" and "Absolutely Sweet Marie," backed by a house band including Booker T. (Jones) and M.G.'s alumni Steve Cropper and Donald "Duck" Dunn.

(Later in the concert, Harrison took a verse in an all-star version of "My Back Pages." "Absolutely Sweet Marie" was included on *Bob Dylan: A 30th Anniversary Celebration Concert*, issued by Sony in the U.S., 24 August 1993. A three-CD German version of the album collects both of Harrison's solo spots.)

23. "A Small Eternity With Yoko Ono" is the title of Frank Zappa's mix of "Au," taken from John and Yoko's appearance with Frank and the Mothers of Invention at New York's Fillmore East, 6 June 1971.

(John and Yoko's "Au" appeared on the "free live jam LP" included with *Sometime in New York City* in 1972. Zappa's mix was issued in 1992 on his Barking Pumpkin label release *Playground Psychotics*. Frank's other title amendment was "Jamrag," which was presented as two tracks, "Say Please" and "Aaawk." Zappa died following a long battle with prostate cancer, 4 December 1993.)

24. For the last forty-nine years, Harrison had been celebrating his birthday on the wrong day.

(George told *Billboard* that he discovered that he was actually born at 11:42 P.M. on 24 February 1943, not 25 February as has been widely noted.)

25. McCartney filmed his *Up Close* special at The Ed Sullivan Theater at Broadway and West 53rd Street in midtown Manhattan.

(On 9 February 1964, CBS Television's Studio 50, as it was then known, was where the Beatles' first live television performance in the U.S. was broadcast on *The Ed Sullivan Show*.)

1993

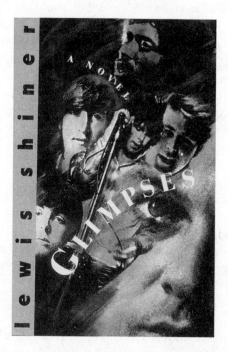

1. McCartney and his band spent the month of January rehearsing at the London Arena, Docklands, in preparation for their New World Tour, which kicked off 14 April at the Sam Boyd Silver Bowl in Las Vegas. Because of the rehearsals, Paul had to decline an invitation to play where, the night of 19 January?

2. What noted poet did Paul ask to "poet proof" read the lyrics to *Off the Ground*?

3. From left to right, whose feet are whose in Clive Arrowsmith's photo for the cover of *Off the Ground*?

4. When MTV premiered its *Up Close* program on Paul McCartney, 3 February, the ninety-minute special offered nineteen of the twenty songs from Macca's set list, selected from the two nights he taped in New York last December. What song was omitted?

5. During a press conference in Las Vegas, 14 April, what major sporting event did Paul say he turned down an invitation to perform at?

6. The pre-concert music on the New World Tour featured several McCartney covers, including "Live and Let Die" by Guns N' Roses, "My Love" by Junior Walker, and a version of "Let 'Em In" by Shinehead. A raucous version of "Monkberry Moon Delight" was also included—who sang it?

7. Headlining a bill at the Hollywood Bowl that included 10,000 Maniacs, Steve Miller, and Don Henley, McCartney's eighty-five minute set at the *Earth Day for the Environment Concert*, 16 April, included an appearance by Ringo during the "Hey Jude" all-star finale. Earlier, a performance of "Hope of Deliverance" featured backing vocals by what noted singer/songwriter?

8. Beginning with the New World Tour's North American leg, 17 April, Richard Lester's opening film from the 1989–1990 World Tour (which had been updated with scenes of the fall of the Berlin Wall, the Gulf War, Margaret Thatcher leaving No. 10 Downing Street, the "Liverpool Oratorio" premiere and Bill Clinton) was replaced by a more controversial one, directed by Kevin Godley. What caused the uproar?

9. Yoko Ono upset many Lennon fans when her exhibit at the Shoshana-Wayne Gallery in Santa Monica, California opened 17 April. Among the objects displayed: a replica of John's blood-stained glasses and a bloody bronze replica of Lennon's bullet-riddled shirt, priced at $25,000 and $35,000, respectively. What was the name of the exhibit?

10. Ringo appeared behind the drumkit backing singer Jonelle Glosser as part of a band assembled by producer Don Was for Together for Our Children, a charity concert held at UCLA's Royce Hall, 23 June. What was the name of Ringo's new band, who had also performed at Farm Aid VI in Ames, Iowa, 24 April?

11. Arnold Shapiro Productions, producer of the William Shatner-hosted series *Rescue 911*, had reportedly targeted a summer debut on CBS-TV for this series pilot to be hosted by Ringo, which would have granted the fantasy wishes of its viewers. While Starr eventually withdrew from the project, what was the show to have been called?

12. The video *Paul McCartney: Movin' On*, issued 26 July, documents rehearsals for the New World Tour and the making of videos for *Off the Ground*. In one sequence, strings arranged by Angelo Badalamenti are shown being laid down at Abbey Road for a track written by McCartney and Hamish Stuart. What is the title of the song?

13. During 1993, Elton John consigned Sotheby's in London to auction his private collection of over 25,000 albums and 23,000 singles. Sold as a single lot, the auction realized approximately $270,000 for AIDS charities. Elton is said to have kept but two albums back for himself, the first an acetate of his July 1970 sessions for Warlock Music publisher Joe Boyd (featuring his covers of Nick Drake songs). The second album was by the Beatles—which one?

14. In Lewis Shiner's novel *Glimpses*, stereo repairman Ray Shackleford can hear rock and roll music in his head that never existed and transfer it to tape. Ray's album "releases" include the Doors' *Celebration of the Lizard* and the Beach Boys' *Smile*, but the first song he recreates is one by the Beatles. What song is it?

15. The European leg of the New World Tour (opening in Berlin at the Waldbuehne, 3 September), saw some changes in the songlist, with Paul replacing "And I Love Her" with the first song he ever composed, age 14, in late '56/early '57. What is the song?

16. Starring Peter Scolari and Pamela Reed, what Beatles song was used as the theme of the sitcom *Family Album*, which premiered on CBS-TV, 24 September?

17. What Beatles song was used as the opening theme of the ABC-TV comedy *Grace Under Fire* starring Brett Butler?

18. In the fifth season opener of *The Simpsons* (30 September), Homer remembers his days in the summer of 1985 as a member of The Be Sharps barbershop quartet. Feeling nostalgic, he assembles the other members, Principal Skinner, Apu, and Barney for a reunion on the roof of Moe's, a la *Let It Be*. As they sing their big hit "Baby on Board" to a gathering crowd on the street below, a limo pulls up. From the back seat, George regards the scene above. Voiced by the real Harrison, what does he say?

19. What is the title of Australian actor John Waters's Lennon theatrical tribute, which opened for a limited run, 18 October, at London's Criterion Theatre?

20. Selected performances and soundchecks from Paul's 1993 New World Tour were first issued by Parlophone in the UK 16 November as *Paul is Live*. The cover shows McCartney reenacting his famous zebra crossing outside of Abbey Road studios, this time with a sheepdog. What is the sheepdog's name?

21. Where did Paul get the idea for calling his New World Tour album *Paul is Live?*

22. What is "transpiritual stomp"?

23. What is the origin of the McCartney/Youth pseudonym "The Fireman"?

24. McCartney's former fiancée, Jane Asher, starred in the TV drama *Closing Numbers*, first broadcast in Britain, 2 December. Its airing on Channel 4 caused quite a stir in the media for the forty-seven-year-old actress—why was that?

25. First issued in December by Thunderbolt/Magnum Music Group in the UK, George added slide guitar to two cuts on Alvin Lee's album *Nineteenninetyfour* (retitled *I Hear You Rockin'* in the U.S.). A Lee composition, "The Bluest Blues," was the first, but for the second, Alvin was covering what Beatles song?

ANSWERS

1. Rehearsals at the London Arena (which cost McCartney £17,000 a day), kept Paul from accepting an invitation to play at President Clinton's Inaugural Gala at the Capitol Centre in Landover, Maryland, 19 January.

(The President had to be content instead with Fleetwood Mac, who reunited for the first time in eight years to play "Don't Stop" [which had been Clinton's campaign theme song] at the event.)

2. Paul asked Liverpool poet Adrian Mitchell "to look through the lyrics as if he was an English teacher checking my homework."

(One of Mitchell's suggestions was for "C'mon People." Adrian asked him if he couldn't find a stronger adjective than "coming" for the line. "We got a future and it's coming in." Paul would revise the lyric to "rushing" and, in a later verse, "charging.")

3. From left to right, the feet on the cover of *Off the Ground* belong to Robbie McIntosh, Linda, Paul, Blair Cunningham, and Hamish Stuart.

4. "Big Boys Bickering" (with its line about said boys "fucking it up for everyone"), was not included in the *Up Close* broadcast.

(A brief rendition of "Jingle Bells" [played before "Hope of Deliverance" on the first night], and a near complete version of "If I Were Not Upon The Stage" [played before "My Love" on the second night], were also excluded.)

5. Noting "it's the kind of thing Michael (Jackson) would be better at," McCartney turned down an invitation from the National Football League to perform at halftime at the Superbowl in Atlanta, 30 January 1994.

(Paul would have had a good crowd; attendance at the Georgia Dome for Superbowl XXVIII between the Dallas Cowboys and the Buffalo Bills was 72,817.)

6. The pre-concert music on the New World Tour included a version of "Monkberry Moon Delight" sung by Jalacy J. Hawkins, better known as Screamin' Jay Hawkins.

(Screamin' Jay's version was first issued in 1979 on the album *Screamin' the Blues*. Hawkins died of internal hemorrhaging following surgery for an obstructed bowel, 12 February 2000 in Neuilly-sur-Seine, a suburb west of Paris. He was seventy.)

7. Backing vocals on "Hope of Deliverance" at the Earth Day concert were handled by k. d. lang.

8. In addition to featuring rare Beatles home movies, Kevin Godley's opening film for McCartney's New World Tour included graphic images of lab animals and vivisections, which many did not consider appropriate viewing for the family audiences Paul's shows were attracting.

(Godley also directed the computer morphing video for "C'mon People" and the Beatles' "Real Love.")

9. Yoko's exhibit at the Shoshana-Wayne Gallery was titled *A Family Album (Blood Objects)*.

10. Featuring Benmont Tench on keyboards, Don Was on guitar and bassist Alex Duvall, Ringo drummed in an ensemble dubbed the New Maroons.

11. Ringo was to have hosted the fantasy wish fulfillment series, *Best Wishes*.

12.   *Movin' On* shows Paul and Hamish Stuart working in Abbey Road (15 December 1992) on their (as yet) unreleased collaboration "Is It Raining In London?"

13.   Elton did not part with his copy of the White Album, signed by all four Beatles.

14.   Ray Shackleford's first mind-to-tape transfer was a version of "The Long and Winding Road"—produced in Abbey Road Studio Number Two by George Martin.

("I got all the pieces together in my head. I could see Paul's face, hear John nervously tapping one booted foot. Ringo putting out a cigarette and laughing at something. It was all there. I nodded and Hudson started the tape. I closed my eyes. Geoff Emerick said, "Long and Winding Road. Take four." I heard Hudson shift in his chair, like I'd scared him. Then Paul started singing.")

15.   "And I Love Her" was replaced on the European leg of the New World Tour with "I Lost My Little Girl."

16.   *Family Album* used "Two of Us" as its opening theme song.

17.   Premiering 29 September, *Grace Under Fire* ran for five seasons on ABC-TV using "Lady Madonna" as its opening theme.

18.   "It's been done."
(Written by Jeff Martin, episode #9F21, "Homer's Barbershop Quartet," is liberally sprinkled with Beatles references:

- When Nigel, The Be Sharps' manager urges the group to replace Chief Wiggum with Barney (an exceptional tenor), there is a brief outcry of "Barney Never, Wiggum Forever" at Barney's debut that evening at "Moe's Cavern," recalling the furor accompanying Pete Best's sacking from the Beatles, 16 August 1962, leading some Best fans to demonstrate outside NEMS with placards declaring "Ringo Never, Pete Forever" and "Pete is Best."
- After recording "Baby on Board," Nigel walks on to the studio floor declaring, "Gentleman, you've just recorded your first number one." On 26 November, 1962, following 18 takes to complete "Please Please Me," producer George Martin would declare over

the talkback in Abbey Road's Studio Two, "You've just made your first number one."

- Nigel's insistence that Homer keep his marriage to Marge a secret refers to Brian Epstein's desire to keep John's marriage to Cynthia a secret to the group's fans and the press.

- The Be Sharps' arrival at John F. Kennedy Airport and subsequent press conference parodies the Beatles' own arrival at JFK, 7 February 1964, down to recreating the Pan Am press lounge reception on the first floor of the main terminal. During the press reception, Principal Skinner is referred to as "The Funny One."

- The Be Sharps' first album, Meet the Be Sharps, parodies Robert Freeman's front cover of Meet the Beatles and Michael Cooper's back cover of Sgt. Pepper, with Homer (like Paul) with his back to the camera. The group's second album, Bigger Than Jesus, parodies the front cover of Abbey Road, with Barney walking barefoot.

- Barney's new girlfriend, Kako, a "Japanese conceptual artist," sports long black hair and dresses in black, a la Yoko Ono, circa January 1969, during the filming of Let It Be. When Barney and Kako go into Moe's for a drink, Kako orders "a single plum, floating in perfume, served in a man's hat."

- When the group are shown listening to Barney's latest experimental tape (Kako alternately reciting "No. 8" as Barney belches), they are parodying the oft-reprinted photo by Ethan Russell of the Beatles and Ono in the basement of Apple during the filming of Let It Be, posed around a recording desk (Lennon with his feet on the console, Yoko standing behind him), looking tired and bored as they listen to a playback.

- For the group's reunion on the roof of Moe's, The Be Sharps dress as the Beatles dressed on the roof of Apple, 30 January, with Homer wearing a red windbreaker (Ringo), Barney donning a brown fur coat (John) and Principal Skinner a black morning suit with a white shirt, sans tie (Paul). Finishing "Baby on Board," Homer acknowledges the crowd's applause: "I'd like to thank you on behalf of the group and I hope we passed the audition." Laughing along with the crowd at Homer's witticism, Barney abruptly stops, declaring, "I don't get it.")

19. John Waters's Lennon tribute was titled Looking Through a Glass Onion.

20. Paul is pictured on the cover of *Paul is Live* with son James's sheep-dog—her name is Arrow.

(Photographer Iain MacMillan took the photo of McCartney, 22 July, which was then computer-grafted onto MacMillan's original cover shot from 8 August 1969. "It was strange to go back to the Abbey Road crossing again," McCartney said in the liner notes accompanying a promo-only sampler for the album. "The deja vu hit in. It was a summer's day again. The cops held the traffic again. The crowd of surprised onlookers gaped again. But the only difference was, instead of the Beatles, it was one man and his dog—but, please, don't start reading anything into that.")

21. On 15 May, filmmaker Allison Anders had planned to begin shooting her movie about a girl coming of age titled *Paul is Dead*, with actor Hugh Grant playing McCartney. When Anders sent the script to Paul for approval, the film's title gave him the idea for *Paul is Live*.

(While Paul approved the script, the film subsequently went into limbo when Grant had second thoughts and pulled out of the project.)

22. "Transpiritual stomp" is the title of the first of nine techo dance remixes featured on *strawberries oceans ships forest* made in early October 1992 by The Fireman, a.k.a. Paul McCartney and producer/remixer and former Killing Joke bassist Youth (Martin Glover). EMI released the album in the UK 15 November, followed (rather reluctantly) by Capitol in the U.S., 22 February 1994.

(Spoken samples on "transpiritual stomp" include two from McCartney's *Back To the Egg* album: "I think I sense the situation" [from John Galsworthy's poem "The Little Man," spoken by Harold Margery in "The Broadcast"], and "tufts of hair, stuck here and there" [from A. P. Herbert's poem "The Poodle and The Pug," spoken by Diedre Margery on "Reception"]. Youth had discovered both poems programmed on one of the discs in Paul's studio Chamberlain synthesizer. The titles of all the mixes originated with Youth, who assigned them quite spontaneously. "transpiritual stomp' had a kind of pagan feel, I could imagine a caveman kicking up the dust to it.")

23. The inspiration for Paul's pseudonym The Fireman came from his father Jim McCartney's stint in Liverpool during the Second World War as a volunteer fireman.

24. Jane Asher did a nude scene in *Closing Numbers*.

(Jane plays a housewife named Anna, happily married for years to Keith [Tim Woodward] until one day she suspects he's having an affair.

Keith's affair is with another man. Anna comes to befriend her husband's lover and his friend, Jim, who is dying of AIDS.)

25.   George added slide guitar to Alvin Lee's cover of "I Want You (She's So Heavy)."

1994

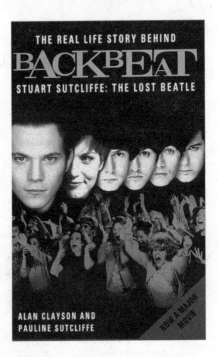

1. During an interview for *Mojo* magazine, Oasis composer/guitarist (and Beatles fan) Noel Gallagher became annoyed: "You know The New Seekers are suing us for 'Shakermaker'—'I want to teach the world to sing,' that bit?" Noel insists that the melody of their second single was actually taken from a Beatles song. No great surprise there—which one?

2. Once the press got wind of the Beatles' reunion recording plans (with columnist Marilyn Beck and *Goldmine* magazine getting wind of things in January), the staff at Apple took to referring to the *Anthology* project as "T.T.T.F.O."—which soon became the common response to the press's constant calls for updates. What did the acronym stand for?

3. Who inducted John Lennon (as a solo artist) into the Rock and Roll Hall of Fame at ceremonies held at New York's Waldorf-Astoria Hotel, 19 January?

4. The Beatles' reunion single "Free As A Bird" was recorded at The Mill, Paul's home recording studio in Sussex, England, during February and March. What was the name of the guitar George used for the bottle-neck playing heard at the start of the song?

5. Linda and Paul were in Fairmont, Minnesota, 25 March, to help promote her line of frozen meatless entrees that Fairmont Foods of Minnesota were introducing to the U.S. market, 1 May. What was the name of the line?

6. Featuring twenty-nine of Ono's songs (including "We're All Water" from *Sometime In New York City* and "Yes, I'm Your Angel" from *Double Fantasy*), what is the title of the off-Broadway musical that Yoko staged at New York's WPA theater, from 30 March to 17 April?

7. Issued by Private Music, 12 April, on whose album does Ringo share lead vocals on a version of "My Little Grass Shack"?

8. The role of John in *Backbeat* was played by twenty-nine-year-old Liverpool actor Ian Hart, who had previously portrayed the 1963 Lennon in *The Hours and Times*. What line in the film did director Ian Softley have the 1962 Lennon utter, despite Hart's efforts to have it removed?

9. Opening in U.S. theaters 15 April, posters and print ads for *Backbeat* included a descriptive tagline about the film in the form of a 5, 4, 3, 2, 1, countdown. What was the tagline?

10. Premiering at The Actor's Playhouse in New York, 19 April, what was the title of this off-Broadway play by Kevin Scott dramatizing the last night of Brian Epstein?

11. In 1994, the Beatles received a star on the Hollywood Walk of Fame. A few weeks later the star was removed—why?

12. Queen Latifah would've done "Lady Madonna" and Public Enemy wanted to rap "Revolution," but Michael Jackson, owner of ATV Music, wouldn't O.K. the album of rap artists recording Lennon/McCartney songs planned by 57/Sunset. Producers at the New York-based label subsequently sued Jackson for $76 million for reneging on an agreement to approve the project. In 1994, Jackson won out, receiving an injunction prohibiting 57/Sunset from using the songs without permission. What was the album to have been titled?

13. Long believed lost, a previously unheard take of "Love Me Do" from the Beatles' first studio session at Abbey Road was discovered in 1994 when this person discovered an acetate copy while cleaning out a cupboard. Who was it?

14. On 23 June, Paul, George, and Ringo convened at Harrison's Friar Park Studios. A number of rock and roll classics were revisited and a jam ensued, all of it filmed by series director Bob Smeaton for possible use in the *Anthology*. "It was just two acoustic guitars and me on brushes," Ringo would say later. One small sequence featured in the *Anthology* shows George sitting on a bench out in his garden with Paul and Ringo, singing what unreleased Harrison composition?

15. Paul still hadn't seen *Backbeat* when he spoke to Tony Bacon in an interview printed in the July/August 1995 issue of *Bass Player*. "But I did see a clip where John's character sings 'Long Tall Sally,' which is a piss-off for me . . ." Why was McCartney unhappy?

16. Formed 19 March 1986 in Stourbridge, England, the Wonder Stuff released four studio albums before disbanding 15 July 1994. A singles compilation, issued by Polydor in the UK 19 September, namechecks the Beatles in its title—what is it?

17. What Paul McCartney composition is featured on the soundtrack of the movie *Threesome*, starring Lara Flynn Boyle, Stephen Baldwin, and Josh Charles?

18. In August, Kewbank Records issued *Open for Engagements* by the Quarry Men, an album of new recordings featuring original members Rod Davis and John "Duff" Lowe. What is the significance of this CD's title?

19. On 18 August, while Linda was busy cooking vegetarian dishes in the kitchen of chef Pierre Franey's Long Island home, Paul was in the den composing what song?

20. It is present day Liverpool where we first meet teenager Dane McGowan one evening, down by the docks smoking a cigarette when two young men dressed in black leathers approach. The men are John Lennon and Stuart Sutcliffe, circa 1961. Stu tells John of his desire to leave the group and return to Hamburg to be with Astrid. "Mr. Lennon," Dane calls out to the Beatle (just as Mark David Chapman would one evening in 1980). John turns in the direction of the voice, but sees no one. This sequence is featured in what DC Comics title by Grant Morrison, which debuted in 1994?

21.   Directed by Quentin Tarantino, *Pulp Fiction* opened in U.S. theaters beginning 14 October. In one scene, Mia Wallace (Uma Thurman) and Vincent Vega (John Travolta) arrive at "Jackrabbit Slim's," a '50s themed restaurant. Mia's comment, "An Elvis man should love this" refers to a scene Tarantino cut earlier from their first meeting at her apartment with a distinct Beatles reference—what was it?

22.   Phish started a new tradition during their show at the Glenn Falls Civic Center in Glenn Falls, New York, 31 October, by covering another artist's album in its entirety in what they called their "Halloween costume." What Beatles album comprised Phish's inaugural costume?

23.   What English group titled their 1994 album after Paul McCartney's composition "Carnival of Light"?

24.   No stranger to the Beatles' sessions for the BBC, Kevin Howlett first assessed the Corporation's holdings for the group in 1982 when he helped produce *The Beatles at the Beeb* radio series. At an EMI news conference to launch *Live at the BBC*, 22 November, Howlett (who wrote the liner notes for the set) was asked at one point if his first search of the BBC archive "was like walking into King Tutankhamen's tomb." "I was astonished by what I found," was his reply. While he didn't elaborate for the journalist, Kevin would have been astonished, but for different reasons—how many Beatles radio sessions did the BBC have in their archive?

25.   Ringo's ex-wife, Maureen Starkey Tigrett (born Mary Cox), died of leukemia, 30 December. Upon receiving the news of her death, what song did Paul write for her?

ANSWERS

1.   Stating that he'd "rather have McCartney suing me as we'd get more press out of it," Noel Gallagher told *Mojo* managing editor Mark Ellen that "Shakermaker" draws its melody from "Flying."
  ("Sing the lyrics over the top, that's what it is.")

2. Beseiged with requests by the world press for updates, Derek Taylor revealed to *Newsweek* in 1995 that the *Anthology* project soon became known to the staff at Apple as "T.T.T.F.O."—"Tell them to fuck off!"

(Derek Taylor died at the age of sixty-five of cancer of the esophagus, 7 September 1997.)

3. Paul inducted John into the Hall, his speech taking the form of "an open letter" to his former partner, after which he brought Yoko Ono and Sean Lennon up onstage.

4. George uses his early '60s Fender Stratocaster "Rocky" (with its bright green "Om" symbol, the phrases "Be Bop A Lula" and "Go Cat Go" painted in white) for the distinctive slide opening on "Free As A Bird."

(John and George both acquired Fender Stratocasters in 1965, first utilized on the sessions for "Nowhere Man" [recorded 21–22 October in Studio Two]. In 1967, Harrison took some Day-Glo paint and some of Pattie's nail varnish and transformed his pale blue Strat into "Rocky," seen to good effect in the "I Am The Walrus" sequence from *Magical Mystery Tour*.)

5. The initial "rollout" of *Linda McCartney's Home Style Cooking* line consisted of nine entrees, seven boil-in-bag and two pre-plated.

6. *New York Rock*.

(With obvious parallels to Ono's own life, the musical's nine-person cast [directed by Philip Oesterman] tells the story of "Bill" [Pat McRoberts] and "Jill" [Lynette Perry], who fall in love. Later in the show Bill is senselessly murdered. An original cast recording of the show was released by Capitol, 2 May 1995.)

7. Ringo shares lead vocals on "My Little Grass Shack" with Leon Redbone, included on the latter's Private Music album, *Whistling in the Wind*.

8. Hart objected to Lennon saying, "It's been a hard day's night," a phrase Ringo wouldn't coin for another two years, feeling that it undermined the film's dramatic tension.

("Those things are just a bit of fun," noted Softley, "for audiences to laugh at the very obvious references.")

9. *Backbeat's* tagline was "5 guys, 4 legends, 3 lovers, 2 friends, 1 band."

10. Starring Albert Macklin in the title role, *Hide Your Love Away: The Ballad of Brian Epstein*, portrays the last night of the Beatles' manager (Saturday, 26 August 1967).

11. The Beatles' star was removed under pressure from Capitol Records, who believed that a ceremony should have been held with at least one of the group present.

(The star was stored in the office of Hollywood's honorary mayor, Johnny Grant, until 1998, when it was restored without fanfare by Walk of Fame officials, 25 December. It is located next to Elvis Presley's star at the gateway to Hollywood Boulevard. John Lennon's star [which Yoko unveiled at a ceremony conducted 30 September 1988] is located near the landmark Capitol Records tower.)

12. 57/Sunset's rap album was to have been tited *Beatlerap*.

13. George Martin's wife Judy discovered the previously unheard take of "Love Me Do" while cleaning out a cupboard at the Martin's home in Wiltshire.

(The take includes Pete Best on drums, recorded in Studio Two, 6 June 1962, his only session for EMI. It was included on disc one of *Anthology 1*, issued in November 1995.)

14. With a little encouragement from Ringo, George, accompanying himself on ukulele, sings his unreleased composition "Dera Dhun."

15. Paul was unhappy with the *Backbeat* John (sung by Greg Dulli of the Afghan Whigs) singing "Long Tall Sally" ". . . because that's a bit of my history. I was the guy who did "Long Tall Sally," and there was no reason why the John character should have sung that—he had plenty of raunchy, rocking songs that they could have had him sing."

16. Polydor's Wonder Stuff compilation is titled *If the Beatles had Read Hunter . . . The Singles*, the Hunter of the title a reference to gonzo journalist Hunter S. Thompson, author of *Fear and Loathing in Las Vegas*.

(Lead singer Miles Hunt once told a writer that the origin of the band's name was essentially a Lennon quote: "When I was a youngster, John Lennon often used to come around to our house. I was just running around the house like a maniac with my friends, and [Lennon] said [to my father], 'Your boy sure has the wonder stuff.' Often as I grew up, my dad used to remind me of this story." In e-mail correspondence with the author, Russ Hunt, Miles's brother, revealed this story to be "absolutely one hundred percent made up."

"Miles was in a hotel room doing phone interviews one after the other with European magazines and was getting very bored," he explained. "When one journalist asked the question 'where does the name Wonder Stuff come from?' Miles and *NME* journalist James Brown concocted the story about John Lennon and Miles as a baby. Wonder Stuff was simply two words that sounded good together.")

17.   The soundtrack of *Threesome* includes The Fireman instrumental "transpiritual stomp."

18.   "Open for Engagements" was the phrase included on the Quarry Men's business cards, which manager Nigel Whalley had printed up in 1957.

19.   While Linda was cooking a vegetarian meal for the noted culinary author (with *New York Times* food writer Bryan Miller and a photographer looking on), Paul was in the den composing "Young Boy," which started under the working title "Poor Boy."

20.   Dane McGowan's encounter with the ghosts of John and Stu (drawn by Steve Yeowell) appears in "Dead Beatles," issue one of the DC Comics title *The Invisibles*.

(This story is included in the collection *The Invisibles: Say You Want A Revolution*, issued by Vertigo/DC Comics in July 1996.)

21.   While interviewing Vincent at her apartment with a hand-held video camera, Mia declares "There's only two kinds of people in the world, Beatles people and Elvis people."

("Now Beatles people can like Elvis, and Elvis people can like Beatles, but *nobody* likes them both equally. Somewhere, you have to make a choice, and that choice tells you who you are.")

22.   As part of a marathon three-set show, Phish played the entire White Album.

(Taking Yoko Ono's quote "If you became naked" seriously, drummer Fish [John Fishman] performed "Revolution 9" for the Glenn Falls audience in the nude. Subsequent "costumes" included The Who's *Quadrophenia*, at Chicago's Rosemont Horizon, 31 October 1995, and *Remain in Light* by The Talking Heads at The Omni in Atlanta, Georgia, 31 October 1996. Phish weren't the first group keen to tackle the entire

White Album. Sonic Youth guitarist Lee Ranaldo confirmed that during the '80s the group had considered it, telling the *Toronto Sun* in 1995, "There was a period when it was something we were seriously talking about doing.")

23. Oxford quartet Ride named their third album *Carnival of Light*, released in the UK on the Creation label.

24. When Howlett first assayed the BBC's tape archive for the Beatles, he only found two programs: the group's second *From Us to You* holiday special (recorded 28 February 1964) and the group's second appearance on *Top Gear* (recorded 17 November 1964). Only the *Top Gear* appearance was complete.

25. Paul composed "Little Willow" for Maureen, which he recorded in November 1995 for his album *Flaming Pie*.

(In the *Flaming Pie* booklet he states, "I wanted to somehow convey how much I thought of her. For her and her kids.")

1995

F R E E   A S   A   B I R D

1. What are "The Blue Shines Through," "Chasing the Cherry," "Mist the Mind," "Trouble Is," and "Velvet Wave?"

2. On 6 February, George convened with Paul, Ringo, producer Jeff Lynne and Beatles engineer Geoff Emerick at The Mill in Sussex. They were there to work on their second reunion single, "Real Love," another of John's unreleased songs from 1979. Harrison contributed acoustic and lead guitar as well as harmony and backing vocals to the finished Beatles version, released as a single in advance of *Anthology 2*, 5 March 1996. But this wasn't the first time during the '90s George had played guitar on a song titled "Real Love"—to whom does that honor go?

3. What is the title of the song Cynthia Lennon released as her debut single, 22 February?

4. When Yoko and Sean visited Waterfall, the McCartney home in Sussex, 11 March, an unplanned recording session at The Mill resulted. What is the name of the song they recorded, with Yoko on lead vocals, from which Paul produced a seven-minute track?

5. Attended by Prince Charles, *An Evening with Paul McCartney and Friends*, held at London's St. James' Palace 23 March as a benefit for the Royal College of Music, featured several memorable performances by Paul, including two songs with song-writing partner Elvis Costello. What did they sing?

6. Who is Anya Alexeyev?

7. On 9 May, Musicmasters ROCK/BMG released *For the Love of Harry: Everybody Sings Nilsson*. Ringo contributed "Lay Down Your Arms," a previously unreleased Nilsson composition. Who does Ringo sing it with?

8. When Chloe Lewis (Kathleen Wilhoite) wakes her sister Susan (Sherry Stringfield) at 4 A.M. on Mother's Day to tell her she's about to have her baby, which Beatles song figures prominently during the delivery in the *ER* episode "Motherhood," directed by Quentin Tarantino?

9. The Westwood One radio network debuted *Oobu Joobu*, Paul McCartney's fifteen-part "wide-screen radio" series, over Memorial Day weekend, 29 May. Where did Paul draw his inspiration for the series' title?

10. On 12 June, Stella McCartney graduated from London's Central St. Martin's College of Art and Design. Her graduation line, modeled gratis by supermodels Kate Moss and Naomi Cambell, was shown to a sound-track of Marlon Brando yelling "Stella!" from *A Streetcar Named Desire* and this song written by Paul. What is the title of this as-yet unreleased recording?

11. Ringo and the 1995 version of his "All-Starr Band" went to Japan for the start of their world tour, opening at the Iwate Kenmin Hall in Morioka, 14 June. Nils Lofgren and Clarence Clemons dropped out this year to work with their old boss, Bruce Springsteen, while Joe Walsh was busy with an Eagles reunion tour. Who was in the band that year?

12. What do Eric Burdon, Flo and Eddie, Roger McGuinn, and Former Elephant's Memory guitarist Wayne "Tex" Gabriel all have in common?

13. On 29 June, Starr was first seen pitching Pizza Hut's Stuffed Crust Pizza, talking of getting "the lads" together during the thirty-second commercial because he thought "the fans would dig it." Who are the "lads" who eventually join Ringo at the end of the spot?

14. What did Ringo Starr, actress Jane Seymour and Olympic gold-medalist runner Florence Griffiths Joyner have in common?

15. On 24 August, Ringo canceled the last four dates of his All-Starr Tour and flew back to England—why?

16. Who are the Smokin' Mojo Filters?

17. Director Joe Massot had originally envisioned directing this group's screen debut or a concert film. While this never materialized, it was while driving down to Bournemouth to see them in concert, 18 September, that Massot got the idea of doing a director's cut of *Wonderwall*, his first feature film. Who was the group?

18. In what film did Julian Lennon make his credited acting debut, playing a bartender in a biker bar?

19. Where did Paul McCartney say, "If you play 'Maybe I'm Amazed' backwards, you'll hear a recipe for a really ripping lentil soup"?

20. On 16 October, Allen Ginsberg gave a poetry reading, *Rebirth of the Reforgotten*, at London's Royal Albert Hall. For one piece, Paul backed Ginsberg on electric guitar. What was the poem's title?

21. On 7 November, Capitol released *Rising*, Yoko Ono's first new album of original songs in ten years (*Starpeace* being the last in November 1985). What was the name of her backing band, which included son Sean?

22. Yoko Ono guested on NBC-TV's *Mad About You*, in an episode titled *Yoko Said*, first aired 12 November. At the Dakota for a business meeting, Paul and Jamie Buchman discuss with Ms. Ono having the Explorer Channel film Yoko's proposed series of film happenings. What Beatles song does Yoko make her entrance to?

23. ABC-TV made much of its exclusive world premiere of the new Beatles song "Free as a Bird," when it aired the reference-laden video directed by Joe Pytka following the first night of *Anthology*, Tuesday, 19 November. However, the song had actually been played publicly a week before in Adelaide, Australia—who was the culprit?

24. John's drawing used on the picture sleeve/CD single insert for "Free as a Bird" is familiar to Lennon fans from a previous appearance—where is that?

25. What Lennon song does Richard Dreyfuss sing in the 1995 film *Mr. Holland's Opus?*

ANSWERS

1. These are the titles of five poems published in the 27 January issue of Britain's *New Statesman & Society* by Paul McCartney, marking his debut as a published poet.

2. In 1992, George played guitar on Jimmy Nail's composition "Real Love" (cowritten with Guy Pratt and Danny Schogger), included on his album *Growing Up in Public*, issued in the U.S. on Atlantic, 29 September 1992.

3. Cynthia Lennon made her debut as a singer with a remake of "Those were the Days."

4. The Ono/Lennon/McCartney session produced "Hiroshima, it's Always a Beautiful Blue Sky."

(As Ono chanted, Paul contributed some vocals as he played his Bill Black stand-up bass; Linda played a Hammond B-3 organ, Sean and Paul's son James played guitars, while daughters Heather, Mary, and Stella added percussion. The song had its world premiere, 6 August [under the title "Hiroshima Sky is Always Blue"], on Japan's NHK television to mark the fiftieth anniversary of the dropping of the first atomic bomb on Hiroshima, 6 August 1945.)

5. Accompanying themselves on acoustic guitars, Paul and Elvis sang "The One After 909" followed by "Mistress and Maid," the latter a co-compositon McCartney included on his 1993 album *Off the Ground*.

6. Twenty-two-year-old Russian pianist Anya Alexeyev opened "An Evening with Paul McCartney and Friends" with the royal world premiere of "a leaf," a ten-minute solo piano piece written by Paul.

(A CD single of Alexeyev's performance was issued as *Paul McCartney's "a leaf"* by EMI Classics in the UK, 24 April.)

7. Ringo sang "Lay Down Your Arms" in duet with Fleetwood Mac's Stevie Nicks.

("Everyone did songs that were already done by Harry," Ringo recalled to Ken Sharp. "And I had this song that nobody had done but he had written it. It was very emotional for me because I was doing it for Harry and it was [about] the gun law and everything else." Nilsson died in his sleep from a heart attack, 15 January 1994. He was fifty-two.)

8. When her tape of the White Album fails to materialize, Chloe delivers her baby daughter while singing "Blackbird."

(Written by Lydia Woodward, "Motherhood" [episode 24], was first aired 11 May 1995.)

9. The name "Oobu Joobu" was inspired by a BBC Third Program production of Alfred Jarry's "Ubu Cocu" (Ubu Cuckolded), aired 10 January 1966, which McCartney had heard while driving to Liverpool in his Aston Martin.

("It was the best radio play I had ever heard in my life," Paul told Barry Miles. "That was one of the big things of the period for me.")

10. "Stella Mayday."

(Stella's fashion line, carried in the U.S. by Bergdorf Goodman and Neiman Marcus, was financed by the sale of her graduation collection of eight designs, which realized $12,000.)

11. Ringo's 1995 "All-Starr Band" featured Randy Bachman (guitar), Felix Cavaliere (keyboards), John Entwistle (bass), Mark Farner (guitar), Billy Preston (keyboards), Max Rivera (sax, percussion, acoustic guitar) and Zak Starkey (drums).

12. All were asked to be part of Ringo's All-Starr band line-up in 1995.

13. Sitting behind his drum kit, Starr is joined by Monkees Micky Dolenz, Davy Jones, and Peter Tork. "Wrong lads," notes Ringo.

(Pizza Hut's commercial with Starr premiered in the U.S. 29 June during NBC-TV's *Mad About You*.)

14. Joyner, Seymour, and Starr all submitted paintings used as designs for the "Private Issue" credit card issued by Discover Card.

(Unveiled at an after hours ceremony at the Guggenheim Museum in New York City, 12 July, Ringo's painting was auctioned for $33,000 to benefit the Make-A-Wish Foundation. The painting, a series of red circles and lines of a face against a blue background was a featured backdrop behind the All-Starr Band during shows that year.)

15. Ringo cancelled the last four dates of the 1995 All-Starr Tour (in Reno, Nevada; Apple Valley, California; San Diego, California, and Las Vegas, Nevada) when he learned that his twenty-four-year-old daughter Lee had lost consciousness shortly after her hand had gone numb while writing.

(Lee was discharged from the London Clinic 1 September after undergoing surgery to drain fluid from her brain. A short time later she entered Boston's Brigham and Women's Hospital where surgery successfully removed a brain tumor. She was released 20 September.)

16. The Smokin' Mojo Filters are Paul Weller (The Jam, Style Council), Paul McCartney and Noel Gallagher (Oasis). The band also included Steve Craddock on guitar, Damon Minchella on bass, Steve White on drums, and singer Carleen Anderson.)

(Paul sang backup to Weller's lead on a cover of "Come Together," just one of the songs recorded [and/or assembled] at Abbey Road during a twenty-four-hour marathon session conducted between the midnights of 3–4 September. The result was *Help!* an album benefiting the Bosnian relief charity War Child, issued just five days later by Go! Discs Limited in the UK, 9 September.)

17. Massot had been inspired by Oasis after receiving a call from his eldest son, Jason, that the group had included a song on their second album, (*What's the Story*) *Morning Glory?* called "Wonderwall."

18. Julian played a bartender in a biker bar in *Leaving Las Vegas*, starring Nicholas Cage and Elizabeth Shue.

19. McCartney's lentil soup recipe can be heard in "Lisa the Vegetarian," episode #3F03 of *The Simpsons*, first aired 15 October.

(The roof of Apu's Kwik-E-Mart supports a thriving garden from which Paul and Linda emerge to counsel Lisa on how to be a respectful vegetarian. Paul, it seems, has known Apu for years: "We met him in India, years ago, during the Marharishi days." In addition to Paul and Linda providing guest voices [the last of the surviving Beatles to do so], McCartney recorded a new version of "Maybe I'm Amazed" for the closing credits in which he reads a recipe for lentil soup that can be understood when played backwards, concluding with "Oh, and by the way, I'm alive.")

20. McCartney backed Ginsberg during his reading of "The Ballad of the Skeletons."

(A CD single featuring three versions of "Skeletons" was issued 8 October 1996 by Mouth Almighty Records/Mercury featuring musical contributions by Paul and Philip Glass.)

21. Yoko's backing band on *Rising* was called Ima.

(Ima would also back Yoko on a subsequent mini tour, which opened at the 9:30 Club in Washington, D.C., 29 February 1996. The three-piece band included Sean Lennon [guitar, piano], Timo Ellis [bass] and Sam Koppelman [drums].)

22. Yoko made her entrance on *Mad About You* to "I Want to Hold Your Hand."

23. During a party for race driver Damon Hill, 12 Novmeber, following his victory at the Australian Grand Prix that afternoon, George instructed the DJ at the Adelaide Hilton's Freezer Club to play "Free as a Bird."

24. The "Free As A Bird" drawing first appeared in 1964 in John's first book *In His Own Write*.

(The illustration actually serves as the book's dedication page. Lennon had intended to dedicate the book to Pete Shotton, his best mate since childhood, with the inscription "To Pete, who got it first." Not wishing to offend his Aunt Mimi by not dedicating the book to her, Lennon substituted the drawing, a caricature of Shotton. Designed by Richard Ward of the London design firm *The Team*, the image selected for "Free As A Bird" was one of three Lennon drawings submitted by Yoko Ono as her preference, with George, Paul, and Ringo all approving the final sleeve.)

25. Richard Dreyfuss sings "Beautiful Boy (Darling Boy)" in *Mr. Holland's Opus*.

(*Opus* also features John's version of "Imagine," included [along with Lennon's version of "Beautiful Boy"] on the original motion picture soundtrack, issued by Polydor, 20 January 1996. Closing the film is "Cole's Song," performed by Julian Lennon, which he cowrote with Justin Clayton and Michael Kamen.)

1996

1. Featuring the restored wall murals painted in 1960 by Stuart Sutcliffe and Rod Murray, the newly refurbished Jacaranda Club in Liverpool hosted what group on its opening night, 25 January?

2. On 30 January, Paul attended the dedication of the Liverpool Institute for the Performing Arts, which he helped found on the cite of the former Liverpool Institute High School for Boys. What room in LIPA was named in his honor?

3. Joan Armatrading, Mark Knopfler, Carly Simon, Vangelis, producers Glyn Johns and Sir George Martin, and former Beyond the Fringe members Dudley Moore and Dr. Jonathan Miller are all patons in something with Sir Paul—what is it?

4. Ringo picked up an $800,000 paycheck in 1996 for doing a TV commercial seen only in Japan. What product was he pitching?

5. Originally scheduled for 27 February, the release of *Anthology 2* was delayed until 18 March—why?

6. The central images in Klaus Voormann and Alfons Kiefer's triptych for the *Anthology* albums include the cover of the Savage Records release *The Savage Young Beatles* on *Anthology 1* and the cover of *Let It Be* on *Anthology 3*. For *Anthology 2*, the central image was based upon a photo of the Beatles performing live—where?

7. Whose face replaced Oscar Wilde's on the portion of the cover of *Sgt. Pepper* visible on the cover of *Anthology 2*?

8. During a private signing session at a hotel in Los Angeles for a line of collectible plates issued by Gartlan USA, 25 April, Ringo mentioned that his own collecting interests included crosses, European dragons, early pirates and owls. He also divulged his lucky number—what is it?

9. Claiming that she was "sharing the words of God," Yoko earned the displeasure of the Archdiocese of New York and the Catholic League when she began tearing pages out of a Bible and handing them to audience members at the edge of the stage during her concert with Ima at Irving Plaza, 14 May. What Beatles song did she quote prior to her dispersement?

10. In *The Rock*, which opened in U.S. theaters 7 June, FBI Special Agent Dr. Stanley Goodspeed (Nicholas Cage) receives a package at work containing a Beatles record he ordered because his girlfriend "thinks it's dumb to spend $600 on an LP." "The girl is right," a fellow agent concurs, "why don't you just spend $13 on a CD, man?" "First of all, it's because I'm a Beatlemaniac," replies Goodspeed, examining the album, "and second, these sound better." What album did Stanley buy?

11. Despite a petition from sixty-four members of Parliament, Paul, George, and Ringo were not among those up for knighthood on the Queen's Birthday Honors List, issued at midnight, 15 June. Another important Beatles person was however—who?

12. While not billed as the Who, the three surviving members reunited for a "MasterCard Masters of Music Concert for the Prince's Trust" at London's Hyde Park, 29 June. Taking up behind the drum kit was Ringo's son, Zak. A crowd estimated at 100,000 watched as Starkey backed Townshend, Daltry, and Entwistle as they performed what album in its entirety?

13. "Driving down to Fiddler's Green to hear a tune or two/I thought I saw John Lennon there, looking kind of blue."

Grateful Dead lyricist Robert Hunter wrote these lyrics for what song, released by a Rykodisc artist in 1996?

14. What McCartney song do the Red House Painters cover on their 1996 Supreme Records/Island album *songs for a blue guitar*?

15. What Lennon song did Stevie Wonder perform during the Closing Ceremonies of the Summer Olympic Games in Atlanta, 4 August?

16. A Sotheby's auction in London 19 September saw Paul McCartney's recording notes for "Hey Jude" fetch £25,300 ($39,030). The mystery buyer turned out not to be a Beatles fan with deep pockets, but someone with more sentimental reasons for acquiring the notes—who was it?

17. This nine-minute film directed by Paul McCartney had its U.S. premiere at the New York Film Festival, 28–29 September. Who was the subject of Macca's film, made from four rolls of stills taken by Linda in 1967–1968?

18. What Lennon song was attempted as the third reunion single to accompany the release of *Anthology 3*?

19. Readers calling the phone number listed in an ad placed in the 14 October issue of *The New Yorker* for this fur dealer heard the voice of Paul McCartney inviting them to leave their name and address for a free fur video "featuring our lively collection of fox, mink and raccoon. You'll be astounded and could save thousands." What was the name of the furrier?

20. A group mind of alien invaders known as The Hive attempt to use the Beatles' appearance on *The Ed Sullivan Show*, 9 February 1964, to trigger a mass suicide in an episode of the NBC-TV science fiction series *Dark Skies*, first aired 26 October. What Beatles soundalike band portrayed the group?

21. The Rutles reunited in 1996, without the participation of Dirk McQuickly. "He gave up music and got into comedy," explained Ron Nasty. A new album was subsequently compiled. "Some of it was stuff I found in my shed, some of it's new and some of it was stuff we buried in a time capsule at the bottom of Barry's garden to thwart bootleggers. And the taxman." While the plan apparently was for the capsule to remain interred for a thousand years, "Barry's dog dug it up." Issued on Virgin Records, 29 October, what is the reunion disc's title?

22. Pete Best was paid £10,000 to do a commercial for this product, where he is seen sitting alone in the Cavern Club. What was he endorsing?

23. George personally overruled Northern Songs Ltd. when they refused British band Kula Shaker permission to borrow the riff from this Harrison song for "Gokula," the B-side of their hit "Govinda," issued by Columbia, 11 November. What song did they use?

24. An exhibit of Linda McCartney's photographs opened at the IPC Gallery in New York, 8 November. With its theme of life on the road in her husband's various bands, what was the exhibit called?

25. Name the two McCartney songs featured on the film soundtrack of *Jerry Maguire*, starring Tom Cruise.

ANSWERS

1. The Pete Best Band played the opening night at the Jacaranda Club.

2. LIPA's 513-seat capacity U-shaped auditorium with a U-shaped balcony is named the Sir Paul McCartney Auditorium.

(Closed in 1985, McCartney launched his drive in June 1990 to reopen the Institute [which he attended in 1957] as a "Fame school," hosting three fundraising launches in January 1992, in addition to contributing $1.5 million of his own money. Building and fit-out were completed in December 1995. Degree programs for its first two-hundred students began 8 January.)

3. All are noted as official "Patrons" of the Liverpool Institute for the Performing Arts, with Sir Paul designated "Lead Patron."

4. Ringo's Japanese commercial was for apple juice, specifically Takara's mashed apple juice, *Suriorosi Ringo*.

(Shot in front of a Mount Fuji backdrop at Barnaby Studios in Vancouver, B.C., Starr's only spoken lines were "Ringo Starr!" and "Ringo Sutta!" [or "mashed apples!"]. "Ringo" [pronounced "leen-gaw"] in Japanese, means "apple.")

5. The original tunestack for disc one of *Anthology 2* had "I'm Down" as track 6. When McCartney requested it be moved to track 3, the revision pushed back the release to 18 March, resulting in the trashing of album components including the pulping of an estimated 2.5 million CD booklets.

6. Executed by Voormann and Kiefer to resemble a concert poster, the central image for *Anthology 2* was based on a photograph taken of the Beatles onstage at the Circus-Kron-Bau in Munich (West) Germany, 24 June 1966.

7. The face of Alfons Kiefer, the artist who collaborated with Klaus Voormann on the *Anthology* cover triptych painting, was substituted for Oscar Wilde on *Anthology 2*.
    (Voormann suggested the modification as a joke for the Beatles to discover and as a way to include the artist in a fashion similar to Voormann's—worked into George's hair just below his drawing of John, a detail from his cover for *Revolver*. Klaus looks as he did in 1966 on *Anthology 2* and circa 1996 on *Anthology 3*.)

8. Ringo's lucky number is 27.

9. Yoko quoted from "Julia."
    ("Half of what I say is meaningless/But I say it just to reach you . . .")

10. Stanley is examining a stereo copy of Capitol's *Meet the Beatles*.
    (Unless the album was autographed, the author is at a loss to explain why the producers of *The Rock* would have a "Beatlemaniac" like Goodspeed dropping $600 on a copy of *Meet the Beatles*, the first of the label's early album releases to which Capitol producer Dave Dexter Jr. added echo.)

11. George Martin, already a C.B.E. (Commander of the British Empire), was honored with knighthood.

12. Zak drummed behind the Who as they performed their 1973 album *Quadrophenia*.

13. Sung by Grateful Dead drummer Mickey Hart, Robert Hunter's lyrics for the song "Down the Road" appear on the Rykodisc CD, *Mickey Hart's Mystery Box*.

14. The Red House Painters covered "Silly Love Songs" in a unique arrangement running to nearly eleven minutes by lead vocalist by Mark Kozelek.

("My whole thing is to take completely retarded songs and turn them into something of my own. What can I bring to a song that's already been done well?" Kozelek told *BAM Magazine* of *blue guitar*'s covers, which also include "All Mixed Up" by The Cars and "Long Distance Runaround" by Yes.)

15. More than 80,000 people in Centennial Olympic Park watched as Stevie Wonder sang "Imagine."

16. McCartney's "Hey Jude" recording notes went to Julian Lennon, who was the song's initial inspiration.

17. McCartney's film was about the Grateful Dead.

(The Juggler Films production, *Grateful Dead—A Photofilm*, was made from Linda's photographs of the group taken at the Dead's house at 710 Ashbury in San Francisco and from a concert in New York's Central Park. The soundtrack features excerpts from "That's It for the Other One," "New Potato Caboose," and "Alligator" from *Anthem of the Sun*, the group's second album, released by Warner Bros. in July 1968.)

18. The third Lennon song attempted was "Now and Then."

(According to McCartney, "George didn't like it. The Beatles being a democracy, we didn't do it.")

19. Paul's Furs.

(McCartney had collaborated with PETA [People for the Ethical Treatment of Animals] who placed the $1,800 ad. "Prospective customers [requesting the video] will see who pays the ultimate price for fur: the animals," said Paul in a PETA statement.)

20. The MopTops portrayed the Beatles on *The Ed Sullivan Show* in the *Dark Skies* episode "Dark Days Night."

21. The Rutles' reunion disc is titled *Archaeology*.

(The Rutles' reunion came about when Neil Innes put together a new group, billed as "The New Rutles" [Innes and Beatles soundalike band The MopTops] to perform a one-off show at the Troubador in Los Angeles, 9 September 1994. Their set was so well-received, a second show was added two days later. With interest in the group piqued [and the Beatles' own *Anthology* reunion imminent], a new Rutles CD resulted. While Eric Idle, as the creator of the Rutles, allowed Innes to use the name, he did not participate in *Archaeology*, believing the original film and album were near-perfect on their own. In early 2000, Idle began touring the U.S. with "Eric Idle Exploits Monty Python," billed as "a rather stupid evening of skits and songs," which included a special guest appearance by *Sir* Dirk McQuickly of the Rutles.)

22. Best picked up a £10,000 paycheck for doing a commercial for Carlsberg lager, touted in the ad as "probably the Pete Best lager in the world."

23. Kula Shaker frontman Crispian Mills (son of actress Hayley), personally appealed to Harrison to use the riff from "Ski-ing" (from *Wonderwall Music*) in "Gokula."

(Kula Shaker issued two CD singles in the UK for "Govinda," each featuring "Gokula." The second single [KULA CD5K] offers a mix of "Govinda" titled "Govinda, Hari & St. George.")

24. Described as "stills from a personal road movie recording a slice of my life," Linda's Bradford exhibit was titled "Roadworks."

(A companion book was first published by Little, Brown in the UK, 7 November.)

25. *Jerry Maguire* featured "Momma Miss America" and "Singalong Junk."

(Originally issued by Apple in April 1970 on *McCartney*, both songs are included on the accompanying Epic Soundtrack CD *Jerry Maguire: Music From the Motion Picture* released in December. "Singalong Junk" is actually take 1 of "Junk," the shorter, vocal version McCartney released being take 2.)

1997

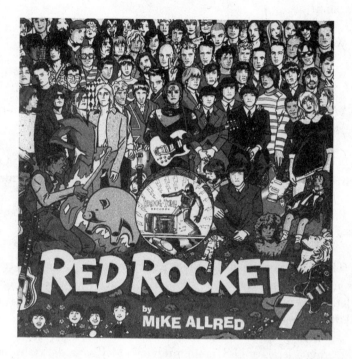

1. In January, Paul obtained an legal injunction against Lily Evans, the widow of Beatles roadie Mal Evans, to prevent her from selling in auction a scrap of paper containing an original draft in McCartney's hand of which Beatles song?

2. Chicago band Veruca Salt (named after a character in Roald Dahl's children's novel *Charlie and the Chocolate Factory*) took the title of their 1994 debut album *American Thighs*, from an AC/DC song. Their second album, issued early in 1997 drew its title from a Beatles castoff. What is it?

3. The morning Paul went to Buckingham Palace to be knighted by Queen Elizabeth II, 11 March, what gift did Linda give him?

4. The same day Paul McCartney made Queen Elizabeth's New Year's Honours list for knighthood (announced 31 December 1996), another former member of Brian Epstein's stable of acts also was up for honors—who?

5. The 1997 edition of Ringo's "All-Starr Band" started their tour 28 April at Seattle's Moore Theater. Who was in this fourth version of Starr's band?

6. Who sponsored Ringo's 1997 All-Starr tour?

7. What are "After Heavy Years" and "He Awoke Startled"?

8. Where did Paul come up with the title for his Capitol album *Flaming Pie*, first issued in the UK, 5 May?

9. A reunion took place during the All-Starr's show at Fiddler's Green in Denver, 7 May, which Ringo dubbed "2% Milk"—who was reunited?

10. Paul McCartney, The Mighty Mighty Bosstones and Reel Big Fish—what do they have in common?

11. The version of "Beautiful Night" on *Flaming Pie* is actually a remake of a song Paul first recorded in 1986. McCartney produced the remake with Jeff Lynne at his studio in Sussex, beginning 13 May 1996. Who produced the original version?

12. During a series of U.S. radio interviews McCartney gave in June to promote *Flaming Pie*, what group did Paul state he thought would be the next Beatles?

13. What Beatles album does Tommy Lee Jones reference in the sci-fi comedy *Men In Black*, which opened in U.S. theaters, 2 July?

14. In July, McCartney agreed to participate in the taping of an MTV *Unplugged* (his second for the series), this time as part of an all-star lineup including Bob Dylan, Patti Smith, Ornette Coleman, Philip Glass, Mark Ribot, and Beck. The show was never made, however—who had *Unplugged* planned to feature?

15. The alien clone title character of Mike Allred's seven-issue graphic novel series (debuting 20 August) was very tight with the Beatles, showing John how to play "Be-Bop-A-Lula" at the Woolton Parish Fête in July 1957, helping Neil Aspinall and George Martin as the group's star rose during 1962–64, even taping the Beatles' legendary jam with Elvis when the two met 27 August 1965. His influence on rock was far reaching, interacting with Elvis, Little Richard, the Rolling Stones, David Bowie, Lou Reed, and many others. Who is he?

16. "It became my last No. 1 and probably my last single," Sir George Martin told *Billboard* magazine in 1999. "It's not a bad one to go out on." After forty-eight years, Sir George Martin retired from music production in 1998, but his last number one single, which he produced and wrote the instrumental score for, was recorded during 1997–what was its title?

17. Released in September, what group closed their fourth album with a cover of "Norwegian Wood (This Bird has Flown)" sung in Punjabi?

18. What band obtained permission from Pauline Sutcliffe to use two of her brother Stuart's paintings for the covers of EPs released on Parlophone in September?

19. On 15 October, Sir Paul, Lady Linda, Ringo, and Barbara were in Paris at the Garnier opera house for the debut of Stella McCartney's new spring-summer ready-to-wear line for Chloe. As top models Kate Moss, Naomi Campbell, and others came down the runway in Stella's creations, what Beatles song introduced the collection?

20. On 4 November, Paul picked up Best Songwriter award at the eighth annual *Q* awards, at London's Park Lane Hotel. Back at Table 10, gong in hand, McCartney was soon reaching for his coat when this man's name was announced as the recipient of the *Q* Special Award. Who did Paul walk out on?

21. An EMI information letter sent to journalists announced a release date of 25 November for a thirtieth anniversary remastered CD of *Sgt. Pepper's Lonely Hearts Club Band*. Without explanation, the release of this limited edition package was withdrawn. *Sgt. Pepper* has been available on CD since it was initially shipped 26 May 1987–what was so special about this release?

22. George Harrison noted that ". . . they don't have much depth. The other bloke's just a pain. I don't think they need him. The one who writes the songs—he can sing them just as well." Paul McCartney seemed to concur, telling Steve Richards of the *New Statesman*, "They're derivative and they think too much of themselves. I hope for their sakes they're right. But they really mean nothing to me." Who were they referring to?

23. "I am personally not afraid of nudity, there's no more in this video than you'd see on any statue anywhere in the world." What video was Paul referring to?

24. Who is Spud?

25. Yoko was quoted in the 28 December edition of *The Sunday Times* as describing Paul McCartney as a musician whose true genius was for organizing John Lennon's talent. Ono went on to compare Lennon's relationship with McCartney to that of which two classical composers?

ANSWERS

1. "With a Little Help from My Friends."

(Lily Evans said she found the manuscript among papers left by her husband. "There is no question that they ever belonged to anyone other than the Beatles," said McCartney in a statement issued 9 January, asserting that Mal was holding the lyrics for the Beatles as their employee. In 1998, Paul would pay Lily £100,000 for Mal's holdings, including "With A Little Help from My Friends" and an original draft of "Yesterday.")

2. Produced by Bob Rock, Veruca Salt's second album was called *Eight Arms to Hold You.*

(The title, first suggested by Ringo, was originally announced, 17 March 1965, as the name of the Beatles' forthcoming second film. In mid-April, the title was changed to *Help!*)

3. The morning Paul became Sir Paul, Linda gave him a silver pocket watch.

(On the back, along with hearts and kisses was the inscription: "To Paul, my knight in shining armour.—Linda.")

4. Cilla Black was made an OBE (Officer of the Order of the British Empire).

5. Ringo's fourth "All-Starr Band" lineup featured Gary Brooker (keyboards), Jack Bruce (bass), Peter Frampton (guitar), Simon Kirke (drums), Dave Mason (guitar), and musical director Mark Rivera (sax, percussion, and guitar).

6. Ringo's 1997 All-Starr Tour was sponsored by Glade air freshener.

7. These are the titles of the first two movements of *Paul McCartney's Standing Stone*, a seventy-five-minute symphonic poem EMI Classics President Richard Lyttelton commissioned McCartney to write to mark the 100th anniversary of the company.

(Lawrence Foster conducted the London Symphony Orchestra and Chorus, recording the album 30 April to 2 May in Abbey Road's Studio One. It was first released by EMI Classics in the U.S., 23 September.)

8. Riding on horseback with Linda in February 1996, Paul was mulling over the lyrics for what would become the album's title track (specifically, searching for a rhyme for "sky"), when he recalled John's story of the origin of the name Beatles, having come ". . . in a vision—a man appeared on a flaming pie and said unto them 'From this day on you are Beatles with an A.' "

(Lennon's man on the flaming pie appears in "Being A Short Diversion on the Dubious Origins of Beatles," an article featured in the first issue of Bill Harry's *Mersey Beat* newspaper, dated July 6–20 1961.)

9. Jack Bruce's "White Room" solo spotlight in Denver turned into a reunion of two-thirds of Cream when drummer Ginger Baker (who lived in Colorado) joined the All-Starrs onstage.

10. All have songs included on the soundtrack of *Father's Day*, starring Robin Williams and Billy Crystal, which opened in U.S. theaters 9 May.

(McCartney contributed two songs from *Flaming Pie*, "Young Boy" and "The World Tonight" [heard over the closing credits]. The Mighty Mighty Bosstones are heard performing "The Impression I Get," while Reel Big Fish are represented with "I'll Never Die.")

11. McCartney and Phil Ramone produced the original version of "Beautiful Night," recorded 21 August 1986 at New York's Power Station.

(McCartney included the original version as part of "Oobu Joobu— Part 5," a bonus track on the first of two "Beautiful Night" CD singles issued by EMI, 15 December 1997.)

12. "I thought they were a really cool band," said Paul, speaking with Atlanta radio station 99X of Nirvana, whom he once thought would be the next band to become as big as the Beatles.

13. *Men In Black* makes reference to *The Beatles* (the White Album).

(While giving Jay [Will Smith] a tour of the headquarters of MIB Special Services, Kay [Tommy Lee Jones] notes that the organization is not government funded. "We own the patents on a few gadgets that we confiscated from out-of-state visitors," he explains. Kay then shows him a small disc about the size of a half-dollar. "This is a fascinating little gadget. It's gonna replace CDs soon. Guess I'll have to buy the White Album again.")

14. Allen Ginsberg.

(Before the show could be taped Ginsberg, who had been battling liver cancer, died 5 April.)

15. *Madman* creator Mike Allred's rock and roll clone is Red Rocket 7.

(Allred has frequently snuck Beatles references into his work. A movie poster for *Help!* shows up in his first book, *Dead Air*. In *Citizen Nocturne*, the story of a reluctant vampire, John makes a cameo in a German dance club, based upon a 1966 photo taken at Candlestick Park by rock photographer Jim Marshall.)

16. George Martin's final number one single was Elton John's tribute to Diana, Princess of Wales, "Candle In the Wind 1997."

(Elton sang the song solo on grand piano at her funeral at Westminster Abbey, 6 September. Following the performance, John went to Martin's AIR Studios to record the single, released in the UK 13 September. A reported 600,000 copies were sold the first day in England, making it the first single in history to enter at No. 1 based on first day sales. Worldwide orders for the single were said to have topped eight million. "Candle" was George's thirtieth number one single in the UK.)

17. Adapted and sung in Punjabi by British Asian Tjinder Singh, with some fine sitar by Anthony Saffery, Cornershop covered "Norwegian Wood" on their album *When I was Born for the 7th Time*.

18. Mansun obtained permission from Pauline Sutcliffe to use two of Stuart's paintings for their *Seven EP Closed for Business* cover art.

(Paul Draper contacted Pauline after attending a retrospective of Stuart's art in Liverpool earlier in the year. The painting on CD1 was signed and dated by Sutcliffe in 1962, the year of his death. Formed in the summer of 1995, the predominantly Liverpudlian Mansun [shortened from A Man Called Sun] also reference the Beatles on the Draper composition "Taxloss," from *Six EP Taxlo$$*, issued by Parlophone 28 April. The song is a play on Albert Tatlock, a character from the long-running British soap opera *Coronation Street*. "The track is a pisstake of the Beatles," notes a Parlophone-run web site on the group, "lyrical references include

Albert's age as seventy-four, as opposed to when I'm sixty-four, he's got long hair and is from Liverpool.")

19.   "All You Need Is Love."

(Stella, who replaced Karl Lagerfeld as the chief designer for the House of Chloe, dedicated the show to her mother.)

20.   Calling it "a Let It Be thing," McCartney walked out on Phil Spector.

(Telling reporters "I'm not a man who forgets," McCartney does not appear to have forgiven Phil for his lush production of *Let It Be*, notably the orchestral and choral tracks added to "The Long and Winding Road" in Studio One, 1 April 1970.)

21.   The remastered CD version of *Sgt. Pepper* announced for release on 25 November would have made these songs available in mono.

(The Beatles considered the mono version of *Sgt. Pepper*, in the words of Richard Lush, "the only real version," and were present for all the mono mix sessions at Abbey Road. By contrast, no Beatles were present for the stereo mixes, which were completed in only a few days by George Martin and engineers Geoff Emerick and Richard Lush.)

22.   These quotes from George and Paul were directed at Oasis.

23.   Jokingly dubbed "Hey Nude" by the press, McCartney's quote was in reference to the controversy over the uncut version of Julien Temple's promotional video for "Beautiful Night," in which twenty-four-year-old actress/model Emma Moore is seen stripping off her gown for a skinny dip in the River Mersey.

24.   Spud is the name of the four-piece band of sixteen-year-old A-level students from Ealing seen playing with Ringo and Paul in the "Beautiful Night" video.

(A scout for video director Julien Temple spotted the group playing a small gig at the Monarch Club.)

25.   "(John) is a visionary and that is why the Beatles happened. (Paul) is put in the position of being a Salieri to a Mozart."

(Yoko was referencing the relationship of Antonio Salieri to that of Wolfgang Amadeus Mozart. Salieri's technically brilliant work was overshadowed in the court of Vienna by that of Mozart. Some believe he plotted against his rival and may even have schemed to poison him.)

1998

1. When Carl Perkins died 19 January at the age of 65 of complications from three strokes he had suffered the previous November and December, George attended his funeral at the R. E. Womack Memorial Chapel in Jackson, Tennessee, 23 January. What song did Harrison perform at the service as a tribute?

2. Debuting 4 March at the Museum of Science in Boston, the soundtrack to the IMAX film *Everest* married orchestral arrangements of Harrison compositions such as "All Things Must Pass," "Give Me Love," "Life Itself," and "This Is Love" (performed by the Norwest Sinfonia Orchestra) to new compositions by film composer/producers Steve Wood and Daniel May. What song, performed live by Harrison, is heard over the film's closing credits?

3. First printed in the April 1998 issue of *Interzone* magazine, this short story by sci-fi author Stephen Baxter details the contents of *God*, a Beatles album (on Apple) that should not exist in this world. Discovered among the possessions of a man referred to as Sick Note, the album's highlight is the group's version of "Maybe I'm Amazed"—sung by John! What is Baxter's short story titled?

4. Who is Mellow T. Ron?

5. "We had a record contract and we were on a roll. The last thing we needed was one little bedroom recording to come out." What was Harrison referring to, during an appearance in London High Court on behalf of Apple, 6 May?

6. What is the name of the band Ringo put together to promote his *Vertical Man* album?

7. Sean Lennon's debut album, *Into the Sun*, was first issued in the UK, 18 May, on the Beastie Boys' Grand Royal label. What was originally announced as the album's title?

8. Who is the "mystery voice" saying "Goodnight Sean" on "Sean's Theme," the last cut on *Into the Sun*?

9. Coincidentally (?), Julian Lennon's fifth album, *Photograph Smile*, was released by Music From Another Room/Rough Trade in the UK the same day *Into the Sun* by half-brother Sean was issued—18 May. Who did Julian dedicate the album to?

10. Who are Schoo and Tinsel?

11. The commercially released version of Ringo's *Vertical Man* album (first issued on Mercury in the U.S., 16 June), doesn't include something featured on advance CD and cassette copies—what is it?

12. Ringo found the title for *Vertical Man* while "reading this huge book of quotes that my step-daughter, Francesca, won at school." The quote Starr discovered is an excerpt from a poem by what poet?

13. *Vertical Man* was one of two titles considered for the album—what was the other?

14. What group makes a brief cameo in the video Ringo made for "La De Da," the first single from *Vertical Man*?

15. What song on *Vertical Man* did Ringo say was written after a walk in Monaco?

16. What is the connection between artists Mary Engelbreit, Maxfield Parrish, Alberto Vargas, and Ringo Starr?

17. This Beatle's former residence, opened to the general public 29 July, was the first building bought and restored by Britain's National Trust because of its significance to twentieth-century popular culture. What house did the NT purchase?

18. Linda McCartney's third collaboration with Argentinian animator Oscar Grillo had its world premiere at the Edinburgh International Film Festival in Scotland, 19 August. What is the film's title?

19. Sean Lennon appeared as the musical guest on the two-hundredth episode of this popular nighttime soap, 14 September. What is the name of the show?

20. Who is Julie Lewis and what is her connection to Paul McCartney?

21. Who is Alistair Donald and what is his relationship to Paul?

22. Who sings the cover of "Getting Better" featured in the Philips Flat TV commercials which began airing in the fall of 1998?

23. Starring Tobey Maguire and Reese Witherspoon, *Pleasantville* had its world premiere 1 October at the Austin Film Festival. What Beatles song is featured on the soundtrack?

24. What is unique about the acoustic version of "New York City" which opens disc two of the *John Lennon Anthology*, the four-CD box set issued by Capitol in the U.S., 3 November?

25. What is the title of the essay by horror writer Poppy Z. Brite that speculates on the social impact of a homosexual relationship between John and Paul?

ANSWERS

1. Harrison sang the Perkins song "Your True Love" at Carl's funeral.

2. A live version of "Here Comes the Sun" is heard over the closing credits of *Everest*, the IMAX documentary of the infamous May 1996 summit attempt of Mt. Everest.

(Included on George's *Live in Japan* album, this version was recorded at the Castle Hall in Osaka, 12 December 1991.)

3. Stephen Baxter's short story is titled "The Twelfth Album."

(Baxter's title presupposes that there are only eleven UK Beatles albums, not including *Yellow Submarine* "which was mostly a George Martin movie score" or *Magical Mystery Tour*, which was first issued as an LP in the U.S.)

4. Paul contributed a version of "A Room With A View" to Pet Shop Boy Neil Tennant's Noël Coward tribute charity album, doing all the instruments himself as Mellow T. Ron and his Mood Men, featuring Slick Willie Guitar.

(In June 1965, Coward attended one of the Beatles' four concerts at the Teatro Adriano in Rome. In his diary entry for 4 July, he related being sickened by the "mob hysteria." "I was truly horrified and shocked by the audience," he wrote. "It was like a mass masturbation orgy . . ." *Twentieth Century Blues: The Songs of Noël Coward*, was issued in the UK by EMI, 13 April.)

5. The "bedroom recording" Harrison was remarking on were the mono recordings made of the Beatles by Adrian Barber at the Star-Club in December 1962.

(On 8 May, Judge Sir David Neuberger ruled that Lingasong Music Ltd. discontinue sales of the recordings and hand over the original tapes and any copies to Apple.)

6. The band Ringo assembled to promote *Vertical Man* are called the Roundheads.

(The Roundheads are band musical director Mark Hudson [guitar, backing vocals]: Joe Walsh [guitar]; Steve Dudas [guitar]; Gary Burr [guitar]; Jim Cox [keyboards]; Jack Blades [bass]; and Simon Kirke [drums]. Starr publicly debuted his new band at the Bottom Line in New York City, 12 May.)

7. *Into the Sun* had originally been announced as forthcoming under the title *Photosynthesis*.

8. Walter Sear, at whose Sear Sound studio in Manhattan *Into the Sun* was recorded, is the mystery voice that says "Goodnight Sean."

("It was a reference to my dad," Sean told *Mojo* magazine, "because he always used to say 'Goodnight Sean' before I went to sleep, like on *Double Fantasy*.")

9. Julian dedicated *Photograph Smile* to his ex-stepfather Roberto Bassanini, whom he notes was "more of a father to me than anyone."

10. After a courageous two-year battle with breast cancer, Linda McCartney died at the family's eighty-acre ranch home northeast of Tucson, Arizona, 17 April. Following Paul's emotional address at her memorial service in London, 8 June, two Shetland ponies named Schoo and Tinsel, which he had given her as Christmas presents the previous year, were led up the aisle of St. Martin's-in-the-Fields Church.

(Paul also played a tape of his version of Jack Lawrence's song "Linda" at the service.)

11. Advance copies of Ringo's *Vertical Man* album include a mix of the Dobie Gray hit "Drift Away" with Alanis Morrissette and Aerosmith's Steven Tyler sharing the lead vocals with Ringo. Columbia Records requested that Tyler's vocals be removed from the final release.

(The reason given was that they did not want the track competing with the two new Aerosmith songs included on the *Armageddon* movie soundtrack. New lead vocals by Tom Petty replaced Tyler's on the commercial release, though he is still credited for his drumming on the track.)

12. Ringo found the title *Vertical Man* in the poem "Shorts," written in 1930 by W. H. (Wystan Hugh) Auden:

> Let us honor if we can
> The vertical man,
> Though we value none
> But the horizontal one.

13. *Vertical Man* coproducer Mark Hudson told *Beatlefan* Contributing Editor Rip Rense that the other title considered was "the old Beatle adage, 'Thanks for Comin'.'"

14. Isaac, Taylor, and Zachary, a trio of brothers from Oklahoma known by their surname, Hanson, are seen briefly in the video for "La De Da."

15. During the taping for VH1's *Storytellers* 13 May, Ringo related that the song "I Was Walkin' " was written after a walk in Monaco.

16. Works by Engelbreit, Parrish, and Vargas are included among the grid of squares comprising the cover of *Vertical Man*.
(A portion of Parrish's 1922 work "Daybreak" is included on the back cover of the *Vertical Man* CD booklet.)

17. In 1995, the National Trust paid £55,000 for the three bedroom 1950s terraced house at 20 Forthlin Road in the Liverpool suburb of Allerton where the McCartney family lived from 1955 to 1964.

18. Linda McCartney conceived and produced *Wide Prairie*, a seven-minute animated short directed by Oscar Grillo.
(Based on the Linda McCartney song of the same name, *Wide Prairie* was screened in Edinburgh, appropriately enough, before the British premiere of the Robert Redford film *The Horse Whisperer*.)

19. Sean Lennon is seen rehearsing and later performing from the stage of the Jazz Club in "The World According to Matt," the two-hundredth episode of the FOX-TV series *Melrose Place*.

20. A photograph of nude model Julie Lewis (taken by pin-up photographer Bunny Yeager) is prominent amongst the artwork used on *Rushes*, the second collaboration between Paul McCartney and Youth as The Fireman, first issued by Hydra/EMI in the UK, 21 September.

21. Television producer Alistair Donald became Paul's son-in-law when he married twenty-seven-year-old Mary McCartney at St. Peter and St. Paul's Church in Peasmarch, 26 September.

22. The version of "Getting Better" used in commercials for Philips Flat TV was recorded by the British group Gomez.
(Gomez were persuaded to do the ad when they were offered the chance to record their version at Abbey Road studios. "We weren't even sure they were gonna like it, it was so ridiculously rushed," said Tom Gray. "But it was just a great opportunity for us to go into Abbey Road and be the Beatles." Rather than being sent to Los Angeles by conventional

means, Gomez's finished song was instead sent digitally over a high speed phone connection.)

23. *Pleasantville* concludes with a version of "Across the Universe" sung by Fiona Apple.

24. The acoustic version of "New York City" on the *John Lennon Anthology* was mastered from a bootleg source.

("Over the years Yoko had some stuff stolen from her," related *Anthology* coproducer/engineer Rob Stevens. "So I took that and I cleaned it up. By the way, I felt no guilt about bootlegging the bootleg.")

25. In "Would You?" Brite details "how much better the world would be if John and Paul had been queer for each other."

1999

1. What Lennon/McCartney song is used as the opening theme of the NBC-TV show *Providence*, starring Melina Kanakaredes and Mike Farrell, debuting in the U.S., 8 January?

2. On 29 January, a day shy of its thirtieth anniversary, this Beatles soundalike band recreated in dress and manner the Beatles' final live performance on the roof of 3 Savile Row, their former Apple Corp. headquarters. What is the name of this group, who played for 25 minutes (with police permission) as a charity fundraiser?

3. Robin is studying old news tapes of the Beatles while Wonder Girl, Impulse, and Secret patrol a Beatles Expo at the Midtown Convention Center attempting to solve a riddle posed by a villain named Harm in this issue of what DC Comics title, dated February 1999?

4. Ringo's fifth All-Starr Band opened its tenth anniversary tour 12 February at the Taj Mahal Casino in Atlantic City, New Jersey. Who was onstage?

5. Paul McCartney was finally inducted into the Rock and Roll Hall of Fame as a solo artist 15 March, at ceremonies at the Waldorf-Astoria Hotel. Who did the honors?

6. In Paul's acceptance speech, he encouraged the Hall of Fame committee to finish the job, "You got me and John in this. What about George and Ringo? C'mon guys." McCartney then brought up his daughter Stella, who delighted the crowd with the phrase printed on the white tank top she wore. What did it say?

7. Who is Arthur Donald?

8. Paul made an unbilled appearance at a tribute concert for Linda, held at London's Royal Albert Hall, 10 April. Hofner in hand, McCartney introduced the first song he sang as "one Linda and I used to listen to—I was in Liverpool, she was in New York, we both listened to it in the '50s." What song did he sing?

9. *Here There and Everywhere, A Concert for Linda,* boasted an impressive roster of acts, including the Pretenders, Neil Finn, and Marianne Faithfull. Tom Jones sang "She's a Woman," George Michael performed "Eleanor Rigby," and Elvis Costello covered two McCartney compositions—what were they?

10. First aired on FOX-TV in the U.S. 25 April, this episode of *The Simpsons* finds Bart required to perform twenty hours of community service at the Springfield Retirement Castle after his actions cost the town its chance to host the Olympic games. When Bart and the seniors escape the home to cavort around Springfield, their antics parody the field scene from *A Hard Day's Night.* What group performed "Can't Buy Me Love" for the sequence?

11. *Paul McCartney Paintings,* an exhibit of seventy-three oil and acrylic works, opened at the Lyz Art Forum in Siegen, Germany, 1 May. The show, which ran through 25 July, also featured a picture-sound installation comprising a six video monitor sculpture designed by McCartney that shows him playing several different guitars and a chainsaw. Original music accompanying the display was heard over twelve tape machines. What was this piece titled?

12. On 10 May, the *London Sun* reported that a "source close to the group" had said that the Beatles had "unearthed" a track recorded in

1968 that had been "completely forgotten." "No new work has been done on it," the source was quoted, "but Paul, George and Ringo have said this will be the last ever Beatles single—there's nothing else left." The source turned out to be Beatles spokesman Geoff Baker who, while not at liberty to reveal the song's title, told the Reuters news agency "it's a real rocker" from the *Yellow Submarine* sessions. "John is singing on it," said Baker. "It is not a 'Free As A Bird' job." Beatle fans smelled something fishy and their suspicions were borne out when the true nature of this "lost" track was revealed to be simply a remix of what song?

13. Sponsored by Linda McCartney Vegetarian Foods, the Linda McCartney Pro Cycling Team was launched in early February in a ceremony in London's Trafalgar Square. Paul composed an exclusive instrumental for the team, recorded at Abbey Road studios, 28 May. At the time of this writing, it could only be heard on the team's web site. What is its title?

14. "I've turned down work all year," Linda told this woman in 1998, "but I'm really excited because (your album) is so strong, and I love strong." Whose album did Linda shoot the cover for, very likely her last portrait, released by Warner Bros. in the U.S., 22 June 1999?

15. A musical tribute to Linda McCartney had its world premiere at the chapel of Charterhouse School in Surrey, England, 18 July. *A Garland for Linda*, a nine-song cycle, was written by eight British composers, including former Apple artist John Tavener. What is the title of the piece Paul composed for the Garland?

16. Premiering 16 August in Warwick, Rhode Island, what McCartney song is featured in the film *Outside Providence*, starring Alec Baldwin, Shawn Hatory, and Amy Smart?

17. A renovated version of *Yellow Submarine* was issued by MGM/UA 14 September, featuring a newly remixed and remastered Dolby Digital 5.1 soundtrack, replacing the film's original mono. The new version also reinstated the animated sequence for "Hey Bulldog," cut from the film following its world premiere at the London Pavilion, 17 July 1968. As a result, what sequence is not included on the DVD/video release?

18. Actress Patsy Kensit, wife of Oasis lead singer Liam Gallagher, delivered a six-pound boy by Caesarean at 8:40 P.M., 14 September, at central London's Portland Hospital. What did Liam name his son, in honor of John Lennon?

19. What do the Beatles, *Catch-22*, *Easy Rider*, the Motown Sound, Pop Art, *Rowan & Martin's Laugh-In*, *Star Trek*, and Woodstock have in common?

20. PETA (People for the Ethical Treatment of Animals) held their Party of the Century and Humanitarian Awards dinner, 18 September, at the Paramount Studios lot in Los Angeles. Paul attended the Millennium Gala, accompanied by daughter Stella, where he performed six songs included on his forthcoming rock oldies album *Run Devil Run*. McCartney also presented the first Linda McCartney Memorial Award—who was the recipient?

21. While in Atlanta in early January to help daughter Heather promote her new line of housewares, Paul was walking around the downtown with son James when he spotted a bottle of "Run Devil Run" bath salts in the window of a drug store. "I thought it was a good title for a song. So when I was on holiday after that, I started thinking of words for it and it came quite easily." A Dave Fine photograph of the store front graces the cover of the album, first issued by Parlophone/EMI in the UK, 4 October, but the name was changed to "Earl's Quick E Drugs." What is the store's actual name?

22. Sessions for *Run Devil Run* commenced at Abbey Road studios, 1 March. What was the first song recorded?

23. Who are Bett and Ted Robbins and what is their connection to *Run Devil Run*?

24. What Beatles song did Ringo remake for his Christmas album *Ringo Starr . . . I Wanna be Santa Claus*, issued by Island/Mercury in the U.S., 19 October?

25. At 23:44 GMT (Greenwich mean time) on 31 December, what Beatles song were guests in Greenwich, London, asked to join the 276-voice Millennium Choir in singing, prior to the Queen's opening of the Millennium Dome?

ANSWERS

1. As performed by Chantal Kreviazuk, *Providence* uses "In My Life" as its opening theme.

2. The Bootleg Beatles.
(The event was organized by the Building Societies Association, 3 Savile Row's current occupants, for their favorite charities.)

3. Harm poses the Riddler-like riddle, "Holy Beatles, Kids," in issue no. 5 of *Young Justice*.
(The answer is St. Swithin's Cathedral, where Harm planned a showdown during a midnight Mass led by Pope *John Paul* II, in a story by Peter David titled "First, Do No Harm." Perhaps best known for his *Star Trek* novels, David references Lennon's song "Beautiful Boy" in his *Next Generation* novel *Triangle: Imzadi II*. Early in the story, the thoughts of Deanna Troi, the *Enterprise*'s counselor, turn to her Imzadi, or "beloved," William Riker: "They were Imzadi, and they were supposed to be together. But life, as an Earth musician had said several centuries earlier, was what happened to you while you were making other plans.")

4. Ringo's fifth All-Starr Band included Gary Brooker (keyboards), Jack Bruce (bass), Timmy Capello (sax), Simon Kirke (drums) and Todd Rundgren (guitar).
(Joe Walsh had originally been announced as lead guitarist for the tour, but an impending Eagles tour caused him to pull out of the ASB two weeks before the start of rehearsals.)

5. Paul was inducted into the Rock and Roll Hall of Fame by Neil Young.
(Sir George Martin was also honored that evening in the non-performer category, inducted by producer Jimmy Iovine.)

6. Stella's tank top declared "About Fucking Time" on the front and "15/3/99" on the back, a reference to the five years Paul waited before joining John in the Hall as a solo artist.

7. On 3 April, Paul's daughter Mary gave birth to Arthur Donald, McCartney's first grandchild, who weighed in at seven pounds at a West London hospital.

8. Paul sang "Lonesome Town," a hit in 1958 for Ricky Nelson.
(McCartney also sang "All My Loving" and "Let It Be.")

9. Elvis sang "Warm and Beautiful" (from *Wings at the Speed of Sound*) and the McCartney/MacManus collaboration "That Day Is Done" (from *Flowers in the Dirt*).
(The concert was a benefit for the Animaline pet charity.)

10. The Providence, Rhode Island-based band NRBQ (New Rhythm and Blues Quartet) covered "Can't Buy Me Love" for "The Old Man and the 'C' Student," episode #AABF16 of *The Simpsons*.

11. Paul's performance art installation at his Siegen art exhibit was titled "Feedback."

12. The "lost" track turned out to be nothing more than a (badly-hyped) remix version of "Hey Bulldog."
(The proposed single was subsequently cancelled.)

13. Featuring a sample from "Penny Lane," Paul's instrumental for the Linda McCartney Pro Cycling Team is titled "Clean Machine."
(Paul dubbed the team "The Clean Machine" as all fifteen riders are vegetarians.)

14. Linda took the photo of Chrissie Hynde that graces the cover of ¡Viva El Amor! (Long Live Love), the eighth studio album by the Pretenders.
("Linda shot the cover—me with my fist in the air—based on those [South American] propaganda images. We did the picture exactly how we discussed it, just the one shot. And then she said, 'I'm going to the States, I'll see you in a couple of weeks.' And a month later she was dead.")

15. Paul's contribution to *A Garland for Linda* is titled "Nova."
(Performed by the thirty-voice Joyful Company of Singers, the piece was conceived by Stephen Connock, chairman of the Ralph Vaughan Williams Society, with performance proceeds benefitting a new charity dubbed the Garland Appeal. Connock was inspired by "A Garland for the Queen," a tribute written by ten British composers for the 1953 Coronation of Queen Elizabeth II. In addition to Paul and Tavener, Linda's "Garland" was written by Michael Berkeley, Judith Bingham, Sir Richard Rodney Bennett, David Matthews, Roxanna Panufnik, John Rutter, and Giles Swayne.)

16. The soundtrack for *Outside Providence* features Paul McCartney and Wings' version of "Band On The Run."

(Based on the novel by Peter Farrelly, the film also includes "No Matter What" by Badfinger. A soundtrack album was issued 24 August by Giant/Warner Bros.)

17. Reinstatement of the "Hey Bulldog" sequence meant the removal of footage that begins with Paul (the voice of Geoffrey Hughes), shouting "Beatles to battle!"

(This transitional sequence was created after the London opening and is not technically part of the original movie. According to "Sub" screenwriter Erich Segal, it was during a meeting with all four Beatles at Abbey Road Studios that Paul suggested that the "Hey Bulldog" footage be removed to improve the film for the U.S. market.)

18. Liam and Patsy named their son Lennon Francis Gallagher.

19. All were nominees in the Art & Entertainment category in the U.S. Postal Service's "Celebrate the Century" competition to select subjects for their decade of the '60s commemorative stamps.

(Voting by official ballot [or online] ran from 1 May to 30 May 1998, with approximately 930,000 ballots cast. The Beatles placed fourth overall; the other Art & Entertainment winners were *Star Trek* and Woodstock. First day of issue for the fifteen Celebrate the Century '60s stamps [with the Beatles' stamp depicting the Yellow Submarine] was 17 September in Green Bay, Wisconsin.)

20. The first Linda McCartney Memorial Award was presented to actress Pamela Anderson Lee for her animal rights work.

21. The Atlanta store front photographed for the cover of *Run Devil Run* is "Miller's Rexall Drugs."

22. The first song Paul recorded at the *Run Devil Run* sessions was Charlie Gracie's "Fabulous," first issued in the UK by Parlophone/EMI, 18 October, as a bonus track on two CD singles for "No Other Baby."

(McCartney first recalled hearing the song as a young man during "a day at the fairground, Sefton Park Fair, when I had on a blue fleck jacket, with a flap on the top pocket, and my mate had a fleck jacket too—I think mine was blue and his was white—it was just great. We thought we were looking cool, and we just walked around the fair, and I remember hearing this playing off the waltzer. . . . That was the first one we actually did, that was the kick-off on the Monday morning.")

23. A Mike McCartney photograph of fifteen-year-old Paul with his cousin Bett and second cousin Ted is featured as the CD tray insert art for *Run Devil Run.*

(Mike's photograph, showing Paul playing his guitar in Ted's pushchair, was taken on the beach during a holiday the McCartney brothers took with their family in September 1957 at the Butlin's Holiday Camp in Filey, Yorkshire.)

24. Ringo's Christmas album includes his remake of the Lennon/McCartney/Harrison/Starkey composition "Christmas Time (Is Here Again)," first recorded by the Beatles in Abbey Road's Studio Three, 28 November 1967, for their fifth fan club Christmas record.

(Ringo's version, coproduced with Mark Hudson, features a guitar solo by Joe Perry of Aerosmith.)

25. Prior to the Queen's opening of the Millennium Dome, those gathered joined the Millennium Choir in singing "All You Need Is Love."

(A four-man panel, which included pianist and TV presenter Jools Holland, chose the song as the anthem to herald the new millennium in Britain. "It expresses the sentiment we all share for the future of the planet, our children, and ourselves," said Mark Fisher, the Dome's creative director. The panel also considered selecting "Let It Be.")

SOURCES

1100-1956

1. Source: *Abbey Road*, by Brian Southall, Peter Vince, and Allan Rouse. Omnibus Press, 1997, page 15.

2. Sources: *The Beatles (Second Revised Edition)*, by Hunter Davies. W. W. Norton & Company, 1996, page 141; *The Ultimate Beatles Encyclopedia*, by Bill Harry. Hyperion, 1992, page 620; *Up the Beatles' Family Tree*, by Cecil R. Humphery-Smith, Michael G. Heenan and Jenifer Mount. Achievements Ltd., 1966, page 8.

3. Source: *John Lennon, My Brother*, by Julia Baird with Geoffrey Giuliano. Henry Holt & Company, 1988, pp. 6–7.

4. Sources: *The Beatles: The Ultimate Recording Guide*, by Allen J. Wiener. Facts On File, 1992, page 1; *Backbeat: Stuart Sutcliffe: The Lost Beatle*, by Alan Clayson and Pauline Sutcliffe. Pan Books, 1994, page 8.

5. Sources: *The Macs: Mike McCartney's Family Album*, by Mike McCartney. Delilah Books, 1981, page 13; *McCartney: The Definitive Biography*, by Chris Salewicz. St. Martin's Press, 1986, page 10.

6. Sources: *Abbey Road*, by Brian Southall, Peter Vince and Allan Rouse. Omnibus Press, 1997, pp. 18–19; *The End of the Beatles?*, by Harry Castleman and Walter J. Podrazik. Pierian Press/Popular Culture Ink, 1985, pp. 403–404.

7. Sources: "The Last Hurrah of the Fifth Beatle," by Ken Sharp. *Goldmine*, 6 November 1998, page 16; *All You Need Is Ears*, by George Martin with Jeremy Hornsby. St. Martin's Press, 1979, page 16.

8. Sources: *Beatle! The Pete Best Story*, by Peter Best and Patrick Doncaster. Plexus Publishing Ltd., 1985, page 13; *Drummed Out! The Sacking of Pete Best*, by Spencer Leigh. Northdown Publishing, 1998, page 37.

Sources

9. Source: *Beatle! The Pete Best Story*, by Pete Best and Patrick Doncaster. Plexus Publishing Ltd., 1985, page 13.

10. Source: "More Lennons?" (Beatlenews Roundup), by William P. King. *Beatlefan*, vol. 19, no. 6, 1998, page 6.

11. Sources: *John, Paul & Me: Before the Beatles*, by Len Garry. Collector's Guide Publishing Inc., 1997, page 42; *The Ultimate Beatles Encyclopedia*, by Bill Harry. Hyperion, 1992, pp. 461, 677.

12. Source: *John Lennon, My Brother*, by Julia Baird with Geoffrey Giuliano. Henry Holt & Company, 1988, page 5.

13. Source: *John Lennon, My Brother*, by Julia Baird with Geoffrey Giuliano. Henry Holt & Company, 1988, pp. 12–13.

14. Source: *The Beatles (Second Revised Edition)*, by Hunter Davies. W. W. Norton & Company, 1996, pp. 143–144.

15. Sources: *John Lennon in My Life*, by Pete Shotton and Nicholas Schaffner. Stein and Day, 1983, page 25; *The Macs: Mike McCartney's Family Album*, by Mike McCartney. Delilah Communications Ltd., 1981, page 35.

16. Sources: *The Paul McCartney World Tour* (program book), Paul Du Noyer, ed. EMAP Metro, 1989, page 8; *The Ultimate Beatles Encyclopedia*, by Bill Harry. Hyperion, 1992, page 349.

17. Source: *Lennon*, by Ray Coleman. McGraw-Hill Book Company, 1984, page 34.

18. Source: *The Beatles (Second Revised Edition)*, by Hunter Davies. W. W. Norton & Company, 1996, pp. 145, 147.

19. Sources: *Beatle! The Pete Best Story*, by Pete Best and Patrick Doncaster. Plexus Publishing Ltd., 1985, page 13; *The Ultimate Beatles Encyclopedia*, by Bill Harry. Hyperion, 1992, page 90.

20. Sources: "McCartney's Liverpool Triumph," *Beatlefan*, vol. 13, no. 3, 1991, page 23; *The Beatles (Second Revised Edition)*, by Hunter Davies. W. W. Norton & Company, 1996, page 29; "Walrus Tales," by Eddie Porter. *Good Day Sunshine*, no. 53, New Years, 1990, page 27.

22. Sources: *John Lennon in My Life*, by Pete Shotton and Nicholas Schaffner. Stein and Day, 1983, pp. 35–36; *McCartney: The Definitive Biography*, by Chris Salewicz. St. Martin's Press, 1986, page 40.

23. Sources: *Rock & Roll Memorabilia*, by Hilary Kay. Fireside Books, 1992, page 21; "Anglophile" (Beatlenews Roundup), by William P. King. *Beatlefan*, vol. 8, no. 5, 1986, page 5.

24. Sources: "Paul McCartney—Meet the Beatle," by Tony Bacon. *Bass Player*, July/August 1995; *The Beatles (Second Revised Edition)*, by Hunter Davies. W. W. Norton & Company, 1996, page 30; "Paul McCartney Reminisces" (from *Oobu Joobu—Part 2*), by Paul McCartney. *Young Boy* (CD single), Parlophone, 1997, track 3.

25. Sources: *John Lennon in My Life*, by Pete Shotton and Nicholas Schaffner. Stein and Day, 1983, page 38; *The Beatles: a diary*, by Barry Miles. Omnibus Press, 1998, page 15.

1957-1959

1. Source: *The Beatles: From Cavern to Star-Club*, by Hans Olof Gottfridsson. Premium Publishing, 1997, page 43.

2. Source: *The Beatles: From Cavern to Star-Club*, by Hans Olof Gottfridsson. Premium Publishing, 1997, page 42.

3. Sources: "An Early Interview With the Beatles," by Peter Jones. *The Beatles Book Appreciation Society Magazine*, Beat Publications Ltd., June 1980, page v; *The Ultimate Beatles Encyclopedia*, by Bill Harry. Hyperion, 1992, page 214.

4. Source: *The Ultimate Beatles Encyclopedia*, by Bill Harry. Hyperion, 1992, pp. 128, 354.

5. Source: *The Day John Met Paul*, by Jim O'Donnell. Penguin Books, 1994, pp. 79–80.

6. Sources: *The Complete Beatles Chronicle*, by Mark Lewisohn. Harmony Books, 1992, page 14; *The Day John Met Paul*, by Jim O'Donnell. Penguin Books, 1994, page 111.

7. Sources: "Beatlenews Roundup," by William P. King. *Beatlefan*, vol. 15, no. 6, 1994, page 4, and vol. 16, no. 1, 1994, page 5; *John, Paul & Me:*

Sources

Before the Beatles, by Len Garry. Collector's Guide Publishing Inc., 1997, page 168.

8. Sources: *The Beatles: From Cavern to Star-Club*, by Hans Olof Gottfridsson. Premium Publishing, 1997, page 26; *The Beatles: a diary*, by Barry Miles. Omnibus Press, 1998, page 15.

9. Sources: *The Best of Cellars*, by Phil Thompson. The Bluecoat Press, 1994, pp. 122, 124; *The Complete Beatles Chronicle*, by Mark Lewisohn. Harmony Books, 1992, page 39.

10. Source: *McCartney: The Definitive Biography*, by Chris Salewicz. St. Martin's Press, 1986, pp. 29, 45–46.

11. Sources: "God in heaven, what was I on?" by Mat Snow. *Mojo*, November 1995, page 59; *Paul McCartney: Many Years from Now*, by Barry Miles. Henry Holt and Company, 1997, page 39.

12. Sources: *The Paul McCartney World Tour* (program book), Paul Du Noyer, ed. EMAP Metro, 1989, page 8; *The Complete Beatles Chronicle*, by Mark Lewisohn. Harmony Books, 1992, page 15.

13. Source: *The Beatles: From Cavern to Star-Club*, by Hans Olof Gottfridsson. Premium Publishing, 1997, page 12.

14. Sources: *The Beatles: From Cavern to Star-Club*, by Hans Olof Gottfridsson. Premium Publishing, 1997, pp. 23, 28, 45, 47. *Anthology 1* (CD booklet notes), by Mark Lewisohn. EMI/Capitol, 1995, pp. 6–7.

15. Sources: *John Lennon in My Life*, by Pete Shotton and Nicholas Schaffner. Stein and Day, 1983, page 61; *John Lennon, My Brother*, by Julia Baird with Geoffrey Giuliano. Henry Holt and Company, 1988, page 44.

16. Source: *John, Paul & Me: Before the Beatles*, by Len Garry. Collector's Guide Publishing Inc., 1997, pp. 190–91.

17. Sources: *The Macs: Mike McCartney's Family Album*, by Mike McCartney. Delilah Books, 1981, page 52; *Lennon*, by Ray Coleman. McGraw-Hill Book Company, 1984, page 93.

18.   Sources: *McCartney: The Definitive Biography*, by Chris Salewicz. St. Martin's Press, 1986, pp. 67–68; *The Ultimate Beatles Encyclopedia*, by Bill Harry. Hyperion, 1992, page 404.

19.   Sources: *Backbeat: Stuart Sutcliffe: The Lost Beatle*, by Alan Clayson and Pauline Sutcliffe. Pan Books, 1994, page 49; *The Ultimate Beatles Encyclopedia*, by Bill Harry. Hyperion, 1992, page 305.

20.   Sources: *The Best Years of the Beatles*, by Pete Best with Bill Harry. Headline Book Publishing, 1996, page 21; *The Complete Beatles Chronicle*, by Mark Lewisohn. Harmony Books, 1992, pp. 13, 17; *The Beatles: An Oral History*, by David Pritchard and Alan Lysaght. Hyperion, 1998, page 21; *The Ultimate Beatles Encyclopedia*, by Bill Harry. Hyperion, 1992, pp. 388, 416.

21.   Sources: *Shout! The Beatles in Their Generation*, by Philip Norman. Simon and Schuster, 1981, page 61; *The Best Years of the Beatles*, by Pete Best with Bill Harry. Headline Book Publishing, 1996, page 21; *The Love You Make: An Insider's Story of the Beatles*, by Peter Brown and Steven Gaines. McGraw-Hill Book Company, 1983, page 41.

22.   Sources: *The Best Years of the Beatles*, by Pete Best with Bill Harry. Headline Book Publishing, 1996, page 26; *The Beatles and Some Other Guys*, by Pete Frame. Omnibus Press, 1997, page 2.

23.   Sources: *The Ultimate Beatles Encyclopedia*, by Bill Harry. Hyperion, 1992, pp. 354, 476; *Stuart: The Life and Art of Stuart Sutcliffe*, by Kay Williams and Pauline Sutcliffe. Genesis Publications Limited, 1996, pp. 94, 98.

24.   Sources: *Stuart: The Life and Art of Stuart Sutcliffe*, by Kay Williams and Pauline Sutcliffe. Genesis Publications Limited, 1996, pp. 93–94; "Setting Harrison Straight on 'The Wild One,'" by Bill Harry. *Beatlefan*, vol. 18, no. 6, 1997, page 17.

25.   Source: *Blinds & Shutters: The Photographs of Michael Cooper*, Brian Roylance, ed. Genesis/Hedley, 1990, page 306.

1960

1.   Source: *The Paul McCartney World Tour* (program book), Paul Du Noyer, ed. EMAP Metro, 1989, page 9.

Sources

2. Sources: *Wildcat!*, by The Beatals (bootleg CD). Madman Records, 1996, disc two, track one; *The Beatles: From Cavern to Star-Club*, by Hans Olof Gottfridsson. Premium Publishing, 1997, pp. 200–203.

3. Source: *The Beatles: From Cavern to Star-Club*, by Hans Olof Gottfridsson. Premium Publishing, 1997, pp. 200–202.

4. Sources: *How They Became the Beatles*, by Gareth L. Pawlowski. E. P. Dutton, 1989, pp. 7, 11; *DK Encyclopedia of Rock Stars*, by Dafydd Rees and Luke Crampton. DK Publishing, Inc., 1996, page 201.

5. Sources: *Shout! The Beatles in Their Generation*, by Philip Norman. Simon and Schuster, 1981, page 73; *The Complete Beatles Chronicle*, by Mark Lewisohn. Harmony Books, 1992, page 19.

6. Sources: *How They Became the Beatles*, by Gareth L. Pawlowski, E. P. Dutton, 1989, page 12; *The Complete Beatles Chronicle*, by Mark Lewisohn. Harmony Books, 1992, page 19.

7. Source: "Touring With the Silver Beetles: Johnny Gentle Recalls His Onetime Backing Band," by Ian Forsyth. *Beatlefan*, vol. 15, no. 5, 1994, page 16.

8. Sources: *The Best Years of the Beatles*, by Pete Best with Bill Harry. Headline Book Publishing, 1996, page 31; *The Complete Beatles Chronicle*, by Mark Lewisohn. Harmony Books, 1992, pp. 19, 27; *Backbeat: Stuart Sutcliffe: The Lost Beatle*, by Alan Clayson and Pauline Sutcliffe. Pan Books, 1994, page 69; *The Beatles: From Cavern to Star-Club*, by Hans Olof Gottfridsson. Premium Publishing, 1997, page 39.

9. Source: *The Complete Beatles Chronicle*, by Mark Lewisohn. Harmony Books, 1992, page 20.

10. Sources: *The Complete Beatles Chronicle*, by Mark Lewisohn. Harmony Books, 1992, pp. 20, 28; *Follow the Merseybeat Road*, by Sam Leach. Eden Publications, 1983, page 25; *The Man Who Gave the Beatles Away*, by Allan Williams and William Marshall. Macmillan Publishing Company, Inc., 1975, page 50.

11. Source: *How They Became the Beatles*, by Gareth L. Pawlowski. E. P. Dutton, 1989, pp. 6, 23.

12. Sources: *Backbeat: Stuart Sutcliffe: The Lost Beatle*, by Alan Clayson and Pauline Sutcliffe. Pan Books, 1994, pp. 57–60; *Stuart: The Life and Art of Stuart Sutcliffe*, by Kay Williams and Pauline Sutcliffe. Genesis Publications Limited, 1996, pp. 110–111.

13. Sources: *Beatle! The Pete Best Story*, by Pete Best and Patrick Doncaster. Plexus Publishing, 1985, page 28; *The Beatles: The Ultimate Recording Guide*, by Allen J. Wiener. Facts On File, 1986, page 4.

14. Source: *The Beatles: From Cavern to Star-Club*, by Hans Olof Gottfridsson. Premium Publishing, 1997, page 52.

15. Source: *The Complete Beatles Chronicle*, by Mark Lewisohn. Harmony Books, 1992, page 21.

16. Sources: "The McCartney Interview" (part one), by Vic Garbarini. *Beatlefan*, vol.2, no. 5, 1980, page 14; *The Complete Beatles Chronicle*, by Mark Lewisohn. Harmony Books, 1992, page 28.

17. Sources: *Backbeat: Stuart Sutcliffe: The Lost Beatle*, by Alan Clayson and Pauline Sutcliffe. Pan Books, 1994, page 79; *The Beatles Live!*, by Mark Lewisohn. Henry Holt & Company, 1986, page 51; *The Complete Beatles Chronicle*, by Mark Lewisohn. Harmony Books, 1992, page 363.

18. Source: *The Rickenbacker Book*, by Tony Bacon and Paul Day. GPI Books, 1994, pp. 28–29.

19. Source: *The Best of Cellars*, by Phil Thompson. The Bluecoat Press, 1994, page 46.

20. Sources: *Backbeat: Stuart Sutcliffe: The Lost Beatle*, by Alan Clayson and Pauline Sutcliffe. Pan Books, 1994, pp. 100–101; *The Complete Beatles Chronicle*, by Mark Lewisohn. Harmony Books, 1992, page 28; *The Beatles: From Cavern to Star-Club*, by Hans Olof Gottfridsson. Premium Publishing, 1997, pp. 54–55.

21. Sources: *Backbeat: Stuart Sutcliffe: The Lost Beatle*, by Alan Clayson and Pauline Sutcliffe. Pan Books, 1994, page 101; "Klaus Voormann: The Old Beatle Pal Behind the 'Revolver' and 'Anthology' Covers," by Rip Rense. *Beatlefan*, vol. 17, no. 5, 1996, page 18; *Hamburg Days*, by Astrid Kirchherr and Klaus Voormann. Genesis Publications Limited, 1999, pp. 47–48.

22. Source: *Backbeat: Stuart Sutcliffe: The Lost Beatle*, by Alan Clayson and Pauline Sutcliffe. Pan Books, 1994, page 105.

23. Sources: *The Beatles: From Cavern to Star-Club*, by Hans Olof Gottfridsson. Premium Publishing, 1997, page 66; *Backbeat: Stuart Sutcliffe: The Lost Beatle*, by Alan Clayson and Pauline Sutcliffe. Pan Books, 1994, page 108; *Hamburg Days*, by Astrid Kirchherr and Klaus Voormann. Genesis Publications Limited, 1999, pp. 18, 87, 122.

24. Source: *McCartney: The Definitive Biography*, by Chris Salewicz. St. Martin's Press, 1986, page 104.

25. Source: *Miller's Rock & Pop Memorabilia*, by Stephen Maycock. Reed Consumer Books Ltd., 1994, page 32.

1961

1. Sources: *The Complete Beatles Chronicle*, by Mark Lewisohn. Harmony Books, 1992, page 23; *Miller's Rock & Pop Memorabilia*, by Stephen Maycock. Reed Consumer Books Ltd., 1994, page 41; *The Beatles: From Cavern to Star-Club*, by Hans Olof Gottfridsson. Premium Publishing, 1997, pp. 53–54.

2. Sources: *The Beatles: From Cavern to Star-Club*, by Hans Olof Gottfridsson. Premium Publishing, 1997, page 66; *The Complete Beatles Chronicle*, by Mark Lewisohn. Harmony Books, 1992, page 40.

3. Sources: *The Complete Beatles Chronicle*, by Mark Lewisohn. Harmony Books, 1992, page 31; *The Best of Cellars*, by Phil Thompson. The Bluecoat Press, 1994, page 49.

4. Source: *The Macs: Mike McCartney's Family Album*, by Mike McCartney. Delilah Books, 1981, page 80.

5. Source: *Hofner Violin "Beatle" Bass*, by Joe Dunn. River Books, 1996, pp. 5–7, 15.

6. Source: *The Beatles: From Cavern to Star-Club*, by Hans Olof Gottfridsson. Premium Publishing, 1997, page 68.

7. Source: *The Complete Beatles Chronicle*, by Mark Lewisohn. Harmony Books, 1992, page 31.

Sources

8. Source: *The Beatles: From Cavern to Star-Club*, by Hans Olof Gott-fridsson. Premium Publishing, 1997, page 177.

9. Source: *The Beatles: From Cavern to Star-Club*, by Hans Olof Gott-fridsson. Premium Publishing, 1997, pp. 77–78, 420.

10. Sources: *Backbeat: Stuart Sutcliffe: The Lost Beatle*, by Alan Clayson and Pauline Sutcliffe. Pan Books, 1994, pp. 125, 151; *Sotheby's Catalogue of Rock & Roll Memorabilia 1956–1983*, 1 September 1983, page 31; *Stuart: The Life and Art of Stuart Sutcliffe*, by Kay Williams and Pauline Sutcliffe. Genesis Publications Limited, 1996, pp. 82–83; 153.

11. Source: *Mersey Beat: The Beginnings of the Beatles*, by Bill Harry. Omnibus Press, 1977, page 19.

12. Sources: *The Ultimate Beatles Encyclopedia*, by Bill Harry. Hyperion, 1992, page 12; *The Beatles Live!*, by Mark Lewisohn. Henry Holt and Company, 1986, page 59.

13. Source: *The Beatles Live!*, by Mark Lewisohn. Henry Holt & Company, 1986, page 76.

14. Source: *Backbeat: Stuart Sutcliffe: The Lost Beatle*, by Alan Clayson and Pauline Sutcliffe. Pan Books, 1994, pp. 138, 160.

15. Source: *Shout! The Beatles in Their Generation*, by Philip Norman. Simon and Schuster, 1981, page 107.

16. Source: *Drummed Out! The Sacking of Pete Best*, by Spencer Leigh. Northdown Publishing Ltd., 1998, page 26.

17. Sources: *Beatle! The Pete Best Story*, by Pete Best and Patrick Don-caster. Plexus Publishing Ltd., 1985, page 123; *Paul McCartney: Many Years From Now*, by Barry Miles. Henry Holt & Company, 1997, page 76.

18. Source: *The Complete Beatles Chronicle*, by Mark Lewisohn. Har-mony Books, 1992, page 47.

19. Sources: *A Cellarful of Noise*, by Brian Epstein. Doubleday and Company, Inc., 1964, page 6; *The Beatles: The Ultimate Recording Guide*, by Allen J. Wiener. Facts on File, 1992, page 7; *Mojo*, July 1997, page 8.

20. Source: "Alistair Taylor recalls how Brian Epstein DISCOVERED THE BEATLES," by Tony Barrow. *The Beatles Book Appreciation Society Magazine*, Beat Publications Ltd., May 1982, page iv.

21. Sources: *The Beatles: From Cavern to Star-Club*, by Hans Olof Gottfridsson. Premium Publishing, 1997, pp. 278, 410.

22. Sources: *The Complete Beatles Chronicle*, by Mark Lewisohn. Harmony Books, 1992, pp. 41, 49; *The Ultimate Beatles Encyclopedia*, by Bill Harry. Hyperion, 1992, pp. 703–704.

23. Sources: *Follow the Merseybeat Road*, by Sam Leach. Eden Publications, 1983, page 4; *The Complete Beatles Chronicle*, by Mark Lewisohn. Harmony Books, 1992, page 36; *The Ultimate Beatles Encyclopedia*, by Bill Harry. Hyperion, 1992, page 371.

24. Source: *How They Became the Beatles*, by Gareth L. Pawlowski. E. P. Dutton, 1989, pp. 41–42, 46.

25. Sources: *The Beatles: From Cavern to Star-Club*, by Hans Olof Gottfridsson. Premium Publishing, 1997, page 68; "Klaus Voormann: One of the Fab Four's Earliest Friends Remembers," by Rick Glover. *Beatlefan*, vol. 20, no. 1, 1998, page 21.)

1962

1. Source: *How They Became the Beatles*, by Gareth L. Pawlowski. E. P. Dutton, 1989, page 62.

2. Sources: *How They Became the Beatles*, by Gareth L. Pawlowski. E. P. Dutton, 1989, page 45; *Stanley Gibbons Postage Stamp Catalogue, Part One: British Commonwealth*, Stanley Gibbons Ltd., 1963, pp. 29–30; *The Complete Beatles Chronicle*, by Mark Lewisohn. Harmony Books, 1992, page 36.

3. Sources: *Backbeat: Stuart Sutcliffe: The Lost Beatle*, by Alan Clayson and Pauline Sutcliffe. Pan Books, 1994, page 149; *The Beatles: From Cavern to Star-Club*, by Hans Olof Gottfridsson. Premium Publishing, 1997, page 73.

4. Sources: *The Complete Beatles Chronicle*, by Mark Lewisohn. Harmony Books, 1992, page 64; *A Cellarful of Noise*, by Brian Epstein. Doubleday and Company, Inc., 1964, page 56.

Sources

5. Sources: *The Beatles at the Beeb: The Story of Their Radio Career, 1962–1965,* by Kevin Howlett. Pierian Press/Popular Culture Ink, 1982, 1983, page 10; *The Complete Beatles Chronicle,* by Mark Lewisohn. Harmony Books, 1992, pp. 65, 67.

6. Sources: *Stuart: The Life and Art of Stuart Sutcliffe,* by Kay Williams and Pauline Sutcliffe. Genesis Publications Ltd., 1996, pp. 204–205; *Backbeat: Stuart Sutcliffe: The Lost Beatle,* by Alan Clayson and Pauline Sutcliffe. Pan Books, 1994, pp. 159–160.

7. Source: *The Beatles: From Cavern to Star-Club,* by Hans Olof Gottfridsson. Premium Publishing, 1997, page 73.

8. Source: *The Cemetery of Rock—The Rock 'n' Roll Graveyard,* by Bert Hilton-Wood, http://www.ruralnet.net.au/~berthw/grave.html.

9. Sources: *Hamburg: The Cradle of British Rock,* by Alan Clayson. Sanctuary Publishing Ltd., 1997, page 71; *The Complete Beatles Chronicle,* by Mark Lewisohn. Harmony Books, 1992, pp. 69–70.

10. Source: *Beatle! The Pete Best Story,* by Pete Best and Patrick Doncaster. Plexus Publishing Ltd., 1985, page 155.

11. Source: *Beatle! The Pete Best Story,* by Pete Best and Patrick Doncaster. Plexus Publishing Ltd., 1985, pp. 157–158.

12. Sources: *The Beatles: From Cavern to Star-Club,* by Hans Olof Gottfridsson. Premium Publishing, 1997, pp. 98–101, 105; "The 'Missing' Polydor Beatles Recording," by Martin C. Babicz. *Beatlefan,* vol. 19, no. 3, 1998, pp. 12–13.

13. Source: *The Man Who Made the Beatles:* An Intimate Biography of Brian Epstein, by Ray Coleman. McGraw-Hill Publishing Company, 1989, page 188.

14. Source: *Remember: Recollections and Photographs of the Beatles,* by Michael McCartney. Henry Holt and Company, 1992, page 93.

15. Sources: *The Man Who Made the Beatles: An Intimate Biography of Brian Epstein,* by Ray Coleman. McGraw-Hill Publishing Company, 1989, page 123; *Drummed Out! The Sacking of Pete Best,* by Spencer Leigh.

Northdown Publishing Ltd., 1998, page 40; *The Complete Beatles Chronicle*, by Mark Lewisohn. Harmony Books, 1992, pp. 59, 75.

16. Source: *The Beatles: From Cavern to Star-Club*, by Hans Olaf Gottfridsson. Premium Publishing, 1997, page 60.

17. Sources: *The Beatles: From Cavern to Star-Club*, by Hans Olaf Gottfridsson. Premium Publishing, 1997, pp. 123, 125; *The Complete Beatles Chronicle*, by Mark Lewisohn. Harmony Books, 1992, pp. 58–59.

18. Sources: *The Man Who Made the Beatles: An Intimate Biography of Brian Epstein*, by Ray Coleman. McGraw-Hill Publishing Company, 1989, pp. 124–125; *Drummed Out! The Sacking of Pete Best*, by Spencer Leigh. Northdown Publishing Ltd., 1998, page 50.

19. Sources: *The Beatles: From Cavern to Star-Club*, by Hans Olof Gottfridsson. Premium Publishing, 1997, page 122; *The Man Who Made the Beatles: An Intimate Biography of Brian Epstein*, by Ray Coleman. McGraw-Hill Publishing Company, 1989, page 124.

20. Sources: "The Truth Behind the Decca Audition," by Tony Barrow. *The Beatles Book Appreciation Society Magazine*, Beat Publications Ltd., March 1982, page vi; *The Complete Beatles Chronicle*, by Mark Lewisohn. Harmony Books, 1992, page 75.

21. Sources: *Drummed Out! The Sacking of Pete Best*, by Spencer Leigh. Northdown Publishing Ltd., 1998, pp. 72–75; *The Complete Beatles Chronicle*, by Mark Lewisohn. Harmony Books, 1992, pp. 77–78.

22. Sources: "The Evolution That Created a Revolution: The Story of John Lennon's J-160E Acoustic Guitar," by Andy Babiuk. *Gibson Musical Instruments*, http://www.gibson.com/products/montana/lennon/fabfour.html; *Mersey Beat: The Beginnings of the Beatles*, by Bill Harry. Omnibus Press, 1977, page 41; *The Beatles: Recording Sessions*, by Mark Lewisohn. Harmony Books, 1988, page 20.

23. Sources: "No Direction Home," by Richard Younger. *Mojo*, December 1995, pp. 96–97, 100; *All Together Now*, by Harry Castleman and Walter J. Podrazik. Pierian Press/Popular Culture Ink, 1975, page 230.

24. Sources: "Touring With The Silver Beetles: Johnny Gentle Recalls His Onetime Backing Band," by Ian Forsyth. *Beatlefan*, vol. 15, no. 5,

1994, page 16; *The Beatles: From Cavern to Star-Club*, by Hans Olof Gott-fridsson. Premium Publishing, 1997, page 335.

25. Source: *Songs, Pictures and Stories of the Fabulous Beatles Records on Vee-Jay*, by Bruce Spizer. 498 Productions, LLC, 1998, pp. 202, 204–205, 207.

1963

1. Source: *Shout! The Beatles in Their Generation*, by Philip Norman. Fireside/Simon and Schuster, 1981, pp. 174–175, 191.

2. Source: *All You Need Is Ears*, by George Martin with Jeremy Hornsby. St. Martin's Press, 1979, pp. 62, 128–129.

3. Sources: "The First Official Mal Evans Story," by Neil Aspinall. *The Beatles Book Monthly*, Beat Publications Ltd., May 1967, pp. 11–12; "Just Out Of Shot," by Paul Du Noyer. *Mojo*, October 1996, page 75; *The Complete Beatles Chronicle*, by Mark Lewisohn. Harmony Books, 1992, pp. 96–97, 118.

4. Source: *Songs, Pictures and Stories of the Fabulous Beatles Records on Vee-Jay*, by Bruce Spizer. 498 Productions, LLC, 1998, pp. 203–204.

5. Sources: *A Hard Day's Write*, by Steve Turner. HarperCollins Publishers, 1994, page 25; *The Playboy Interviews with John Lennon & Yoko Ono*, by David Sheff. Playboy Press, 1981, page 140.

6. Sources: *The Beatles: Recording Sessions*, by Mark Lewisohn, Harmony Books, 1988, page 26; *The Complete Beatles Chronicle*, by Mark Lewisohn. Harmony Books, 1992, page 99.

7. Source: *The Beatles: Recording Sessions*, by Mark Lewisohn. Harmony Books, 1988, page 32.

8. Sources: *The Beatles: Recording Sessions*, by Mark Lewisohn. Harmony Books, 1988, page 28. *Paul McCartney: Many Years from Now*, by Barry Miles. Henry Holt and Company, 1997, page 149.

9. Sources: *The Beatles at the Beeb: The Story of Their Radio Career, 1962–1965*, by Kevin Howlett. Pierian Press/Popular Culture Ink, 1982, 1983, page 112; *The Complete Beatles Chronicle*, by Mark Lewisohn. Harmony Books, 1992, pp. 107–108.

Sources

10. Sources: *The Ultimate Beatles Encyclopedia*, by Bill Harry. Hyperion, 1992, page 194; *The Beatles at the Beeb: The Story of Their Radio Career, 1962–1965*, by Kevin Howlett. Pierian Press/Popular Culture Ink, 1982, 1983, pp. 84, 87, 112.

11. Source: *The Beatles: a diary*, by Barry Miles. Omnibus Press, 1998, page 70.

12. Sources: *Songs, Pictures and Stories of the Fabulous Beatles Records on Vee-Jay*, by Bruce Spizer. 498 Productions, LLC, 1998, pp. 11–12; *The Ultimate Beatles Encyclopedia*, by Bill Harry. Hyperion, 1992, page 598.

13. Source: *The Complete Beatles Chronicle*, by Mark Lewisohn. Harmony Books, 1992, pp. 113, 167.

14. Sources: "Tales of Abbey Road: Beatles Producer George Martin Reminisces," by Mark Lewisohn. *Beatlefan*, vol. 15, no. 2, 1994, page 15; *The Beatles: Recording Sessions*, by Mark Lewisohn. Harmony Books, 1988, page 32.

15. Sources: *The Beatles: Recording Sessions*, by Mark Lewisohn. Harmony Books, 1988, page 32. *Paul McCartney: Many Years from Now*, by Barry Miles. Henry Holt and Company, 1997, page 151; *The Beatles Complete Scores*, Hal Leonard Publishing Corporation, 1989, 1993, page 472.

16. Sources: *Shout! The Beatles in Their Generation*, by Philip Norman. Fireside/Simon and Schuster, 1981, pp. 193, 196; *The Ultimate Beatles Encyclopedia*, by Bill Harry. Hyperion, 1992, page 630.

17. Sources: *The Beatles: a private view*, by Robert Freeman. Mallard Press, 1990, page 56; *The Complete Beatles Chronicle*, by Mark Lewisohn. Harmony Books, 1992, page 119; *Paul McCartney: Many Years from Now*, by Barry Miles. Henry Holt & Company, 1997, page 156.

18. Source: *The Macs: Mike McCartney's Family Album*, by Mike McCartney. Delilah Books, 1981, page 114.

19. Sources: "Fandango" (Beatlenews Roundup), William P. King. *Beatlefan*, vol. 16, no. 3, 1995, page 7; *The Beatles: a diary*, by Barry Miles. Omnibus Press, 1998, pp. 82–83.

20.   Sources: "The Beatles' Christmas Fan Club Discs," by Tony Barrow. *The Beatles Book Appreciation Society Magazine*, Beat Publications Ltd., December 1980, page iii; *The Complete Beatles Chronicle*, by Mark Lewisohn. Harmony Books, 1992, page 125.

21.   Source: "With The Beatles Again!" by Tony Barrow. *The Beatles Book Appreciation Society Magazine*, Beat Publications Ltd., June 1982, page vi.

22.   Sources: *The Beatles: a private view*, by Robert Freeman. Mallard Press, 1990, pp. 56, 78; *The Beatles London*, by Piet Schreuders, Mark Lewisohn and Adam Smith. St. Martin's Press, 1994, page 78.

23.   Sources: *All Together Now*, by Harry Castleman and Walter J. Podrazik. Pierian Press/Popular Culture Ink, 1975, pp. 15, 19; *Songs, Pictures and Stories of the Fabulous Beatles Records On Vee-Jay*, by Bruce Spizer. 498 Productions, LLC, 1998, page 3.

24.   Source: *MPL Communications*, http://www.mplcommunications.com.

25.   Sources: *The Beatles: a diary*, by Barry Miles. Omnibus Press, 1998, page 93; *The Beatles at the Beeb*, by Kevin Howlett. Pierian Press/Popular Culture Ink, 1983, page 50.

1964

1.   Source: *The Complete Beatles Chronicle*, by Mark Lewisohn. Harmony Books, 1992, page 142.

2.   Sources: Press release from http://www.best.com/~abbeyrd; "Carnegie Hall," by Allan Kozinn, 6 September 1998; *Beatles Reference Library*, http://www.getback.org.

3.   Sources: *The Beatles File*, by Andy Davis. CLB International, 1998, page 40; *Fifty Years Adrift*, by Derek Taylor. Genesis Publications Ltd., 1984, page 108.

4.   Source: *Spin Again—Board Games from the Fifties and Sixties*, by Rick Polizzi and Fred Schaefer. Chronicle Books, 1991, page 73.

5.   Sources: *Richard Lester and the Beatles*, by Andrew Yule. Donald I. Fine, 1994, pp. 5, 37, 39; *Beatles at the Movies*, by Roy Carr. HarperPerennial, 1997, pp. 30–31; *French Dressing: IMDb* [Internet Movie Database], http://us.imdb.com.

Sources

6. Sources: *Richard Lester and the Beatles,* by Andrew Yule. Donald I. Fine, 1994, page 8; *Mrs. Brown, You've Got a Lovely Daughter: IMDb* [Internet Movie Database], http://us.imdb.com.

7. Sources: *A Hard Day's Night: A Complete Pictorial Record of the Film,* J. Philip Di Franco, ed. Chelsea House, 1977, page 20; *Richard Lester and the Beatles,* by Andrew Yule. Donald I. Fine, 1994, pp. 34, 36.

8. Sources: "Beatle Movie Memories: Talking With Norman Rossington of 'Norm and Shake,' " by Ian Forsyth. *Beatlefan,* vol. 16, no. 3, 1995, page 18; *The Complete Beatles Chronicle,* by Mark Lewisohn. Harmony Books, 1992, page 149.

9. Sources: *Beatles at the Movies,* by Roy Carr. HarperPerennial, 1996, page 40; *The Complete Beatles Chronicle,* by Mark Lewisohn. Harmony Books, 1992, pp. 150, 158.

10. Source: *The Beatles: a private view,* by Robert Freeman. Mallard Press, 1990, page 118.

11. Sources: *Richard Lester and the Beatles,* by Andrew Yule. Donald I. Fine, 1994, page 11; *Beatles at the Movies,* by Roy Carr. HarperPerennial, 1997, page 39; *The Complete Beatles Chronicle,* by Mark Lewisohn. Harmony Books, 1992, page 156.

12. Sources: *Richard Lester and the Beatles,* by Andrew Yule. Donald I. Fine, 1994, page 13; *The Complete Beatles Chronicle,* by Mark Lewisohn. Harmony Books, 1992, page 153.

13. Sources: *Richard Lester and the Beatles,* by Andrew Yule. Donald I. Fine, 1994, page 3; *Beatles at the Movies,* by Roy Carr. HarperPerennial, 1997, page 40; *The Ultimate Beatles Encyclopedia,* by Bill Harry. Hyperion, 1992, page 287; "Beatlefan Trivia Quiz," *Beatlefan,* vol. 4, no. 5, 1982, page 12; "Trivia Quiz Winners & Answers," *Beatlefan,* vol. 4, no. 6, 1982, page 7.

14. Source: *The Complete Beatles Chronicle,* by Mark Lewisohn. Harmony Books, 1992, page 131.

15. Sources: *Richard Lester and the Beatles,* by Andrew Yule. Donald I. Fine, 1994, pp. xiii, 11; *The Complete Beatles Chronicle,* by Mark Lewisohn. Harmony Books, 1992, page 157; *The Beatles London,* by Piet Schreuders, Mark Lewisohn and Adam Smith. St. Martin's Press, 1994, page 93.

Sources

16.   Source: *The Man Who Made the Beatles: An Intimate Biography of Brian Epstein*, by Ray Coleman. McGraw-Hill Publishing Company, 1989, pp. 173–174.

17.   Sources: *The Complete Beatles Chronicle*, by Mark Lewisohn. Harmony Books, 1992, page 159; *The Complete Works of Shakespeare*, updated 4th edition, David Bevington, ed. Longman, 1997, page 150; *Paul McCartney: Many Years from Now*, by Barry Miles. Henry Holt and Company, 1997, page 263.

18.   Sources: *Rock & Roll Memorabilia*, by Hilary Kay. Fireside Books, 1992, page 137.

19.   Sources: *Lennon*, by Ray Coleman. McGraw-Hill Book Company, 1984, page 274; *The Beatles: Recording Sessions*, by Mark Lewisohn. Harmony Books, 1988, page 32.

20.   Sources: *The Beatles Live!* by Mark Lewisohn. Henry Holt and Company, 1986, pp. 168, 177.

21.   Source: *The Playboy Interviews with John Lennon and Yoko Ono*, by David Sheff. Playboy Press, 1981, page 147.

22.   Source: *Completely Mad: A History of the Comic Book and Magazine*, by Maria Reidelbach. Little, Brown and Company, 1991, page 53.

23.   Sources: *The Official Price Guide to the Beatles Records and Memorabilia*, by Perry Cox and Joe Lindsay. House of Collectibles, 1995, page 72; *The Beatles Live!* by Mark Lewisohn. Henry Holt and Company, 1988, page 132; "Buried Treasure," by Kingsley Abbot. *Mojo*, October 1998, page 155.

24.   Sources: *The Beatles File*, by Andy Davis. CLB International, 1998, page 77; "Screaming Lord Sutch" [Real Gone], by Johnny Black. *Mojo*, August 1999, page 32.

25.   Sources: "The Untold, Real, True, Inside Story of the Beatles' Sgt. Pepper's Lonely Hearts Club Band," by [Barry] Miles. *High Times*, October 1979, page 54; *Lennon*, by Ray Coleman. McGraw-Hill Book Company, 1984, page 239; *The Beatles: a private view*, by Robert Freeman. Mallard Press, 1990, pp. 81, 84.)

1965

1. Sources: *The Beatles London*, by Piet Schreuders, Mark Lewisohn, and Adam Smith. St. Martin's Press, 1994, page 59; "Behind the Spotlight," by Billy Shepherd (Peter Jones) and Johnny Dean. *The Beatles Book Monthly*, Beat Publications Ltd., February 1967, page 21.

2. Source: *Richard Lester and the Beatles*, by Andrew Yule. Donald I. Fine, 1994, page 95.

3. Sources: *Beatles at the Movies*, by Roy Carr. HarperPerennial, 1996, pp. 60, 74; *The Beatles Files*, by Andy Davis. CLB International, 1998, page 85.

4. Source: *Richard Lester and the Beatles*, by Andrew Yule. Donald I. Fine, 1994, page 103.

5. Source: *The Beatles: Recording Sessions*, by Mark Lewisohn. Harmony Books, 1988, page 193.

6. Sources: *The Complete Beatles Chronicle*, by Mark Lewisohn. Harmony Books, 1992, page 188; *The Official Doctor Who & the Daleks Book*, by John Peel and Terry Nation. St. Martin's Press, 1988, pp. 31–32.

7. Sources: *The Beatles: a diary*, by Barry Miles. Omnibus Press, 1998, page 160; "Real Gone" (Allen Ginsberg obituary), by (Barry) Miles. *Mojo*, June 1997, page 161.

8. Source: *Rock & Roll Memorabilia*, by Hilary Kay. Fireside Books, 1992, page 131.

9. Sources: "The First Official Mal Evans Story," by Neil Aspinall. *The Beatles Book Monthly*, Beat Publications Ltd., May 1967, page 12; *The Complete Beatles Chronicle*, by Mark Lewisohn. Harmony Books, 1992, page 197.

10. Sources: "At The Premiere," by Elizabeth Sacks. *The Beatles Book Monthly*, Beat Publications Ltd., September 1965, page 27; *The Beatles: a diary*, by Barry Miles. Omnibus Press, 1998, page 167.

11. Source: *The Official Prisoner Companion*, by Matthew White and Jaffer Ali. Warner Books, 1988, pp. 109, 115.

12. Sources: "The Beatles in New York," by Bernice Young. *The Beatles Book Monthly*, Beat Publications Ltd., November 1965, page 14; *The Complete Beatles Chronicle*, by Mark Lewisohn. Harmony Books, 1992, pp. 198–199.

13. Source: *Careless Love: The Unmaking of Elvis Presley*, by Peter Guralnick. Little, Brown and Company, 1999, page 211.

14. Sources: *The Beatles (Second Revised Edition)*, by Hunter Davies. W. W. Norton and Company, 1996, pp. 358–359; "It's Zak, But It Could Have Been Lee" (Beatle News). *The Beatles Book Monthly*, Beat Publications Ltd., October 1965, page 29.

18. Sources: "The Beatles Cartoons and Me," by Christopher Cook. *Beatlefan*, vol. 3, no. 5, 1981, pp. 4–5, 9; *The Ultimate Beatles Encyclopedia*, by Bill Harry. Hyperion, 1992, pp. 74, 631; *Beatletoons: The Real Story Behind The Cartoon Beatles*, by Mitchell Axelrod. Wynn Publishing, 1999, pp. 80–81, 126, 135, 138, 145, 150.

19. Sources: *The Beatles: Recording Sessions*, by Mark Lewisohn. Harmony Books, 1988, page 63; *Paul McCartney: Many Years from Now*, by Barry Miles. Henry Holt and Company, 1997, page 270.

20. Sources: *Like the Night: Bob Dylan and the Road to the Manchester Free Trade Hall*, by C. P. Lee. Helter Skelter Publishing, 1998, pp. 78, 113; "Judas Christ Superstar," by Andy Gill. *Mojo*, November 1998, page 52.

21. Source: "Lennon on the Air: Listen to This Article," by Thomas Rehwagen. *Beatlefan*, vol. 16, no. 3, 1995, page 23.

22. Sources: "A Big Hand for the Quiet One," by Mark Ellen. *Q*, January 1988, page 59; *I Me Mine*, by George Harrison. Genesis Publications/Simon and Schuster, 1980, page 90.

23. Source: *Paul McCartney: Many Years from Now*, by Barry Miles. Henry Holt and Company, 1997, page 274.

24. Source: *The Complete Beatles Chronicle*, by Mark Lewisohn. Harmony Books, 1992, page 67.

25. Sources: "McCartney Answers Fans," *Beatlefan*, vol. 16, no. 2, 1995, page 7; *Paul McCartney: Many Years fFrom Now*, by Barry Miles. Henry Holt and Company, 1997, page 218.

1966

1. Source: *The Beatles (Second Revised Edition)*, by Hunter Davies. McGraw-Hill, Inc., 1985, page xv; *DK Encyclopedia of Rock Stars*, by Dafydd Rees and Luke Crampton. DK Publishing, Inc., 1996, page 649.

2. Sources: *Beatles Undercover*, by Kristofer K. Engelhardt. Collector's Guide Publishing Inc, 1998, pp. 28–29.

3. Sources: *The Complete Beatles Chronicle*, by Mark Lewisohn. Harmony Books, 1992, page 215; "Bob Whitaker: Behind the Scenes With the 'Butcher' Cover Photographer," by Juan Agueras and Javiro Tarazona. *Beatlefan*, vol. 18, no. 6, 1997, page 21; *Unseen Beatles*, by Bob Whitaker and Martin Harrison. HarperCollins Publishers, 1991, page 142.

4. Sources: "The Untold, Real, True, Inside Story of the Beatles' Sgt. Pepper's Lonely Hearts Club Band," by (Barry) Miles. *High Times*, October 1979, page 50; *Paul McCartney: Many Years from Now*, by Barry Miles. Henry Holt and Company, 1997, page 238.

5. Sources: *Paul McCartney: Many Years From Now*, by Barry Miles. Henry Holt and Company, 1997, page 190.

6. Source: *The Beatles: Recording Sessions*, by Mark Lewisohn. Harmony Books, 1988, pp. 72–73.

7. Source: *The Playboy Interviews with John Lennon & Yoko Ono*, by David Sheff. Playboy Press, 1981, page 151.

8. Sources: "Triumphant Return!" (by Johnny Dean). *The Beatles Book Monthly*, Beat Publications Ltd., August 1966, pp. 2, 7; *Paul McCartney: Many Years from Now*, by Barry Miles. Henry Holt and Company, 1997, page 269.

9. Source: *I Me Mine*, by George Harrison. Genesis Publications/Simon and Schuster, 1980, page 95.

Sources

10. Sources: *The Paul McCartney World Tour* (program book), Paul Du Noyer, ed. EMAP Metro, 1989, page 9; *The Beatles Recording Sessions*, by Mark Lewisohn. Harmony Books, 1988, page 76.

11. Source: *The Beatles: Recording Sessions*, by Mark Lewisohn. Harmony Books, 1988, page 77.

12. Sources: *The Complete Beatles Chronicle*, by Mark Lewisohn. Harmony Books, 1992, pp. 221–222; "The Unseen Beatles: A Talk With the Man Behind the Camera for the 'Butcher Cover,' " by George Watts. *Beatlefan*, vol. 13, no. 5, 1992, page 26.

13. Sources: "Neil's Column," by Neil Aspinall and "New Stage Outfits" (Beatle News). *The Beatles Book Monthly*, Beat Publications Ltd., July 1966, pp. 25, 29; *The Beatles: a diary*, by Barry Miles. Omnibus Press, 1998, page 215.

14. Sources: *The Making of Pet Sounds*, by David Leaf. *The Pet Sounds Sessions* (box set booklet), Capitol Records, 1996, pp. 123–124, 126; *Moon: The Life and Death of a Rock Legend*, by Tony Fletcher. Spike/Avon Books, Inc., 1999, page 169.

15. Source: *The Beatles: Recording Sessions*, by Mark Lewisohn. Harmony Books, 1988, page 81.

16. Source: "Triumphant Return!" (by Johnny Dean). *The Beatles Book Monthly*, Beat Publications Ltd., August 1966, page 9.

17. Source: *Unseen Beatles*, by Bob Whitaker and Martin Harrison. HarperCollins Publishers, 1991, pp. 77, 110.

18. Source: "The Beatles: Live at Budokan," William Bartone and Daniel Green, ed., *The Smoking Gun,* http://www.thesmokinggun.com/archive/beatles1.shtml.

19. Source: *Tomorrow Never Knows: The Beatles' Last Concert*, by Eric Lefcowitz. Terra Firma Books, 1987, pp. 13, 15.

20. Source: *Hey, Hey, We're the Monkees*, Harold Bronson, ed. General Publishing Group, Inc., 1996, page 35.

21. Source: *Tomorrow Never Knows: The Beatles' Last Concert*," by Eric Lefcowitz. Terra Firma Books, 1987, pp. 7, 44, 48, 60.

22. Sources: "Beatlebeat," by Bill Harry. *Beatlefan*, vol. 17, no. 2, 1996, page 11; *Paul McCartney: Many Years from Now*, by Barry Miles. Henry Holt and Company, 1997, page 124.

23. Source: "Beatle Movie memories: Talking With Norman Rossington of 'Norm and Shake,'" by Ian Forsyth. *Beatlefan*, vol. 16, no. 3, 1995, page 19.

24. Sources: "Time Machine October 1966: Meanwhile . . ." *Mojo*, October 1996, page 37; *The Ultimate Beatles Encyclopedia*, by Bill Harry. Hyperion, 1992, page 238.

25. Source: *The Complete Beatles Chronicle*, by Mark Lewisohn. Harmony Books, 1992, page 232.

1967

1. Source: *The Beatles Recording Sessions*, by Mark Lewisohn. Harmony Books, 1988, page 94.

2. Source: *Blinds & Shutters: The Photographs of Michael Cooper*, Brian Roylance, ed. Genesis/Hedley Publications, 1990, page 307.

3. Sources: *The Beatles: Recording Sessions*, by Mark Lewisohn. Harmony Books, 1988, page 114; *The Complete Beatles Chronicle*, by Mark Lewisohn. Harmony Books, 1992, page 242.

4. Sources: *Paul McCartney: Many Years from Now*, by Barry Miles. Henry Holt and Company, 1997, pp. 259, 308–309; *The Complete Beatles Chronicle*, by Mark Lewisohn. Harmony Books, 1992, page 240.

5. Sources: *A Hard Day's Write*, by Steve Turner. HarperCollins Publishers, 1994, page 128; *The Complete Beatles Chronicle*, by Mark Lewisohn. Harmony Books, 1992, pp. 242–243; *Blinds & Shutters: The Photographs of Michael Cooper*, Brian Roylance, ed. Genesis/Hedley Publications, 1990, page 275.

6. Source: *Songs in the Rough*, by Stephen Bishop. St. Martin's Press, 1996, page 29.

Sources

7.   Source: *John, Paul & Me: Before the Beatles*, by Len Garry. Collector's Guide Publishing Inc., 1997, page 199.

8.   Sources: *Songs in the Rough*, by Stephen Bishop. St. Martin's Press, 1996, page 28; *Paul McCartney: Many Years from Now*, by Barry Miles. Henry Holt and Company, 1997, page 320.

9.   Sources: *A Hard Day's Write*, by Steve Turner. HarperCollins Publishers, 1994, pp. 125–127; *Blinds & Shutters: The Photographs of Michael Cooper*, Brian Roylance, ed. Genesis/Hedley Publications, 1990, pp. 44, 360; *Paul McCartney: Many Years from Now*, by Barry Miles. Publications Henry Holt and Company, 1997, page 316.

10.   Sources: *Paul McCartney: Many Years From Now*, by Barry Miles. Henry Holt and Company, 1997, page 312; *A Hard Day's Write*, by Steve Turner. HarperCollins Publishers, 1994, pp. 122–123; *The Playboy Interviews with John Lennon & Yoko Ono*, by David Sheff. Playboy Press, 1981, page 153; *The Annotated Alice*, by Lewis Caroll and Martin Gardner. Wings Books, 1960, pp. 252–264.

11.   Source: *The Beatles: Recording Sessions*, by Mark Lewisohn. Harmony Books, 1988, page 101.

12.   Sources: *I Me Mine*, by George Harrison. Genesis Publications/Simon and Schuster, 1980, page 112; *A Hard Day's Write*, by Steve Turner. HarperCollins Publishers, 1994, page 129.

13.   Sources: *Paul McCartney: Many Years from Now*, by Barry Miles. Henry Holt & Company, 1997, pp. 316–317; *The Beatles: Recording Sessions*, by Mark Lewisohn. Harmony Books, 1988, pp. 103, 128.

14.   Source: *Blinds & Shutters: The Photographs of Michael Cooper*, Brian Roylance, ed. Genesis/Hedley Publications, 1990, page 19.

15.   Sources: *Blinds & Shutters: The Photographs of Michael Cooper*, Brian Roylance, ed. Genesis/Hedley Publications, 1990, page 56; *Miller's Rock & Pop Memorabilia*, by Stephen Maycock. Reed Consumer Books Ltd., 1994, page 77.

16.   Sources: *The Beatles Files*, by Andy Davis. CLB International, 1998, page 116; "Beatle Bits" (The Official Beatles Fan Club, July Newsletter), by Freda Kelly. *The Beatles Book Monthly*, Beat Publications Ltd., July 1967, page 5.

17. Sources: *Unsurpassed Masters Vol. 3* (bootleg CD), by the Beatles. Yellow Dog Records, 1989, track 10; *The Complete Beatles Chronicle*, by Mark Lewisohn. Harmony Books, 1992, pp. 257, 259–260.

18. Source: "Four View Points of the Magical Mystery Tour," by Sylvia Nightingale, et al. *The Beatles Book Monthly*, Beat Publications Ltd., November 1967, page 11.

19. Sources: *The Complete Beatles Chronicle*, by Mark Lewisohn. Harmony Books, 1992, page 263; *The Beatles Album*, by Julia Delano. Smithmark Publishers, 1991, page 193; "Filming the Magical Mystery Tour," by Tony Barrow. *The Beatles Book Monthly*, Beat Publications Ltd., October 1987, page 7.

20. Sources: "A Rutle Remembers: Talking With Neil Innes," by Ken Sharp. *Beatlefan*, vol. 10, no. 1, 1987, page 18; *The Complete Beatles Chronicle*, by Mark Lewisohn. Harmony Books, 1992, page 266.

21. Sources: "Cash for Questions: Paul McCartney," by Robert Yates. *Q*, January 1998, page 18; "McCartney Answers Fans" (Beatlenews Roundup), by William P. King. *Beatlefan*, vol. 16, no. 2, 1995, page 7.

22. Source: "The Faces of Time" (advertisement), *Time*, 8 June 1998.

23. Source: *Hey, Hey, We're the Monkees*, Harold Bronson, ed. General Publishing Group, Inc., 1996, page 90.

24. Source: *The Complete Beatles Chronicle*, by Mark Lewisohn. Harmony Books, 1992, page 245

25. Source: *The Beatles Movies*, by Bob Neaverson. Cassell, 1997, page 65.

1968

1. Sources: *Wonderwall Movie* website, http://www.wonderwallfilm.co.uk; *Beatles Undercover*, by Kristofer K. Engelhardt. Collector's Guide Publishing Inc., 1998, page 395.

2. Source: *They Can't Hide Us Anymore*, by Richie Havens with Steve Davidowitz. Spike/Avon, 1999, pp. 166–167.

Sources

3. Source: *The Beatles Encyclopedia,* by Bill Harry. Hyperion, 1992, page 204.

4. Sources: *The Beatles File,* by Andy Davis. CLB International, 1998, page 132; "Your Album Queries," by Mal Evans. *The Beatles Book Monthly,* Beat Publications Ltd., February 1969, page 7.

5. Sources: *Fifty Years Adrift,* by Derek Taylor. Genesis Publications Ltd., 1984, page 359; *The Longest Cocktail Party,* by Richard DiLello. Playboy Press, 1972, page 103; *Dear Mr. Fantasy,* by Ethan A. Russell. Houghton Mifflin Company, 1985, page 117.

6. Sources: *The Paul McCartney World Tour* (program book), Paul Du Noyer, ed. EMAP Metro, 1989, page 9; *The Beatles Recording Sessions,* by Mark Lewisohn. Harmony Books, 1988, page 137.

7. Source: *The Beatles Files,* by Andy Davis. CLB International, 1998, page 139.

8. Sources: *A Hard Day's Write,* by Steve Turner. HarperCollins Publishers, 1994, pp. 153–154; *Paul McCartney: Many Years from Now,* by Barry Miles. Henry Holt and Company, 1997, page 419; *The Complete Beatles Chronicle,* by Mark Lewisohn. Harmony Books, 1992, page 288.

9. Sources: "Life in the Yellow Submarine: The Making of the Movie," by Dr. Bob Hieronimus. *Goldmine,* 6 November 1998, page 144; *The Encyclopedia of the American Theatre 1900–1975,* by Edwin J. Bronner. A. S. Barnes & Company, Inc., 1980, page 99.

10. Source: "Life in the Yellow Submarine: The Making of the Movie," by Dr. Bob Hieronimus. *Goldmine,* 6 November 1998, page 138.

11. Sources: "The Making of Yellow Submarine," by Bob Hieronimus. *Beatlefan,* vol. 19, no. 4, 1998, pp. 15–16; "Life in the Yellow Submarine: The Making of the Movie," by Dr. Bob Hieronimus. *Goldmine,* 6 November 1998, page 138.

12. Source: "Life in the Yellow Submarine: The Making of the Movie," by Dr. Bob Hieronimus. *Goldmine,* 6 November 1998, page 142.

13. Sources: "The McCartney Interview" (part one), by Vic Garbarini. *Beatlefan,* vol. 2, no.5, 1980, page 13; *A Hard Day's Write,* by Steve Turner.

Sources

HarperCollins Publishers, 1994, page 167; *Paul McCartney: Many Years from Now*, by Barry Miles. Henry Holt and Company, 1997, page 487.

14. Sources: *The Beatles London*, by Piet Schreuders, Mark Lewisohn and Adam Smith. St. Martin's Press, 1997, pp. 33–35, 37, 45–46; "The Mad Day Out," by Paul Du Noyer. *Mojo*, October 1996, page 60.

15. Sources: "This Just In," *Mojo*, October 1998, page 12; "Incoming," *Q*, October 1998, page 32; "Briefly" (Beatlenews Roundup), by William P. King. *Beatlefan*, vol. 19, no. 6, 1998, page 10; *Sotheby's* website, http://www.sothebys.com.

16. Sources: *I Me Mine*, by George Harrison. Genesis Publications/Simon & Schuster, 1980, page 138; *The Beatles: Recording Sessions*, by Mark Lewisohn. Harmony Books, 1988, pp. 147–148.

17. Source: *Revolution in the Head: The Beatles' Records and the Sixties*, by Ian MacDonald. Henry Holt and Company, 1994, page 262.

18. Sources: *A Hard Day's Write*, by Steve Turner. HarperCollins Publishers, 1994, page 165; "Judas Christ Superstar," by Andy Gill. *Mojo*, November 1998, page 46.

19. Sources: *The Beatles: Recording Sessions*, by Mark Lewisohn. Harmony Books, 1988, page 150; "McCartney Answers Fans" (Beatlenews Roundup), by William P. King. *Beatlefan*, vol. 16, no. 2, 1995, page 7.

20. Source: *Fifty Years Adrift*, by Derek Taylor. Genesis Publications Ltd., 1984, page 360.

21. Sources: *A Hard Day's Write*, by Steve Turner. HarperCollins Publishers, 1994, page 155; *Rock & Roll Memorabilia*, by Hilary Kay. Fireside Books, 1992, page 38.

23. Source: *Wonderwall Music* (CD liner notes), by Derek Taylor. Apple Records, 1992, pp. 7–8.

24. Source: *Paul McCartney: Many Years from Now*, by Barry Miles. Henry Holt and Company, 1997, page 527.

25. Sources: *Blinds & Shutters: The Photographs of Michael Cooper*, Brian Roylance, ed. Genesis Publications, 1990, page 99; *Paul McCartney:*

Many Years from Now, by Barry Miles. Henry Holt and Company, 1997, page 500.

1969

1.   Source: *Get Back: The Unauthorized Chronicle of the Beatles' Let It Be Disaster*, by Doug Sulpy and Ray Schweighardt. St. Martin's Press, 1997, pp. 196–198.

2.   Source: *Get Back: The Unauthorized Chronicle of the Beatles' Let It Be Disaster*, by Doug Sulpy and Ray Schweighardt. St. Martin's Press, 1997, pp. 153, 188–189.

3.   Source: *Get Back: The Unauthorized Chronicle of the Beatles' Let It Be Disaster*, by Doug Sulpy and Ray Schweighardt. St. Martin's Press, 1997, pp. 158–161.

4.   Sources: *Linda McCartney's Sixties—Portrait of an Era*, by Linda McCartney. Bulfinch Press, 1992, page 153; *Paul McCartney: Many Years from Now*, by Barry Miles. Henry Holt and Company, 1997, pp. 230–231.

5.   Sources: *Get Back: The Unauthorized Chronicle of the Beatles' Let It Be Disaster*, by Doug Sulpy and Ray Schweighardt. St. Martin's Press, 1997, page 216; *The Complete Beatles Chronicle*, by Mark Lewisohn. Harmony Books, 1992, page 348; *Carry On Line*, by Andrew Davidson, http://www.carryonline.com.

6.   Sources: *The Beatles: An Oral History*, by David Pritchard and Alan Lysaght. Hyperion, 1998, pp. 277–278; "Mal's Diary," by Mal Evans. *The Beatles Book Monthly*, Beat Publications Ltd., March 1969, page 15.

7.   Source: *Blinds & Shutters: The Photographs of Michael Cooper*, Brian Roylance, ed. Genesis Publications/Hedley, 1990, pp. 89–90.

8.   Sources: "George Harrison Gets 'Undercover,'" by Paul Cashmere. *Undercover* (CD-ROM magazine), issue 2, 1996; *I Me Mine*, by George Harrison. Genesis Publications/Simon & Schuster, 1980, page 152.

9.   Sources: "Lennon and Yoko turned back at port," *Daily Mail*, 17 March 1969 (article included in "The Press" booklet included with the *Wedding Album*); *Lennon*, by John Robertson. Omnibus Press, 1995, page 64.

Sources

10. Source: *The Long & Winding Road: A History of the Beatles on Record,* by Neville Stannard. Virgin Books, 1983, page 10.

11. Source: *The Complete Beatles Chronicle,* by Mark Lewisohn. Harmony Books, 1992, page 319.

12. Source: *The Beatles: Recording Sessions,* by Mark Lewisohn. Harmony Books, 1988, page 174.

13. Sources: *The Longest Cocktail Party,* by Richard DiLello. Playboy Press, 1972, page 169; *Lennon,* by Ray Coleman. McGraw-Hill Book Company, 1984, page 392.

14. Sources: *Nick Drake,* by Patrick Humphries. Bloomsbury Publishing, 1997, page 185; *The Beatles London,* by Piet Schreuders, Mark Lewisohn and Adam Smith. St. Martin's Press, 1994, page 100.

15. Sources: "Daddy Has Gone Away Now: Let It Be," by Jonathan Cott and David Dalton. *Rolling Stone,* 9 July 1970; *Fifty Years Adrift,* by Derek Taylor. Genesis Publications Ltd., 1984, page 398.

16. Sources: "Derek Taylor Makes a Radio Teleprinter Call From the QE2," by Derek Taylor. *The Beatles Book Monthly,* Beat Publications Ltd., July 1969, page 12; *Black Market Beatles,* by Jim Berkenstadt and Belmo (Scott Belmer). Collector's Guide Publishing, 1995, page 79; *Fifty Years Adrift,* by Derek Taylor. Genesis Publications Ltd., 1984, page 368.

17. Sources: *Fifty Years Adrift,* by Derek Taylor. Genesis Publications Ltd., 1984, page 413; *Lennon,* by Ray Coleman. McGraw-Hill Book Company, 1984, pp. 452–453; *Dear Mr. Fantasy,* by Ethan A. Russell. Houghton Mifflin Company, 1985, pp. 200, 204.

18. Source: *The Beatles: Recording Sessions,* by Mark Lewisohn. Harmony Books, 1988, page 181.

19. Sources: *Paul McCartney: Many Years from Now,* by Barry Miles. Henry Holt and Company, 1997, page 555. *Miller's Rock & Pop Memorabilia,* by Stephen Maycock. Reed Consumer Books Ltd., 1994, page 33.

20. Sources: "People" (Beatlenews Roundup), by William P. King. *Beatlefan,* vol. 14, no. 1, 1992, page 7; " 'Paul Is Live' Released" (Beatlenews Roundup), by William P. King. *Beatlefan,* vol. 15, no. 1, 1993, page 5.

21. Sources: *Belmo's Beatleg News*, vol. 4, nos. 1–2, 1990, page 9; *The Beatles: Recording Sessions*, by Mark Lewisohn. Harmony Books, 1988, page 194.

22. Source: *Beatles Undercover*, by Kristofer K. Engelhardt. Collector's Guide Publishing, 1998, pp. 316, 404.

23. Sources: "Hoaxers Unmasked" [Enlightenment], by Fred Dellar. *Mojo*, May 1999, page 125; *All Together Now*, by Harry Castleman and Walter J. Podrazik. Pierian Press/Popular Culture Ink, 1975, page 288; *The Ultimate Beatles Encyclopedia*, by Bill Harry. Hyperion, 1992, page 441.

24. Sources: *Black Market Beatles*, by Jim Berkenstadt and Belmo [Scott Belmer]. Collector's Guide Publishing, 1995, pp. 76–79; *Bootleg: The Secret History of the Other Recording Industry*, by Clinton Heylin. St. Martin's Press, 1995, page 57.

25. Sources: *Peter Sellers*, by Alexander Walker. MacMillan Publishing Company, 1981, page 195; *The Life and Death of Peter Sellers*, by Roger Lewis. Applause Books, 1997, pp. 39, 63; *The Beatles London*, by Piet Schreuders, Mark Lewisohn and Adam Smith. St. Martin's Press, 1994, page 117.

1970

1. Source: *Without You: The Tragic Story of Badfinger*, by Dan Matovina. Frances Glover Books, 1997, pp. 65–67.

2. Sources: *Fifty Years Adrift*, by Derek Taylor. Genesis Publications Ltd., 1984, pp. 390, 428; *The Longest Cocktail Party*, by Richard DiLello. Playboy Press, 1972, page 242.

3. Sources: *Paul McCartney: Many Years from Now*, Barry Miles. Henry Holt and Company, 1997, page 538; "The Songs," by Mark Lewisohn. *Club Sandwich*, no. 82, Summer 1997, MPL Communications, http://www.mplcommunications.com.

4. Source: *Paul McCartney: Many Years from Now*, by Barry Miles. Henry Holt and Company, 1997, page 539.

5. Source: *The Complete Beatles Chronicle*, by Mark Lewisohn. Harmony Books, 1992, page 343.

Sources

6.   Source: *The Longest Cocktail Party*, by Richard DiLello. Playboy Press, 1972, page 255.

7.   Sources: *The Playboy Interviews with John Lennon & Yoko Ono*, by David Sheff. Playboy Press, 1981, page 183; *Paul McCartney: Many Years from Now*, by Barry Miles. Henry Holt and Company, 1997, page 183.

8.   Source: *The Complete Beatles Chronicle*, by Mark Lewisohn. Harmony Books, 1992, page 345.

9.   Source: *The Longest Cocktail Party*, by Richard DiLello. Playboy Press, 1972, page 254.

10.   Sources: *Dark Horse: The Private Life of George Harrison*, by Geoffrey Giuliano. Dutton, 1990, pp. 2, 122; *The Beatles (Second Revised Edition)*, by Hunter Davies. W. W. Norton, 1996, page 360; "Beatles '79: A Diary of Recent News and Events," by Mark Lewisohn. *The Beatles Book Appreciation Society Magazine*, December 1979, page v.

11.   Source: *The Longest Cocktail Party*, by Richard DiLello. Playboy Press, 1972, page 233.

12.   Sources: *Beatles Undercover*, by Kristofer K. Engelhardt. Collector's Guide Publishing Inc., 1998, pp. 41–42; *The Complete Beatles Chronicle*, by Mark Lewisohn. Harmony Books, 1992, page 334.

13.   Source: "Ringo Goes Single," by Jack Hamilton. *Look*, 10 February 1970, page 41.

14.   Source: "FBI: The John Lennon Investigation" [copy of John Lennon's FBI files]. From *John Lennon Pages—Beatles Net Link*, http://www.beatles.miningco.com.

15.   Source: *Bob Dylan: The Recording Sessions 1960–1994*, by Clinton Heylin. St. Martin's Griffin, 1996, pp. 84, 87.

16.   Source: *Dear Mr. Fantasy*, by Ethan A. Russell. Houghton Mifflin Company, 1985, pp. 103, 119, 177, 179, 183, 209, 235–236.

17.   Sources: *I Me Mine*, by George Harrison. Genesis Publications/Simon & Schuster, 1980, pp. 164–165; *Bob Dylan: A Life in Stolen Moments*, by Clinton Heylin. Book Sales Ltd., 1996, page 114.

18. Source: *I Me Mine*, by George Harrison. Genesis Publications/Simon & Schuster, 1980, pp. 182–183.

19. Sources: *The Longest Cocktail Party*, by Richard DiLello. Playboy Press, 1972, page 258; "Production Bio: Neil Aspinall," *The Beatles Anthology* [press packet], 1995.

20. Source: "The Beatles in Graphic Terms," by Rick Glover. *Beatlefan*, vol.21, no. 2, 2000, page 19.

21. Source: *Ringo Starr Home Page*, by Gary Schultz, http://web2.airmail.net.

22. Sources: *Lennon*, by Ray Coleman. McGraw-Hill Book Company, 1984, page 381; *Sotheby's London Rock and Roll Memorabilia 1956–1984* (auction catalogue), 1985, page 35.

23. Source: *Janis* by Janis Joplin. Columbia/Legacy, 1993, disc three, track nine; *DK Encyclopedia of Rock Stars*, by Dafydd Rees and Luke Crampton. DK Publishing, Inc., 1996, page 471.

24. Sources: *Scrooge* (and) *Darling Lili: IMDb* (Internet Movie Database), http://us.imdb.com; *The Beatles: The Ultimate Recording Guide*, by Allen J. Wiener. Facts On File, 1992, page 47.

25. Source: *Careless Love: The Unmaking of Elvis Presley*, by Peter Guralnick. Little, Brown and Company, 1999, pp. 420, 425–426, 704.

1971

1. Sources: *Skywriting by Word of Mouth*, by John Lennon. Harper & Row, 1986, page 25; *Lennon*, by John Robertson. Omnibus Press, 1995, page 80.

2. Sources: *Moon: The Life and Death of a Rock Legend*, by Tony Fletcher. Spike/Avon, 1999, pp. 295–296; *Beatles Undercover*, by Kristofer K. Engelhardt. Collector's Guide Publishing Inc., 1998, page 519.

4. Source: "Affidavit of Allen Klein" (1970 M. No. 6315), 12 February 1971, http://www.rockmine. music.com.uk.

6. Sources: *The Complete Beatles Chronicle*, by Mark Lewisohn. Harmony Books, 1992, pp. 345, 347; "A Starr Is Reborn," by Mark Brown. *Orange County Register*, 3 May 1997, http://www.ocregister.com.

8. Sources: *Without You: The Tragic Story of Badfinger*, by Dan Matovina. Frances Glover Books, 1997, pp. 136–138; *Straight Up* (CD booklet notes), by Andy Davis. Apple/Capitol, 1993, page 7.

9. Sources: "More With Ringo Starr!" by Ken Sharp. *Beatlefan*, vol. 20, no. 2, 1999, page 18; *The Beatles After the Breakup 1970–2000*, by Keith Badman. Omnibus Press, 1999, page 35.

10. Source: *John Lennon: In His Own Words*, by [Barry] Miles. Quick Fox, 1981, page 99.

11. Source: *I Am Also a You*, by Jay Thompson. Clarkson N. Potter, Inc., 1971.

12. Source: *The Playboy Interviews with John Lennon & Yoko Ono*, by David Sheff. Playboy Press, 1981, page 172.

13. Source: *Without You: The Tragic Story of Badfinger*, by Dan Matovina. Frances Glover Books, 1997, page 143.

14. Source: *Without You: The Tragic Story of Badfinger*, by Dan Matovina. Frances Glover Books, 1997, pp. 143–144.

15. Sources: *Rock Names: From Abba To ZZ Top: How Rock Bands Got Their Names*, by Adam Dolgins. Citadel Press, 1998, pp. 293–294; *The Ultimate Beatles Encyclopedia*, by Bill Harry. Hyperion, 1992, page 457; "Beatle Again Is Father of Girl" (from the Associated Press), *The Sacramento Bee*, 19 September 1971; *Linda McCartney: A Portrait*, by Danny Fields. Renaissance Books, 2000, pp. 32, 35, 37.

16. Source: *John Lennon: In His Own Words*, by [Barry] Miles. Quick Fox, 1981, page 98.

17. Sources: *The Art & Music of John Lennon*, by John Robertson. Omnibus Press, 1990, page 144; *Lennon*, by John Robertson. Omnibus Press, 1995, pp. 85–86; "It's Time for Lennon's CLOCK" (CD bootleg review), by Belmo (Scott Belmer). *Belmo's Beatleg News*, February 1997, page 1; *The Beatles After The Breakup 1970–2000*, by Keith Badman. Omnibus Press, 1999, page 49.

18. Sources: "The McCartney Interview" (part one), by Vic Garbarini. *Beatlefan*, vol. 2, no. 5, 1980, page 13; *Blackbird: The Life and Times of Paul McCartney* (Updated Edition), by Geoffrey Giuliano. Da Capo Press, 1997, pp. 163–164; *Bob Dylan: The Recording Sessions 1960–1994*, by Clinton Heylin. St. Martin's Griffin, 1996, page 73.

19. Sources: *The Art & Music of John Lennon*, by John Robertson. Omnibus Press, 1990, pp. 144–145; *The Beatles After the Breakup 1970–2000*, by Keith Badman. Omnibus Press, 1999, pp. 50–51.

20. Sources: *Dharma Lion: A Biography of Allen Ginsberg*, by Michael Schumacher. St. Martin's Press, 1992, pp. 523, 556–557, 732; *Not For Sale: The Beatles' Musical Legacy as Archived on Unauthorized Recordings*, by Belmo [Scott Belmer]. The Hot Wacks Press, 1997, pp. 270–271.

21. Sources: *Lennon*, by John Robertson. Omnibus Press, 1995, page 86. *The Beatles After The Break-up 1970–2000*, by Keith Badman. Omnibus Press, 1999, page 51.

22. Sources: "Identity Crisis" [Joe Massot], by Bleddyn Butcher. *Mojo*, October 1996, page 146; *Zachariah: IMDb* (Internet Movie Database), http://us.imdb.com.

24. Source: *Lennon*, by John Robertson. Omnibus Press, 1995, page 87.

25. Source: "FBI: The John Lennon Investigation" Lennon's FBI Files, (article by Bill Gray in the *Detroit News*, 13 December 1971), *John Lennon Pages—Beatles Net Link*, http://www.beatles.miningco.com.

1972

1. Sources: *Beatles Undercover*, by Kristofer K. Engelhardt. Collector's Guide Publishing Inc., 1998, pp. 111–112; *I Me Mine*, by George Harrison. Genesis Publications/Simon & Schuster, 1980, page 234.

2. Source: *Beatles Undercover*, by Kristofer K. Engelhardt. Collector's Guide Publishing Inc., 1998, pp. 234–235.

3. Sources: UPI, Washington Capitol News Service, 17 June 1975.

Sources

4. Source: "Wings First Flight," by Shelley Turner. *Wings Over Europe*, (concert program), McCartney Productions, 1972, page 8.

5. Source: "John and Yoko on Mike Douglas," by Bonnie Kent. *Instant Karma*, no. 8, 1983.

6. Source: "FBI: The John Lennon Investigation" [copy of John Lennon's FBI files]. *John Lennon Pages—Beatles Net Link*, http://www.beatles.miningco.com.

7. Source: *Beatles Undercover*, by Kristofer K. Engelhardt. Collectors Guide Publishing, 1998, page 341.

8. Sources: *Lennon*, by John Robertson. Omnibus Press, 1995, page 85; *The Lost Lennon Tapes, Volume 21* (bootleg LP). Bag Records, 1991, side two, track six.

9. Source: *VH1 Storytellers* (CD), by Ringo Starr. Mercury Records, 1998, track 4.

12. Source: *Lennon*, by John Robertson. Omnibus Press, 1995, page 89.

13. Source: *Beatles Undercover*, by Kristofer K. Engelhardt. Collectors Guide Publishing Inc. 1998, pp. 518–520.

14. Source: *Wings Over Europe*, by Gordon House and John Nun. McCartney Productions, 1972, page 4.

15. Source: *McCartney: The Definitive Biography*, by Chris Salewicz. St. Martin's Press, 1986, page 231.

16. Source: *All Together Now*, by Harry Castleman and Walter J. Podrazik. Pierian Press/Popular Culture Ink, 1975, page 115.

17. Sources: *The Beatles: The Ultimate Recording Guide*, by Allen J. Wiener. Facts On File, 1992, pp. 50–51; *Listen to These Pictures: Photographs of John Lennon*, by Bob Gruen. William Morrow and Company, 1985, page 13.

19. Sources: *Listen to These Pictures: Photographs of John Lennon*, by Bob Gruen. William Morrow and Company, 1985, page 14; *Lennon*, by John Robertson. Omnibus Press, 1995, page 90; *The Beatles Again*, by Harry

Castleman and Walter J. Podrazik. Pierian Press/Popular Culture Ink, 1977, page 169.

20. Source: *Beatles Undercover*, by Kristofer K. Engelhardt. Collector's Guide Publishing Inc., 1998, pp. 447–448.

21. Source: *All Together Now*, by Harry Castleman and Walter J. Podrazik. Pierian Press/Popular Culture Ink, 1975, page 118.

23. Sources: *Starring Fred Astaire*, by Stanley Green and Burt Goldblatt. Dodd, Mead & Company, 1973, page 468; *The Beatles After The Break-Up 1970–2000*, by Keith Badman. Omnibus Press, 1999, pp. 47, 86.

24. Source: *Traveller Chess Sites*, http://misc.traveller.com/chess/graphics/yoko.htm.

25. Source: *Fear and Loathing in Las Vegas*, by Hunter S. Thompson. Random House, 1972, page 21.

1973

1. Source: *Fifty Years Adrift*, by Derek Taylor. Genesis Publications Ltd., 1984, pp. 448–451.

3. Sources: *The Pink Floyd Encyclopedia*, by Vernon Fitch. Collector's Guide Publishing Inc. 1998, pp. 77–78, 191; " 'Intelligent vs pigheaded . . . ,' " by Peter Henderson. *Mojo*, March 1998, page 81.

4. Sources: *The Dark Side of the Moon: Twentieth Anniversary Edition* [CD]. EMI, 1993, track 9; *The Pink Floyd Encyclopedia*, by Vernon Fitch. Collector's Guide Publishing Inc. 1998, page 91.

5. Source: *Moon: The Life and Death of a Rock Legend*, by Tony Fletcher. Spike/Avon Books, 1999, pp. 343–344, 395.

6. Source: "Far East Man: George Harrison and the Road to 'Live In Japan,' " by Timothy White. *Goldmine*, 27 November 1992, page 17.

7. Sources: *Life at the Dakota*, by Stephen Birmingham. Random House, 1979, pp. 78–79; "Love-hate relationship exists for tenants of famous Dakota," by Marian Christie. *The Oregonian* [LA Times-Washington Post Service], 23 October 1979.

8.   Source: "The Recording of Band on the Run," by Mark Lewisohn. *Band on the Run: 25th Anniversary Edition* [CD], Capitol Records, 1999, page 4 (and) "Dustin Hoffman (Dialogue)," CD2, track eighteen.

11.   Source: *McCartney: The Definitive Biography*, by Chris Salewicz. St. Martin's Press, 1986, pp. 236–239.

12.   Source: *All You Need Is Ears*, by George Martin and Jeremy Hornsby. St. Martin's Press, 1979, page 231.

13.   Source: *The John Lennon Anthology*, by John Lennon. Capitol Records, 1998, disc two, tracks 14, 15.

14.   Source: *Absolute Elsewhere* [CD bootleg box set], by John Lennon. Vigotone, 1998, disc one, track eleven.

15.   Source: *Absolute Elsewhere* [CD bootleg box set], by John Lennon. Vigotone, 1998, disc three, track one.

16.   Source: "Paul Simon Song Book" [review], by Paul McCartney. *Punch*, 8 August 1973, reprinted in *With a Little Help From My Friends*, no. 42, April 1983, pp. 10–11.

17.   Source: "Out of adversity . . ." *The Paul McCartney World Tour* (program book), Paul Du Noyer, ed. EMAP Metro, 1989, page 75.

18.   Sources: "The Recording of Band on the Run," by Mark Lewisohn. *Band on the Run: 25th Anniversary Edition* [CD], Capitol Records, 1999, page 8; "Fela Kuti: 1938–1997" [Real Gone], by Neil Spencer. *Mojo*, October 1997, page 29; *The Beatles After the Break-Up 1970–2000*, by Keith Badman. Omnibus Press, 1999, page 107.

19.   Sources: *The Beatles London*, by Piet Schreuders, Mark Lewisohn, and Adam Smith. St. Martin's Press, 1994, page 100; *The Beatles After the Break-up 1970–2000*, by Keith Badman. Omnibus Press, 1999, page 108.

20.   Source: "The Goon Show Scripts" [review], by John Lennon. *The New York Times Book Review*, 30 September 1973, reprinted in *With a Little Help From My Friends*, no. 42, April 1983, page 10.

21.   Source: "The Cover Photo," by Mark Lewisohn. *Band on the Run: 25th Anniversary Edition* [CD], Capitol Records, 1999, page 8.

22. Source: *Lennon*, by John Robertson. Omnibus Press, 1995, page 93.

23. Source: *The Official Price Guide to the Beatles Records and Memorablilia*, by Perry Cox and Joe Lindsay. House of Collectibles, 1995, page 234.

25. Source: *Without You: The Tragic Story of Badfinger*, by Dan Matovina. Frances Glover Books, 1997, page 210.

1974

1. Source: *Rocket Man: Elton John From A-Z*, by Claude Bernardin and Tom Stanton. Praeger Publishers, 1996, pp. 124, 192.

2. Source: "Far East Man: George Harrison and the Road To 'Live In Japan,'" by Timothy White. *Goldmine*, November 27, 1992, page 18.

3. Source: *Rock Names: From Abba to ZZ Top: How Rock Bands got Their Names*, by Adam Dolgins. Citadel Press, 1998, page 212.

4. Source: *Fifty Years Adrift*, by Derek Taylor. Genesis Publications Ltd., 1984, pp. 457, 459–460.

5. Source: *Moon: The Life and Death of a Rock Legend*, by Tony Fletcher. Spike/Avon Books, 1999, page 439.

6. Source: *Personal Best: The Harry Nilsson Anthology* (CD booklet notes), by Dawn Eden. RCA, 1994, page 23.

7. Sources: *Loving John*, by May Pang and Henry Edwards. Warner Books, 1983, pp. 247–248; "Macca News," August 1997, *Macca Central Website*, http://www.macca-central.com//macca-news.

8. Source: Checker proof sheet from Composition Arts Company, September 4, 1974. *Mitch McGeary's Songs, Pictures and Stories of the Beatles Website*, http://www.rarebeatles.com.

9. Source: *Beatles Undercover*, by Kristofer K. Engelhardt. Collector's Guide Publishing Inc., 1998, pp. 78, 123.

10. Source: *Listen to These Pictures: Photographs of John Lennon*, by Bob Gruen. William Morrow and Company, 1985, page 63.

Sources

11. Source: "Listen to This Interview," by John Lennon. *Mitch McGeary's Songs, Pictures and Stories of the Beatles Website*, http://www. rarebeatles.com.

12. Sources: *Lennon*, by Ray Coleman. McGraw-Hill Book Company, 1984, page 509; *Todd Rundgren Connection Website*, http://www.roadkill. com/todd/trconn.

13. Source: *Beatles Undercover*, by Kristofer K. Engelhardt. Collector's Guide Publishing Inc., 1998, pp. 235–236.

15. Source: "Dark Horsing Around," by Bill King and Peter C. Palmiere. *Beatlefan*, vol. 16, no. 1, 1994, page 12.

16. Sources: *The First 28o Years of Monty Python*, by Kim "Howard" John-son. St. Martin's Press/Griffin, 1999, pp. 99–100, 212; "Dateline Burbank: George Harrison Can't Shake That 33⅓!" (advertisement for Warner Bros. Records), *Rolling Stone*, 13 January 1977.

17. Source: "Dark Horsing Around," by Bill King and Peter C. Palmiere. *Beatlefan*, vol. 16, no. 1, 1994, pp. 11–13.

18. Source: "Dark Horsing Around," by Bill King and Peter C. Palmiere. *Beatlefan*, vol. 16, no. 1, 1994, page 13.

19. Source: *Ringo Starr Homepage*, by Gary Schultz, http://web2.air-mail.net.

20. Sources: *Rocket Man: Elton John From A-Z*, by Claude Bernardin and Tom Stanton. Praeger Publishers, 1996, pp. 126, 184; *Lennon*, by John Robertson. Omnibus Press, 1995, page 95.

21. Sources: *I Me Mine*, by George Harrison. Genesis Publications/Simon & Schuster, 1980, page 280; *Tennyson: A Selected Edition*, Christopher Ricks, ed. University of California Press, 1989, page 453.

22. Sources: *The Macs: Mike McCartney's Family Album*, by Mike McCartney. Delilah Books, 1981, pp. 44–45; *The Beatles: An Oral History*, by David Pritchard and Alan Lysaght. Hyperion, 1998, page 26; *The Ultimate Beatles Encyclopedia*, by Bill Harry. Hyperion, 1992, page 404; *I Me Mine*, by George Harrison. Genesis Publications/Simon & Schuster, 1980, page 23.

23. Source: "A big hand for The Quiet One," by Mark Ellen. *Q*, January 1988, page 66.

25. Source: "Harrison's 'Extra Texture': Read All About It," by Paul Gambaccini. *Rolling Stone*, 23 October 1975, page 15.

1975

1. Source: "Inside Wings: An Interview With Ex-Drummer Joe English," by William P. King. *Beatlefan*, vol. 1, no. 1, 1978, page 3.

2. Source: "The Private Years," by Chet Flippo. *The Ballad of John and Yoko*, Rolling Stone Press/Doubleday and Company, 1982, page 164.

3. Source: "Wide Prairie" (featured album), *MPL Communications Website*, http://www.mplcommunications.com.

4. Sources: "Mojo Wall of Sound 6" (photo insert), by Jurgen Vollmer. *Mojo*, May 1997; *The Beatles After the Break-Up 1970–2000*, by Keith Badman. Omnibus Press, 1999, page 151.

5. Source: *The Beatles: The Ultimate Recording Guide*, by Allen J. Wiener. Facts on File, 1992, page 116.

6. Source: "The Private Years," by Chet Flippo. *The Ballad of John and Yoko*, Rolling Stone Press/Doubleday and Company, 1982, page 163.

7. Source: *The Beatles Again?*, by Harry Castleman and Walter J. Podrazik. Pierian Press/Popular Culture Ink, 1977, pp. 214–215.

8. Source: *The Beatles After the Break-Up 1970–2000*, by Keith Badman. Omnibus Press, 1999, page 153.

10. Sources: *Beatles Undercover*, by Kristofer K. Engelhardt. Collector's Guide Publishing Inc., 1998, page 297; *Moon: The Life and Death of a Rock Legend*, by Tony Fletcher. Spike/Avon Books, 1999, page 426.

11. Sources: *Fifty Years Adrift*, by Derek Taylor. Genesis Publications Ltd., 1984, pp. 475–476; *The Beatles: Now and Then*, by Harry Benson. Universe Publishing, 1998, pp. 114–117; *Beatles Undercover*, by Kristofer K. Engelhardt. Collector's Guide Publishing Inc., 1998, page 207; *The Beatles After the Break-Up 1970–2000*, by Keith Badman. Omnibus Press, 1999, page 156.

12. Source: *The Beatles: The Ultimate Recording Guide*, by Allen J. Wiener. Facts on File, 1992, page 58.

13. Sources: *Rock Names: From Abba to ZZ Top: How Rock Bands Got Their Names*, by Adam Dolgins. Citadel Press, 1998, page 226; *The Beatles Tapes Vol. II: Early Beatlemania 1963–1964* [CD]. Jerden Records/Great Northwest Music Company, 1993, track 14.

14. Source: *Moon: The Life and Death of a Rock Legend*, by Tony Fletcher. Spike/Avon Books, 1999, page 447.

15. Sources: "Harrison's 'Extra Texture': Read All About It," by Paul Gambaccini. *Rolling Stone*, 23 October 1975, page 15; *Beatles Undercover*, by Kristofer K. Engelhardt. Collector's Guide Publishing Inc., 1998, pp. 457–458; *The Beatles After the Break-Up 1970–2000*, by Keith Badman. Omnibus Press, 1999, page 25.

19. Source: "Long Night's Journey Into Day," by Pete Hamill. *Rolling Stone*, 5 June 1975.

20. Source: *Drummed Out! The Sacking of Pete Best*, by Spencer Leigh. Northdown Publishing Ltd., 1998, page 11.

21. Sources: *The Beatles After the Break-Up 1970–2000*, by Keith Badman. Omnibus Press, 1999, page 158; *Beatles Undercover*, by Kristofer K. Engelhardt. Collector's Guide Publishing Inc., 1998, pp. 123–124.

22. Sources: *I Me Mine*, by George Harrison. Genesis Publications/Simon & Schuster, 1980, page 308; *Melissa Manchester (Official Website)*, http://www.melissa-manchester.com.

23. Source: "Harrison's 'Extra Texture': Read All About It," by Paul Gambaccini. *Rolling Stone*, 23 October 1975, page 15.

24. Source: "Harrison's 'Extra Texture': Read All About It," by Paul Gambaccini. *Rolling Stone*, 23 October 1975, page 15.

1976

1. Sources: *Paul McCartney: Many Years from Now*, by Barry Miles. Henry Holt and Company, 1997, pp. 600–601; *Without You: The Tragic Story of Badfinger*, by Dan Matovina. Frances Glover Books, 1998,

Sources

pp. 303–304; *The Beatles After the Break-Up 1970–2000*, by Keith Badman. Omnibus Press, 1999, page 175.

3. Source: "Wide Prairie" (featured album), *MPL Communications website*, http://www.mplcommunications.com

4. Sources: *The Playboy Interviews with John Lennon & Yoko Ono*, by David Sheff. Playboy Press, 1981, page 69; "Carl Perkins: The Beatles Connection," by Tom Frangione and Ken Michaels. *Goldmine*, 6 November 1998, page 70; *The Beatles After the Break-Up 1970–2000*, by Keith Bedman. Omnibus Press, 1999, page 182.

5. Source: *Beatles Undercover*, by Kristofer K. Engelhardt. Collector's Guide Publishing Inc., 1998, pp. 483–485.

6. Sources: "Ringo Remembers," by Paul Gambaccini. *Rolling Stone*, 18 November 1977, page 33; "Paul Won't Rest His Wings," by Paul Gambaccini. *Rolling Stone*, 16 December 1977.

7. Sources: "New Albums from Paul and Wings and George Harrison," by Johnny Dean. *The Beatles Book Appreciation Society Magazine*, Beat Publications Ltd., January 1977, page iv; *I Me Mine*, by George Harrison. Genesis Publications/Simon & Schuster, 1980, page 108.

8. Source: *Moon: The Life and Death of a Rock Legend*, by Tony Fletcher. Spike/Avon Books, 1999, page 447.

9. Sources: "Imagine: John Lennon Legal," by Chet Flippo. *Rolling Stone*, 9 September 1976; *Lennon*, by Ray Coleman. McGraw-Hill Book Company, 1984, page 485.

10. Source: *The Beatles After the Break-Up 1970–2000*, by Keith Badman. Omnibus Press, 1999, page 189.

11. Sources: "FBI: The John Lennon Investigation" (copy of Lennon's FBI file). From *John Lennon Pages—Beatles Net Link*, http://www.beatles.mingco.com; *Lennon*, by John Robertson. Omnibus Press, 1995, pp. 91, 103.

13. Sources: *I Me Mine*, by George Harrison. Genesis Publications/Simon & Schuster, 1980, page 228; *The Beatles: The Ultimate Recording Guide*, by Allen J. Wiener. Facts On File, 1992, pp. 137, 159, 235; "Ringo Starr:

Sources

The Hit Parader Interview," by Lisa Robinson. *Hit Parader*, December 1976, page 38.

14.   Source: *Ringo Starr Home Page*, by Gary Schultz, http://web2.air-mail.net.

15.   Source: "Random Notes," *Rolling Stone*, 18 November 1976.

17.   Sources: *Moon: The Life and Death of a Rock Legend*, by Tony Fletcher. Spike/Avon Books, 1999, pp. 495–496; "All This and World War II" (advertisement), *Rolling Stone*, 16 December 1977, page 39; "Beatles Drafted for WWII Soundtrack" (Back Pages: New York), by Peter Crescenti. *Circus Magazine*, 14 February 1977, page 53.

18.   Source: *Beatles Undercover*, by Kristofer K. Engelhardt. Collector's Guide Publishing Inc., 1998, pp. 175–176.

19.   Source: *Beatles Undercover*, by Kristofer K. Engelhardt. Collector's Guide Publishing Inc., 1998, pp. 360–361, 476–477.

20.   Source: *Rocket Man: Elton John From A-Z*, by Claude Bernardin and Tom Stanton. Praeger Publishers, 1996, pp. 11, 145, 187–188.

22.   Source: *I Me Mine*, by George Harrison. Genesis Publications/Simon & Schuster, 1980, page 321.

23.   Source: *I Me Mine*, by George Harrison. Genesis Publications/Simon & Schuster, 1980, page 334.

24.   Source: *I Me Mine*, by George Harrison. Genesis Publications/Simon & Schuster, 1980, page 330.

25.   Source: *The End of the Beatles?*, by Harry Castleman and Walter J. Podrazik. Pierian Press/Popular Culture Ink, 1985, page 12.

1977

1.   Source: *Fifty Years Adrift*, by Derek Taylor. Genesis Publications Ltd., 1984, page 496.

2.   Sources: *The Beatles: From Cavern to Star-Club*, by Hans Olaf Gottfridsson. Premium Publishing, 1997, pp. 179–180; *Beatles Undercover*, by Kristofer K. Engelhardt. Collector's Guide Publishing, 1998, pp. 162–165.

Sources

3. Sources: *Rude Studio Demos* (CD bootleg), by Paul McCartney. Columbus Records, 1989, track 16; *The Beatles: The Ultimate Recording Guide*, by Allen J. Wiener. Facts on File, 1992, pp. 61, 247.

4. Source: *The First 28 Years of Monty Python*, by Kim "Howard" Johnson. St. Martin's Griffin, 1999, pp. 310, 318.

5. Sources: *Songs, Pictures and Stories of the Beatles Website*, by Mitch McGeary, http://www.rarebeatles.com; *The Complete Beatles Chronicle*, by Mark Lewisohn. Harmony Books, 1992, pp. 169–170, 200–202.

6. Sources: *Songs, Pictures and Stories of the Beatles Website*, by Mitch McGeary, http://www.rarebeatles.com; *The 910's Guide to the Beatles' Outtakes*, by Doug Suply. The 910, 1996, pp. 182–183.

7. Source: *Beatles Undercover*, by Kristofer K. Engelhardt. Collector's Guide Publishing Inc., 1998, page 230.

8. Sources: "'London Town': The Story Behind Paul's Latest Album," by Rosie Horide. *The Beatles Book Appreciation Society Magazine*, Beat Publications Ltd., March 1978, page v; *Not For Sale: The Beatles' Musical Legacy as Archived on Unauthorized Recordings*, by Belmo [Scott Belmer]. The Hot Wacks Press, 1997, page 397; *The Beatles: The Ultimate Recording Guide*, by Allen J. Wiener. Facts on File, 1992, page 62.

9. Source: *Beatles Undercover*, by Kristofer K. Engelhardt. Collector's Guide Publishing Inc., 1998, page 108.

10. Sources: *The End of the Beatles?*, by Harry Castleman and Walter J. Podrazik. Pierian Press/Popular Culture, Ink, 1985, page 24; *The Beatles After the Break-Up 1970–2000*, by Keith Badman. Omnibus Press, 1999, page 209.

11. Sources: "Transistion," *Newsweek*, 26 September 1977; "Things We Said Today," by Joe Pope. *Strawberry Fields Forever*, no. 26, 1977, page 21.

12. Source: "Suzy & the Red Stripes: "Seaside Woman" [New on the Charts], *Billboard*, reprinted in *The Write Thing*, no. 19, August/September 1977, page 23.

13. Source: *I Me Mine*, by George Harrison. Genesis Publications/Simon & Schuster, 1980, page 322.

Sources

14. Source: *Meet the Residents: America's Most Eccentric Band!*, by Ian Shirley. SAF Publishing Ltd. 1998, pp. 40–42, 44, 61.

15. Sources: *All You Need Is Ears*, by George Martin and Jeremy Hornsby. St. Martin's Press, 1979, pp. 216–217; "The Big Beat: Conversations with Rock's Great Drummers" [Beatle Bookshelf], by Sue Felder. *Beatlefan*, vol. 6, no. 5, 1984, page 23; *The Beatles From Cavern to Star-Club*, by Hans Olof Gottfridsson. Premium Publishing, 1998, pp. 332–333, 352–353.

17. Source: "The Private Years," by Chet Flippo. *The Ballad of John and Yoko*, Rolling Stone Press/Doubleday and Company, 1982, pp. 174–175.

18. Sources: *Ringo Starr Home Page*, by Gary Schultz, http://web2.airmail.net; "Ringo Starr: The Hit Parader Interview," by Lisa Robinson. *Hit Parader*, December 1976, page 38.

19. Source: *The End of the Beatles?*, by Harry Castleman and Walter J. Podrazik. Pierian Press/Popular Culture, Ink, 1985, page 10.

20. Source: "Paul McCartney: Hip, Fab and Groovy," by Ray Bonici. *Trouser Press*, February 1978, page 14.

21. Source: *Lennon*, by John Robertson. Omnibus Press, 1995, pp. 105–106.

22. Sources: *DK Encyclopedia of Rock Stars*, by Dafydd Rees and Luke Crampton. DK Publishing, Inc., 1996, page 796; "Inside Wings: An Interview With Ex-Drummer Joe English," by William P. King. *Beatlefan*, vol. 1, no. 1, 1978, page 3.

23. Sources: *Cold Cuts* [CD bootleg], by Paul McCartney. Pegboy, 1996, track three; *The Beatles: The Ultimate Recording Guide*, by Allen J. Wiener. Facts on File, 1992, page 62.

24. Source: *The Beatles After the Break-Up 1970–2000*, by Keith Badman. Omnibus Press, 1999, page 215.

25. Source: *The End of the Beatles?*, by Harry Castleman and Walter J. Podrazik. Pierian Press/Popular Culture Ink, 1985, pp. 16–17.

1978

1. Source: *Skywriting by Word of Mouth*, by John Lennon. Harper & Row, 1986, page 25.

2. Source: *Mae West: A Biography*, by George Eells and Stanley Musgrove. William Morrow and Company, 1982, pp. 300, 304–305.

3. Sources: "Sextette" [Shock Cinema Archives], by Steve Puchalski. *Shock Cinema Website*, http://members.aol.com/Shockcin; *Mae West: A Biography*, by George Eells and Stanley Musgrove. William Morrow and Company, 1982, pp. 304–305.

5. Source: *The Rutles* [CD], Rhino, 1990.

6. Source: *Rehearsal*, by the Rutles [CD-R bootleg]. Goldtone, 1997, track 13.

7. Sources: *The Rutles*, by the Rutles [LP], Warner Bros., 1978; "Briefly . . ." (Beatlenews Roundup), by William P. King. *Beatlefan*, vol. 18, no. 1, 1996, page 6.

8. Sources: "Wings" [Pop Star of the Month], Dave Gelly. *Song Hits Magazine*, September 1978, page 8; Interview with Paul McCartney by Radio Luxembourg DJ Tony Prince, transcription by Tony Luscombe. *The Write Thing*, August/September 1978, page 22.

10. Sources: *The End of the Beatles?*, by Harry Castleman and Walter J. Podrazik. Pierian Press/Popular Culture Ink, 1985, page 28; *Beatles Undercover*, by Kristofer K. Engelhardt. Collector's Guide Publishing, Inc., 1998, page 501; "Meet the Fans," by Mary Ann Dolphin. *The Write Thing*, May/June 1978, pp. 21–22.

12. Sources: "Laurence Juber: Taking Off With Wings," by David Lawrenson. *International Musician and Recording World*, October 1979, page 85; "Lawrence [sic] Juber—Guitar," *Club Sandwich*, June/July 1978, page 7.

14. Sources: *The End of the Beatles?*, by Harry Castleman and Walter J. Podrazik. Pierian Press/Popular Culture Ink, 1985, page 22; *The Beatles: The Ultimate Recording Guide*, by Allen J. Wiener. Facts On File, 1992, page 242.

15. Source: *The Playboy Interviews With John Lennon & Yoko Ono*, by David Sheff. Playboy Press, 1981, page 183.

16. Source: *The Complete Beatles Chronicle*, by Mark Lewisohn. Harmony Books, 1992, pp. 190–191.

17. Sources: *All You Need Is Ears*, by George Martin with Jeremy Hornsby. St. Martin's Press, 1979, page 216; "Sgt. Pepper—The Story Behind A $30 Million Movie Gamble," *The Star*, 8 August 1978, page 3.

18. Source: "The Annotated 'I Do the Rock,'" by Linda Fletcher. *The Complete Tim Curry Website*, http://www.geocities.com.

19. Source: *The First 28⊗ Years of Monty Python*, by Kim "Howard" Johnson. St. Martin's Griffin, 1999, page 308.

20. Source: *Paperback Writer*, by Mark Shipper. Fred Jordan Books/Sun Ridge Press, 1978, page 95.

21. Sources: "Hawthorne is second home to ex-Beatle" [news article], *The Write Thing*, January/February 1979, page 22; *The Beatles: The Ultimate Recording Guide*, by Allen J. Wiener. Facts on File, 1992, page 63.

22. Sources: *Cold Cuts* [CD bootleg], by Paul McCartney. Pegboy, 1996, page 22; *Same Time Next Year: IMDb* [Internet Movie Database], http://us.imdb.com.

23. Sources: "Beatlenews Roundup," by William P. King. *Beatlefan*, vol. 1, no. 1, 1978, page 3 [and] vol. 1, no. 5, 1979, page 8; *The Beatles: The Ultimate Recording Guide*, by Allen J. Wiener. Facts on File, 1992, page 63.

24. Source: *The Beatles After the Break-Up 1970–2000*, by Keith Badman. Omnibus Press, 1999, page 227.

25. Source: "Beatlenews Roundup," by William P. King. *Beatlefan*, vol. 1, no. 2, 1979, page 15.

1979

1. Source: "'George Harrison': The Album Reviewed," by Mark Lewisohn. *The Beatles Book Appreciation Society Magazine*, Beat Publications Ltd., 1979, page v.

Sources

2. Source: "Far East Man: George Harrison and the Road to 'Live In Japan,'" by Timothy White. *Goldmine*, 27 November 1992, page 19.

3. Source: *I Me Mine*, by George Harrison. Genesis Publications/Simon & Schuster, 1980, page 355.

4. Sources: "George Harrison: On the Record," *Beatlefan*, vol. 1, no. 3, 1979, page 10; *I Me Mine*, by George Harrison. Genesis Publications/Simon & Schuster, 1980, pp. 352–353.

5. Sources: "George Harrison, Brazil, 1979," *Meet the Beatles*, 1998, http://members.tripod.com/~holysm0ke; "Beatlenews Roundup," by William P. King. *Beatlefan*, vol. 1, no. 3, 1979, page 2.

6. Sources: "Beatlenews Roundup," by William P. King. *Beatlefan*, vol. 16, no. 2, 1995, page 12 [and] vol. 16, no. 3, 1995, page 8; *Songs, Pictures and Stories of the Beatles Website*, by Mitch McGeary, http://www.rarebeatles.com.

7. Sources: *Lennon*, by Ray Coleman. McGraw-Hill Book Company, 1984, page 530; *The Last Days of John Lennon*, by Frederic Seaman. Birch Lane Press, 1991, pp. 51–52; *The Beatles After the Break-Up 1970–2000*, by Keith Badman, Omnibus Press, 1999, page 231.

8. Sources: "Beatlenews Roundup," by William P. King. *Beatlefan*, vol. 1, no. 4, 1979, page 2; *DK Encyclopedia of Rock Stars*, by Dafydd Rees and Luke Crampton, DK Publishing, 1996, page 190.

9. Source: "Plenty Of Yolks!" interviews compiled by Tony Luscombe. *The Write Thing*, August/September 1979, page 29.

10. Sources: "Beatlenews Roundup," by William P. King. *Beatlefan*, vol. 1, no. 4, 1979, page 4; "Laurence's Guitar Corner," by Laurence Juber. *Club Sandwich*, no. 14, April/May 1979, page 6.

11. Sources: "Back to the Egg," *Beatlefan*, vol. 1, no. 4, 1979, page 5; *The Beatles: The Ultimate Recording Guide*, by Allen J. Wiener. Facts On File, 1992, page 119.

12. Source: "Plenty of Yolks!" interviews compiled by Tony Luscombe. *The Write Thing*, August/September 1979, page 29.

Sources

13. Source: "Back to the Egg" (review), by William P. King. *Beatlefan*, vol. 1, no. 4, 1979, page 57.

14. Source: "Laurence Juber: The Last Days of Wings," by Bill De Young. *Beatlefan*, vol. 19, no. 4, 1998, page 21.

15. Source: *The First 28⊗ Years of Monty Python*, by Kim "Howard" Johnson. St. Martin's Griffin, 1999, pp. 228–229, 232–233.

16. Source: *Lennon*, by John Robertson. Omnibus Press, 1995, page 106.

17. Source: *Lennon*, by John Robertson. Omnibus Press, 1995, page 106.

18. Source: *Wills of the Rich & Famous*, by Herbert E. Nass, Esq. Warner Books, 1991, pp. 78–82.

19. Source: *The Beatles After the Break-Up 1970–2000*, by Keith Badman. Omnibus Press, 1999, page 238.

20. Sources: *Lennon*, by John Robertson. Omnibus Press, 1995, page 107; "John Lennon, Where Are You?" by Laurence Shames. *Esquire*, November 1980, page 32; *The Last Days of John Lennon*, by Frederic Seaman. Birch Lane Press, 1991, page 78.

21. Sources: "Birth of The Beatles" (reviews), by William P. King and Al Sussman, *Beatlefan*, vol. 2, no. 1, 1979, pp. 14–15; *I Me Mine*, by George Harrison, Genesis Publications/Simon & Schuster, 1980, page 84; *The Complete Beatles Chronicle*, by Mark Lewisohn. Harmony Books, 1992, page 119; *The Ultimate Beatles Encyclopedia*, by Bill Harry. Hyperion, 1992, page 107.

22. Sources: "Birth of the Beatles," by Al Sussman. *Beatlefan*, vol. 2, no. 1, 1979, page 15; *How They Became the Beatles*, by Gareth L. Pawlowski. E. P. Dutton, 1989, page 22; *The Beatles: The Authorized Biography*, by Hunter Davies. William Heinemann Ltd., 1968, page 157.

23. Source: *The Complete Beatles Chronicle*, by Mark Lewisohn. Harmony Books, 1992, pp. 52, 63.

24. Source: *Beatles Undercover*, by Kristofer K. Engelhardt. Collector's Guide Publishing Inc., 1998, page 241.

25. Source: "Confessions of a Beatle Bootlegger," by Amos 'n' Isaac. *Beatlefan*, vol. 13, no. 6, 1992, pp. 29–31.

1980

1. Sources: "Wanted!" *Beatlefan*, vol. 2, no. 2, 1980, pp. 1, 4–5; *Blackbird: The Life and Times of Paul McCartney*, by Geoffrey Giuliano. Da Capo Press, Inc, 1997, page 236; *DK Encyclopedia of Rock Stars*, by Dafydd Rees and Luke Crampton. DK Publishing, Inc., 1996, page 560.

2. Sources: "Paul's Pot Bust Shocker makes him a Jailhouse Rocker," by Harry Wasserman. *High Times*, July 1980; "Beatlenews Roundup," by William P. King. *Beatlefan*, vol. 2, no. 1, 1980, page 22.

3. Sources: *The End of the Beatles?*, by Harry Castleman and Walter J. Podrazik. Pierian Press/Popular Culture Ink, 1985, pp. 305, 307; "Beatlenews Roundup," by William P. King. *Beatlefan*, vol. 2, no. 1, 1980, page 22.

4. Sources: "Barbara Bach keeps Him Going, says Ringo Starr, Still Banging the Drum Slowly for John," by Salley Rayl. *People*, 23 February 1981, page 34; "A Starr for Ringo," by Richard Sanders. *Us*, 28 April 1981, page 41.

5. Sources: "The True Story of 'Collector's Items' and 'Casualties,'" by Mark Wallgren. *The Write Thing*, no. 42, February/March 1984, pp. 17–18; "The Beatles Rarities," by Wally Podrazik. *Beatlefan*, vol. 2, no. 3, 1980, pp. 1, 4; *Bootleg: The Secret History of the Other Recording Industry*, by Clinton Heylin. St. Martin's Press, 1995, pp. 183–186.

6. Sources: "Every Little Thing: The Story Behind *Rarities*, the 'new' Beatles LP," by Nicholas Schaffner. *Trouser Press*, June 1980, page 16; *The Beatles London*, by Piet Schreuders, Mark Lewisohn and Adam Smith. St. Martin's Press, 1994, page 1.

7. Source: "The McCartney Interview," by Paul Gambaccini. *Club Sandwich*, no. 19, 1980, page 3.

8. Source: *The End of the Beatles?* by Harry Castleman and Walter J. Podrazik. Pierian Press/Popular Culture Ink, 1985, page 96.

9. Sources: "McCartney II," by Mark Lewisohn. *The Beatles Book Appreciation Society Magazine*, Beat Publications Ltd., July 1980, page iii; "Beatles '80: A Diary of Recent News and Events," by Mark Lewisohn.

Sources

The Beatles Book Appreciation Society Magazine, Beat Publications Ltd., November 1980, page xi.

10. Source: *The Last Days of John Lennon*, by Frederic Seaman. Birch Lane Press, 1991, pp. 133, 147.

11. Sources: *Rupert The Bear Demo Soundtrack* (CD bootleg), Library Product, 1990, tracks 2, 6, 9; "Beatles '80: A Diary of Recent News and Events," by Mark Lewisohn. *The Beatles Book Appreciation Society Magazine*, Beat Publications Ltd., July 1980, page x; "Previewing Standing Stone" (Beatlenews Roundup), by William P. King. *Beatlefan*, vol. 18, no. 6, 1997, page 5; *The Beatles After the Break-Up 1970–2000*, by Keith Badman. Omnibus Press, 1999, page 266.

12. Sources: *The Playboy Interviews with John Lennon & Yoko Ono*, by David Sheff. Playboy Press, 1981, page 187; *Lennon*, by John Robertson. Omnibus Press, 1995, pp. 107–108.

13. Sources: *The Last Days of John Lennon*, by Frederic Seaman. Birch Lane Press, 1991, page 158; *The Beatles After the Break-Up 1970–2000*, by Keith Badman. Omnibus Press, 1999, page 252.

14. Sources: *Lennon*, by John Robertson. Omnibus Press, 1995, page 108; *The Last Days of John Lennon*, by Frederic Seaman. Birch Lane Press, 1991, page 167.

15. Sources: *I Me Mine*, by George Harrison. Genesis Publications/Simon & Schuster, 1980, page 11; "I Me Mine" (Beatle Bookshelf), by Nicholas Schaffner. *Beatlefan*, vol. 2, no. 6, 1980, page 19.

16. Source: "Beatlenews Roundup," by William P. King. *Beatlefan*, vol. 6, no. 3, 1984, page 4.

17. Source: *The Beatles After the Break-Up 1970–2000*, by Keith Badman. Omnibus Press, 1999, page 256.

18. Sources: *Lennon*, by John Robertson. Omnibus Press, 1995, page 109; *The Last Days of John Lennon*, by Frederic Seaman. Birch Lane Press, 1991, page 200; "Lennon's Last Sessions: Producer Jack Douglas on Recording 'Double Fantasy,'" by Ken Sharp. *Beatlefan*, vol. 20, no. 2, 1999, page 14.

19. Sources: *Fifty Years Adrift*, by Derek Taylor. Genesis Publications Limited, 1984, pp. 518–519; *The Beatles: The Ultimate Recording Guide*, by Allen J. Wiener. Facts on File, 1992, page 65.

20. Sources: *Abbey Road*, by Brian Southall, Peter Vince and Allan Rouse. Omnibus Press, 1997, page 139; "Beatles '80: A Diary of Recent News and Events," by Mark Lewisohn. *The Beatles Book Appreciation Society Magazine*, Beat Publications Ltd., December 1980, page viii; "Beatles For Sale: Abbey Rd Auctions," by Richard Buskin. *Come Together*, vol. 2, no. 9, 1981, pp. 10–11.

21. Source: *The Last Days of John Lennon*, by Frederic Seaman. Birch Lane Press, 1991, page 200.

22. Sources: *The Playboy Interviews with John Lennon & Yoko Ono*, by David Sheff. Playboy Press, 1981, page 35; *The Beatles: The Ultimate Recording Guide*, by Allen J. Wiener. Facts On File, 1992, page 245.

23. Sources: *Paul McCartney: Many Years from Now*, by Barry Miles. Henry Holt & Company, 1997, pp. 593–594; "Barbara Bach Keeps Him Going, Says Ringo Starr, Still Banging the Drum Slowly for John," by Salley Rayl. *People*, 23 February 1981, page 32; "A Starr for Ringo," by Richard Sanders. *Us*, 28 April 1981, page 43; *BeatleBlitz '93 Presents an Interview with Louise Harrison* (CD), by Richard Farrar and Steve Whitt. Hello Goodbye Productions, 1993, track 1.

24. Sources: *The Beatles: The Ultimate Recording Guide*, by Allen J. Wiener. Facts on File, 1992, page 68; *Paul McCartney: Many Years From Now*, by Barry Miles. Henry Holt and Company, 1997, pp. 593–594.

25. Source: *Richard Lester and the Beatles*, by Andrew Yule. Donald I. Fine, 1994, page 107.)

1981

1. Sources: "A Starr for Ringo," by Richard Sanders. *Us*, 28 April 1981, page 44; "Beatlenews Roundup," by William P. King. *Beatlefan*, vol. 3, no. 2, 1981, page 2.

2. Sources: "Finishing Note," by Yoko Ono (picture sleeve for "Walking On Thin Ice"), 24 January 1981; *The End of the Beatles?* by Harry Castleman and Walter J. Podrazik. Pierian Press/Popular Culture Ink, 1985, page 132.

Sources

3. Sources: *Elvis Costello: A Biography*, by Tony Clayton-Lea. Fromm International, 1998, page 124; "Geoff Emerick: Beatles Master," by Mr. Bonzai. *Mix*, October 1992, pp. 147–148.

4. Source: *DK Encyclopedia of Rock Stars*, by Dafydd Rees and Luke Crampton. DK Publishing, Inc., 1996, pp. 749–750.

5. Sources: "Can Paul McCartney Get Back?" by James Henke. *Rolling Stone*, 15 June 1989, page 44; (interview), by Steve Grant, *Time Out*, 11–17 October 1984, excerpted in *With a Little Help from My Friends*, no. 48, October 1984, page 4; *The Beatles After the Break-Up 1970–2000*, by Keith Badman. Omnibus Press, 1999, page 282.

6. Source: "Beatles '81: A Diary of Recent News and Events," by Mark Lewisohn. *The Beatles Book Appreciation Society Magazine*, Beat Publications Ltd., June 1981, page viii.

7. Source: *Caveman* (movie ads), *The Oregonian*, 16 April [and] 24 April 1981.

8. Sources: "Beatlefan Extra" (insert containing UPI wire report of the wedding), *Beatlefan*, vol. 3, no. 3, 1981; "Ringo's Wedding," *The Beatles Book Appreciation Society Magazine*, Beat Publications Ltd., June 1981, page xi; "Barbara Bach keeps him Going, says Ringo Starr, still Banging the Drum Slowly for John," by Salley Rayl. *People*, 23 February 1981, page 32.

9. Source: "Ringo's Wedding," *The Beatles Book Appreciation Society Magazine*, Beat Publications Ltd., June 1981, page xi.

11. Sources: *I Me Mine*, by George Harrison. Genesis Publications/ Simon & Schuster, 1980, page 28; *The Beatles After the Break-Up 1970–2000*, by Keith Badman. Omnibus Press, 1999, page 254.

15. Source: "Ono's album faces John's death, reality," by John Palmer. *The Fresno Bee*, 18 August 1981, page A7; *The End of the Beatles?*, by Harry Castleman and Walter J. Podrazik. Pierian Press/Popular Culture Ink, 1983, pp. 289–290.

16. Source: "Beatles '81: A Diary of Recent News and Events," by Mark Lewisohn. *The Beatles Book Appreciation Society Magazine*, Beat Publications Ltd., November 1981, page x.

17. Source: "Beatles '81: A Diary of Recent News and Events," by Mark Lewisohn. *The Beatles Book Appreciation Society Magazine*, Beat Publications Ltd., September 1981, page ix.

18. Source: *Databank Transcription Team*, http://www.dttlyrics.com

19. Source: "Beatles '81: A Diary of Recent News and Events," by Mark Lewisohn. *The Beatles Book Appreciation Society Magazine*, Beat Publications Ltd., September 1981, page ix.

23. Source: "Starrstruck," by Mark Wallgren. *Beatlefan*, vol. 11, no. 1, 1988, page 16.

24. Sources: *The Beatles: The Ultimate Recording Guide*, by Allen J. Wiener. Facts on File, 1992, page 246; *The End of the Beatles?*, by Harry Castleman and Walter J. Podrazik. Pierian Press/Popular Culture Ink, 1985, page 160.

25. Sources: "Things We Said Today," *Strawberry Fields Forever*, no. 37, 1980, page 27; "Liverpool Has Decided to Put the Beatles on the Map," by the Associated Press. *San Francisco Chronicle*, 27 November 1981; "Beatlenews Roundup," by Eddie Porter and William P. King. *Beatlefan*, vol. 4, no. 5, 1982, page 16; "City honors Beatles" (from the Associated Press), *The Oregonian*, 17 August 1982.

1982

1. Sources: "Anglophile" (Beatlenews Roundup), by William P. King. *Beatlefan*, vol. 4, no. 3, 1982, page 14; "Beatles '82: A Diary of Recent News and Events," by Mark Lewisohn. *The Beatles Book Appreciation Society Magazine*, February 1982, page vii; *DK Encyclopedia of Rock Stars*, by Dafydd Rees and Luke Crampton. DK Publishing, Inc., 1996, page 559.

2. Source: "Paul McCartney Castaway," *Club Sandwich*, no. 26, 1982, page 5.

3. Sources: Interview in the *Daily Mirror*, 16 May 1983, reprinted in *With A Little Help from my Friends*, no. 43, July 1983, page 15; "Paul McCartney's Latest is Exquisite but Flawed," by Robert Palmer. The *New York Times*, April 25, 1982, page 19.

4. Sources: *The Official Price Guide to the Beatles Records and Memorabilia*, by Perry Cox and Joe Lindsay. House of Collectibles, 1995, pp. 261,

282, 284; "A Look at a Forgotten Format: "8-Track Tape," by Martin C. Babicz. *Beatlefan*, vol. 19, no. 6, 1998, pp. 16–17.

5. Source: *The End of the Beatles?*, by Harry Castleman and Walter J. Podrazik. Pierian Press/Popular Culture Ink, 1985, page 252.

6. Source: "Tug of War," by Andy Mackay. *Club Sandwich*, no. 26, 1982, page 3.

7. Sources: "McCartney Answers Fans," *Beatlefan*, vol. 16, no. 2, 1995, page 7; "Life on the Wave . . . ,," photographs by Henry Diltz and Linda McCartney. *Club Sandwich*, no. 3, June/July 1977, page 5.

9. Sources: *The End of the Beatles?*, by Harry Castleman and Walter J. Podrazik. Pierian Press/Popular Culture Ink, 1985, page 174; "The Gospel According to Paul," by Jeff Silverman. *Los Angeles Herald Examiner*, 5 January 1983, page A2.

10. Sources: "Beatles '82: A Diary of Recent News and Events," by Mark Lewisohn. *The Beatles Book Appreciation Society Magazine*, Beat Publications Ltd. February 1982, page vii (and) June 1982, page viii; "Beatlesnews Roundup," by William P. King. *Beatlefan*, vol. 4, no. 4, 1982, pp. 21–22 (and) vol. 2, no. 4, 1980, page 30; "Linda Wins!" *Club Sandwich*, No. 20, 1980, page 1.

11. Source: "One Hand Clapping" (Beatles Video), by John Sosebee. *Beatlefan*, vol. 8, no. 3, 1986, page 18.

12. Sources: "Take It Away," by Mark Lewisohn. *The Beatles Book Appreciation Society Magazine*, August 1982, pp. iii–v; "Beatlenews Roundup," by William P. King. *Beatlefan*, vol. 4, no. 5, 1982, page 2.

13. Source: "Take It Away," by Mark Lewisohn. *The Beatles Book Appreciation Society Magazine*, August 1982, page viii.

14. Source: *The Transmigration of Timothy Archer*, by Philip K. Dick. Timescape/Simon & Schuster, 1982.

15. Source: "Beatlenews Roundup," by William P. King. *Beatlefan*, vol. 5, no. 3, 1983, page 21.

16.   Source: "Beatlenews Roundup," by William P. King. *Beatlefan*, vol. 5, no. 3, 1983, page 18.

17.   Sources: "Shining Starr," *Billboard*, 30 October 1982; "Ringo Down Under," by John McMahon. *The Write Thing*, no. 39, March/April 1983, pp. 7–8.

18.   Sources: " 'Lennon' comes to New York," *Rolling Stone*, 16 September 1982, page 35; "Boy From Liverpool," by Frank Rich. *The New York Times*, 6 October 1982, page C23.

19.   Source: "I Read The News Today . . . ," by Barb Fenick. *The Write Thing*, no. 40, March/April 1983, page 25.

20.   Source: *The End of the Beatles?*, by Harry Castleman and Walter J. Podrazik. Pierian Press/Popular Culture Ink, 1985, page 210.

22.   Source: *Joanie Loves Chachi*, http://www.sitcomsonline.com/joaniechachi.html.

23.   Source: *The End of the Beatles?*, by Harry Castleman and Walter J. Podrazik. Pierian Press/Popular Culture Ink, 1985, pp. 216–217.

24.   Sources: "Israel gets First Single in Five Years," *Billboard*, 18 December 1982; "Israel gets its second McCartney single," *USA Today*, 21 December 1982.

25.   Source: "The Family Way: The Cynthia Lennon Interview," by William P. King. *Beatlefan*, vol. 4, no. 2, 1982, pp. 5, 14.

1983

1.   Sources: "The Day They Shot John Lennon" (Resident Legit Reviews), by Hari. *Variety*, 9 March 1983, page 138; "The Day they Shot John Lennon" (review), by Al Sussman. *Beatlefan*, vol. 5, no. 2, 1983, page 21.

2.   Source: "Beatlenews Roundup," by William P. King. *Beatlefan*, vol. 5, no. 2, 1983, page 2.

3.   Source: "Richie & His Pals" (review), by Mark Wallgren. *The Write Thing*, no. 40, June/July 1983, pp. 7–8.

4.   Source: *The Anubis Gates*, by Tim Powers. Ace Books, 1983, page 138.

Sources

5. Source: *The End of the Beatles?*, by Harry Castleman and Walter J. Podrazik. Pierian Press/Popular Culture Ink, 1985, pp. 246–247.

6. Source: *The End of the Beatles?*, by Harry Castleman and Walter J. Podrazik. Pierian Press/Popular Culture Ink, 1985, page 246; *The Beatles After the Break-Up 1970–2000*, by Keith Badman. Omnibus Press, 1999, page 301.

7. Source: *The End of the Beatles?*, by Harry Castleman and Walter J. Podrazik. Pierian Press/Popular Culture Ink, 1985, pp. 246–247.

8. Source: *The End of the Beatles?* by Harry Castleman and Walter J. Podrazik. Pierian Press/Popular Culture, Ink, 1985, page 247.

9. Sources: "Random Notes," *Rolling Stone*, 23 June 1983; "Ono Completing LP Sessions," by Jeffrey Peisch. *Record*, November 1983, page 8.

10. Sources: *Abbey Road*, by Brian Southall, Peter Vince and Allan Rouse. Omnibus Press, 1982, 1997, pp. 169–170; *The End of the Beatles?*, by Harry Castleman and Walter J. Podrazik. Pierian Press/Popular Culture Ink, 1985, pp. 403–404.

11. Sources: *DK Encyclopedia of Rock Stars*, by Dafydd Rees and Luke Crampton. DK Publishing, Inc., 1996, page 560; "Fabscreen" (Beatlenews Roundup), by William P. King. *Beatlefan*, vol. 5, no. 6, 1983, page 5.

12. Sources: "The Peace Museum," by Mike Hockinson. *The Write Thing*, no. 43, June/July 1984, page 12; *Lennon*, by John Robertson. Omnibus Press, 1995, page 67; *John Lennon: One Day at A Time*, by Anthony Fawcett. Grove Press, Inc., 1976, page 25.

13. Source: *The Art of the Beatles*, by Mike Evans. Anthony Blond/Merseyside City Council, 1984, page 115.

14. Source: *Melody Maker*, 25 June 1983, reprinted in *With a Little Help from my Friends*, no. 43, July 1983, page 14.

15. Source: "Beatlenews Roundup," by William P. King. *Beatlefan*, vol. 5, no. 2, 1983, page 27.

18. Source: "Pipes of Peace Special Feature," by Patrick Humphries. *Club Sandwich*, no. 31, 1983, page 17.

19. Sources: "Say Say Say," by John Hammond. *Club Sandwich*, no. 31, 1983, page 5; *The Beatles: The Ultimate Recording Guide*, by Allen J. Wiener. Facts on File, 1992, page 72.

20. Sources: "Beatlenews Roundup," by William P. King. *Beatlefan*, vol. 6, no. 5, 1984, page 4; *The Beatles: The Ultimate Recording Guide*, by Allen J. Wiener. Facts on File, 1992, pp. 70–71; "How It was Done," *Club Sandwich*, no. 35, 1984, page 25.

21. Sources: "Anglophile" (Beatlenews Roundup), by William P. King. *Beatlefan*, vol. 5, no. 4, 1983, page 16; *The Beatles: The Ultimate Recording Guide*, by Allen J. Wiener. Facts on File, 1992, page 70; *The Beatles After the Break-Up 1970–2000*, by Keith Badman. Omnibus Press, 1999, page 309.

22. Sources: "Ringo is outrageous in 'Daisy'," by Jack Curry. *USA Today*, 3 November 1983; *The Beatles: The Ultimate Recording Guide*, by Allen J. Wiener. Facts on File, 1992, page 70; *Princess Daisy*, by Judith Krantz. Crown Publishing, 1980.

23. Source: *Beatles Undercover*, by Kristofer K. Engelhardt. Collector's Guide Publishing Inc., 1998, page 510.

24. Sources: "Cash for Questions" (Ringo Starr), by Andrew Collins. *Q*, September 1998, page 17; *The Beatles: The Ultimate Recording Guide*, by Allen J. Wiener. Facts on File, 1992, page 72; Beatlenews Roundup, by William P. King. *Beatlefan*, vol. 10, no. 5, 1988, page 5.

25. Source: "Beatlenews Roundup," by William P. King. *Beatlefan*, vol. 11, no. 2, 1989, page 5.

1984

1. Source: "Anglofile" (Beatlenews Roundup), by William P. King. *Beatlefan*, vol. 6. no. 2, 1984, page 5.

2. Source: *The Last Days of John Lennon*, by Frederic Seaman. Birch Lane Press, 1991, pp. 190–191.

3. Sources: "McCartneys fined $200," *San Jose Mercury News*, 17 January 1984, page 3A; "McCartneys' 2nd Pot Bust In Two Days," by the United Press. *San Francisco Chronicle*, 18 January 1984; "Ex-Beatles Wife Fined" (*People*), *The Oregonian*, 25 January 1984, page E2.

Sources

4.   Sources: *The Beatles: The Ultimate Recording Guide,* by Allen J. Wiener. Facts on File, 1992, page 249; "Anglophile" (Beatlenews Roundup), by William P. King. *Beatlefan,* vol. 6, no. 2, 1984, page 5.

5.   Sources: "Beatlenews Roundup," by William P. King. *Beatlefan,* vol. 6, no. 3, 1984, page 5; *DK Encyclopedia of Rock Stars,* by Dafydd Rees and Luke Crampton. DK Publishing, Inc., 1996, page 464.

6.   Source: *The Pink Floyd Encyclopedia,* by Vernon Fitch. Collector's Guide Publishing Inc., 1998, pp. 9–10, 208.

7.   Source: *The Pink Floyd Encyclopedia,* by Vernon Fitch. Collector's Guide Publishing Inc., 1998, pp. 244, 352.

8.   Source: "Anglofile" (Beatlenews Roundup), by William P. King. *Beatlefan,* vol. 6, no. 4, 1984, page 4.

9.   Sources: "Sotheby's New York Auction," by Al Sussman. *Beatlefan,* vol. 6, no. 5, 1984, page 11; "Beatlenews Roundup," by William P. King. *Beatlefan,* vol. 6, no. 4, 1984, page 4; "Collector's Carrousel" (auction pamphlet), Sotheby's New York, June 1984.

11.   Sources: "The Original Unpublished Manuscript for a Book by John Lennon" (Lot 356), *Rock & Roll Memorabilia 1955–1984* (auction catalogue). Sotheby's, 30–31 August 1984, pp. 48–49; (item), *The Oregonian,* 1 September 1984.

13.   Sources: "Are Paul's Beatles Songs Sacred?" (Talent), by Paul Grein. *Billboard,* 1 December 1984; *The Complete Beatles Chronicle,* by Mark Lewisohn. Harmony Books, 1992, page 349.

14.   Sources: "Paul McCartney: The *Beatlefan* interview" (part one), by Bill King. *Beatlefan,* vol. 7, no. 1, 1984, page 12; "Beatlenews Roundup," by William P. King. *Beatlefan,* vol. 1, no. 2, 1979, page 18; vol. 1, no. 3, 1979, page 2; vol. 1, no. 5, 1979, page 92; "Once There Was A Way To Get Back Homeward . . . , by Deborah Frost. *Record Magazine,* September 1984; 'Band On The Run: The True Story,' by Eddie Porter. *Good Day Sunshine,* no. 53, 1990, pp. 28–29; "Ex-Beatle Paul McCartney casts doubts aside to make film," by Steve Morse. *The Oregonian,* 28 October 1984, page 16.

15. Source: "Beatlenews Roundup," by William P. King. *Beatlefan*, vol. 6, no. 6, 1984, page 4.

16. Source: "McCartney: The *Beatlefan* Interview" (part one), by Bill King. *Beatlefan*, vol. 7, no. 1, 1984, page 11.

17. Sources: "Briefly . . ." (Beatlenews Roundup), by William P. King. *Beatlefan*, vol. 20, no. 2, 1999, page 8; "Giant Haystacks" (obituary). *The British Wrestling Website*, http://freepayes.pavilion.net; "Give My Regards to Broad Street Biographies," *Club Sandwich*, no. 35, 1984, pp. 42–43.

18. Source: "McCartney: The *Beatlefan* Interview" (part two), by Bill King. *Beatlefan*, vol. 7, no. 2, 1985, page 10.

19. Source: "Woke up, Got Out of Bed . . ." (*Q* Diary), by Paul McCartney. *Q*, October 1993, page 67.

21. Sources: *Conferment of the Honorary Freeman of the City of Liverpool upon Paul McCartney M.B.E. 28th November 1984* (program), Elliott Brothers & Yeoman Ltd., 1984, page 7; "Liverpool Premiere + Freedom of The City," *Club Sandwich*, no. 35, 1984, page 14; "Chuffed!" *Liverpool Echo*, 29 November 1984, page 4 (pull-out supplement); *The Beatles: The Authorized Biography*, by Hunter Davies. William Heineman Ltd., 1968, page 27; "Paul Simon Song Book" (review), by Paul McCartney. *Punch*, 8 August 1973. Reprinted in *With a Little Help from My Friends*, no. 42, April 1983, page 11.

22. Sources: "Beatlenews Roundup," by William P. King. *Beatlefan*, vol. 7, no. 1, 1984, page 4; *The Beatles: The Ultimate Recording Guide*, by Allen J. Wiener. Facts on File, 1992, page 75; "George sends his regards," article reprinted in *With a Little Help From My Friends*, no. 48, October 1984, page 25 (and) "Last Minute Dept., Part 2" (news item), page 26.

23. Sources: "Beatlenews Roundup," by Bill King and Mark Gunter. *Beatlefan*, vol. 7, no. 1, 1984, page 4; "Fabscreen" (Beatlenews Roundup), by William P. King. *Beatlefan*, vol. 7, no. 2, 1985, page 6.

24. Sources: "Michael Jackson says 'The Girl is Mine' is his," by Maurice Possley. *The Oregonian*, 7 December 1984, page E15; "Jury Finds hit song not lifted," *The Oregonian*, 15 December 1984, page A22.

Sources

25. Sources: *DK Encyclopedia of Rock Stars*, by Dayfydd Rees and Luke Crampton. DK Publishing, Inc., 1996, pp. 64–65; "Charting" (Beatlenews Roundup), by William P. King. *Beatlefan*, vol. 7, no. 2, 1985, page 5.

1985

1. Sources: "Beatlenews Roundup," by William P. King. *Beatlefan*, vol. 7, no. 2, 1985, page 6; *Beatles Undercover*, by Kristofer K. Engelhardt. Collector's Guide Publishing Inc., 1998, pp. 99–100, 194–195.

2. Source: "Ex-Beatle's Son Weds in Secret" (People), *The Oregonian*, 26 January 1985.

3. Source: "The Beatles Album that Almost Was," by Allan Kozinn. *Beatlefan*, vol. 7, no. 3, 1985, page 14.

4. Sources: " 'Sessions' LP: Here Come the Beatles—Maybe," by Rip Rense. *Los Angeles Times*, 14 April 1985, page 54; "The Road to Sessions" by Dinsdale P, http://dinsdalep@aol.com.

5. Sources: *Bob Dylan: A Life in Stolen Moments*, by Clinton Heylin. Music Sales Ltd., 1996, page 114; *The Beatles: The Ultimate Recording Guide*, by Allen J. Wiener. Facts on File, 1992, page 121.

6. Source: *Beatles Undercover*, by Kristofer K. Engelhardt. Collector's Guide Publishing Inc., 1998, page 235.

7. Source: *Beatles Undercover*, by Kristofer K. Engelhardt. Collector's Guide Publishing, 1998, pp. 480–482.

8. Sources: "Fabscreen" (Beatles Video), by William P. King. *Beatlefan*, vol. 7, no. 3, 1985, page 18; *The Beatles: The Ultimate Recording Guide*, by Allen J. Wiener. Facts on File, 1992, page 76; *The Beatles After the Break-Up 1970–2000*, by Keith Badman. Omnibus Press, 1999, page 354.

9. Sources: *Lennon*, by John Robertson. Omnibus Press, 1995, page 124; "Anglophile" (Beatlenews Roundup), by Bill King and Mark Gunter. *Beatlefan*, vol. 7, no. 4, 1985, page 6.

10. Source: *Beatles Undercover*, by Kristofer K. Engelhardt. Collector's Guide Publishing Inc., 1998, page 106.

Sources

11. Sources: "Beatlenews Roundup," by Bill King and Mark Gunter. *Beatlefan*, vol. 7, no. 5, 1985, page 5 (and) vol. 7, no. 6, 1985, page 4.

12. Sources: "Beatlenews Roundup," by Bill King and Mark Gunter. *Beatlefan*, vol. 7, no. 5, 1985, page 5; "Reunion Not Julian's Idea Atlantic VP States" (Grapevine: New York), by Jeff Tamarkin. *Goldmine*, 13 September 1985, page 6.

13. Source: "Beatlenews Roundup," by Bill King and Mark Gunter. *Beatlefan*, vol. 7, no. 5, 1985, page 5.

15. Source: "The Long and Winding Road," by Robert Hilburn. *The Los Angeles Times*, 22 September 1985, (*Calendar* supplement), pp. 60, 69.

16. Source: "Spies Like Us: The Official File," by Patrick Humphries. *Club Sandwich*, no. 39, 1985, page 5.

17. Sources: "Spies Like Us: The Official File," by Patrick Humphries. *Club Sandwich*, no. 39, 1985, page 6; "What's News," *With a Little Help From my Friends*, no. 53, January 1986, page 16.

18. Sources: *The Beatles: The Ultimate Recording Guide*, by Allen J. Wiener. Facts on File, 1992, page 78; *The Beatles After the Break-Up 1970–2000*, by Keith Badman. Omnibus Press, 1999, page 358; *You Can't Do That: Beatles Bootlegs & Novelty Records*, by Charles Reinhart. Contemporary Books, Inc., 1981, pp. xxiv–xxv.

19. Sources: "Meadow dedicated to Lennon," by Rick Hampson (from the Associated Press). *The Oregonian*, 10 October 1985; "Garden Dedicated to John Lennon" (People), *USA Today*, 10 October 1985, page 2D.

20. Source: "Thanks to Carl Perkins, Harrison's Back!" by William P. King. *Beatlefan*, vol. 8, no. 1, 1985, pp. 8–9.

21. Sources: "Fabscreen" (Beatlenews Roundup), by William P. King. *Beatlefan*, vol. 8, no. 3, 1986, page 7; "Beatlenews Roundup," by William P. King. *Beatlefan*, vol. 8, no. 6, 1986, page 6.

22. Sources: *The Beatles: Second Revised Edition*, by Hunter Davies. W. W. Norton, 1996, pp. 368, 370; "McCartney: Try to see things my way," by David Zimmerman and Jeffrey Peisch. *USA Today*, 6 November

1985, pp. 1–2D; "No one ever goes on about the times John hurt me," by Hunter Davies. *Woman*, 9 November 1985, page 29.

23. Source: *Beatles Undercover*, by Kristofer K. Engelhardt. Collector's Guide Publishing Inc., 1998, pp. 24–25.

24. Sources: "Lewis Carroll Goes Hollywood," by Monica Collins. *USA Today*, 9 December 1985, page 1D; "Faces & Places," *Us*, 15 July 1985, page 11.

25. Sources: "Beatlenews Roundup," by William P. King. *Beatlefan*, vol. 8, no. 1, 1985, page 4; "People," *The Oregonian*, 17 December 1985; "What's News," *With a Little Help from my Friends*, no. 53, January 1986, page 19.)

1986

1. Sources: *Lennon*, by John Robertson, Omnibus Press, 1995, page 125; "Rock & Roll Hall of Fame: A Retrospective," by Sheila Rogers. *Rolling Stone* (Insert), 8 February 1990, page 5.

2. Source: *Go, Cat, Go! The Life of Carl Perkins The King of Rockabilly*, by Carl Perkins and David McGee. Hyperion, 1996, pp. 359–360.

3. Source: "Yoko Ono: Report from the Road," by Peter Schuster. *Beatlefan*, vol. 8, no. 2, 1986, page 17.

4. Source: "Madonna, George Meet the Press" (People), *USA Today*, 7 March 1986, page 2D.

5. Source: *Mad Angels: The Plays of Larry Kirwan*, by Larry Kirwan. Forty Seven Books, 1993, pp. 9–79.

6. Sources: "Beatlenews Roundup," by William P. King. *Beatlefan*, vol. 8, no. 3, 1986, page 4; *John Lennon/bag one* (exhibition catalog). Lee Nordness Galleries, 1970, page 7; *The Beatles After the Break-Up 1970–2000*, by Keith Badman. Omnibus Press, 1999, page 370.

7. Source: "Beatlenews Roundup," by William P. King. *Beatlefan*, vol. 8, no. 4, 1986, page 4.

8. Source: "Beatlenews Roundup," by William P. King. *Beatlefan*, vol. 8, no. 4, 1986, page 5.

Sources

9. Sources: "Beatlenews Roundup," by William P. King. *Beatlefan*, vol. 8, no. 5, 1986, page 4; "Only the Beatles . . ." (review), by Mark Wallgren. *Beatlefan*, vol. 8, no. 6, 1986, page 22; *The Beatles: The Ultimate Recording Guide*, by Allen J. Wiener. Facts on File, 1992, page 186.

10. Source: "Beatlenews Roundup," by William P. King. *Beatlefan*, vol. 8, no. 4, 1986, page 5.

11. Sources: "Making that "Press" video," *Club Sandwich*, no. 42, Autumn 1986, page 12; "Press" (Beatles Video), by William P. King. *Beatlefan*, vol. 8, no. 4, 1986, page 21; "Hot Off the Press!" *The Beatles Book Monthly*, Beat Publications Ltd., August 1986, page 33.

12. Source: "Beatlenews Roundup," by William P. King. *Beatlefan*, vol. 8, no. 6, 1986, page 5.

13. Source: "Beatleworld" (Beatlenews Roundup), by William P. King. *Beatlefan*, vol. 13, no. 2, 1992, page 16.

15. Source: "Press to Play: Track by Track," *Club Sandwich*, no. 42, Autumn 1986, page 5.

16. Sources: *Beatles Undercover*, by Kristofer K. Engelhardt. Collector's Guide Publishing Inc., 1998, page 503; *The Beatles: The Ultimate Recording Guide*, by Allen J. Wiener. Facts on File, 1992, page 250.

17. Sources: "Beatles '87: A Diary of Recent News and Events," by Mark Lewisohn. *The Beatles Book Monthly*, Beat Publications Ltd., March 1987, page 32; *The Ultimate Beatles Encyclopedia*, by Bill Harry. Hyperion, 1992, page 447; *MPL Communications*, http://www.mplcommunications.com; *Beatles Undercover*, by Kristofer K. Engelhardt. Collector's Guide Publishing, 1998, page 271; *DK Encyclopedia of Rock Stars*, by Dafydd Rees and Luke Crampton. DK Publishing, Inc. 1996, pp. 448–449.

18. Sources: "Beatles '87: A Diary of Recent News and Events, by Mark Lewisohn. *The Beatles Book Monthly*, Beat Publications Ltd., January 1987, page 37; "Ringo Meets The Press," by Bill King. *Beatlefan*, vol. 8, no. 6, 1986, page 7.

19. Sources: *Peter Gabriel: An Authorized Biography*, by Spencer Bright. Sidgwick and Jackson Ltd., 1988, pp. 234–235; *Not for Sale: The Beatles'*

Musical Legacy As Archived On Unauthorized Recordings, by Belmo (Scott Belmer). The Hot Wacks Press, 1997, page 400.

20. Sources: "Paul McCartney: The Videos," *Club Sandwich*, no. 43, Winter 1986/87, page 3; *Gabrielle Anwar: IMDb* (Internet Movie Database), http://us.imdb.com.

21. Sources: "McCartney Answers Fans" (Beatlenews Roundup), by William P. King. *Beatlefan*, vol. 16, no. 2, 1995, page 7; "Beatles '87: A Diary of Recent News and Events," by Mark Lewisohn. *The Beatles Book Monthly*, Beat Publications Ltd., January 1987, page 32; *Not For Sale: The Beatles' Musical Legacy as Archived on Unauthorized Recordings*, by Belmo (Scott Belmer). The Hot Wacks Press, 1997, pp. 326, 328; *The Beatles After the Break-Up 1970–2000*, by Keith Badman. Omnibus Press, 1999, page 379.

22. Source: "Paul In Royal Variety Show," by Mark Lewisohn. *The Beatles Book Monthly*, Beat Publications Ltd., January 1987, page 41.

24. Source: "The Dream Is Over" (Beatles Video), by Roger Ellis. *Beatlefan*, vol. 9, no. 1, 1986, page 20.

25. Sources: "Beatlenews Roundup," by William P. King. *Beatlefan*, vol. 8, no. 6, 1986, page 4; "Beatlenews Roundup," by William P. King. *Beatlefan*, vol. 9, no. 1, 1986, pp. 4–5.

1987

1. Sources: *Ringo Starr: Straight Man or Joker?* by Alan Clayson. Sidgwick & Jackson, 1991, pp. 245–267; "The Great Lost Albums Part 2," by Roy Carr, et al. *Vox*, November 1990, page 34; *The Beatles: The Ultimate Recording Guide*, by Allen J. Wiener. Facts on File, 1992, page 82; *The Beatles After the Break-Up 1970–2000*, by Keith Badman. Omnibus Press, 1999, pp. 385, 387.

2. Source: *Beatles Undercover*, by Kristofer K. Engelhardt. Collector's Guide Publishing Inc., 1998, page 165.

3. Sources: *Concrete Angels: IMDb* (Internet Movie Datebase), http//us.imdb.com; *The Complete Beatles Chronicle*, by Mark Lewisohn. Harmony Books, 1992, page 171.

Sources

4. Sources: *Beatles Undercover*, by Kristofer K. Engelhardt. Collector's Guide Publishing Inc., 1998, pp. 43–44; "Beatles '87: A Diary of Recent News and Events," by Mark Lewisohn. *The Beatles Book Monthly*, Beat Publications Ltd., May 1987, page 35.

5. Source: "Beatlenews Roundup," by William P. King. *Beatlefan*, vol, 9, no. 4, 1987, page 4.

6. Sources: *Beatles Undercover*, by Kristofer K. Engelhardt. Collector's Guide Publishing Inc., 1998, page 359; *The Beatles: Recording Sessions*, by Mark Lewisohn. Harmony Books, 1988, page 20.

7. Source: "Return to Pepperland: The 'Lost' McCartney Album from the Phil Ramone Sessions," by William P. King. *Beatlefan*, vol. 20, no. 4, 1999, page 18.

8. Sources: *Beatles Undercover*, by Kristofer K. Engelhardt. Collector's Guide Publishing Inc., 1998, pp. 145–148; *The Beatles After the Break-Up 1970–2000*, by Keith Badman. Omnibus Press, 1999, pp. 385–386.

9. Sources: "The First Beatles Cassette Single," *The Beatles Book Monthly*, Beat Publications Ltd., August 1987, pp. 20–21; "Beatles '87: A Diary of Recent News and Events," by Mark Lewisohn. *The Beatles Book Monthly*, Beat Publications Ltd., January 1985, page 34.

10. Source: "Beatles '87: A Diary of Recent News and Events," by Mark Lewisohn. *The Beatles Book Monthly*, Beat Publications Ltd., September 1987, page 37.

11. Source: "Can Paul McCartney Get Back?" by James Henke. *Rolling Stone*, 15 June 1989, page 44.

12. Source: Liner notes for "Once Upon A Long Ago" (extended version), by Roy Carr. Parlophone, 1987.

13. Source: *Elvis Costello: A Biography*, by Tony Clayton-Lea. Fromm International, 1998, page 126.

14. Source: "McCartney on McCartney: Talking About Flowers in the Dirt," *Beatlefan*, vol. 11, no. 4, 1989, page 17.

15. Source: *Disorderlies: IMDb (Internet Movie Database)*, http://us. imdb.com.

16. Source: "Beatles '87: A Diary of Recent News and Events," by Mark Lewisohn. *The Beatles Book Monthly*, Beat Publications Ltd., October 1987, page 33.

17. Source: "The First Beatles Bootleg CDs," by Mitch McGeary. *Songs, Pictures and Stories of the Beatles Website*, http://www.rarebeatles.com.

18. Sources: "George Harrison Talks About Old Guitars, New Songs and When We Were Fab," Dark Horse Records press release for *Cloud Nine*, September 1987, page 2; "George Harrison Gets Back," by Anthony DeCurtis. *Rolling Stone*, 22 October 1987, page 42.

19. Sources: "George Harrison Gets Back," by Anthony DeCurtis. *Rolling Stone*, 22 October 1987, page 42; *The Beatles: The Ultimate Recording Guide*, by Allen J. Wiener. Facts on File, 1992, pp. 81, 84, *The Beatles After the Break-Up 1970–2000*, by Keith Badman. Omnibus Press, 1999, page 374.

20. Source: *Dark Horse: The Private Life of George Harrison*, by Geoffrey Giuliano. Dutton, 1990, page 188.

22. Sources: "George Harrison Talks About Old Guitars, New Songs and When We Were Fab," Dark Horse Records press release for *Cloud Nine*, September 1987, page 2; "Just for Today" (bookmark), Al-Anon Family Group Headquarters, Inc., 1972.

23. Sources: "George Harrison Gets Back," by Anthony DeCurtis. *Rolling Stone*, 22 October 1987, pp. 42, 44; "George Harrison Gets 'Undercover,' " by Paul Cashmere. *Undercover* (CD-ROM magazine), Issue 2, 1996.

24. Sources: "A big hand for The Quiet One," by Mark Ellen. *Q*, January 1988, page 65; "George Harrison Gets Back," by Anthony DeCurtis. *Rolling Stone*, 22 October 1987, page 42.

1988

1. Source: *2061: odyssey three*, by Arthur C. Clarke. Del Ray, January 1988, pp. 220, 228.

Sources

2. Source: "Beatlenews Roundup," by William P. King. *Beatlefan*, vol. 10, no. 2, 1988, page 4.

3. Sources: "Beatlenews Roundup," by William P. King. *Beatlefan*, vol. 10, no. 2, 1988, page 4; *Lennon*, by John Robertson. Omnibus Press, 1995, page 124.

4. Sources: *The Commitments*, by Roddy Doyle. William Heinemann Ltd., 1988, pp. 24–25; *The Beatles: Recording Sessions*, by Mark Lewisohn. Harmony Books, 1988, pp. 93, 120; *Rock & Roll Memorabilia*, by Hilary Kay. Fireside Books, 1992, page 39.

5. Source: *The Official Weird Al Web site*, http://www.weirdal.com.

6. Source: *Red Hot Chili Peppers*, by Dave Thompson. St. Martin's Press, 1993, page 157.

10. Source: *Peter's Wonder Years Guide*, by Peter Reynders, http://our-world.compuserve.com.

11. Source: *Peter's Wonder Years Guide*, by Peter Reynders, http://our-world.compuserve.com.

12. Sources: "The Life of Lennon—On Film," by Mark Lewisohn. *The Beatles Book Monthly*, Beat Publications Ltd., April 1987, page 47; "The Lennon Phenomenon" (Beatlenews Roundup), by William P. King. *Beatlefan*, vol. 10, no. 6, 1988, page 5.

13. Sources: "Introducing the Wilbury Brothers," *Time*, 24 October 1988, page 104; "The Second Coming of Jeff Lynne," *Rolling Stone*, 4 October 1990, page 94.

14. Sources: "Wilburys, a.k.a. super rockers," *USA Today*, 17 October 1988; "Death of a Wilbury," *Beatlefan*, vol. 11, no. 1, 1988, page 5; *Dark Horse: The Private Life of George Harrison*, by Geoffrey Giuliano. Dutton, 1990, page 190.

15. Sources: *The Beatles Live*, by Mark Lewisohn. Henry Holt and Company, Inc., 1986, page 132; *The Beatles: Recording Sessions*, by Mark Lewisohn. Harmony Books, 1988, page 161; *Bob Dylan: A Life in Stolen Moments*, by Clinton Heylin. Book Sales Limited, 1996, pp. 55, 63; "The Second Coming of Jeff Lynne," *Rolling Stone*, 4 October 1990, page 95.

Sources

16. Sources: *Dark Star—The Roy Orbison Story*, by Ellis Amburn. Lyle Stuart, 1990, page 220; "Outlaw Blues," by Tom Hibbert. *Q*, July 1989, page 50; "Tributes," *Rolling Stone*, 26 January 1989, page 32.

17. Source: *Rolling Stone*, 26 January 1989, page 24.

18. Source: *Wanted Man: In Search of Bob Dylan*, John Bauldie, ed. Citadel Press, 1991, page 186.

19. Sources: *Only the Lonely—Roy Orbison's Life and Legacy*, by Alan Clayson. St. Martin's Press, 1989, page 206; *Richard Lester and the Beatles*, by Andrew Yule. Donald I. Fine, 1994, page 42.

20. Source: *The Beatles: The Ultimate Recording Guide*, by Allen J. Wiener. Facts on File, 1992, page 147.

21. Source: "Paul McCartney's "Choba b CCCP" Album: A Translation of the Liner Notes," by Yuri Victorovich Popov. *Goldmine*, 17 November 1989, pp. 38, 137.

22. Sources: "Don't remind me," by Robert Sandall. *Q*, January 1991, page 57; "Rehabilitation for Ringo" (Beatlenews Roundup), by William P. King. *Beatlefan*, vol. 11, no. 1, 1988, page 4.

23. Sources: *Bootleg: The Secret History of the Other Recording Industry*, by Clinton Heylin. St. Martin's Press, 1995, pp. 282–283; *Black Market Beatles*, by Jim Berkenstadt and Belmo (Scott Belmer). Collector's Guide Publishing Inc., 1995, page 95.

24. Sources: "Death of a Wilbury" (Beatlenews Roundup), by William P. King. *Beatlefan*, vol. 11, no. 1, 1988, page 5; *The Beatles: The Ultimate Recording Guide*, by Allen J. Wiener. Facts on File, 1992, page 188; "New Wilburys Video" (Beatlenews Roundup), by William P. King. *Beatlefan*, vol. 11, no. 2, 1989, page 6; "2nd Wilburys Album Rumored" and "Anglophile" (Beatlenews Roundup), by William P. King. *Beatlefan*, vol. 11, no. 2, 1989, pp. 4, 8; "Anglophile" (Beatlenews Roundup), by William P. King, *Beatlefan*, vol. 11, no. 5, 1989, page 10 *The Beatles After the Break-Up 1970–2000*, by Keith Badman. Omnibus Press, 1999, page 416.

25. Source: *Moonwalker: IMDb (Internet Movie Database)*, http://us.imdb.com.

Sources

1989

1.   Source: "Starrstruck," by Mark Wallgren. *Beatlefan*, vol. 11, no. 1, 1988, page 16.

2.   Source: "Starrstruck," by Mark Wallgren. *Beatlefan*, vol. 11, no. 1, 1988, page 16.

3.   Source: "Beatle Pal Victor Spinetti a Crowd Pleaser," by Brad Hundt and Rick Glover. *Beatlefan*, vol. 11, no. 3, 1989, page 21.

4.   Sources: *Beatles Undercover*, by Kristofer K. Engelhardt. Collector's Guide Publishing Inc., 1998, pp. 375–376; *The Beatles: The Ultimate Recording Guide*, by Allen J. Wiener. Facts on File, 1992, page 87; "2nd Wilburys Album Rumored" (Beatlenews Roundup), by William P. King. *Beatlefan*, vol. 11, no. 3, 1989, page 4.

5.   Source: "McCartney on McCartney: Talking About 'Flowers in the Dirt,'" *Beatlefan*, vol. 11, no. 4, 1989, pp. 17–18.

6.   Source: "Can Paul McCartney Get Back?" by James Henke. *Rolling Stone*, 15 June 1989, page 48.

8.   Source: "Maybe I'm Amazed," by Paul Du Noyer. *Q*, July 1989, page 70.

9.   Sources: "Some Kind of Mystery: The Art of Songwriting" (from *The Paul McCartney World Tour* program book), Paul Du Noyer, ed. EMAP Metro, 1989, page 78; *The Macs: Mike McCartney's Family Album*, by Mike McCartney. Delilah Communications Ltd., 1981, page 32.

10.   Source: "'Flowers' Looks Promising" (Beatlenews Roundup), by William P. King. *Beatlefan*, vol. 11, no. 4, 1989, page 6.

11.   Sources: "Anglophile" (Beatlenews Roundup), by William P. King. *Beatlefan*, vol. 11, no. 5, 1989, page 10; "Modern Roses: Hybrid Tea Rose," by Wynn Wagner III. *Wynn's Rose Garden*, http://www.global.org/wynn/roses/modern/mccartney.

12.   Source: "New McCartney Tour Dates" (Beatlenews Roundup), by William P. King. *Beatlefan*, vol. 12, no. 1, 1990, page 4.

13.   Source: "Ringo Starr Tour Begins July 23" (Beatlenews Roundup), by William P. King. *Beatlefan*, vol. 11, no. 4, 1989, pp. 4, 5.

15. Source: *Beatles Undercover*, by Kristofer K. Engelhardt. Collector's Guide Publishing Inc., 1998, page 467.

16. Source: "McCartney World Tour" (Beatlenews Roundup), by William P. King. *Beatlefan*, vol. 11, no. 5, 1989, pp. 4–6.

18. Source: "One For The Road," by David Fricke. *Rolling Stone*, 8 February 1990, page 44.

19. Sources: "Macca Plans U.S. Mini-Tour?" (Beatlenews Roundup), by William P. King. *Beatlefan*, vol. 11, no. 4, 1989, page 5; *Guitar Player*, July 1990, page 32.

20. Source: "Talking With McCartney," by Allan Kozinn. *Beatlefan*, vol. 12, no. 5, 1990, page 7.

21. Source: "What did you do in the Crawdaddy?" by Mark Paytress. *Mojo*, June 1998, pp. 16, 18.

22 Source: "Beatlefax," by Leslie King. *Beatlefan*, vol. 11, no. 6, 1989, page 9.

23. Source: "Beatle News and Other Interesting Views," by Charles F. Rosenay!!! *Good Day Sunshine*, no. 52, November 1989, page 16.

24. Sources: *The Beatles: The Ultimate Recording Guide*, by Allen J. Wiener. Facts on File, 1992, pp. 176–177; "Talking With McCartney," by Allan Kozinn. *Beatlefan*, vol. 12, no. 6/vol. 13, no. 1, 1991, page 28.

25. Sources: "New McCartney Tour Dates" (Beatlenews Roundup), by William P. King. *Beatlefan*, vol. 12, no. 1, 1990, page 4; "One for the Road," by David Fricke. *Rolling Stone*, 8 February 1990, page 44.

1990

1. Sources: "Paul MacCartney—Meet the Beatle," by Tony Bacon. *Bass Player*, July/August 1995; "Lifeline: Paul McCartney," *The Paul McCartney World Tour*, Paul Du Noyer, ed. EMAP Metro, 1989, page 9.

2. Source: "Talking With McCartney," by Allan Kozinn. *Beatlefan*, vol. 12, no. 5, 1990, page 7.

Sources

3. Source: *Vineland*, by Thomas Pynchon. Little, Brown and Company, 1990, pp. 377–378.

4. Source: "Macca at the Grammys" (Beatlenews Roundup), by William P. King. *Beatlefan*, vol. 12, no. 2, 1990, page 6.

5. Sources: *The Beatles: The Ultimate Recording Guide*, by Allen J. Wiener. Facts on File, 1992, pp. 123, 189; "New Beatles Medley Released" (Beatlenews Roundup), by William P. King. *Beatlefan*, vol. 12, no. 2, 1990, page 5.

6. Source: "Paragon Crafts HandMade Buy," by Edwin Riddell. *Hollywood Reporter*, 18 May 1994.

7. Sources: "Anglophile" (Beatlenews Roundup), by William P. King. *Beatlefan*, vol. 12, no. 3, 1990, page 9; *The Beatles: The Ultimate Recording Guide*, by Allen J. Wiener. Facts on File, 1992, page 68; *Not for Sale: The Beatles' Legacy as Archived on Unauthorized Recordings*, by Belmo (Scott Belmer). The Hot Wacks Press, 1997, page 399.

8. Source: *The Beatles: The Ultimate Recording Guide*, by Allen J. Wiener. Facts on File, 1992, page 189.

9. Sources: *DK Encyclopedia of Rock Stars*, by Dafydd Rees and Luke Crampton. DK Publishing, Inc., 1996, pp. 456, 657, 673–674, 681; *The Beatles: The Ultimate Recording Guide*, by Allen J. Wiener. Facts on File, 1992, page 123; "The Last Temptation of Elvis: Paul Contributes to a Unique Compilation," by Patrick Humphries. *Club Sandwich*, no. 54, Spring 1990, page 19.

10. Sources: *Beatles Undercover*, by Kristofer K. Engelhardt. Collector's Guide Publishing, 1998, pp. 94, 298–299; *The Beatles: The Ultimate Recording Guide*, by Allen J. Wiener. Facts on File, 1992, page 178.

11. Sources: "Come Together" (Stories), Q, August 1990, page 32; *The Beatles Live!*, by Mark Lewisohn. Henry Holt & Company, Inc., 1986, pages 62–63; "What's on track for charity record," *USA Today*, 25 July 1990; *The Beatles: From Cavern to Star-Club*, by Hans Olof Gottfridsson. Premium Publishing, 1997, pp. 77, 248.

12. Sources: "McCartney's Stadium Tour" by Bill King. *Beatlefan*, vol. 12, no. 3, 1990, page 18; *The Guinness Book of World Records 1997*, Guin-

Sources

ness Publishing Ltd., 1996, page 137; "End of World Tour Party" (Beatlenews Roundup), by William P. King. *Beatlefan*, vol. 12, no. 6/vol. 13, no. 1, 1991, page 10.

13.   Sources: "That Lennon Concert In Full!" by Tom Hibbert. *Q*, July 1990, page 31; *Lennon*, by John Robertson. Omnibus Press, 1995, page 126; "Liverpool Lennon Tribute" (Beatlenews Roundup), by William P. King. *Beatlefan*, vol. 12, no. 3, 1990, pp. 5–6.

14.   Source: *Beatles Undercover*, by Kristofer K. Engelhardt. Collector's Guide Publishing Inc., 1998, pp. 191–192.

15.   Sources: *The Beatles: The Ultimate Recording Guide*, by Allen J. Wiener. Facts on File, 1992, pp. 62, 126; "Tripping the Live Fantastic!" by Bill King, et al. *Beatlefan*, vol. 12, no. 4, pp. 17–18; "Glascow To Knebworth: A Week Is a Long Time In the Rock Business," by Geoff Baker. *Club Sandwich*, no. 55/56, Winter 1990/91, page 8.

16.   Sources: *The Beatles: The Ultimate Recording Guide*, by Allen J. Wiener. Facts on File, 1992, page 94; "Tripping the Live Fantastic!" by Bill King, et al. *Beatlefan*, vol. 12, no. 4, 1990, pp. 18–19.

17.   Source: "Beatleworld" (Beatlenews Roundup), by William P. King. *Beatlefan*, vol. 12, no. 4, 1990, page 13.

18.   Sources: "Come Together" (Stories), *Q*, August 1990, page 32; "Mediawatch" (Beatlenews Roundup), by William P. King. *Beatlefan*, vol. 12, no. 4, 1990, page 11.

20.   Source: *Paul McCartney* paintings, http://www.siegen-wittgenstein.de/kultur/pmc/indexb.htm.

21.   Sources: "Lynne doesn't look for the limelight," *USA Today*, 7 November 1990, page 4D; *Volume Four*, The Traveling Wilburys (CD bootleg). House Party, 1991.

23.   Source: "Briefly . . ." (Beatlenews Roundup), by William P. King. *Beatlefan*, vol. 12, no. 6/vol. 13, no. 1, 1991, page 12.

24.   Source: A jar of said confection, issued by Warner Bros. during the promotion of *Vol. 3*.

25. Source: "Harrison Sues Tabloid" (Beatlenews Roundup), by William P. King. *Beatlefan*, vol. 13, no. 4, 1991, pp. 5–6.

1991

1. Sources: "Give Peace a Chance" (Beatlenews Roundup) and "Give Peace a Chance" (Record Reviews), by William P. King. *Beatlefan*, vol. 12, no. 6/vol. 13, no. 1, 1991, pp. 9, 43; *The Beatles After the Break-Up 1970–2000*, by Keith Bedman, Omnibus Press, 1999, page 459.

2. Source: "Macca's 'MTV Unplugged' to Yield Live Album" (Beatlenews Roundup), by William P. King. *Beatlefan*, vol. 12, no. 6/vol. 13, no. 1, 1991, page 4.

3. Source: "A Grammy For Lennon" (Beatlenews Roundup), by William P. King. *Beatlefan*, vol. 12, no. 6/vol. 13, no. 1, 1991, page 6.

4. Sources: "Anglophile" (Beatlenews Roundup), by William P. King. *Beatlefan*, vol. 13, no. 2, 1991, page 11; "Anglophile" (Beatlenews Roundup), by William P. King. *Beatlefan*, vol. 13, no. 3, 1991, page 16; "Beatles Top Chart for 3 Weeks!" (Beatlenews Roundup), by William P. King. *Beatlefan*, vol. 17, no. 2, 1996, page 6; *Jumpin' Jim's '60s Uke-In*, by Jim Beloff. Flea Market Music, Inc., 1999, page 3.

5. Source: "Mediawatch" (Beatlenews Roundup), by William P. King. *Beatlefan*, vol. 13, no. 2, 1991, pp. 12–13.

6. Sources: *The Simpsons: The Complete Guide to our Favorite Family*, Ray Richmond and Antonia Coffman, ed. HarperCollins Publishers, 1997, pp. 53, 91, 110, 215; "Cash for Questions: Ringo Starr," by Andrew Collins. *Q*, September 1998, page 17.

7. Source: "Anglofile" (Beatlenews Roundup), by William P. King. *Beatlefan*, vol. 13, no. 2, 1991, page 11.

8. Sources: "Stories," by Phil Sutcliffe. *Q*, August 1991, page 12; *Lennon*, by John Robertson. Omnibus Press, 1995, page 127.

9. Source: "McCartney Playing Surprise Club Dates!" (Beatlenews Roundup), by William P. King. *Beatlefan*, vol. 13, no. 2, 1991, page 4.

10. Source: "Briefly . . ." (Beatlenews Roundup), by William P. King. *Beatlefan*, vol. 13, no. 2, 1991, pp. 8–9.

Sources

11.   Source: "More McCartney-MacManus Tunes" (Beatlenews Roundup), by William P. King. *Beatlefan*, vol. 12, no. 6/vol. 13, no. 1, 1991, page 8.

12.   Source: "People" (Beatlenews Roundup), by William P. King. *Beatlefan*, vol. 12, no. 6/vol. 13, no. 1, 1991, page 18.

13.   Source: "People" (Beatlenews Roundup), by William P. King. *Beatlefan*, vol. 13, no. 3, 1991, page 15.

14.   Source: "Far East Man: George Harrison and the Road 'To Live in Japan,' " by Timothy White. *Goldmine*, 27 November 1992, page 16.

15.   Source: "McCartney's Liverpool Triumph," by Bill and Leslie King. *Beatlefan*, vol. 13, no. 3, 1991, pp. 23–27.

16.   Sources: *John, Paul & Me: Before the Beatles*, by Len Garry. Collector's Guide Publishing Inc., 1997, page 39; *The Ultimate Beatles Encyclopedia*, by Bill Harry, Hyperion, 1992, page 404; *Liverpool Institute for the Performing Arts*, http://www.lipa.ac.uk; "McCartney's Liverpool Triumph," by Bill and Leslie King. *Beatlefan*, vol. 13, no. 3, 1991, page 23.

17.   Source: *Treefort*, by Dutchwmm and Elzool, http://www.bnl.org/html.

18.   Source: "Macca's 'Secret Gigs' " (Beatlenews Roundup), by William P. King. *Beatlefan*, vol. 13, no. 3, 1991, page 8.

19.   Sources: *Video Movie Guide 1999*, by Mick Martin and Marsha Porter. Ballantine Books, 1998, page 813; *The Beatles Down Under: The 1964 Australia and New Zealand Tour*, by Glenn A. Baker with Roger Dilernia. Pierian Press/Popular Culture Ink, 1985, page 55.

20.   Sources: "People" (Beatlenews Roundup), by William P. King. *Beatlefan*, vol. 13, no. 3, 1991, page 15; "Briefly" (Beatlenews Roundup), by William P. King. *Beatlefan*, vol. 13, no. 4, 1991, page 7; *Beatles Undercover*, by Kristofer K. Engelhardt. Collector's Guide Publishing, 1998, page 237.

21.   Source: *The Greatest Hits*, by Cheap Trick. Epic/Sony Entertainment Inc., 1991, track one.

22.   Source: "Ringo Does Song for Film" (Beatlenews Roundup), by William P. King. *Beatlefan*, vol. 13, no. 4, 1991, page 5.

Sources

23. Sources: *Richard Lester and the Beatles*, by Andrew Yule. Donald I Fine, 1994, page 343; *The Beatles: The Ultimate Recording Guide*, by Allen J. Wiener. Facts on File, 1992, page 97.

24. Source: "Harrison on Tour!" by Gen Onoshima. *Beatlefan*, vol. 13, no. 4, 1991, pp. 12, 14, 15.

25. Source: "Harrison on Tour!" by Gen Onoshima. *Beatlefan*, vol. 13, no. 4, 1991, page 15; "Harrison-Clapton: A Tour Wrap-Up," by Gen Onoshima, et al. *Beatlefan*, vol. 13, no. 5, 1992, page 12.)

1992

1. Sources: "Briefly . . ." (Beatlenews Roundup), by William P. King. *Beatlefan*, vol. 14, no. 3, 1992, page 5; *DK Encyclopedia of Rock Stars*, by Dafydd Rees and Luke Crampton. DK Publishing, Inc., 1996, pp. 376, 891.

2. Source: " 'Onobox' Released" (Beatlenews Roundup), by William P. King. *Beatlefan*, vol. 13, no. 5, 1992, page 6.

3. Sources: "McCartney Still In Studio" (Beatlenews Roundup), by William P. King. *Beatlefan*, vol. 13, no. 6, 1992, page 6; *DK Encyclopedia of Rock Stars*, by Dafydd Rees and Luke Crampton. DK Publishing, Inc., 1996, page 561; *Beatles Undercover*, by Kristofer K. Engelhardt. Collector's Guide Publishing Inc., 1998, pp. 299–300.

4. Source: "Harrison Fills the Albert Hall," by Simon J. Rogers, Carl Rehm, et al. *Beatlefan*, vol. 13, no. 6, 1992, pp. 12–15.

5. Sources: "The Hours and Times" (film review), *Film.com*, http://www.film.com; *Lennon*, by John Robertston. Omnibus Press, 1995, page 17; *The Beatles After the Break-Up 1970–2000*, by Keith Badman. Omnibus Press, 1999, page 478.

6. Sources: *Lennon*, by John Robertson. Omnibus Press, 1995, page 127; "Briefly . . ." (Beatlenews Roundup), by William P. King. *Beatlefan*, vol. 13, no. 6, 1992, pp. 6–7.

8. Sources: *Flaming Pie* (CD booklet notes), by Mark Lewisohn. Capitol Records, 1997, page 19; "Talking with Ringo," by Allan Kozinn. *Beatlefan*, vol. 13, no. 6, 1992, page 16; "McCartney does Song for Ringo" (Beatlenews Roundup), by William P. King. *Beatlefan*, vol. 13, no. 4, 1991, page 5.

Sources

9. Source: "A *Beatlefan* reader writes a song for Ringo," by Rick Suchow. *Beatlefan*, vol. 14, no. 1, 1992, page 15.

10. Source: "In Honour of Honore," by Mark Lewisohn. *Club Sandwich*, no. 62, summer 1992, pp. 8–9.

11. Sources: *Polar Music Prize*, http://www.polarmusicprize.se; "Beatle-world" (Beatlenews Roundup), by William P. King. *Beatlefan*, vol. 13, no. 6, 1992, page 10.

12. Source: "More All-Starr Dates Announced" (Beatlenews Roundup), by William P. King. *Beatlefan*, vol. 13, no. 6, 1992, page 4.

13. Sources: "Anglophile" (Beatlenews Roundup), by William P. King. *Beatlefan*, vol. 13, no. 6, 1992, page 8; *The Beatles After the Break-Up 1970–2000*, by Keith Badman. Omnibus Press, 1999, pp. 483–484.

14. Source: "Briefly . . ." (Beatlenews Roundup), by William P. King. *Beatlefan*, vol. 14, no. 1, 1992, page 5.

15. Sources: "Beatleworld" (Beatlenews Roundup), by William P. King. *Beatlefan*, vol. 14, no. 1, 1992, page 6; "Beatleworld" (Beatlenews Roundup), by William P. King. *Beatlefan*, vol. 12, no. 6/vol. 13, no. 1, 1991, page 24.

17. Source: *Alternate Kennedys*, edited by Mike Resnick. Tor Books, 1992, pp. 119, 124.

18. Sources: *In Dreams*, Paul J. McAuley and Kim Newman, editors. Victor Gollancz Ltd., 1992, page 413; *Lennon*, by Ray Coleman. McGraw-Hill Book Company, 1984, pp. 14–15.

19. Sources: *Fatherland*, by Robert Harris. Random House, Inc., 1992, page 35; *The Complete Beatles Chronicle*, by Mark Lewisohn. Harmony Books, 1992, pp. 86, 155, 227.

20. Sources: "More All-Starr Dates Announced" (Beatlenews Roundup), by William P. King. *Beatlefan*, vol. 13, no. 6, 1992, page 4; "Starr Time!" by Al Sussman, Alan Wright, Mark Wallgren and Matt Hurwitz. *Beatlefan*, vol. 14, no. 1, 1992, pp. 11–14; "Starr Trekking!" by William P. King, et al. *Beatlefan*, vol. 14, no. 2, 1992, pp. 14–15.

21. Source: "Starr Trekking!" by William P. King, et al. *Beatlefan*, vol. 14, no. 2, 1992, page 22.

22. Sources: "Beatlenews Roundup," by William P. King. *Beatlefan*, vol. 14, no. 1, 1992, page 4 (and) vol. 14, no. 6, 1993, page 5.

23. Source: *Beatles Undercover*, by Kristofer K. Engelhardt. Collector's Guide Publishing Inc., 1998, pp. 518, 520–521.

24. Sources: "Billboard Honors Harrison" (Beatlenews Roundup), by William P. King. *Beatlefan*, vol. 14, no. 2, 1992, page 24; *The Beatles: a diary*, by Barry Miles. Omnibus Press, 1998, page 10.

25. Sources: " 'Up Close' With McCartney," by William P. King, et al. *Beatlefan*, vol. 14, no. 3, 1992, page 8; *Looking for Changes* (CD bootleg), by Paul McCartney. Yellow Cat, 1993, track 2; *The Complete Beatles Chronicle*, by Mark Lewisohn. Harmony Books, 1992, pp. 144–145.

1993

1. Sources: "U.S. Tour Dates Announced!" (Beatlenews Roundup), by William P. King. *Beatlefan*, vol. 14, no. 3, 1993, page 4; *DK Encyclopedia of Rock Stars*, by Dafydd Rees and Luke Crampton. DK Publishing, Inc., 1996, page 329.

2. Source: "And it All Happened like This," by Laura Gross. *Club Sandwich*, no. 65, Spring 1993, page 3.

3. Source: "And it All Happened like This," by Laura Gross. *Club Sandwich*, no. 65, Spring 1993, pp. 4–5.

4. Sources: "Mediawatch" and "Devil's Radio" (Beatlenews Roundup), plus "Up Close With McCartney," by William P. King, et al. *Beatlefan*, vol. 14, no. 3, 1993, pp. 6, 8–9.

5. Source: "Briefly . . ." (Beatlenews Roundup), by William P. King. *Beatlefan*, vol. 14, no. 6, 1993, page 5.

6. Sources: "The Fireman Cometh" (Beatlenews Roundup), by William P. King. *Beatlefan*, vol. 15, no. 2, 1994, page 5; "Screamin' Jay Hawkins (Real Gone)," by Stuart Colman. *Mojo*, April 2000, page 30.

7. Source: "Planet McCartney: Live In the New World," by William P. King, et al. *Beatlefan*, vol. 14, no. 5, 1993, page 9.

8. Sources: "Paul McCartney: The New World Tour," by William P. King, et al. *Beatlefan*, vol. 14, no. 4, 1993, pp. 9–10, 16; "Planet McCartney: Live in the New World," by William P. King, et al. *Beatlefan*, vol. 14, no. 5, 1993, page 11.

9. Sources: "Publishers' Notes," by William P. King. *Beatlefan*, vol. 15, no. 1, 1993, page 3; *Lennon*, by John Robertson. Omnibus Press, 1995, page 127.

10. Sources: "Ringo Onstage—a New Band?" (Beatlenews Roundup), by Peter Palmiere and Matt Hurwitz. *Beatlefan*, vol. 14, no. 5, 1993, page 5; *The Beatles After The Break-Up 1970–2000*, by Keith Badman. Omnibus Press, 1999, pp. 506–507.

11. Sources: "Wishing for Ringo" (Beatlenews Roundup), by William P. King. *Beatlefan*, vol. 14, no. 4, 1993, page 5; "Mediawatch" (Beatlenews Roundup), by William P. King. *Beatlefan*, vol. 14, no. 6, 1993, page 6.

12. Sources: " 'Raining' May Be Macca Single" (Beatlenews Roundup) and "Paul McCartney: Movin' On" (review), by William P. King. *Beatlefan*, vol.14, no. 5, 1993, pp. 5, 27.

13. Sources: *Nick Drake*, by Patrick Humphries. Bloomsbury Publishing, 1997, page 145; *Rocket Man: Elton John From A–Z* by Claude Bernardin and Tom Stanton. Praeger Publishers, 1996, page 3.

14. Source: *Glimpses*, by Lewis Shiner. William Morrow and Company, Inc., 1993, pp. 17, 35–36.

15. Source: "McEuroshows: Macca's New World Tour Hits the Old World," by William P. King, et al. *Beatlefan*, vol. 15, no. 1, 1993, page 12.

16. Source: "Briefly . . ." (Beatlenews Roundup), by William P. King. *Beatlefan*, vol. 14, no. 6, 1993, page 6.

18. Sources: *The Simpsons: The Complete Guide to Our Favorite Family*, Ray Richmond and Antonia Coffman, eds. HarperCollins Publishers, 1997, page 120; *The Man Who Made the Beatles: An Intimate Biography of Brian Epstein*, by Ray Coleman. McGraw-Hill Publishing Company, 1989, page 126; *The Beatles: Recording Sessions*, by Mark Lewisohn. Harmony Books, 1988, page 23.

19.   Source: " 'Briefly . . ." (Beatlenews Roundup), by William P. King. *Beatlefan*, vol. 15, no. 1, 1993, page 6.

20.   Sources: "1969 + 24 – 4 + 1 + a dog = 1993," *Club Sandwich*, no. 68, Winter 1993, page 3; "Why Did the Beatle Cross the Road?" (Beatlenews Roundup), by William P. King. *Beatlefan*, vol. 14, no. 6, 1993, page 5; " 'Paul is Live' Released" (Beatlenews Roundup), by William P. King. *Beatlefan*, vol. 15, no. 1, 1993, pp. 4–5.

21.   Source: "Fabscreen" (Beatlenews Roundup), by William P. King. *Beatlefan*, vol. 15, no. 4, 1994, page 9.

22.   Sources: "Back To the Egg," *Beatlefan*, vol. 1, no. 4, 1979, page 5; "The Fireman Cometh" (Beatlenews Roundup), by William P. King. *Beatlefan*, vol. 15, no. 2, 1994, page 5; "The Fireman Rushes in," by Mark Lewisohn. *Club Sandwich*, 1994, (from *Beatles Reference Library*, http://www.getback.org).

23.   Source: "Paul: 'Linda will have the last laugh,' " *Mojo*, November 1998, page 11.

24.   Sources: "Mediawatch" (Beatlenews Roundup), by William P. King. *Beatlefan*, vol. 15, no. 2, 1993, page 6; *Closing Numbers: IMDb* (Internet Movie Database), http://uk.imdb.com.

25.   Source: *Beatles Undercover*, by Kristofer K. Engelhardt. Collector's Guide Publishing Inc., 1998, pp. 233–235.

1994

1.   Source: "Through The Past Darkly," by Mark Ellen. *Mojo*, January 1995, page 58.

2.   Sources: "Come Together," by Jeff Giles. *Newsweek*, 23 October 1995, page 66; "Fab 3 Finish Lennon Song!" (Beatlenews Roundup), by William P. King. *Beatlefan*, vol. 15, no. 3, 1994, page 4.

3.   Source: "Hall of Fame Notes and Quotes" (Beatlenews Roundup), by William P. King. *Beatlefan*, vol. 15, no. 3, 1994, page 5.

Sources

4. Sources: "Careful with that axe, Leonardo," by Clive Prior. *Mojo*, March 1998, page 17; *Pirate Songs*, by George Harrison (CD bootleg). Vigotone Records, 1995, page 16.

5. Source: "Linda Launches U.S. Food Line" (Beatlenews Roundup), by William P. King. *Beatlefan*, vol. 15, no. 4, 1994, pp. 5–6.

6. Source: "Ono Musical has New York Run" (Beatlenews Roundup), by William P. King. *Beatlefan*, vol. 15, no. 4, 1994, page 6.

7. Source: *Beatles Undercover*, by Kristofer K. Engelhardt. Collector's Guide Publishing Inc., 1998, page 394.

8. Source: "A Bit of Slap and a Wig," by Mat Snow. *Q*, May 1994, page 58.

9. Source: "*Backbeat* Off to Good Start" (Beatlenews Roundup), by William P. King. *Beatlefan*, vol. 15, no. 4, 1994, pp. 5–6.

10. Source: "Epstein's Last Night Dramatized" (Beatlenews Roundup), by William P. King. *Beatlefan*, vol. 15, no. 4, 1994, page 6.

11. Source: "Briefly . . ." (Beatlenews Roundup), by William P. King. *Beatlefan*, vol. 20, no. 2, 1999, page 8.

12. Sources: "Briefly . . ." (Beatlenews Roundup), by William P. King. *Beatlefan*, vol. 14, no. 4, 1993, page 6; "Briefly . . ." (Beatlenews Roundup), by William P. King. *Beatlefan*, vol. 14, no. 5, 1993, page 6; "Jacko Puts Wrap on 'Beatlerap'" (Beatlenews Roundup), by William P. King. *Beatlefan*, vol. 15, no. 5, 1994, page 5.

13. Sources: *The Complete Beatles Chronicle*, by Mark Lewisohn. Harmony Books, 1992, page 70; "The Fab Four: the Remix!," by Jim Irvin. *Mojo*, December 1995, page 32.

14. Source: *The Beatles Anthology*, Chips Chipperfield, producer. Pioneer/Apple Corps Ltd., 1996, disc 7, track 6.

15. Source: "Paul McCartney—Meet the Beatle," by Tony Bacon. *Bass Player*, July/August 1995.

16. Sources: *The Wonder Stuff*, by Curtis Malasky, http://www.enteract.com/~shabadoo/Stuff.html; *Rock Names: From Abba to ZZ Top: How Rock Bands got their Names*, by Adam Dolgins. Citadel Press, 1998, pp. 294–295.

17. Source: *Threesome: IMDb* (Internet Movie Database), http://us.imdb.com.

18. Source: *The Beatles: From Cavern to Star-Club*, by Hans Olof Gottfridsson. Premium Publishing, 1997, pp. 201, 410.

19. Source: "The Songs," by Mark Lewisohn. *Club Sandwich*, no. 82, Summer 1997.

21. Source: *Pulp Fiction* (Special Collector's Edition), Miramax Films, 1996.

22. Sources: "The Month in Phish History: October 1994," *Phish: The Official Website*, http://www.phish.com/; "Rockers rollin' to the Beatles tune," by Jane Stevenson. *Toronto Sun*, 10 November 1995, *The Beatles Music Database Homepage*, http://www.canoe.ca/JamMusicBeatles/rockers.html.

23. Source: "Nuggets," by Myles Patten. *Mojo*, November 1995, page 150.

24. Sources: "Live at the BBC: Did Apple/EMI botch this first archival release?" by Allan Kozinn. *Beatlefan*, vol. 16, no. 2, 1994, pp. 15–16; "A Complete Catalog Of The Beatles' UK Radio Broadcasts, Part Two," by Mark Lewisohn. *The Beatles Book Appreciation Society Magazine*, Beat Publications Ltd., April 1980, pp. viii, x.

25. Sources: "Beatlenews Roundup," by William P. King. *Beatlefan*, vol. 16, no. 2, 1995, page 4; " 'Flaming Pie' Tastier With Each Serving!" by William P. King. *Beatlefan*, vol. 18, no. 4, 1997, page 12.

1995

1. Source: "Poetry," by Paul McCartney. *New Statesman & Society*, 27 January 1995, page 41.

2. Sources: *Beatles Undercover*, by Kristofer K. Engelhardt. Collector's Guide Publishing, Inc., 1998, page 300; *Anthology 2* (booklet liner notes), by Mark Lewisohn. EMI/Capitol, 1996, page 4; *The Beatles After The Break-Up 1970–2000*, by Keith Badman. Omnibus Press, 1999, page 527.

Sources

3. Source: *Lennon*, by John Robertson. Omnibus Press, 1995, page 128.

4. Sources: *Lennon*, by John Robertson. Omnibus Press, 1995, page 128; "Beatlenews Roundup," by William P. King. *Beatlefan*, vol. 16. no. 4, 1995, pp. 5, 7; "Mediawatch" (Beatlenews Roundup), by William P. King. *Beatlefan*, vol. 16, no. 6, 1995, page 6; *The Beatles After the Break-Up 1970–2000*, by Keith Badman. Omnibus Press, 1999, pp. 528, 538.

5. Sources: "Royal Premiere for Macca" (Beatlenews Roundup), by William P. King. *Beatlefan*, vol. 16, no. 3, 1995, page 5; "Macca Classical Release" (Beatlenews Roundup), by William P. King. *Beatlefan*, vol. 16, no. 4, 1995, page 6.

6. Sources: "Royal Premiere for Macca" (Beatlenews Roundup), by William P. King. *Beatlefan*, vol. 16, no. 3, 1995, page 5; "Macca Classical Release" (Beatlenews Roundup), by William P. King. *Beatlefan*, vol. 16, no. 4, 1995, page 6.

7. Source: "All Starr: New York Q&A," by Ken Sharp. *Beatlefan*, vol. 16, no. 5, 1995, page 19.

8. Source: *ER*: "Motherhood," summary/review by Scott Hollifield, http://www.digiserve.com.

9. Sources: " 'Oobu Joobu' Set to Start" (Beatlenews Roundup), by Bill King. *Beatlefan*, vol. 16, no. 4, 1995, page 8; *Paul McCartney: Many Years from Now*, by Barry Miles. Henry Holt and Company, 1997, page 230.

10. Sources: "Mac Women In Spotlight" (Beatlenews Roundup), by William P. King. *Beatlefan*, vol. 16, no. 5, 1995, pp. 5–6; "Mediawatch" (Beatlenews Roundup), by William P. King. *Beatlefan*, vol. 18, no. 3, 1997, page 8; "Stella!" (Beatlenews Roundup), by William P. King. *Beatlefan*, vol. 18, no. 4, 1997, page 6.

11. Source: "All-Starr Band Itinerary Released" (Beatlenews Roundup), by William P. King. *Beatlefan*, vol. 16, no. 4, 1995, page 5.

12. Sources: "All-Starr World Tour Planned" (Beatlenews Roundup), by William P. King. *Beatlefan*, vol. 16, no. 1, 1994, page 5; *Beatles Undercover*, by Kristofer K. Engelhardt. Collector's Guide Publishing Inc., 1998, page 151.

13. Source: "Ringo: 'Wrong Lads' " (Beatlenews Roundup), by William P. King. *Beatlefan*, vol. 16, no. 5, 1995, page 6.

14. Source: "On the Road with Ringo Starr," by Denise McCann Beck, http://web2.airmail.net~gschultz/ontherd.html.

15. Sources: "Family Emergency Ends Tour" (Beatlenews Roundup), by William P. King. *Beatlefan*, vol. 16, no. 6, 1995, page 5; "Beatlenews Roundup," by William P. King. *Beatlefan*, vol. 17, no. 1, 1995, page 5: *The Beatles After the Break-Up 1970–2000*, by Keith Badman, Omnibus Press, 1999, pp. 534–535.

16. Sources: "Briefly . . ." (Beatlenews Roundup), by William P. King. *Beatlefan*, vol. 16, no. 6, 1995, page 6; "Pop, What Is It Good For?" by Martin Aston. *Q*, November 1995, pp. 20–21; *Abbey Road*, by Brian Southall, Peter Vince and Allan Rouse. Omnibus Press, 1997, pp. 186–187.

17. Source: *Wonderwall Movie Website*, http://www.wonderwallfilm.co.uk/history.html.

18. Source: *Leaving Las Vegas: IMDb* (Internet Movie Database), http://us.imdb.com.

19. Sources: *The Simpsons: The Complete Guide to Our Favorite Family*, Ray Richmond and Antonia Coffman, eds. HarperCollins Publishers, 1997, page 185; "Beatlenews Roundup," by William P. King. *Beatlefan*, vol. 16, no. 6, 1995, page 6 (and) vol. 17, no. 1, 1995, page 6.

20. Source: *Beatles Undercover*, by Kristofer K. Engelhardt. Collector's Guide Publishing, 1998, pp. 178–179.

21. Sources: "New & Upcoming Releases" (Beatlenews Roundup), by William P. King. *Beatlefan*, vol. 17, no. 1, 1995, page 4; "Yoko and Ima: A Review," by Rick Glover. *Beatlefan*, vol. 17, no. 3, 1996, page 5 (and) "Yoko, Sean on Tour" (Beatlenews Roundup), by William P. King, page 6.

22. Source: "Yoko Sunday: Two Reviews," by Edward S. Chen, 16 November 1995. *Beatles Reference Library*, http://www.getback.com.

23. Sources: "Beatles Top Charts for 3 Weeks!" (Beatlenews Roundup), by William P. King. *Beatlefan*, vol. 17, no. 2, 1996, page 6;

The Beatles After the Break-Up 1970–2000, by Keith Badman. Omnibus Press, 1999, page 543.

24. Sources: *John Lennon In My Life*, by Pete Shotton and Nicholas Schaffner. Stein and Day, 1983, page 86; "Back To the Future: Beatles 45 Sleeves In the '90s," by Charles Szabla. *Goldmine*, 6 November 1998, page 20.

25. Source: *Mr. Holland's Opus: IMDb* (Internet Movie Database), http://us.imdb.com.

1996

1. Sources: "Briefly . . ." (Beatlenews Roundup), by William P. King. *Beatlefan*, vol. 17, no. 3, 1996, page 7; *The Beatles: From Cavern to Star-Club*, by Hans Olof Gottfridsson. Premium Publishing, 1997, page 31.

2. Sources: "McCartney Dedicates LIPA" (Beatlenews Roundup), by William P. King. *Beatlefan*, vol. 17, no. 3, 1996, page 6; *Liverpool Institute for the Performing Arts*, http://www.lipa.ac.uk.

3. Source: *Liverpool Institute for the Performing Arts*, http://www.lipa.ac.uk.

4. Sources: "Beatlenews Roundup," by William P. King. *Beatlefan*, vol. 17, no. 3, 1996, pp. 7–8; "Devil's Radio," by Norm & Shake. *Beatlefan*, vol. 17, no. 4, 1996, page 7; *The Beatles After the Break-Up 1970–2000* by Keith Badman. Omnibus Press, 1999, page 552.

5. Sources: "Preview of *Anthology 2*" (Beatlenews Roundup), by William P. King. *Beatlefan*, vol. 17, no. 2, 1996, page 4; "Anthology Notes" (Beatlenews Roundup), by William P. King. *Beatlefan*, vol. 17, no. 3, 1996, page 5.

6. Source: *The Beatles: Memories and Memorabilia*, by Richard Buskin. Crescent Books, 1994, page 9.

7. Source: "Klaus Voormann: The Old Beatle Pal Behind *Revolver* and *Anthology* Covers," by Rip Rense. *Beatlefan*, vol. 17, no. 5, 1996, page 17.

8. Source: "Ringo Signs Collectibles" (Beatlenews Roundup), by Diane Carnevale Jones. *Beatlefan*, vol. 17, no. 4, 1996, page 4.

Sources

9. Sources: "Instant News: Archive, September 1996," *Instant Karma!*, http://www.instantkarma.com.); "Ono, Ima on Tour" (Beatlenews Roundup), by William P. King. *Beatlefan*, vol. 17, no. 5, 1996, page 6.

11. Source: "Queen Snubs Beatles!" (Beatlenews Roundup), by William P. King. *Beatlefan*, vol. 17, no. 5, 1996, pp. 4–5.

12. Sources: *Moon: The Life and Death of a Rock Legend*, by Tony Fletcher. Spike/Avon Books, Inc., 1999, page 575; *DK Encyclopedia of Rock Stars*, by Dafydd Rees and Luke Crampton. DK Publishing, Inc., 1996, page 924.

14. Source: "Red House Painters' Blue Period," by Rob O'Connor. *BAM Magazine*, 9 August 1996.

15. Source: "A Curtain Call in Atlanta," by Jennifer Frey. *Washingtonpost.com*, 5 August 1996, http://www.washingtonpost.com/wp-srv/sports/olympics/daily/aug/05/close5.htm.

16. Sources: "Jude's sad song makes better than £25,000," *Electronic Telegraph*, Issue 485, 20 September 1996, http://www.telegraph.co.uk; "Instant News: Archive, September 1996," *Instant Karma!*, http://www.instantkarma.com.

17. Source: "*Dead* Film Released" (Beatlenews Roundup), by William P. King. *Beatlefan*, vol. 18, no. 1, 1996, page 5.

18. Sources: "Recording with the Fab Three," by Rip Rense. *Beatlefan*, vol. 17, no. 1, 1995, page 20; "Cash for Questions," by Robert Yates. *Q*, January 1998, page 18.

19. Source: "Was it Paul? Fur Sure!" (Beatlenews Roundup), by William P. King. *Beatlefan*, vol. 18, no. 1, 1996, page 5.

20. Sources: "Briefly . . ." (Beatlenews Roundup), by William P. King. *Beatlefan*, vol. 18, no. 1, 1996, page 6; *Unofficial Dark Skies Homepage*, http://www.patriotcom.com/darkskies.

21. Sources: "Phone Home: Ron Nasty of the Rutles," by Jim Irvin. *Mojo*, October 1996, page 21; *The First 28⊗ Years of Monty Python*, by Kim "Howard" Johnson. St. Martin's Griffin, 1999, pp. 59, 347; "Briefly . . ." (Beatlenews Roundup), by William P. King. *Beatlefan*, vol. 16, no. 1, 1994, page 5; [print ad for "Eric Idle Exploits Monty Python"], *Willamette Week*, vol. 26, no. 16, 23 February 2000, page 45.

22. Sources: "Out of the Beatles into the Shadows," by Jan Moir. *Electronic Telegraph*, issue 535, 9 November 1996, http://www.telegraph.co.uk; "Mediawatch" (Beatlenews Roundup), by William P. King. *Beatlefan*, vol. 17, no. 2, 1996, page 9.

23. Sources: "Briefly . . ." (Beatlenews Roundup), by William P. King. *Beatlefan*, vol. 18, no. 2, 1997, page 7; *The Official Kula Shaker Website*, http://www.kulashaker.co.uk.

24. Source: "Linda switches focus from cancer," by John Gaskell and Julia Llewllyn Smith. *Electronic Telegraph*, issue 508, 13 October 1996, http://www.telegraph.co.uk; *The Beatles After the Break-Up 1970–2000*, Keith Badman. Omnibus Press, 1999, page 560.

25. Source: *The Longest Cocktail Party*, by Richard DiLello. Playboy Press, 1972, page 254.

1997

1. Sources: Associated Press wire report, 9 January 1997; "Briefly . . ." (Beatlenews Roundup), by William P. King. *Beatlefan*, vol. 19, no. 6, 1998, page 10.

2. Sources: "Eight Arms to Hold You" (Recordings), by Rob O'Connor. *Rolling Stone*, 20 February 1997, page 66; *The Complete Beatles Chronicle*, by Mark Lewisohn. Harmony Books, 1992, pp. 186, 189.

3. Source: "Why I Didn't Tell Linda She was Dying," by Rebecca Hardy. *Daily Mail*, 17 October 1998.

4. Sources: "Beatlenews Roundup," by William P. King. *Beatlefan*, vol. 18, no. 2, 1997, page 4 (and) vol. 18, no. 3, 1997, page 5.

5. Source: "All Starr Itinerary Released!" (Beatlenews Roundup), by William P. King. *Beatlefan*, vol. 18, no. 3, 1997, page 4.

6. Source: "All Starr Itinerary Released!" (Beatlenews Roundup), by William P. King. *Beatlefan*, vol. 18, no. 3, 1997, page 4.

Sources

7. Source: "Previewing *Standing Stone*" (Beatlenews Roundup), by William P. King. *Beatlefan*, vol. 18, no. 6, 1997, page 4.

8. Sources: *Flaming Pie* (CD booklet notes), by Paul McCartney. Capitol Records, 1997, page 11; *Mersey Beat: The Beginnings of the Beatles*, Bill Harry, ed. Omnibus Press, 1977, page 17.

9. Source: "Ringo Starr & The All-Starrs Road Report #3," by Peter Frampton, http://www.frampton.com.

10. Source: *Father's Day: IMDb* (Internet Movie Database), http://us.imdb.com.

11. Sources: *Flaming Pie* (CD booklet), by Geoff Baker. Capitol, July 1997, page 20; "Beautiful Night" (CD single liner notes), EMI/Parlophone, December 1997; (Beatlenews Roundup,) by William P. King. *Beatlefan*, vol. 8, no. 5, 1986, page 4.

12. Sources: "Beatlenews Roundup," by William P. King. *Beatlefan*, vol. 18, no. 5, 1997, page 5.

14. Source: "Real Gone" (Allen Ginsberg obituary), by (Barry) Miles. *Mojo*, June 1997, page 161.

15. Sources: *Dead Air*, by M. Dalton Allred. Slave Labor Books, 1989, page 66; *Citizen Nocturne*, by M. Dalton Allred. Brave New Words, 1992, page 16; *Tomorrow Never Knows: The Beatles' Last Concert*, by Eric Lefcowitz. Terra Firma Books, 1987, page 47.

16. Sources: "George Martin: The Billboard Interview," by Paul Sexton. *Billboard*, 11 April 1999, http://www.billboard-online.com/sr/martin/; *Cornflakes & Classics—A History of Elton John (1997)*, by Paul Maclachlan, 1 March 1999, http://www.vex.net/~paulmac/elton/ej1997.html.

18. Sources: "Mansun News," *Mansun: The Website*, http://www.mansun.co.uk/dave/six.html; "Mansun: Did You Know?" *Parlophone Fanbase '98*, http://www.parlophone.co.uk/.

19. Sources: "A Big Week for the McCartneys!" (Beatlenews Roundup), by William P. King. *Beatlefan*, vol. 19, no. 1, 1997, pp. 5–6; "Stella!" (Beatlenews Roundup), by William P. King. *Beatlefan*, vol. 18, no. 4, 1997, page 6.

20. Sources: "The Q Awards" by Danny Eccleston and Lucy O'Brien. *Q*, January 1998, pp. 46, 54, 56; "Briefly . . ." (Beatlenews Roundup), by William P. King. *Beatlefan*, vol. 19, no. 1, 1997, page 8; *The Complete Beatles Chronicle*, by Mark Lewisohn. Harmony Books, 1992, page 349.

21. Sources: "Where have you gone, Sgt. Pepper?" by Terry Ott. *National Post*, 13 January 1999, *National Post Online*, http://www.nationalpost.com; *The Beatles: Recording Sessions*, by Mark Lewisohn. Harmony Books, 1988, page 108.

22. Sources: "Beatlenews Roundup," by William P. King. *Beatlefan*, vol. 19, no. 1, 1997, page 7; "Big Brother is Watching You," by Nick Kent. *Mojo*, December 1997, page 84.

23. Source: "Beatlenews Roundup," by William P. King. *Beatlefan*, vol. 19, no. 2, 1998, pp. 5–7.

24. Sources: "Beatlenews Roundup," by William P. King. *Beatlefan*, vol. 19, no. 2, 1998, page 6; "Make It a Beautiful Night for Me," *Club Sandwich*, no. 84, Winter 1997.

25. Source: "McCartney 'No Mozart'—Yoko," by Nicholas Hellen. *The Times and Sunday Times*, 28 December 1997, http://www.sunday-times.co.uk/news/pages/.

1998

1. Source: "Harrison at Perkins Rites" (Beatlenews Roundup), by William P. King. *Beatlefan*, vol. 19, no. 3, 1998, page 5.

2. Source: *Everest* Uses Harrison Music (Beatlenews Roundup), by William P. King. *Beatlefan*, vol. 19, no. 3, 1998, pp. 5–6.

3. Source: *Year's Best SF 4*, edited by David G. Hartwell. HarperPrism, June 1999, pp. 103–117.

4. Sources: "Lessons from the Master," by Neil Tennant. *Electronic Telegraph*, issue 1044, 4 April 1998, http://www.telegraph.co.uk; "A Room With A View" (Record Reviews), by Dieter Hoffman. *Beatlefan*, vol. 19, no. 5, 1998, page 29.

5. Source: "Beatles want bootleg record banned," by Colin Randall. *Electronic Telegraph*, issue 1077, 7 May 1998 (and) "Judge bans "drunken"

Sources

Beatles CD," *Electronic Telegraph*, issue 1079, 9 May 1998, http://www.
telegraph.co.uk.

6. Source: "Ringo Performs At Bottom Line!" (Beatlenews Roundup),
by William P. King. *Beatlefan*, vol. 19, no. 4, 1998, page 4.

7. Source: "Updating Other Projects" (Beatlenews Roundup), by
William P. King. *Beatlefan*, vol. 19, no. 2, 1998, page 6.

8. Source: "Groovin' up slowly," by James McNair. *Mojo*, June 1998,
page 102.

9. Source: "Two New Junior Lennon Albums" (Beatlenews Roundup),
by William P. King. *Beatlefan*, vol. 19, no. 4, 1998, page 7.

10. Sources: "Why I Didn't Tell Linda She Was Dying," by Rebecca
Hardy. *Daily Mail*, 17 October 1998; "Sir Paul Pays Tribute to Linda"
(Beatlenews Roundup), by William P. King. *Beatlefan*, vol. 19, no. 5, 1998,
page 5.

11. Sources: "Tyler's *Vertical* Vocals Removed!" (Beatlenews Roundup),
by William P. King. *Beatlefan*, vol. 19, no. 4, 1998, page 6; "Making
Ringo's New Album," by Rip Rense. *Beatlefan*, vol. 19, no. 2, 1998, page
15; "Briefly . . ." (Beatlenews Roundup), by William P. King. *Beatlefan*,
vol. 19, no. 5, 1998, page 7.

12. Sources: "Making Ringo's Album," by Rip Rense. *Beatlefan*, vol. 19,
no. 2, 1998, page 14; *Collected Poems*, by W. H. Auden. Vintage International, 1991, pp. 52–53; *Mercury Records: Ringo Starr*, http://www.mer-
curyrecords.com/cgi_bin/mercury/artists.cgi?url=ringo_starr.

13. Source: "Making Ringo's New Album," by Rip Rense. *Beatlefan*, vol.
19, no. 2, 1998, page 14.

15. Source: "Taping Ringo's 'Storytellers' (Beatlenews Roundup), by
William P. King. *Beatlefan*, vol. 19, no. 4, 1998, page 5.

17. Sources: "Sir Paul 'chuffed' with history house," *BBC News*, 21 July
1998, http://news.bbc.co.uk; "House where it will always be yesterday," by
Nigel Bunyan. *Electronic Telegraph*, issue 1153, 22 July 1998, http://www.
telegraph.co.uk.

18.   Source: "Linda's last film premieres to packed house," *BBC News*, 20 August 1998, http://news.bbc.co.uk.

19.   Source: *Melrose Place TV*, http://www.melrosetv.com.

20.   Source: *Bunny's Honeys: Bunny Yeager, Queen of Pin-Up Photography*, Burkhard Riemschneider, ed. Benedikt Taschen, 1994, pp. 88–89.

21.   Source: "Briefly . . ." (Beatlenews Roundup), by William P. King. *Beatlefan*, vol. 19, no. 6, 1998, page 10.

22.   Source: *MTV News Gallery*, http://www.mtv.com/news/gallery/b/ beatles981109.html.

23.   Source: *MTV News Gallery*, http://www.mtv.com/news/gallery/b/ beatles.html.

24.   Source: "Imagine There's a Box Set," by Blair Jackson. *Mix*, February 1999, pp. 220–221.

25.   Source: "Would You?" by Poppy Z. Brite. *Nerve: Literate Smut*, Genevieve Field and Rufus Griscom, editors. Broadway Books, 1998, pp. 160–164.

1999

1.   Source: *Providence: IMDb* (Internet Movie Database), http://us. imdb.com.

2.   Sources: "Fab Four Tribute Raises the Roof" (Entertainment), *BBC News Online Network*, http://news.bbc.co.uk, 29 January 1999; *The Beatles After the Break-Up 1970–2000*, by Keith Badman. Omnibus Press, 1999, page 616.

3.   Sources: "First, Do No Harm," by Peter David, Todd Nauck, and Larry Stucker. *Young Justice*, no. 5, DC Comics, February 1999, pp. 4, 6–7, 10–11; *Triangle: Imzadi II*, by Peter David. Pocket Books, October 1998, page 70.

4.   Sources: "All-Starr Band Tour Dates!" (Beatlenews Roundup), by William P. King. *Beatlefan*, vol. 20, no. 2, 1999, pp. 5–6; "All Starr Band Tour Report" (and) "Ringo Meets the Press" (Beatlenews Roundup), by William P. King. *Beatlefan*, vol. 20, no. 3, 1999, pp. 6, 8.

Sources

5. Source: "Macca, Martin Enter Hall of Fame" (Beatlenews Roundup), by William P. King. *Beatlefan*, vol. 20, no. 3, 1999, page 4.

6. Source: "Macca, Martin Enter Hall of Fame" (Beatlenews Roundup), by William P. King. *Beatlefan*, vol. 20, no. 3, 1999, page 4.

7. Sources: "Macca Performs at Linda Tribute!" (Beatlenews Roundup), by William P. King. *Beatlefan*, vol. 20, no. 4, 1999, page 6; *The Beatles After the Break-Up 1970–2000*, by Keith Badman. Omnibus Press, 1999, page 621.

8. Source: "Macca Performs at Linda Tribute!" (Beatlenews Roundup), by William P. King. *Beatlefan*, vol. 20, no. 4, 1999, page 6.

9. Source: "A Concert for Linda" (Live Shows), *Mojo*, June 1999, pp. 144–145.

10. Source: *The Simpsons Forever! A Complete Guide To Our Favorite Family . . . Continued!* Scott M. Gimple, ed. HarperPerennial, 1999, page 74.

11. Sources: "McCartney Art Opening Set" (Beatlenews Roundup), by William P. King. *Beatlefan*, vol. 20, no. 3, 1999, pp. 5–6; "Sir Paul the Painter in Germany!" (Beatlenews Roundup), by William P. King. *Beatlefan*, vol. 20, no. 4, 1999, page 5.

12. Sources: " 'New' Beatles Track Not So New!" (Beatlenews Roundup), by William P. King. *Beatlefan*, vol. 20, no. 4, 1999, page 4; "Final Beatles Song Marks End of Millennium" (Beatle News), vol. 3, no. 5, 30 May 1999. *The Beatles on Abbey Road*, http://webhome.idirect.com~faab/AbbeyRoad/.

13. Source: *Linda McCartney Pro Cycling Team*, http://www.lindamc-cartney-pct.co.uk.

14. Source: "Raw Hynde," by Evelyn McDonnell. *Interview*, July 1999, page 72.

15. Sources: "Two New Paul McCartney Albums this Year" (Macca-News), 19 May 1999, *Macca-Central*, http://www.macca-central.com/macca-news; "A Garland for Linda" (Macca-News), 18 July 1999, *Macca-Central*, http://www.macca-central.com/macca-news; "A Garland for Linda Premieres" (Beatlenews Roundup), by William P. King. *Beatlefan*, vol. 20, no. 5, 1999, pp. 5–6.

16. Sources: *Outside Providence: IMDb* (Internet Movie Database), http://us.imdb.com; *Outside Providence*, http://www.outsideprovidence.com.

17. Sources: "It All Began with a five-year-old Girl . . ." *Beatlefan*, vol. 20, no. 6, 1999, page 18; "Fantastic Voyage," by Clark Collins. *Mojo*, October 1999, page 58.

18. Source: "Oasis singer names his baby after Beatle John," by Nicole Martin. *Electronic Telegraph*, issue 1573, 15 September 1999, http://www. telegraph.co.uk.

19. Sources: http://stampvote.msn.com; "*Yellow Sub* Marketing Blitz Set!" (Beatlenews Roundup), by William P. King. *Beatlefan*, vol. 20, no. 5, 1999, page 4.

20. Source: "PETA Gala site," by Mike Kovacich, et al. *Macca-Central*, http://www.macca-central.com/macca-events/peta/gala/.

21. Source: "Salty Dog" (Beatle News), vol. 3, no. 8, 3 October 1999. *The Beatles on Abbey Road*, http://webhome.idirect.com~faab/ AbbeyRoad.

22. Sources: "I'm Not Giving Up, Man!" (Paul McCartney Interview— Part One), by Patrick Humphries. *MUSIC365*, http://www.music365. co.uk; "New McCartney Releases" (Beatlenews Roundup), by William P. King. *Beatlefan*, vol. 20, no. 6, 1999, page 6.

23. Sources: *Remember: Recollections and Photographs of the Beatles*, by Michael McCartney. Henry Holt & Company, 1992, page 24; *The Macs: Mike McCartney's Family Album*, by Mike McCartney. Delilah Books, 1981, pp. 57, 59, 61; *The Beatles: a diary*, by Barry Miles. Omnibus Press, 1999, page 16.

24. Sources: "Credits for 'Santa'!" (Beatlenews Roundup), by William P. King. *Beatlefan*, vol. 20, no. 6, 1999, page 5; *The Beatles: Recording Sessions*, by Mark Lewisohn. Harmony Books, 1988, page 131.

25. Sources: "Beatles Anthem Is Millennium Song" (Entertainment), 18 December 1999, *BBC News*, http://news2.thls.bbc.co.uk; "UK bids farewell to 20th Century," 31 December 1999, *BBC News*, http://news2. thls.bbc.co.uk.

CORRECTIONS TO
THE ULTIMATE BEATLES QUIZ BOOK

"Thanks for buying me book,

it was very handy."

—John Lennon

The author offers the following corrections, clarifications and amendments to his first book, *The Ultimate Beatles Quiz Book*, published in 1992 by St. Martin's Press:

(page 6)
9. The *Let It Be* movie soundtrack medley mentioned in this answer also includes the Little Richard song "Miss Ann" and should be listed as "Kansas City/Miss Ann/Lawdy Miss Clawdy."

(page 57)
5. In addition to The Bachelors and Tex Roberg and the Graduates, *Roy Young* also appeared with the Beatles at their first gig at the Star-Club.

(page 68)
21. John aired "Too Many Cooks" (complete title: "Don't Ever Change (Too Many Cooks)") during an interview with Tom Donahue on San Francisco's KSAN-FM in September 1974.

(page 83)
1. Song title "Your Gonna Lose that Girl" should read "You're Gonna Lose that Girl."

(page 84)

16. Filming on *Let It Be* began 2 *January* 1969 at Twickenham Film Studios, London.

(page 88)

24. Mr. King called in the "black marias" to halt the Beatles' *final* live performance together on the roof of Apple, 3 *Savile Row*, 30 January 1969.

(page 109)

20. While George and Paul have both suggested that the name Beatles may have originated from the 1954 film *The Wild One* (where Chino [Lee Marvin] refers to the motorcycle club's female members as "beetles"), evidence to the contrary suggests that at the time the group were looking for a name (1960), the film was still under a ban in Britain "stemming from the fear that its depiction of hooligans and violence might incite adolescents to imitate them." The ban would not be lifted until 1968.

(pp. 136, 140)

16. Poco guitarist Rusty Young has stated in an interview that John Lennon had nothing to do with the country-rock band's name change from Pogo to Poco. "Walt Kelly, the comic's creator, sued us, so we had to stop using the name Pogo. And I actually suggested, from my high school Spanish, 'Why don't we call ourselves Poco? It doesn't mean anything, really."

(page 139)

6. While Ed Sullivan lived and had an office at New York's Delmonico Hotel, he did not own it.

(page 141)

25. On 21 August 1990, Sotheby's in London auctioned Lennon's Warhol collage for nearly $42,000.

(page 155)

16. Paul has also played his Hofner Violin 500/1 bass in promotional videos for "Coming Up," "Take It Away," "My Brave Face," and "This One."

(page 160)

6. Rain (additional entry).
   "I Am The Walrus"
   (". . . you get a tan from standing in the English rain.")

Corrections to *The Ultimate Beatles Quiz Book*

(page 194)
15. Paul's "Fool On the Hill" sequence, the last to be filmed for *Magical Mystery Tour*, was shot in Nice, France *30–31 October 1967.*

(page 224)
3. "You Know My Name (Look Up the Number)" is also available on the compilation CD *Past Masters, Volume Two.*

(page 225)
15. Geronimo (additional entry).
"Good Times Coming/Feel the Sun"
("Pack up your bags and yell Geronimo!" From the album *Press to Play.*)

(page 259)
7. "Love You Too" should read "Love You To."

(page 298)
17. The original title for Monty Python's *The Life of Brian* was *Brian of Nazareth. (Jesus Christ: Lust for Glory* was a joke title thought up by Eric Idle, when asked near the end of shooting on *Monty Python and the Holy Grail* what their follow-up would be.)

(page 327)
3. Linda Eastman first photographed the Beatles at the press launch for *Sgt. Pepper* held 19 May 1967 at Brian Epstein's Georgian town house, 24 Chapel Street, Belgravia, London.

(page 357)
6. The Beatles' first meeting with Bob Dylan was at the Delmonico Hotel on 28 August 1964.
(There is one Beatles reference book that states that Dylan had first met them in New York the previous February but during those days the Beatles' itinerary placed them in the city [7–10, 12 February], Dylan was in the South, giving a concert at Emory University in Atlanta on the 7th, working on "Chimes of Freedom" while driving through Mississippi on the 9th and arriving in New Orleans on the 10th to enjoy Mardi Gras the following day. Departing the morning of the 12th for Tougaloo, Missouri, Dylan and his band would play an unscheduled set at Tougaloo College that afternoon.)

SOURCES

20. Sources: *Paul McCartney: Many Years from Now*, by Barry Miles. Henry Holt and Company, 1997, pp. 52–53; "Setting Harrison Straight on 'The Wild One,'" by Bill Harry. *Beatlefan*, vol. 18, no. 6, 1997, page 17; *Brando*, by Robert Tanitch. Studio Vista, 1994, page 50.

16. Source: *Rock Names: From Abba to ZZ Top: How Rock Bands got their Names*, by Adam Dolgins. Citadel Press, 1998, pp. 199–200.

15. Source: *The Complete Beatles Chronicle*, by Mark Lewisohn. Harmony Books, 1992, page 270.

17. Source: *The First 280 Years of Monty Python*, by Kim "Howard" Johnson. St. Martin's Griffin, 1999, page 228.

6. Source: *Bob Dylan: A Life in Stolen Moments*, by Clinton Heylin. Book Sales Ltd., 1996, page 55.